Race, Front and Center:
Perspectives on Race among
Puerto Ricans

Race, Front and Center: Perspectives on Race among Puerto Ricans

Edited by Carlos Vargas-Ramos

Centro
Press

Library of Congress Cataloging-in-Publication Data
Names: Vargas-Ramos, Carlos, editor of compilation. | Hunter College. Centro de
Estudios Puertorriqueños.
Title: Race, front and center : perspectives on race among Puerto Ricans /
    edited by Carlos Vargas-Ramos.
Description: New York, NY : Centro Press, Center for Puerto Rican Studies,
    Hunter College, CUNY, [2017] | Includes bibliographical references and
    index.
Identifiers: LCCN 2016030601 (print) | LCCN 2016038299 (ebook) | ISBN
    9781945662003 (paperback : alkaline paper) | ISBN 9781945662010 (ePub) | ISBN
    9781945662010
Subjects: LCSH: Puerto Rico--Race relations. | United States--Race relations.
    | Puerto Ricans--Attitudes. | Race awareness--Puerto Rico. |
    Nationalism--Puerto Rico. | Puerto Ricans--Race identity--United States. |
    Puerto Ricans--Cultural assimilation--United States. | Puerto
    Rico--Emigration and immigration--Social aspects. | United
    States--Emigration and immigration--Social aspects.
Classification: LCC F1983.A1 R33 2016 (print) | LCC F1983.A1 (ebook) | DDC
    305.80097295--dc23
LC record available at https://lccn.loc.gov/2016030601

Published by
Centro Press
Center for Puerto Rican Studies
Hunter College, CUNY
695 Park Avenue, E-1429
New York, NY 10065
centrops@hunter.cuny.edu
http://centropr.hunter.cuny.edu

TABLE OF CONTENTS

ix　Acknowledgements

11　Introduction
　　Carlos Vargas-Ramos

Section I. Racial Formation in Building a Nation

41　**Chapter 1.** Un hombre (negro) del pueblo: José Celso Barbosa and the Puerto Rican "Race" Toward Whiteness
　　Miriam Jiménez-Román

61　**Chapter 2.** Puerto Rico: The Pleasures and Traumas of Race
　　Alan West-Durán

77　**Chapter 3.** AfroPuerto Rican Cultural Studies: Beyond *cultura negroide* and *antillanismo*
　　Juan A. Giusti Cordero

91　**Chapter 4.** *Nanas negras:* The Silenced Women in Rosario Ferré and Olga Nolla
　　Mary Ann Gosser-Esquilín

102　**Chapter 5.** Brothels, Hell and Puerto Rican Bodies: Sex, Race, and Other Cultural Politics in 21st Century Artistic Representations
　　Hilda Lloréns

Section II. Racialization in Migration: Modes of Incorporation

113　**Chapter 6.** Afro-Puerto Rican Radicalism in the United States: Reflections on the Political Trajectories of Arturo Schomburg and Jesús Colón
　　Winston James

133　**Chapter 7.** Remembering Pura Belpré's Early Career at the 135th Street New York Public Library: Interracial Cooperation and Puerto Rican Settlement During the Harlem Renaissance
　　Victoria Núñez

145　**Chapter 8.** Resisting the Racial Binary? Puerto Ricans' Encounter with Race in Depression-Era New York City
　　Lorrin Thomas

Section III. A Nuyorican Perspective

161　**Chapter 9.** Nuyorican Visionary: Jorge Soto and the Evolution of an Afro-Taíno Aesthetic at Taller Boricua
　　Yasmin Ramírez

172　**Chapter 10.** Central Park Rumba: Nuyorican Identity and the Return to African Roots
　　Berta Jottar

182　**Chapter 11.** Slipping and Sliding: The Many Meanings of Race in Life Histories of New York Puerto Rican Return Migrants in San Juan
　　Eileen J. Findlay

Section IV. The Insidious and Ineffable Violence of Racial Discrimination

197 **Chapter 12.** The Social and Educational Inequalities of Black Students Studying English in Rural Puerto Rico
Elena González Rivera

210 **Chapter 13.** Slippery Semantics: Race Talk and Everyday Uses of Racial Terminology in Puerto Rico
Isar P. Godreau

225 **Chapter 14.** Domestic Work and Racial Divisions of Women's Employment in Puerto Rico, 1899-1930
Elizabeth Crespo

233 **Chapter 15.** Policing the Crisis in the Whitest of All the Antilles
Kelvin Santiago-Valles

Section V. The Racialization of Place and the Place for Racialization

247 **Chapter 16.** De la disco al caserío: Urban Spatial Aesthetics and Policy to the Beat of Reggaetón
Zaire Z. Dinzey-Flores

255 **Chapter 17.** All This Is Turning White Now: Latino Constructions of "White Culture" and Whiteness in Chicago
Ana Y. Ramos-Zayas

Section VI. Institutional Racialization and the Racialization of Self

273 **Chapter 18.** Changed Identities: A Racial Portrait of Two Extended Families, 1909-Present
Gabriel Haslip-Viera

284 **Chapter 19.** Acculturation under Duress: The Puerto Rican Experience at the Carlisle Indian Industrial School, 1898-1918
Pablo Navarro-Rivera

Section VII. Is Race in the Genes?

305 **Chapter 20.** The Politics of Taíno Revivalism: The Insignificance of Amerindian mtDNA in the Population History of Puerto Ricans
Gabriel Haslip-Viera

312 **Chapter 21.** Amerindian mtDNA in Puerto Rico: When Does DNA Matter?
Jorge Estevez

322 **Chapter 22.** Amerindian mtDNA Does Not Matter: A Reply to Jorge Estevez and the Privileging of Taíno Identity in the Spanish-speaking Caribbean
Gabriel Haslip-Viera

330 References

372 Notes

395 Index

ACKNOWLEDGEMENTS

The publication of a book is never an individual effort, but rather the collection of contributions from many people. They may not always get the credit, but their effort must be acknowledged and their involvement thanked. Here I do so.

An anthology is impossible without the contributions of the original authors. Therefore, I am grateful to the authors of the works collected in this anthology for producing them in the first place and contributing to a growing body of knowledge from which we have been able to draw. Their work has made our work easier.

Preparing the manuscript for publication required the dedicated editorial assistance of Cindy Rodriguez and Leah Stauber. At Centro Publications I recognize the work of assistant editors Yamila Sterling, Noraliz Ruiz and Madeline Friedman, designers Imani Núñez and Kenneth J. Kaiser, and the exceptional direction of its editor, Xavier F. Totti. I am also grateful to an anonymous reviewer for their pertinent commentary and suggestions.

To all, my heartfelt gratitude.

Carlos Vargas-Ramos
New York
November 2016

INTRODUCTION
By Carlos Vargas-Ramos

*They are very well-built people, with handsome bodies and very
fine faces, [...] very broad heads and foreheads, more so that I
have ever since in any other race. Their eyes are large and
very pretty, and their skin is the color of Canary Islanders
or of sunburned peasants, not at all black, [...]. [...]
their legs, with no exceptions, are quite straight,
and none of them has paunch. They are, in fact,
well proportioned. Their hair is not kinky,
but straight and coarse like horsehair.*

—Christopher Columbus, 12 October 1492[1]

Race has been an organizing identity of American societies since the first Europeans
arrived on its shores more than five hundred years ago. As an organizing identity it
has sustained principles of social organization in Puerto Rico, in the United States
and elsewhere in the hemisphere. Race has served to differentiate colonial societies
on the basis of physical characteristics of individuals and groups of individuals. It has
served as well to assign social value to those individuals and groups of individuals,
the legacy of which we live with to this day. Moreover, race continues to inform
and structure social life, with direct and indirect implications for how people fare
materially, morally, spiritually and psychologically. Yet, it is a subject of analysis that
is often subsumed or sidelined in the analysis of conditions in Puerto Rican life.

Race, Front and Center: Puerto Rican Perspectives on Race engages directly how
social differentiation based on physical characteristics has impacted Puerto Ricans
singly and collectively; and it does so in a manner in which race as a social identity is
foregrounded and centrally addressed with the purpose of highlighting inequalities
and unequal treatment that persists among Puerto Ricans. The works we have
collected in this anthology provide us with a panoramic view of how race has been
constructed, portrayed, interpreted and performed among Puerto Ricans both in
Puerto Rico and in the United States.

These works form part of the body of knowledge that has been individually produced over the past two decades by authors at the forefront of the study of race among Puerto Ricans. They were originally published as full-length articles in *Centro: The Journal of the Center for Puerto Rican Studies*, which itself has been under uninterrupted publication over the past thirty years as the leading vehicle for the dissemination of knowledge on the Puerto Rican experience. We have collected redacted versions of these articles in this anthology to facilitate the dissemination of this knowledge even more broadly. The collection does not represent in any way the complete breadth of works on race among Puerto Ricans. What it does is present the reader with the multifaceted ways in which this social identity has been brought under scholarly analysis.

The anthology is a collection of twenty-two chapters divided thematically into seven sections that address how Puerto Ricans as a people are conceived racially; how the migration experience has served to inform our collective understandings of racial identity and racial differentiation; what the effects of racial differentiation and discrimination are; and the actual locations, institutions and mechanisms by which racial differentiation takes place.

Section I–Racial Formation in Building a Nation–sets the stage with essays by Miriam Jiménez-Román, Alan West-Durán, Juan A. Giusti-Cordero, Mary A. Gosser-Esquilín and Hilda Lloréns. These scholars, from disciplines such as history, sociology and anthropology, as well as language and literature, coincide in a cultural analysis of the role of race in the construction and characterization of Puerto Rican identity. This approach is very fitting given how salient cultural production, particularly in literature (e.g., *la generación del treinta* and the reaction to it), has been in the interpretation of Puerto Rican identity and the place of race in it. The contributions of these authors provide us with, among other things, the racial contours of Puerto Rican identity; contours that have often left black Puerto Ricans and other Puerto Ricans of African descent with a tenuous standing in the nation.

The focus of Section I is largely on Puerto Rico and how the cultural production of a racialized Puerto Rican identity evolved on the island. But a significant and increasingly important component of the Puerto Rican experience takes place away from Puerto Rico, extending to the United States. Sections II and III of the anthology broach how Puerto Ricans, perceived in the United States as a foreign, decidedly non-white people, grapple with their insertion in a different racial system. In Racialization in Migration: Modes of Incorporation (Section II), Winston James, Victoria Núñez and Lorrin Thomas use a historical approach to analyze and interpret the process by which Puerto Rican migrants inserted themselves in the United States. Some times incorporation happened with ease and cooperatively (see

Núñez); at other times, it was more conflicted (see Thomas); and it did not always entail remaining within the orbit of a Puerto Rican identity (see James).

In Section III—A *Nuyorican* Experience—Yasmin Ramirez, Berta Jottar and Eileen J. Findlay go beyond the migrant generation of Puerto Ricans who left the island for the United States and examine the experience of their children and grandchildren, perhaps born, but certainly raised in the United States. These authors show the continuities, but above all the discontinuities of a racialized Puerto Rican identity. The discontinuities of the Nuyorican generation tended to highlight or privilege the indigenous and African heritages of Puerto Ricans in reaction to not only the discrimination they experienced at the hand of the non-Hispanic white American majority to which they were exposed in the United States, but also in relation to strains of Puerto Rican characterizations that rejected Puerto Ricans born and/or raised in the United States as inauthentic. Ramirez and Jottar delve into these themes through the lenses of the arts (visual and musical, respectively) as readily accessible vehicles of identity expression. Findlay approaches this generation of Puerto Rican from a different vantage point. She focuses on another dimension of the migration experience, one that entailed not the migration from Puerto Rico to the United States, but rather the migration of these Puerto Ricans from the United States to a Puerto Rico that did not always accept them with ease.

The Insidious and Ineffable Violence of Racial Discrimination (Section IV) presents the works of Elena González Rivera, Isar P. Godreau, Elizabeth Crespo and Kelvin Santiago-Valles, sociologists and anthropologists, who provide direct empirical evidence of how Puerto Ricans of different racial make-up have seen their life opportunities limited at the hands of other Puerto Ricans, in Puerto Rico specifically. González Rivera provides a contemporary portrayal of children in a community identified as black, who are marginalized, not only by their peers, but also in deed or by neglect by school authorities charged with their care. Crespo makes use of aggregate census data to underscore how early in the twentieth century black Puerto Rican women appeared unable to make the transition from service occupations to manufacturing at a historical moment when industrial production was gaining a foothold in Puerto Rico's economy. Santiago-Valles provides an interpretative analysis of how disruptions in the Puerto Rican economy led to policing strategies by government authorities that affected Puerto Ricans of African descent disproportionately. Godreau engages in the interpretation of interpersonal exchanges from her ethnographic studies to highlight the ways solidarity or antagonism are elicited with racial terminology or racialized language, whether used ambiguously and inconsistently or more distinctly and concretely, in the context of clear racial hierarchies in Puerto Rico.

Section V—The Racialization of Place and the Place for Racialization—literally grounds the assignation of racial categories and racializing characteristics in physical locations. People engage in the process of attributing social value according to racial designations in concrete locations. Zaire Dinzey-Flores' content analysis of reggaetón lyrics as the source of descriptions of urban spaces zeroes in on a genre that has been associated variously with the city, the streets, *barriadas* and public housing projects, the struggles of poverty and violence, and blackness. The characterization of these places with black (or non-white) inhabitants racializes these places in particular ways that distinguishes them from other physical locations, for instance, *urbanizaciones*. Ana Y. Ramos-Zayas's ethnographic work in a transitioning (i.e., gentrifying) Puerto Rican neighborhood in Chicago offers a complementary account to the racialization of place. In her account, it is Puerto Ricans who engage in the racialization of another group—non-Hispanic whites; a novel twist since, in the racialization process, whites are often treated or portrayed implicitly as agents with the capacity, authority or simply the entitlement to racialize others.

Racialization takes place not simply in physical locations, but also in concrete institutions in which individuals and groups or individuals find themselves, which then become the locations of racialized social interaction. In Section VI—Institutional Racialization and the Racialization of Self—historians Gabriel Haslip-Viera and Pablo Navarro-Rivera provide us with two stark examples of how Puerto Ricans have faced and dealt with racializing institutions. Navarro-Rivera's account of the experience of Puerto Ricans in the Carlisle Indian Industrial School shows the mechanism by which the United States government attempted to stamp out the cultural vestiges of what in the eyes of its bureaucrats were inferior non-white peoples. Haslip-Viera, in a complementary but contrasting fashion, offers an account of how inconsistent the racializing treatment (e.g., racial identification) by U.S. governmental institutions at the local, state and federal levels can be, and how individual Puerto Ricans react and manage the outcomes of that racializing treatment.

Section VII—Is Race in the Genes?—closes the anthology with a polemic between historian Gabriel Haslip-Viera and self-styled Taíno culture researcher and curator Jorge Estevez over the findings by biologist Juan Carlos Martínez-Cruzado regarding the contributions to the Puerto Rican genome that different population groups in Puerto Rico have made. Haslip-Viera challenges the validity and reliability of the genetic analysis, while Estevez questions the historical record regarding the presence and absence of Taínos from present-day Puerto Rico and among Puerto Ricans. At stake is the role that genomics may play in the construction of racial identity, and its implications for the construction of a national identity.

Race, Front and Center: Perspectives of Race among Puerto Ricans therefore grapples with this fraught subject matter from a variety of perspectives and scholarly approaches, offering the reader a vantage point with a broad outlook from which to engage and understand how Puerto Ricans have differentiated themselves along the lines of physical characteristics, with labels we term races, and how these differentiations have affected their lives.

Race: The Subject

Race is one of those social identities that have been used to arrange and organize social relations, most certainly in the Western Hemisphere, since it was incorporated into the orbit of the Western world in the fifteenth century. The understanding of distinctions and ascription between human beings that members of a society have assigned each other based on physical characteristics began with the European colonization of the Americas in the sixteenth century. The judgments and attributions of moral value and social standing took place at the same time. Assigning distinctions in any society is done relationally; that is to say, socially, in interactions among people across space and time. However, assigning distinction among members of a society based on physical characteristics is not done based on the simple aggregation of opinions about what races are; but, rather, this assigning is mediated by the power different members of a society have relative to one another, so that the opinion of some members of that society carries more weight or sanction than the opinion of others. Those opinions, even if not unanimous, consensual or majoritarian, can become and are often formally codified by political processes and institutional practices governing a society. Those opinions may also prevail informally. Collectively they regulate and mediate social relations.

In the context of Puerto Rico and among Puerto Ricans this dynamic racialization of society has been marked by the experience of Europeans meeting the indigenous populations they encountered by chance in their voyages of exploration and commercial expansion, and whom they decided to subdue in their occupation of the native inhabitants' territory, along with other population groups subject to the powerful European intervention. The dynamics were bound by the context of the conquest and then colonization of the island by the Spaniards, their subjugation of the native population and the importation of forced labor from other lands (both Africa and other areas of the Western Hemisphere). Puerto Ricans still live with the legacy of that founding arrangement, even as it has evolved over the centuries and historical circumstances. There may be a new colonial sovereign (i.e., the United States), and the migration of a large number of Puerto Ricans from the Caribbean may have altered the contours of the process of assigning social value to different members of society based on their physical characteristics or phenotype. But the dynamic that privileges those Puerto Ricans of European origin or descent over those of African origin or descent, as well as those of mixed European, Indigenous and African background, remains.

Despite political discourses of equality and egalitarianism that have underscored another social identity—one based on the concept of the nation—notable and persistent differences and unequal outcomes persist among Puerto Ricans due to their socially defined physical distinctions (Rogler 1948; Seda Bonilla 1961, 1973). Puerto Ricans of African descent, and black Puerto Ricans in particular, have been notably subject to unequal treatment (Rodríguez Cruz 1965). The differential treatment they have experienced historically persists to this day (Godreau and Vargas-Ramos 2009). Racist and discriminatory practices and their effects have been amply documented in myriad aspects of Puerto Rican social life: in employment (Hernández 2002; Rivera-Ortiz 2001; Withey 1977); in the household and among relatives (Franco-Ortiz 2003); in the education system (Godreau et al. 2008); in the mass media (Rivero 2005); in law enforcement (Santiago-Valles 1996); in localities and spatial arrangements (Godreau 1999, 2015; Mills-Boccachica 2003; Dinzey-Flores 2013; Lloréns 2014); in everyday formal and informal speech (Godreau 2008, 2015); in public health (Landale and Oropesa 2004; Gravlee, Dressler and Bernard 2005; Rodriguez-Silva 2012); and in the formation of a national identity (Roy-Fequiere 2004; Godreau 1999; Guerra 1998; Carrión 1996; González 1985; Zenón Cruz 1974; Pedreira 1934 [1992]; Géliga-Vargas et al. 2009).

The project of crafting that imagined community that is the nation has largely come at the expense of populations deemed non-white in American countries (Marx 1998). In the context of Puerto Rico, the expendable national group has been Puerto Ricans of African descent. The crafting of an identity congruent with the idea of the nation was a project of the political, economic and intellectual elites for the political, economic and intellectual elites. As non-whites were seldom constituent members of those elites, their representation in the nation became subordinate. Attempts to highlight race as an acceptable identity to advance claims, particularly among such subordinate groups, have been historically rebuffed and condemned by national elites as antithetical to the nation-building project, even anti-national or divisive (Labrador-Rodríguez 1999). As a result, it has been in the context of privileging national identity that unequal treatment of Puerto Ricans of African descent in a wide number of social spheres, as noted above, has taken place. This unequal treatment and the unequal position that Puerto Ricans of African descent occupy as a result is often perpetuated when asserting that there is no racial prejudice within the Puerto Rican nation, either by neglecting, ignoring, minimizing or denying such unequal treatment and its consequences (Betances 1972, 1973).

Privileging identities: nation hides race

The process of group identity formation based on and associated with a geographical area characterized by specific cultural commonalities (i.e., nation-building) began as a political project of localized political, economic and intellectual elites, who attempted to carve out a space for political action and agency in the face of colonial overrule. In most countries of the Western Hemisphere, this struggle for space to operate and influence the political arena resulted in nationalist projects that sought independence from colonial rule and the building of a state based on the concept of nation, influenced by liberal ideologies.

In the case of Puerto Rico, in spite of some nationalist tendencies within the political and intellectual elites, the predominant manifestation of group singularity took the form of *autonomismo*, increased local self-rule without severing completely political, economic and even cultural ties with the colonial sovereign. Yet the project to construct a group identity based on the concept of "the nation" is said to have developed fully, even if it did not seek to extend it to the political project of creating an independent nation-state (Duany 2002). Puerto Rican elites accomplished group distinction and separation, first, from Spain and Spaniards, and, subsequently, by resisting the United States and "Americanization." The process began in the middle of the nineteenth century; by the middle of the twentieth century it was well rooted and established.

Self-characterization and self-description took a prominent role during this "nation-building" century. After all, for most of its history, the inhabitants of Puerto Rico had been portrayed and characterized by outsiders, including government or ecclesiastical officials as well as foreigners at the service of the Spanish crown or travelers (e.g., Ledru, Abbad y Lasierra, Flinter). What or who would capture and symbolize an entire people required a long period of crafting and contouring as the images of the people-nation were created in the service of political goals (Martínez-Echazábal 1998; Rodríguez-Silva 2012). This crafting and contouring was punctuated by historical events of political importance (Martínez-Echazábal 1998). In Puerto Rico, the political junctures were the struggle for the abolition of slavery, the fight for an autonomy charter from Spain, the U.S. occupation of Puerto Rico and the creation of the Estado Libre Asociado (Rodríguez-Silva 2012).

According to Ileana Rodríguez-Silva, the abolition of slavery in Puerto Rico required *criollo* elites convincing the Spanish government that emancipation would not have a destabilizing effect, whether in the labor market, politically or socially. This was accomplished by highlighting the numerically marginal number of slaves in the population as well as their social compliance and the racial predominance of white Puerto Ricans. Autonomy required minimizing the mixed race background of very large segments of the island's population; doing so by underscoring the white segments and their attributes, and unequivocally portraying the elites as white and Spanish in inspiration and evocation. This whitewashing required greater effort and tenacity under U.S. colonialism, given the very early and persistent description of the population by U.S. colonial administrators, chroniclers and travelers as decidedly non-white (Duany 2002; Thompson 2007; Rodríguez-Silva 2012). The trope and symbol of the *jíbaro* as a direct white descendant of Spanish settlers ensconced in the hinterland played a crucial role in this regards (Guerra 1998). So did the silencing strategies deployed at those historical junctures that elided black Puerto Ricans specifically (Rodríguez-Silva 2012; Géliga-Vargas 2015), ultimately culminating in the unassailable formulation of the Puerto Rican people as *la gran familia puertorriqueña*. The deployment of *mestizaje*, much maligned and regretted by liberal criollo elites during the second half of the nineteenth century and the first third of the twentieth century, to include the vast segment of the Puerto Rican people into a broader group identity, would buttress the nation-building project from mid-twentieth century on. But it would also serve to deracialize the political discourse (Martínez-Echazábal 1998).

Racial formation in building a nation

Race, Front and Center: Perspectives of Race among Puerto Ricans opens with the works of Miriam Jiménez-Román and Alan West-Durán, who contribute to contextualize how race has been interpreted in the process of building of a national identity, a most salient social and political process in Puerto Rico and among Puerto Ricans. In the process of creating a Puerto Rican *imagined community*, the construction and shaping of a national identity has been particularly marked by the literary production of the intellectual and the literati class (Roy-Fequiere 2004). This construction of a national identity took place crucially in the period between the middle of the nineteenth century to the middle of the twentieth, often, in the later period, involving the direct intervention of the *criollo* colonial State (i.e., the Commonwealth government). Therefore, it is fitting that the works that have focused on the literary production of the Puerto Rican intellectual classes, which have both shaped but also contested how the Puerto Rican people have been racialized within the context of a Puerto Rican national identity, open this anthology. Jiménez-Román focuses on the work of a political leader and academic cultural critics, while West-Durán focuses more narrowly on the work of literary writers.

In "Un hombre (negro) del pueblo: José Celso Barbosa and the Puerto Rican 'Race' Toward Whiteness," Jiménez-Román uses the figure of Barbosa, a leading political figure at the turn of the twentieth century as Puerto Rico's colonial status shifted between colonial metropolitan powers –Spain and the United States– to highlight the fraught, conflicting and at times contradictory positions that a black Puerto Rican, a self-made professional, member of the Puerto Rican political and civic elite that often snubbed him, had to manage, endure and grapple with both as an individual, as leader of a number of political movements (i.e., *autonomista* under Spanish colonialism, *anexionista* under U.S. colonialism), and as inspiration to a marginalized segment of the Puerto Rican population (i.e., black Puerto Ricans and other Puerto Ricans of African descent). Jiménez-Román's starting point for her description is the process of Spanish conquest and colonization of Puerto Rico that set the stage for the process of racial formation in which peninsular Spaniards subjugated the local indigenous inhabitants until their virtual disappearance from the social, economic and political scenes and their substitution by forced labor from Africa in the form of commercialized slaves. The forceful subjugation by the Spaniards created a hierarchy that situated them—the *peninsulares*—at the top, followed by their *criollo* descendents (both groups collectively categorized as *blancos*), the free populations of color, whether they were of indigenous origin, African origin or a mix of these populations with Europeans (i.e., *pardos* and *morenos*), and the slave population of mostly, but not exclusively, African origin (i.e. *negros* and *mulatos*).

Jiménez-Román's review of that early Spanish conquest and colonialism period alerts us to the fact that a racialization of the people of Puerto Rico had already occurred and was firmly in place by the time the United States obtained Puerto Rico as booty from the Cuban-Spanish-American War of 1898. This point is very relevant because coming under the direct rule of the United States has been used to minimize the local system of social exclusion and marginalization based on physical appearance that was already in place among Puerto Ricans. Minimizing the local system of social exclusion was relatively simple because the United States' own racialization process has been contrasted markedly with that of Puerto Rico and the rest of the Caribbean and Latin America as much more malign in its consequence for conquered, colonized and enslaved peoples. But Puerto Rico already had a racialized society with its own prejudices and discriminatory practices prior to the U.S. occupation and colonial administration of the island. José Celso Barbosa himself lived them and described them.

The historical background Jiménez-Román provides serves as context for her discussion of the literary and intellectual generation that shaped the intellectual and ideological construction of race and nation among Puerto Ricans, represented in her chapter by Tomás Blanco and *la generación del treinta*. This intellectual generation relied on an idealized and mythologized Spanish colonial past, including its race relations, to reaffirm a local Hispanic identity facing the forceful attempts by the United States to remake the Puerto Rican people in its own people's image in as much as that might be possible. Identifying with Spain, its legacy and culture served as a bulwark for these Puerto Rican intellectuals facing the "Americanization" campaign unleashed by the United States government. The dichotomy built around race relations was that the United States had a truly racist society; in Puerto Rico, if there was any discrimination or prejudice, it was experienced or manifested at the individual level not systemically. As Jiménez-Román tells us, these constructs

"...don't allow for protest from those that are excluded because in theory there is no exclusion. Those who have protested racially motivated exclusions and injustices and demanded full and dignified membership in '*la familia*' have been labeled overtly sensitive, as suffering from an inferiority complex, or unwitting victims of an imported, i.e., alien, racial ideology. In a society which devalues blackness, black Puerto Ricans are trapped in the paradoxical situation of being doubly silenced, largely absent from the family portrait and yet prohibited from mentioning the slight under penalty of even greater ostracism." (p. 43)

What results from this race relations dynamic, Jiménez-Román explains, is a situation which may have led many black Puerto Ricans to take an accommodationist stance; one that, in the case of Barbosa, perhaps explains some political and social positions that seem paradoxical and even contradictory.

Likewise, in "Puerto Rico: The Pleasures and Traumas of Race," Alan West-Durán highlights the relevance of *la generación del treinta*'s view of Puerto Ricans' race and identity. He also uses the work of historian and essayist Tomás Blanco to underscore the impact that generation of intellectuals had on current understandings of national identity and the role race played in it, but contrasting it, as Jiménez-Román does, with that of Isabelo Zenón Cruz, who was also a university-based cultural critic and writer from a later generation who labored unrelentingly to demystify those prevailing understandings. However, West-Durán's exposition provides a broader view, both in time and space, presenting portrayals of race relations in Puerto Rico harking back to the 1860s and extending them to the 1990s, with examples of how race has been lived by Puerto Ricans in the United States as well.

Three of the works West-Durán discusses centered on *mulatas*, perhaps the paradigmatic character in the process of *mestizaje* in the Caribbean; and in two of these works (i.e., *La cuarterona* and *Maldito amor*) such characters are presented under the theme of the "tragic mulatto" even as the works were written more than one hundred years apart. This tragic mulatto theme, common in U.S. literature (and later film) in the nineteenth and early twentieth century, entailed characters who did not properly fit into the normatively regulated social order of the dominant classes. The theme focuses on the purported transgression of miscegenation in racially pluralistic societies, as Jiménez-Román indicates in her description of *pardos*, but one that is even more salient in racially bi-polar societies. This is a theme surrounding racially mixed populations manifest throughout the hemisphere. While Puerto Rico (and other countries in the Caribbean and Latin America) may not have a racially bi-polar society, as the United States is purported to be, it is nevertheless a society in which those of mixed ancestry have occupied tenuous and uncertain spaces over the decades and centuries. The boundaries of race, particularly the protection of whiteness, have been monitored to greater or lesser extent, and with greater or lesser success; for instance, under the concept of *pureza* or *limpieza de sangre*, and the practice of registering births/baptisms, weddings and deaths in the racially appropriate ministerial ledgers. The mixed-race women depicted by their respective (white) authors in West-Durán's account find themselves thwarted by social conventions that restrict their desires, agency, and social and material positions; tragically, one —Julia—dies, and the other one—Gloria—ends up debased working as a prostitute.

The third work presented by West-Durán, that of Palés Matos's *Tuntún de pasa y grifería*, also presents a mixed-race woman (or, rather, her allegory), joining the other two works discussed in highlighting one crucial characteristic of these women: their physical desirability, generally, and specifically, their desirability to white men. In Palés Matos's work, this desirability for a mixed-race woman is most blunt and reaches its zenith, making use of stereotypes and prejudices, many revolving around exuberant sensuality, that had been used to devalue these women by those of "proper society or station." Palés Matos turns those stereotypes on their head and makes them into attractive attributes. Yet they are still stereotypes that often border on caricatures of actual human beings. Moreover, they are rather figments of the (white) author's imagination (Davis 1979). The resulting character is the embodiment of a type of woman often sought after by (white) Latin American men.

In fact, West-Durán's original essay (as well as Hilda Lloréns') quotes the maxim by an early exponent of the Latin America racial democracy myth and benevolent race relations, Gilberto Freyre, that encapsulates the privileged Latin American man's thinking about his choice of women: white woman to marry, mulata to fornicate with and black woman to do work (Freyre 1986: 13).

Mary Ann Gosser-Esquilín's analysis in *"Nanas negras*: The Silenced Women in Rosario Ferré and Olga Nolla" further reiterates this point about the desirability of mixed-race women (along with the socially advantageous position of white women and the relegation of black women to menial work). One of Gosser-Esquilín's salient points, in addition to the silencing or evanescing of Puerto Ricans of African descent and especially black women in Puerto Rican literature, is how women of African descent are stereotypically depicted as sexually alluring. Moreover, for these women it is a sexuality that is judged, and needs to be policed and intervened with; unlike what happens in contrast with literary portrayals of a higher-class status white woman's sexuality. Gosser-Esquilín makes this contrast clear in her discussion of Olga Nolla's novel *El manuscrito de Miramar*, in which a black female character— Toñita—becomes pregnant out of wedlock, for which she loses her job as a nanny working in an upper-class white family's home. Her employer—Sonia—takes it upon herself to question Toñita, and to confront the father-to-be to take responsibility and marry Toñita. All the while Sonia is presented as a modern, liberated woman who engages in an extramarital affair that results in a pregnancy, but suffers no social, personal or material consequence after getting an abortion.

The social judgment and policing of a black woman's sexuality is presented even more prominently and strikingly in "Brothels, Hell and Puerto Rican Bodies: Sex, Race, and Other Cultural Politics in 21st Century Artistic Representations," Hilda Lloréns' analysis of Mayra Santos Febres' *Our Lady of the Night*. This is not entirely surprising given that the subject of the story is the fictionalized life of Isabel Luberza Oppenheimer, a black woman, who rose to notoriety as the owner of several brothels until her violent death in 1974. The transgressive nature of the lead character stems from the fact that she rises from and often continues to operate at the margins of social propriety as a resourceful and well-off black woman who owns a successful if reproachable establishment. Luberza, by virtue of her race, gender, holdings and the activities surrounding her livelihood, challenged such social propriety. Lloréns underscores this by making the point of dwelling on Isabel, *La Negra*'s dark skin tone, as does Santos Febres, referring to her as *una negra, negra*. Lloréns explains that, in doubling up a word, the speaker gives emphasis to that characteristic—Isabel's skin— which, for Santos Febres, was a provocation. In this emphasis on a person's body, with its markers of "socio-cultural belonging and boundaries," Lloréns' (and Santos Febres') focus on the physical attributes of a person serves to show how race, and the differential treatment that may come along with it, operates in an unspoken but nevertheless evident way to prime social interaction between interlocutors.

The theme of the desirable woman of African descent is further depicted in Santos Febres' "*Marina y su olor.*" But instead of portraying a desirable mulata, a common theme in Caribbean and Latin American literature, this black Puerto Rican female author makes a young black woman the subject of desire of a privileged white man. Unlike the previous female characters in the works described by West-Durán (or Gosser Esquilín), this young black woman is not simply at the mercy of circumstances beyond her control or by which she is irremediably constrained; rather, Marina makes use of her natural attributes and abilities to cope with adversity and to reassert her position. Moreover, she is a fully constructed character, not a stereotype or archetype. West-Durán also remarks on Santos Febres' use of a persistent racist stereotype around black people and smell to turn it into a weapon of self-defense and empowerment. This is in marked contrast to Palés Matos, who, in hindsight, ultimately fails at his attempt to enhance blackness in his depictions for using essentialized characterizations of people of African descent that often are the core of negative stereotypes; an inherently rickety and suspect approach.

The ultimately marginalizing characterization of black Puerto Ricans at the core of *poesía negroide*, exemplified in the works of Palés Matos, and which to an extent also afflicts *antillanismo* in later aesthetic generations, is one of the subjects of Juan Giusti Cordero's work. In "AfroPuerto Rican Cultural Studies: Beyond *cultura negroide* and *antillanismo*," Giusti calls for a more expansive and inclusive view of Afro-Puerto Rican culture. The abundant limitations on the behavior of these Puerto Ricans to characterizations that border on caricature or remain uncomplicated and unidimensional in this form of literary production is supplemented by the spatial limitations to which black Puerto Ricans are subject to in the popular imaginary, as the work of Zaire Dinzey-Flores and Lloréns also make manifest. By identifying and marking specific locations as black, as it is the case for instance of municipalities such as Loíza or Guayama, those inhabitants and locations tend to be placed outside of the norm (Godreau 2015). These limitations in effect contribute to excise black Puerto Ricans from what is understood as being Puerto Rican; they are made into the "other," and, in the process of "othering," these Puerto Ricans are de-nationalized.

In contrast to essentialist characterizations of Puerto Ricans of African descent that pervaded the works of Palés Matos, the lived experience manifest in the works of Barbosa, as described by Jiménez-Román, and Santos Febres, as described by

West-Durán, is just as pronounced in Tato Laviera's poem *Negrito*. It is, after all, autobiographical. The poem highlights in the starkest of terms the jolting contrast in perceptions of race and race relations that Puerto Ricans in general experience on migrating to the United States. However, in this case it is more so for a black Puerto Rican asked by his aunt to keep away from African Americans, whom, to Laviera, look just like him. The dissonance around what a Puerto Rican understands about his own identity and that of others around him and what he encounters in a new, culturally and socially different terrain clashes to the point of confusion.

Racialization in migration: Modes of incorporation

The migrant's capacity to manage such a transition is tested as Puerto Ricans cross cultural, social and political borders, very often in trying circumstances; yet, migrants adapt. This adaptation takes many forms, as the experiences of Arturo Alfonso Schomburg and Jesús Colón show in the chapter by Winston James. In "Afro-Puerto Rican Radicalism in the United States: Reflections on the Political Trajectories of Arturo Schomburg and Jesús Colón," James explains that Schomburg and Colón came to live and became incorporated in the United States in distinct manners given by how race was constructed and understood within the Caribbean. James in fact provides a complementary explanation to racial formation in Puerto Rico to that offered by Jiménez Román. He attributes this specific racial construction in the Hispanic Caribbean to the comparatively larger proportion of the white population in Cuba, Puerto Rico and the Dominican Republic, as well as the larger proportion of free and freed non-white populations that resulted from these Spanish colonies joining late the world capitalist production and trading systems based on labor-intensive commodity agriculture (e.g., sugarcane).

The social system that developed in the islands between the middle of the sixteenth century and the late eighteenth century, and in which specific forms of race relations developed, yielded, James tells us, extensive white-owned small-holdings (as opposed to large plantations), an extensive free black peasantry, and relative autonomy from the colonial apparatus that was in marked contrast to the regimented and closely monitored labor regimes extant in the Dutch, English and French Caribbean colonies. For James, the resulting social system yielded less occupational and social distance between the white and non-white laboring groups in the Spanish-speaking island territories, a relatively greater bonding across racial lines, and "high levels of black mobilization and enthusiasm for nationalist projects." These social dynamics around race relations, James argues, resulted in black Puerto Ricans entering the United States "with relatively low 'race' or black consciousness."

As a result, black Latin Americans were less likely to join black nationalism movements, unless those black Latin Americans were descendants themselves of Caribbean migrants from non-Spanish-speaking territories, as was the case with Carlos Cook, Carlos Moore or Arturo Alfonso Schomburg.

James's analysis of Schomburg brings to light the issue of, not cross-ethnic, but rather race-based relations and alliances between Puerto Ricans and others in the United States (and in Puerto Rico). The literature shows how English-speaking Caribbeans (*West-Indians*) and their descendants have been instrumental or at the forefront of black-affirmation and advocacy movements, such as black nationalism (e.g., Marcus Garvey, Stokely Carmichael/Kwame Ture, Malcolm X). However, this had been less the case for people of African descent in the Spanish-speaking regions of the hemisphere. Schomburg's intellectual migration from a Puerto Rican-oriented political focus to one centered exclusively on the broader African diaspora resulted, James argues, from Schomburg's personal connection with and affinity toward the English-speaking Caribbean. Schomburg, in James's interpretation, was an outlier among Puerto Ricans. Jesús Colón, on the other hand, was the norm: a black Puerto Rican, whose social and political concerns centered on the Puerto Rican, or perhaps the broader Latin American, community, with connections to other struggles related to workers' rights and advocacy for the dispossessed, and therefore removed from exclusively race-centered struggles.

James' comparison between Schomburg and Colón would give a reader the impression that this strict bifurcation was the likely paths of social integration and political activism that Puerto Ricans arriving in the United States took, and one in which Puerto Ricans would mostly interact within a Puerto Rican or Latino or Latin American context, avoiding African Americans or Afro-Caribbeans. But Victoria Núñez shows us an alternative path across the ethno-racial divide in the United States with her description of Pura Belpré's life as a librarian in the New York Public Library system.

"Remembering Pura Belpré's Early Career at the 135th Street New York Public Library: Interracial Cooperation and Puerto Rican Settlement During the Harlem Renaissance," Núñez's description of Belpré's life in New York City, provides a glimpse at how Puerto Ricans, in this specific case one of African descent, navigated the racial politics in the city in her interactions with both non-Hispanic blacks and whites on an on-going basis. Núñez sees cooperation across racial lines at this elite city institution, one that benefitted African Americans and Puerto Ricans both as employees of the library and as patrons of it. Her chapter then serves as a sort of corrective, if in narrow contexts, to the view that interactions involving Puerto Ricans with others of different ethnoracial background were inherently conflictual or adversarial.

Lorrin Thomas provides us a broader context in which the first large wave of Puerto Rican migrants arrived in New York City, and how they fit (or not) into the extant system of racial relations. In "Resisting the Racial Binary? Puerto Ricans' Encounters with Race in Depression-Era New York City," Thomas describes how Puerto Ricans came to be racialized in the United States and how their own elites reacted to the process of racialization they experienced. It highlighted both the role and agency the Puerto Rican civic elites played in the process of navigating the social system depending on what side of the racial divide Puerto Ricans occupied or may have been assigned to by non-Puerto Ricans. It showed how non-Puerto Ricans saw Puerto Ricans (rendering their ethnicity invisible by focusing on Puerto Ricans' race) and, in turn, how Puerto Rican elites attempted to shape those perceptions, at least within the Spanish-speaking community. It is a process that highlights a more conflictual set of relations than what Victoria Nuñez presents in her description of Pura Belpré's life. This is not surprising given the choice of events Thomas uses initially to illustrate her point: a race riot in which positions become polarized and are therefore shown in sharper relief.

As they settled in the United States, Puerto Rican elites (made up mostly of whites and the "pretenders to whiteness" Barbosa had castigated during his time) did not want Puerto Ricans to be "confused" for black Americans, and in making the case, those elites often sidestepped, hid or disguised those Puerto Ricans of African descent in attempts to distance the larger Puerto Rican group from a population that was widely perceived as marginal and one to be avoided (as decades later Tato Laviera's aunt suggested to him, as described in *Negrito*). This was a process already under way and even manifest in Puerto Rico, as exemplified by burgeoning attempts of *la generación del treinta* and its intellectual predecessors, to portray Puerto Ricans as a culturally Hispanic people with marginal and insignificant contributions from other cultural groups, whether of African or indigenous origins. But the process to depict Puerto Ricans as non-black, in the hopes or expectation of being considered white, became more fraught and contentious when the physical appearance of Puerto Ricans in the United States fit different social formulations from those that Puerto Rican elites wanted Puerto Ricans to occupy.

A *Nuyorican* perspective

The attempts by this segment of the Puerto Rican elite in New York to situate themselves away from black Americans and as close to full-fledged "citizens" (i.e., white Americans) as possible involved Puerto Rican migrants who had been born and raised in Puerto Rico and were encountering notably different racial dynamics than those they observed or experienced in the island. However, the children and grandchildren of that pioneer migrant generation observed and experienced racial dynamics from a different lens. Those children and grandchildren may have been taught or learned in the home and the smaller social circles of relatives and acquaintances how racial dimensions may have been perceived or were like in Puerto Rico or among Puerto Ricans more generally. But the U.S.-born and -raised generation(s) also experienced and observed on their own how racial dynamics operated in the United States. Their perspective was informed by what they learned at home and in local Puerto Rican institutions. However, their perspective, based on their own lived experience, contrasted with that of their forebears and from Puerto Ricans in the island. This perspective among U.S.-born and/or -raised Puerto Ricans is exemplified in chapters by Berta Jottar and Yasmin Ramírez.

In "Nuyorican Visionary: Jorge Soto and the Evolution of an Afro-Taíno Aesthetic at Taller Boricua," Ramírez explains how artists affiliated with the Taller Boricua school interpreted and re-interpreted images and understandings about Puerto Rican identity they unearthed from what they learned within the local New York community and what they were taught and learned in and from Puerto Rico. This reliance on Puerto Rico as a font of authority about Puerto Rican identity explains the continuity in Puerto Rican understandings of racial identity that pervades Nuyorican interpretations of that identity. Yet, it was not an interpretation accepted whole and uncritically or unquestioned or un-adapted to the realities those U.S.-born and/or -raised Puerto Ricans experienced first hand; on the contrary.

Ramirez, for instance, focuses on Jorge Soto's reinterpretation of Puerto Rican cultural productions, such as paintings or logos, to underscore how U.S.-born and/or -raised Puerto Ricans viewed those same representations. In describing Soto's aesthetics and understandings of Puerto Rican identity, Ramírez highlights how the native inhabitant (i.e., the Taíno) and the African loomed larger than the Western influence in Puerto Rican culture that Spain, Hispanists and Hispanophiles provided. In search for rootedness, these Puerto Ricans in the United States searched for it not in the locations identified by island's cultural elites as the proper or correct ones (Spain or Hispanized América), but, rather, in what those elites had identified as secondary and marginal sources (folklorized indigenous cultures native to the Western Hemisphere, and a stereotyped Africa); sources that nevertheless were closer to the lives these Puerto Ricans were experiencing in the United States. This experience included living alongside other peoples from the African diaspora, and being exposed, for instance, to their spiritual beliefs or, as Jottar later described, their musical production.

The *Nuyorican* perspective illustrated by Soto's work then is a notable departure from how those cultural contributions were viewed in Puerto Rico, particularly among the cultural elite in the island. This is one of many reasons why U.S.-born and/or -raised Puerto Ricans were derided and questioned in the island as true or authentic Puerto Ricans, since they did not appear to conform to the normatively sanctioned understanding of Puerto Rican culture, identity and history. They were then often perceived in Puerto Rico as unauthentic or ersatz, and their perspectives undermined when not infrequently dismissed or ignored. Yet, this was an understanding of Puerto Rican identity grounded in specific articulations of racial identity and cultural contributions as lived and experienced by these Puerto Ricans in the United States, characterized by economic, social, racial and cultural marginalization against which they were struggling. It is an understanding in conversation, at times contentious, with those in Puerto Rico.

In "Central Park Rumba: Nuyorican Identity and The Return to African Roots," Berta Jottar similarly highlights how U.S.-born and/or raised Puerto Ricans in New York City reaffirmed Puerto Ricans' African roots by using and adapting the musical traditions of other Caribbean populations in the United States, such as Cubans, in conjunction with other groups, such as African Americans, in a process of cultural exchange and bond-making. The process of cultural borrowing and adaptation that underscored the hybrid musical productions of Nuyoricans provides an insight as to how these Puerto Ricans affirmed cultural pride and negotiated inter-racial relations in a distinct milieu. Jottar's interlocutors' commentary about the little regard Afro-Puerto Rican forms, such as *bomba* and *plena*, had in Puerto Rico generally and the decline in popularity they experienced by the 1960s and 1970s, is noteworthy in accounting for that Nuyorican generation's reliance on Afro-Cuban musical forms to express their identity in the United States. Just as important is these Nuyoricans' reaction to their perception as unworthy recipients of "authentic" Puerto Rican cultural forms when cultural gatekeepers questioned their authenticity as Puerto Ricans.

The lived Nuyorican experience, and how race and race relations were understood by these Puerto Ricans, were not limited to what they witnessed and lived while in the United States. As Ramírez mentions when discussing his trajectory, Jorge Soto travelled to and resided in Puerto Rico on a number of occasions, not an uncommon practice among Puerto Ricans, regardless of birthplace. The circulation to and from, and the standing connections with Puerto Rico contributed to a cultural cross-fertilization among Puerto Ricans in Puerto Rico and in the United States; cultural remittances, according to Juan Flores. It also added another layer of understanding in how Puerto Ricans born and/or raised in the United States understood race relations among Puerto Ricans and in relation to other groups in the United States.

One noteworthy finding by Eileen Findlay in "Slipping and Sliding: The Many Meanings of Race in Life Histories of New York Puerto Rican Return Migrants in San Juan" is the relatively reduced importance of race as a marker of exclusion within the Nuyorican generation, as they experienced it in the United States in relation to how they perceived it in Puerto Rico or among their forebears' generation, which was made up of island-born and -raised migrants. Findlay surmises the need for internal solidarity in these U.S.-born and/or raised Puerto Ricans as a reason why race, as a potential cleavage, did not appear to have the relevance and impact in their interactions with other Puerto Ricans in the United States relative to how race relations were perceived and played out on the island and among island-born migrants to the United States.[2] Findlay tells us, "[t] hrough their discussions of racial prejudice and mixing among Puerto Ricans, and in their comments about racial and ethnic confrontation in the United States, the narrators simultaneously insisted on their legitimacy as Puerto Ricans, critiqued the U.S., and differentiated themselves from island Puerto Ricans" (p. 185).

The insidious and ineffable violence of racial discrimination

Findlay's analysis of her interviewees' experiences with race in Puerto Rico highlights the degree of awareness and active role race played in social interactions in Puerto Rico, particularly in the realm of private socializing. Elena González Rivera, however, shows us in "The Social and Educational Inequalities of Black Students Studying English in Rural Puerto Rico" the just-as-insidious effects racial differentiation and social isolation and ostracism may have on life chances in Puerto Rico. While Findlay's interviewees highlight the virulent, sometimes violent manifestations of prejudice and racism in the United States, and the implicit social distance black Puerto Ricans tend to be consistently subject to in Puerto Rico, González Rivera's accounts underscores the silent violence that differential treatment on the basis of racial distinctions has on the life chances of Puerto Ricans of African descent. This differential treatment is then compounded by the indifference those Puerto Ricans are subject to socially and politically. Their physical appearance is present for all neighbors, students, teachers, professionals and paraprofessionals, and administrators to see. It may remain unmentioned; but it is not invisible. Social difference on the basis of race is simply noted and conveyed in different manners.

González Rivera's account of the social isolation of the black members of a rural barrio in the highlands of Puerto Rico shows how local governmental neglect, indifference and ridicule on the part of many educational system staff members, and actual personal interactions between black and white children in a school context result in survival practices that lead to endogamy, limited education attainment and a general closing of ranks among members of extended families. While black children in this community also endured physical violence while being kept away from even the most basic socializing opportunities (e.g., playtime), just as insidious is the labeling that takes place throughout the community (e.g, *fuerza de choque*, riot squad). Seemingly non-racial, the term nevertheless captured these children's apparent imposing physical appearance but also their perceived limited cognitive abilities. The result was categorization that limited attention to their educational needs and consequently reduced prospects for their performance's improvement.

In "Slippery Semantics: Race Talks and Everyday Uses of Racial Terminology in Puerto Rico," Isar Godreau delves more centrally on the use of indirect language or inconsistent terminology in everyday speech to address or sidestep, as the case may be, race and racialization in Puerto Rico. Slippery semantics, as Godreau explains, "upsets the semantic stability of race as an identity," making that social cleavage difficult at times to pin down in social exchanges among Puerto Ricans. This ambivalence is useful in the process of creating solidarity or social distance between interlocutors. These semantics are nevertheless still laden with racial meaning, if perhaps imprecisely. Moreover, Godreau argues and illustrates that ambivalence imbued in racial terminology based on racial continuum (such as those in the Caribbean and Latin America) may nevertheless coexist in Puerto Rico with stark dichotomizations of racial identities inherent in societies with saliently bi-polar racial constructions (such as in the United States). These purported alternative binary and ambiguous models of race-talk may yet form part of the same cultural environment. The context in which these expressions of bi-polarity or continuum appear in everyday conversation is varied and manifold. Godreau suggests that dichotomizing racial categories in Puerto Rican race-talk may surface in situations of evident racism, whether to practice it or to combat it; or in reference to the historical past. Ambiguity, on the other hand, seems to prevail in more formal settings.

The chapters by Elizabeth Crespo and Kelvin Santiago-Valles contribute arguments about how Puerto Ricans of African descent and particularly black Puerto Ricans have faced and continue to endure unequal and inequitable treatment in the labor market and in law enforcement. Crespo in particular shows, in "Domestic Work and Racial Division of Women's Employment in Puerto Rico 1899-1930," how black women, who tended to be overrepresented in the labor market during the first third of the twentieth century, engaged in domestic work overwhelmingly, but appeared to be unable to make a proportional transition from such type of service work to the relatively more remunerative light industrial work that was staffed disproportionately by white women. It appears that in the historical moment, as industrialization was beginning to expand its presence in Puerto Rico, black women in the aggregate were unable to translate their exposure to (and experience with) the labor market toward better paying industrial work, suggesting bias in the labor market. Black women maintained steady their labor force participation, but occupying disproportionately domestic work positions.

The economic dislocation that resulted from another transformation of the economy of Puerto Rico from the mid-1960s on—shifting from the light manufacturing that characterized the economy from the 1930s through the 1950s to capital-intensive manufacturing that required fewer but more highly skilled workers (and a burgeoning service sector)—affected non-white Puerto Ricans disproportionately, according to Kelvin Santiago-Valles in "Policing the Crisis in the Whitest of All the Antilles." The increasing immiseration of this segment of the population resulted in the growth of alternative subsistence practices that were in turn criminalized, resulting in a disproportionate monitoring and policing of communities of people of African descent. Consequently, Santiago-Valles argues further, Puerto Ricans of African descent and black Puerto Ricans in particular tend to be overrepresented among those who are prosecuted and punished by the criminal justice system, in an attempt to control the economic crisis and the social dislocations that result from it. This monitoring by the law enforcement apparatus was often geographically based, singling communities that have been racialized as black neighborhoods or communities "of color."

The racialization of place and the place for racialization

The racialization of communities in Puerto Rico to which Santiago-Valles refers may seem paradoxical, given that residential segregation on the basis of racial difference is not a phenomenon that appears to afflict Puerto Rican society (Denton and Villarrubia 2007). But as the chapters by Giusti Cordero and González Rivera indicate, this is common practice in Puerto Rican society. It begins with the broad racialization of the island that is pervasive in both popular and academic accounts about Puerto Rico: predominance of the non-white population in the coastal plains, particularly in the northeast and southeast of the island, and a white predominance in the interior highlands (Lloréns 2015; Guerra 1998; Rodríguez-Silva 2012). As Giusti Cordero indicated in his analysis of Puerto Rican culture, Loíza appeared front and center in *poesía negroide*, while Piñones (a rural barrio of Loíza) was prominently featured in *antillanista* literature. Orocovis, on the other hand, would not be commonly associated as a location for a black community in Puerto Rico.

How physical locations are visualized and depicted, for instance, in musical forms, is the subject of Zaire Dinzey-Flores's "De la disco al caserío: Urban Spatial Aesthetics and Policy to the Beat of Reggaetón." Dinzey-Flores's focus is on how the city and the concept of the urban have been associated with violence, poverty, masculinity and blackness in reggaetón (and earlier forms of rap/hip-hop that developed in Puerto Rico). These themes are not unique to Puerto Rico, but rather consistent with how hip-hop overall delves in the same subjects and images, underscoring the broader appeal of that musical form. In Puerto Rico, Dinzey-Flores argues, the association of this musical form with the poor and dark-skinned populations not only imbues places or localities with racialized attributes. For *reggaetoneros* this association with the urban also offers authenticity, and therefore legitimacy. Reggaetón also offers some poor and dark-skinned Puerto Ricans the opportunity to denounce their social, economic and political conditions, and, albeit indirectly, when used in government-sponsored public-service campaigns, they may take part of the governing process.

The significance of physical space and its association with specific populations is also the emphasis of Ana Y. Ramos-Zayas's "All This Is Turning White Now: Latino Constructions of 'White Culture' and Whiteness in Chicago." Ramos-Zayas highlights the process of racialization as a physical location undergoing rapid population change, rather than remaining in staid continuity, in Chicago, Illinois. Whereas some regions, towns, neighborhoods or housing forms may be identified over the long term with specific population groups (e.g., Puerto Rico's coastal plains v. its highlands, Loíza v. Orocovis, Ponce's Barrio San Antón v. San Juan's Condado, *caseríos/residenciales* v. *urbanizaciones*), the increasingly rapid transition in some urban neighborhoods in the United States characterized by specific population groups showcases power dimensions that are dynamic rather than static or settled (e.g., Chicago's West Town, New York City's *Loisaida*, Miami's Wynwood). The shrinking Puerto Rican population from Chicago's Near Northwest Side neighborhoods and its replacement with other groups, most notably non-Hispanic whites, serve as the background to their racialization by Puerto Ricans. After all, the process of racialization is not unidirectional, with just non-Hispanic whites creating the parameters of social distinction on the basis of physical difference. Rather, Ramos-Zayas underscores how Puerto Ricans themselves partake in the process of the describing the racial (and ethnic) "other."

Ramos-Zayas's emphasis on Chicago Puerto Ricans' characterization of non-Hispanic whites, particularly those of higher status (e.g., *yuppies*, artists), as cultureless serves as a counterpoint to the culturally distinct (ethnic) "others" who tend to occupy lower status. The implicit normalcy of whiteness, not just in its being socially normative and prevalent, but also insofar as what is socially acceptable and pervasive, imbues it with a lack of distinctiveness or blandness that may lead some *whites* to want to appropriate attractive traits of "others." Some Puerto Ricans in Chicago may feel threatened by the physical encroachment of *whites* who want to occupy their living and social space as well as partake of their ways. Those Puerto Ricans size up those whites, and using indicators of class and status assign whites to categories along an axis of social power (e.g., *yuppies*, artists, ethnic whites and *hillie-billies*).

Institutional racialization and the racialization of self

If Ramos-Zayas broaches how Puerto Ricans racialize other groups they interact with in the United States, Gabriel Haslip-Viera trains his attention in an autobiographical microanalysis on how Puerto Ricans racialize themselves within the context and bounds of institutional forces assigning racial identities on an inconsistent basis. "Changed Identities: A Racial Portrait of Two Extended Families, 1909-Present," Gabriel Haslip-Viera's family history of shifting racial assignation, is pertinent because it reveals how inconsistently race was assigned by governmental authorities in the United States, at least in the New York City area (but also in Puerto Rico), at a time of heightened sensitivities to racial difference and xenophobia in the decades before and after World War I and then through the struggle for civil rights after World War II. It appears as if the boundary between white and non-white was diffused enough to allow the same person to be identified as white or black in different bureaucratic contexts. The inconsistencies in assigning race revealed in this self-referent microscopic study are remarkable given the generalized impression of the rigidity in racial classification and categorical assignation in the United States.

Just as revealing is how individuals navigate these bureaucratic contexts to assert a given identity, as may have been the case with Haslip-Viera's father insisting on assigning a particular racial category to his children at birth. Also noteworthy is how within one's family the stage for an implicit racial identification is established by the primary relations those family members form, particularly around marriage. The spouses they choose will inform how they themselves may be assigned to given racial categories and how their offsprings may identify racially. Those members of Haslip-Viera's family who married black spouses gravitated towards a black identity, while those who married white spouses gravitated towards a white identity; in both instances following what may be expected by an "classic" assimilation process marked by bi-polar race relations. Then there are those who marry within the (Puerto

Rican) group, who end up assuming an "undifferentiated Puerto Rican identity," in effect racializing one's ethnicity. Here Puerto Ricans work as agents in the process of challenging existing arrangements of social identity based on race, whereby a Hispanic ethnicity (e.g., Mexican, Puerto Rican, Latino) comes to stand in for race as well.

While Haslip-Viera's account of his family's haphazard racial categorization by governmental authorities in the United States challenges the much repeated notion that the United States system of racialization was a rigid and immutable one, Pablo Navarro-Rivera's account of Puerto Rican students at the Carlisle Indian Industrial School, provides evidence that an institutionalized system based on such formulation of racial subordination and categorization did exist. In fact, both "approaches" co-existed. Not very many Puerto Ricans attended Carlisle—four dozens. What is noteworthy however is that, as the United States took over Puerto Rico and attempted a process of cultural transformation of its people under American tutelage, the United States resorted to standing institutions that its government officials had created in the United States for the same purpose but directed at other colonized peoples, as was the case with Native Americans.

In "Acculturation Under Duress: The Puerto Rican Experience at the Carlisle Indian Industrial School 1898-1918," Navarro-Rivera argues that Puerto Ricans students were sent to Carlisle not because Puerto Ricans in general or those Puerto Ricans who were actually sent to Carlisle specifically were Indian, as United States officials and intellectuals might have conceived them, or as those students might have identified themselves. Rather, these students were sent to Carlisle and the Tuskegee Institute or Hampton Institute or Cornell University because Puerto Ricans were collectively perceived as not-white by those U.S. government officials and the intellectuals supporting their efforts, and therefore their culture needed to be expunged and replaced by another compatible with Anglo American values, in order for these new "charges" to be able to participate in U.S. society and its political institutions to the extent their cultural assimilation of those Anglo American values permitted it (Del Moral 2013). Carlisle was founded so that they could stamp the Indian out of the man; that is, to expunge the cultural attributes that made Native Americans detestable and unassimilable in the eyes of Anglo Americans. Students from Puerto Rico (and Cuba) were sent to these institutions created to "uplift" these lesser peoples perceived as degraded so, upon graduation, they could become agents of American acculturation (i.e. civilization).

Is race in the genes?

In spite of Navarro-Rivera's statement that Puerto Rican students were sent to Carlisle not because they were Indian or were identified as Indians but simply because they were seen by U.S. authorities as non-whites, recent research on the genomics of Puerto Ricans has raised the question of the nature of Puerto Ricans' racial origins. Are Puerto Ricans Indian? Are there (still) Indians in Puerto Rico? These are in part some of the questions taken up by Gabriel Haslip-Viera and Jorge Estevez in their exchange surrounding the genetic research of Juan Carlos Martínez-Cruzado.

In two studies in 2001 and in 2005, teams of researchers in biology and medical sciences led by Martínez-Cruzado attempted to establish the genetic origins of the Puerto Rican population (Martínez-Cruzado et al. 2001; Martínez-Cruzado et al. 2005). The first study analyzed mitochondrial DNA, genetic material that is passed unaltered from mother to daughter through the generations. The study indicated that 63 percent of the genetic material of all the people studied in the sample overall conducted in Puerto Rico showed markers associated with Native American ancestry, and 37 percent that was not associated with such Native American ancestry (Martínez-Cruzado et al. 2001, Table 3). In a subsequent study Martínez-Cruzado and a different team of researchers replicated the analysis of mitochondrial DNA and found essentially the same proportions of ancestry contribution among this sample: 61 percent "Amerindian," 27 percent "African" and 11.5 percent "West Eurasian." Since that time other studies have established similar proportions of genetic ancestry. For instance, Vilar and colleages (2014) found that analysis of mitochondrial DNA indicated 52 percent of the genetic material was consistent with "Native American" markers; 26 percent with "Sub-Saharan African" markers; and 17 percent with markers associated with "West Eurasia and North Africa."

In "The Politics of Taíno Revivalism: The Insignificance of Amerindian mtDNA in the Population History of Puerto Ricans," Haslip-Viera criticizes the conclusions by Martínez-Cruzado and his teams for the overarching inferences they make, particularly in the mass media, claiming a large Amerindian genetic inheritance among Puerto Ricans. In Haslip-Viera's estimation, Martínez-Cruzado and his team overreach for concluding there is such a large contribution of Amerindian DNA to modern Puerto Ricans' genome. Estevez does not advance his own argument when, in "Amerindian mtDNA in Puerto Rico: When Does DNA Matter?," he misinterprets Martínez-Cruzado's research results and states the research team "demonstrated that up to 61 percent of Puerto Ricans have Amerindian ancestors" (p. 312). Haslip-Viera further criticizes the inferences the research by Martínez-Cruzado and his teams lead to, particularly given the limited scope in ascertaining a person's full ancestral genetic contribution. Haslip-Viera points to unpublished results by Martínez-Cruzado's team research that finds that analysis of genetic contributions by male ancestors are 70 percent of European origin, 20 percent of African origin and only 10 percent of Amerindian origin.

In fact, in more recent analyses of genetic material that is only passed down the male line (i.e., Y-chromosome), Vilar and his colleagues find that, for the sample overall, 85 percent of the genetic markers present are of "West Eurasian origin and approximately 15% of Sub-Saharan origin, while none were clearly indigenous" (Vilar et al. 2014: 363). These results do not necessarily contradict those from mtDNA results, presented by Martínez-Cruzado or Vilar themselves. Rather, they do highlight the limited information that, on their own, these mtDNA or Y-chromosome results alone provide. More saliently, as Gabriel Haslip-Viera remarks both in "The Politics of Taíno Revivalism" and "Amerindian mtDNA Does Not Matter: A Reply to Jorge Estevez and the Privileging of Taíno Identity in the Spanish-speaking Caribbean," the partial information mtDNA (or Y-chromosome) results do provide is further reduced given by the fact that they capture the genetic ancestry of one person in one's lineage, ignoring the contributions that other thousands of ancestors in that person's family tree may have contributed (Shriver and Kittles 2004).

What these handful of studies using these limited techniques show is how extensive is the mixture in the genetic ancestry of present-day Puerto Ricans. In fact, Haslip-Viera states Martínez-Cruzado and his team's own results provide "strong evidence for demonstrating that the Puerto Rican population is thoroughly mixed" (p.323). But this is nothing new! The historical record, sociological and anthropological studies have substantiated this fact. Moreover, genetic ancestry analyses using a different approach, based on the proportions of genetic markers associated with large geographical regions of the globe a given person's genome may show (i.e., autosomal DNA analysis), indicate that estimates of the sub-Saharan African cluster in a given Puerto Rican's ancestry ranged from 24 percent (Risch et al. 2009; Bryc 2010) to 29 percent (Parra et al. 2004). Native American ancestry represents 14 percent (Risch et al. 2009) or 18 percent (Parra et al. 2004) of the genetic make-up in samples of Puerto Ricans. Eurasian genetic heritage accounts for 53 percent (Parra et al. 2004) to 62 percent (Risch et al. 2009).

The analyses the teams led by Martínez-Cruzado and Vilar launched have been presented, however, as explicit challenges directed at the extant historiography, which to a greater or lesser extent has categorically established that a discrete "Indian" population in Puerto Rico, whether Taíno/Arawak or otherwise, had disappeared from Puerto Rico either through death, emigration or cultural and/or biological amalgamation, by the end of the seventeenth century, as Haslip-Viera points out. While scholars conducting genetic ancestry research may not "prove" that Taínos did not disappear from the island post-Columbus, the fact that they provide evidence that Indians "live" within virtually all Puerto Ricans in their genetic makeup gives some, if perhaps misguided, substantiation to essentialist and essentializing claims such as those made by Estevez.

Final thoughts

In closing, *Race, Front and Center: Perspectives on Race among Puerto Ricans* provides a panoramic survey of this salient social identity as a still wide open subject of scholarly inquiry relative to the broad academic production in Puerto Rican Studies. It has presented examples of approaches to the understanding of race among Puerto Ricans from a latter generation of scholars in Anthropology, Economics, Art and Social History, Literature and Literary Criticism as well as Sociology. But much more remains to be analyzed whether from a Political Science perspective or Theology or Legal Theory. More research is also needed from a comparative perspective involving other population groups in the United States, the Caribbean or elsewhere in the Western Hemisphere. What this anthology also hopes to accomplish is to maintain the sustained attention that is needed on a subject that historically and socially is often obscured and neglected.

SECTION I.

Racial Formation in Building a Nation

CHAPTER 1

Un hombre (negro) del pueblo: José Celso Barbosa and the Puerto Rican "Race" Toward Whiteness

By Miriam Jiménez Román

It has long been part of official ideology and popular lore that racism does not exist in Puerto Rico, indeed cannot exist given the overwhelming "racial" mixture that defines the Island's people. The biological and cultural fusion of the Indian, Spaniard and African, it is claimed, has created a distinct Puerto Rican "Creole" society where the social (and more specifically, the cultural) takes precedence over the "racial" and where the nation is presented as a homogeneous whole. Neither black nor white, Puerto Ricans are described as the quintessential "rainbow people" a nation of mestizos free of the "racial" concerns and conflicts so rampant in the United States. If there should be any acknowledgment of racial *prejudice*[1] it is with the caveat of its being merely a survival or "vestige" of slavery or, more commonly, of its coming to the Island as a recent, foreign (read United States) import. Always, there is the insistence on the uniquely non-hostile nature of "race relations" in Puerto Rico.

Juxtaposed to this mestizo construct is a widely accepted belief in the superiority of "whiteness,"—and its corollary, the inferiority of "blackness"— popularly expressed in the notion of *"mejoramiento de la raza"* [improvement of the race]. Thus in 1995, on the occasion of the 122nd anniversary of abolition, Luís Díaz Soler, author of the only comprehensive study of slavery on the Island (Díaz Soler 1970) emphasized the small population of "negros" (sic) during the 19th century and the Spanish "tolerance" for intermarriage which encouraged widespread mestizaje, "and breezily predicted that "in two centuries, there will hardly be any blacks in Puerto Rico."[2] In the same article, anthropologist and cultural promoter Ricardo Alegría offered his own prediction consistent with the argument that Puerto Rico is the "whitest" of the Antilles: in the race toward whiteness the Dominican Republic will come in second and Cuba will finish dead last. Such "predictions" are neither

Originally published in *CENTRO: Journal of the Center for Puerto Rican Studies* 8(1&2): 9-29, 1996.

new or unusual; rather, they have been a mainstay of the race discourse for the past century, presented as the "final solution," without any apparent awareness of the racist implications of such a formulation. From this perspective, *mestizaje* is only laudable—or even acceptable—as a transitional phase and not, as the "rainbow people" construct would seem to suggest, as an end in itself.

That racist expressions and practices continue to coexist alongside its almost adamant denial is a testament to the often contradictory nature of racism itself. Racism, as it is manifested in Puerto Rico, and much if not all of Latin America, is indeed different from that which operates in the United States or South Africa. But for Latin Americans generally, and for Puerto Ricans specifically, difference is typically translated into its non-existence/absence. For most of this century Puerto Ricans have compared themselves (and been compared) with the giant to the North and, finding neither Jim Crow segregation nor lynchings, they have declared themselves free of racism. Despite the changes brought about by the civil rights movement of the sixties and seventies which have significantly reduced the more overt expressions of racism in the United States, this ideology of racial harmony continues to hold sway and most Puerto Ricans continue to object to any suggestion that, in matters of "race," the two countries are more alike than dissimilar. This stance, then, serves to buttress all the other distinctions which the colony asserts, over and against the metropole. Puerto Rican racial exceptionalism has rested on the implicit view that there is only one kind of racism, one way of being racist, with the United States serving as the primary point of reference.[3]

With rare exceptions,[4] students of "race relations" in Puerto Rico have not been immune to this United States-centric perspective on "race." In an attempt to capture different manifestations of what is essentially the same phenomenon, some have taken recourse in the term "social race," as though "race" were anything other than a social construction.[5] As a social construction it has been adaptable to the particular exigencies of the moment, taking on innumerable guises, responding to local, regional and international demands and influences. Yet this range of possibilities, across time and space, actually makes visible certain consistencies and continuities. That Puerto Ricans continue to express derogatory notions about people of visible[6] African ancestry is far from an aberration; they are quite simply expressing the commonplace truisms on matters of "race" as constructed in their particular context(s). In Puerto Rico, these truths have been articulated within a colonial context spanning 500 years and imposed by two "white" imperial powers, with an almost seamless continuity in the transition.

For Puerto Ricans "race" has always functioned on various levels simultaneously and often in contradiction to one another. There is the institutionally sanctioned and popularly reinforced belief in distinct races with identifiable, essential traits, with a corresponding notion of a "multiracial" society whose citizens enjoy harmonious relations, not least because of their evolutionary trek toward "whiteness." On the other hand there is the idea of homogeneity articulated through the rhetoric of "*la gran familia puertorriqueña*," a "race" of mestizos that shares a common culture, language, and history. Trapped between the desire to demonstrate the capacity for self-governance to their colonial overlords and the equally strong striving for national unity and cultural dignity in the face of colonial domination, Puerto Ricans have opted for ambiguity and general avoidance whenever the subject of "race" comes up. As with gender, sexuality, and class, "race" is an issue that threatens the core beliefs of the "family" paradigm, the pillar of much of Puerto Rico's national rhetoric, both anticolonial and annexationist.

Until recently, the discussion of "race" among the Island's political and intellectual elite (whatever their racial classification or political sympathies) has offered up seemingly incompatible arguments based on remarkably similar premises and arriving at predictably similar conclusions. Flowing through all the narratives is a reluctance to acknowledge the existence of racism as anything but an aberration attributable to the baser instincts of a few ignorant, misguided individuals. Interestingly, these "individual" culprits have included "whites," "pretenders to whiteness," and "upstart Negroes"—suggesting the pervasiveness of the very racism which is being denied.

Certainly what is most problematic about the prevailing constructs is that they don't allow for protest from those that are excluded because in theory there is no exclusion. Those who have protested racially motivated exclusions and injustices and demanded full and dignified membership in "*la familia*" have been labeled overly sensitive, as suffering from an inferiority complex, or unwitting victims of an imported, i.e., alien, racial ideology. In a society which devalues blackness, black Puerto Ricans are trapped in the paradoxical situation of being doubly silenced, largely absent from the family portrait and yet prohibited from mentioning the slight under penalty of even greater ostracism. In such a climate it is hardly surprising that few black voices have been raised in protest, or that even those rare attempts at articulating the lived experience of racism have been suppressed or ignored. More commonly, though, black Puerto Ricans have struck an accommodationist chord, downplaying "race" in the interest of national unity, eager to demonstrate their Puerto Ricanness by acquiescing in the very racist ideology that denies them full membership.

What follows is a preliminary discussion of the positions regarding "race" taken by a few prominent members of the Island's national elite, with special attention to the writings of the illustrious political leader, José Celso Barbosa (1857–1922). Barbosa appears as a unique figure in several respects. In a society where African ancestry and Blackness are not understood to be necessarily the same thing, and where phenotype, i.e. appearance, determines "race," Barbosa was unequivocally *un negro*. Of very humble working class origins, Barbosa directly experienced his "race" during the last quarter century of Spanish rule, achieving notable success despite overwhelming social and economic obstacles. During the first decades of United States rule Barbosa was the epitome of the "self-made man," exercising considerable political power within the limited spaces available to the national elite. Barbosa, whose personal experiences left him with few illusions about the social and political system bequeathed the Island by Spain, was a fervent admirer of the Republican democratic ideals represented by the United States, and actively struggled to make Puerto Rico a state at a time when de jure segregation ruled the South and lynching was the national pastime. Most significantly, Barbosa left a record of his experiences and opinions regarding "race," publishing numerous newspaper articles over a span of 25 years, most aimed at explaining the seeming incongruity of a black man wanting political annexation to an openly racist country.

But while Barbosa is unique in his straddling of colonial regimes, his crossing of class lines, and in the documentation that he left behind, in the final analysis his position is quite representative of the contradictions faced by many of those who are both black and Puerto Rican. Throughout his life Barbosa operated under many of the same constraints which still function to silence black Puerto Ricans today. The opinions he put forth were already informed by ideas which would be refined and become officially inscribed during the cultural debates of the 1930s, a period of social, economic and political crises on the Island. Most glaringly, since he directly experienced both regimes, Barbosa would precede *La generación de los treinta* in his selective remembrances of life under Spanish colonialism, ultimately succumbing to the same line of defense against the perceived threats of United States racism and colonialism: the cultural distinctiveness of Puerto Ricans. Because "memories" of Spanish colonialism play such a crucial role in Barbosa's discussions of "race," and continue to serve as the basis for subsequent postulations, it is first necessary to briefly examine the historical context out of which springs the "race" discourse articulated by these, and other, men in twentieth century Puerto Rico.[7]

Historical Background

Far from being a recent import, Puerto Rico was racialized at birth. The Spanish conquerors rationalized the enslavement and extermination of the native Taínos by reference to their "infidel" status, their physical weakness and their lack of "civilization." As is the case with the rest of the Americas, estimates as to the number of indigenous peoples at the moment of contact are varied, fragmented and often exaggerated. For Borikén the numbers range from (an unlikely) high of one million people to a low of 16,000 (Moscoso 1986: 408–10). We find much greater consensus among chroniclers and later scholars as to the fate of the Taínos: within a century of the conquest their numbers had been decimated.

Over 90 percent of the approximately 10 million enslaved Africans brought to the Americas during the more than three centuries of the transatlantic slave trade were taken to Latin America and the Caribbean. The Island of Puerto Rico received approximately one percent (about 100,000), certainly a small figure when compared to Brazil's 38%, or even to the 4.6% received by what is now the territory of the United States. [...] In addition to receiving proportionately greater numbers of enslaved Africans, Puerto Rico's small size and settlement patterns (the first Spanish towns were established in the southwest and northeast, and by the mid-18th century the Island's population was "so scattered" that houses could be found "everywhere") also encouraged a greater dispersal of its black population (Abad 1994: 27).

The *ladino* (i.e. Christianized African) slaves who first accompanied the Spanish conquerors were initially used as domestic servants and then, as the supply of Indian labor continued to dwindle, as miners alongside the Taínos. Just as had occurred in the earliest colony in Hispaniola, *ladino* slaves joined with Taínos and escaped the Spanish settlements. The so-called *bozales*, enslaved Africans who were brought directly from the Niger-Congo region to the Island begin with the first Royal license in 1519, also engaged in organized rebellion in alliance with the Taínos and the *ladinos*. The intimacy of these relations during the first years of Spanish settlement has led at least one student of the subject to observe that any indigenous cultural survivals present today are probably traceable to this early period of isolated fugitive communities of Africans and Taínos. In any event, as an identifiable group, the Taínos had all but disappeared by the 17th century,[8] while *bozales* continued to arrive for another 200 years and Spanish adventurers, repelled by the miserable conditions on the Island and seduced by the promise of wealth on the mainland, continued to leave. Rebellion and subversion of Spanish authority was a mainstay of the developing nation, as reflected at every level of Island society, from the frequent escapes from slave-worked plantations[9] to the resentment of the *criollos*,[10] who increasingly identified their interests as distinct from those of Spain.

Concern with the racial composition of the island was evident from the earliest years of colonization. A 1581 report on the Island population listed more than twice as many Blacks, *mulatos* and mestizos as there were whites. Almost 200 years later, the French naturalist, André Pierre Ledrú, observed that "pure whites without mixture of strange blood are extremely rare" (1935: 75). Despite earnest attempts in the 19th century to rectify what was considered a dangerous imbalance of the "races" through the promotion of European immigration to the Island, the colony's first three centuries resulted in a population predominantly composed of people classified as *negro* and *mulato* or *pardo*. European immigration never approached the numbers of black people who, taking advantage of the Spanish offer to accept slave runaways from rival European powers, escaped from the British (and to a lesser extent, Dutch and Danish) colonies and settled as free men and women on the Island.

The elaborate racial caste system developed by the Spanish showed an obsessive concern with, and dependence on, lineage as a means of controlling their colonies.[11] Membership in a particular *casta* not only determined one's standing within the pecking order but also one's relations with the other castes. Despite the complexity of its classification and terminology the caste system essentially established the superiority and authority of Spaniards. Anyone who was not a Spaniard, or could not claim some affiliation with "Spanish blood,"—which was extended to include its "civilizing" culture—was, by definition, inferior and powerless.

In Spain's attempt at imperial consolidation, "Hispanization" was encouraged; *bozales*, for example, became *negros criollos* within one generation. Accepting the Spanish language and Roman Catholicism did not, however, protect Creole slaves from the abuses of their masters. Notwithstanding what is considered the most "benevolent" of the European slave codes, slave owners acted with impunity, whipping, maiming and even killing their slaves for real or imagined infractions. Slaves were scarce and expensive but the fear of rebellion was greater, and demonstrations of force and authority were a fundamental means of maintaining discipline and obedience. The denigration of Africans and their descendants was the other essential aspect of this control. [...]

Free Blacks, and *pardos* (*mulatos* and other *castas*), as descendants of slaves, were legally and socially discriminated against. Representing the vast majority of the Island's population, they were restricted in the work they could do, in their freedom of movement, the places they could attend and live in, whom they could marry, the bearing of arms, their access to institutions, the clothing they could wear—in short every aspect of their lives was carefully regulated (Wagenheim and Jiménez de Wagenheim 1994: 261-72.). White apprehension that such discriminatory treatment could lead to possible alliances between free and enslaved Blacks and *pardos* is evident in the legislation of the 19th century dealing with slave insurrections; these always included penalties against free Blacks and *pardos*. The steady stream of newly enslaved Africans (many entering through the contraband trade which defied the Crown's regulatory decrees) and the frequently "brutal intimacy"[12] inflicted on the enslaved women by the slave owners, substantially increased the numbers of those classified as *pardos*. *Pardos* were thus stigmatized for both their origins as Africans and as illegitimate offspring. Within the context of a rigid patriarchal morality prescribed by the Catholic Church and enforced by the State, *pardas* were particularly vulnerable, regarded as naturally lacking in moral rectitude, and therefore as the instigator, rather than the victim, of (white and black) male and (white) female aggression. Almost all *pardos* and *pardas* were free,[13] albeit only conditionally; ultimately they were not *blancos*, their loyalties were never certain, and they were not deemed deserving of the same considerations as *blancos*.

Most prevalent among *blancos* was the belief that *pardos* were suspect and had to be watched. We thus find that even in the (ostensibly) Church-based segregated "*cofradías*" and "*hermandades*" that were common throughout the Island well into the 19th century, the officers were always *blancos*; Blacks and *pardos* could not aspire beyond simple membership (López Cantos 1986: 292). As representatives of the Spanish Crown and primary beneficiaries of the colony's resources, Spaniards were not only the most privileged *blancos*, but all so classified automatically were assured deference from the other castes. [...]

Because deference was not limited to matters of social etiquette but included access to employment, goods and services, the "rewards" of whiteness made it a much sought-after classification. In an attempt to control the forging and "fixing" of documents so prevalent in the colonies, the Church and state periodically passed regulations establishing the criteria for membership in one or another caste. None was guarded more closely than the classification as *blanco*, even as its legitimacy was clearly being regarded with increasing suspicion. By the mid-18th century visitors reported that Puerto Rico had "a lack of families of refined and pure ancestry" and that even among the scant white families there were few "without mixture of all types of bad blood" (López Cantos 1986: 244).

[...]

Cross-caste marriages particularly for women, often the best course for attaining upward caste mobility[14]—were discouraged but occurred with enough frequency to expose ever greater contradictions in the caste system itself. In 1757, for example, clerics were instructed in how to register births, marriages and deaths in the two parish ledgers, one for *blancos* and another for *negros* and *pardos*, free or enslaved. In the event of a cross-caste marriage between a *blanco* and a *pardo* whose parents were free, it was to be registered in the "white" ledger. If either parent had been a slave, and the *pardo* was male, the marriage would be listed in the "black" ledger; if it was the female, then the marriage would be in the "white" book.[15] Any children of the marriage would then be classified according to the ledger in which the marriage had been registered. These regulatory prescriptions suggest a certain receptivity to *pardas* legalizing their unions with *blancos* and can be seen as both an accommodation to the popular preference for "colored" women as (fetishized) sexual partners (a preference which had much to do with their numerical preponderance), and as indicative of the greater value placed on the male's racial caste position. Thus the private woman, and the product of her womb, is defined by the public man.

When the biological and the social collided, adjustments were made to accommodate both in the interest of maintaining the political and ideological status quo. Because these practices were well-known, the "whiteness" of *blancos* was continually under scrutiny and contestation. "Whiteness," clearly referring to more than just "blood," or even appearance, required other signifiers, other "proofs" of one's superiority that were consistent with notions of origins, and indeed served to reinforce them. For the *criollos*, education and training, available exclusively to the wealthy, reinforced the notion of their superiority over the lower castes while simultaneously establishing their capacity to rule. [...]

[...]

The *criollo* elite had insisted on their equality with Spaniards and their ability to rule autonomously, but there was never any question as to who would rule this proposed new nation. Thus, these "scientific" new ideas [i.e., biological essentialism contained in social Darwinism] could be received by an Island intellectual elite as viable rationalizations for their continued position of privilege in the social hierarchy.

Before this national project could be realized, the invasion by the United States in 1898 made even more urgent a reconfiguration of the national identity. The North Americans promptly re-named the Island "Porto Rico," and, holding out the promise of industry and prosperity, proceeded to assume its pre-ordained "destiny" as one of the most "advanced races" and bring "enlightened civilization" to the "natives."[16] At the same time, it was necessary to make these inferior "colored people" as palatable as possible to "whites" in the United States, who were not expected to welcome the burden of more "Negroes" among them.

It is interesting that only two years earlier, in the infamous case of *Plessy v Ferguson*, the U.S. Supreme Court had rejected the plea of a Louisiana octoroon that his seventh-eighths "white blood" should qualify him for a seat on a railroad "white" car. The historic decision firmly established the legitimacy of white supremacy and the inferiority of those known to have the slightest trace of African ancestry. Both the new colonizers and the elite of the twice-colonized Puerto Rico had reason for concern over the Island's racial composition and the implications for future relations; from the beginning, it was in their common interest to downplay the issue of "race" and to minimize the black presence on the Island.

The resulting efforts were wrought with incongruities. One of the earliest colonial reports on conditions in Puerto Rico, *Our Islands and Their People* (1899), offered a wealth of photographic proof of Puerto Rican "coloredness"—along with a text that disputed the evidence: Puerto Ricans were described as pertaining to three "distinct types, or races": "Spanish," "white or light mulatto," and "pure-blooded Africans," the latter group described as "few" in number and essentially confined to "a colony at one end of the island..." (Bryan 1899: 297). Apparently concerned that even a "few" Blacks might be cause for alarm, the author reassured his readers, "[b]ut the African race is declining, and will eventually either disappear or be amalgamated with the white race" (Bryan 1899: 284).

[...]

Coming at the matter from different directions, colonizer and colonized converged in their shared values and beliefs regarding the economic and political superiority of the United States, and either implicitly or explicitly attributed it to biology. Where there was disagreement it was in the social sphere, articulated by the national elite in terms of Spain's "ancient civilization," the foundation for Puerto Rico's superior culture. Indeed, as a colony of a "really white" imperial power, with a different language and different racial codes, Puerto Rican "culture" would have to serve double-duty: the Island's superior "culture" also accounted for its "flexible" racial attitude which seemed so incomprehensible to the North Americans. The banner of the "cultural" homogeneity of Puerto Ricans would also be raised whenever internal social tensions and contradictions threatened to surface. It would provide the moral higher ground that exempted Puerto Ricans from accepting a United States construction of race that basically disenfranchised a whole people.

Barbosa: un hombre (negro) del pueblo

For José Celso Barbosa, founder and leader of the Republican Party, this emphasis on "culture" helped resolve what would appear to have been a fundamental contradiction: his support for annexation to the United States and his being *un negro*.

Born free, poor, and black in 1857, the son of a sporadically employed Puerto Rican brickmason and a Venezuelan who had immigrated to the Island as a young girl, Barbosa was able to study at the Island's only secondary educational institution, thanks to the dogged determination of his aunt and despite the obvious hostility of his teachers and fellow students.[17] The victim of frequent humiliations,[18] Barbosa managed to graduate from the colony's Jesuit seminary and soon thereafter left the Island to pursue further studies in the United States. This was already a distinctly different route than that taken by his more affluent classmates, who were able to follow the Island elite tradition of a European university education. At the University of Michigan at Ann Arbor, where he obtained his medical degree in 1880, Barbosa enjoyed an active intellectual and social life (including the attentions of a German girlfriend) and, reportedly, "did not find that cloud of racial prejudices which he had left behind" on the Island.[19]

[...]

Although Michigan's black population never rose above one percent throughout the 19th century, the state's black residents included a large number of highly educated and successful African-Americans, and the community exerted significant economic and political influence in certain counties. By 1880 Blacks were being elected into office in those towns where they represented the majority of voters. A relatively tolerant racial climate led to the repeal, in 1883, of Michigan's anti-miscegenation laws, and two years later to passage of a series of laws banning discrimination in public accommodations. Since Barbosa had left Michigan by 1880 it is safe to conclude that, along with imbibing the ideas of the times, he also personally experienced racial segregation. Certainly he would leave the United States identifying the Republican Party as the savior and future hope of the black masses.

Returning to Puerto Rico, Barbosa began his medical practice, joining the ranks of the neglected colony's professional class which clamored for greater political and economic autonomy from Spain. He became a member of a Masonic lodge, a crucial site (as in the rest of the Americas) for subversive political activity, and joined the Partido Autonomista. A staunch anti-monarchist, by 1897 Barbosa had become the principal figure among Los Ortodoxos, a group which proposed a government which represented the "will of the people"—under the leadership of the educated vanguard, as opposed to hereditary rule by the Creole elite. Emphasizing the need for popular democracy and social equality, Barbosa attained considerable influence among the urban working class, many of whose leaders were also black.[20]

Barbosa's medical practice, which included the dispensing of free services to San Juan's indigent, also flourished—although he was not officially licensed to practice medicine by the Spanish authorities until 1890 when he was subjected to a grueling series of exams by a hostile medical court that included one member who refused to wear his robes "for a colored man." After passing these exams he was admitted to El Ateneo, the Island's first institution to offer post-secondary instruction, where he taught medicine (including classes in midwifery), and soon was serving on its Board.

In addition to his political and pedagogical activities, Barbosa was one of the founders, in 1893, of the Island's cooperatist movement and a regular contributor to the Island newspapers. All indications are that he was also an avid reader who kept abreast of events in Europe as well as the United States. His readings included the writings of W.E.B. DuBois and Booker T. Washington and he appears to have been a subscriber to (though not a sympathizer of) *The Messenger*; until 1922 one of the most widely circulated of the radical black publications in the United States. He also read *The Crisis*, the official organ of the National Association for the Advancement of Colored People. Like other black Puerto Ricans, Barbosa demonstrated a keen interest in "Negro literature and history," and necessarily filled much of this need with material produced in the United States.

Barbosa and his party played a key role in Puerto Rico's transition from Spanish to United States colony, serving as counterforce to the Creole elite's political aspirations. Most notably, during the period of *las turbas republicanas* ("the Republican mobs") that extended from 1900 to 1904, Barbosa's sympathizers among the urban poor and recently arrived peasants launched an often violent campaign against the (till then) dominant Federal Party, which led to the resounding defeat of the Federales in the municipal elections of 1902. Barbosa continued to enjoy the patronage of the United States colonial government, serving on the advisory Executive Council (1900–1917) and as a senator (1917–1921) until his death.[21]

A founding member of the Island's Republican Party, Barbosa often expressed a concern for the urban professional and working classes and advocated a "modernization" process which would free the Island of the sociopolitical practices left behind by Spain.[22] In addition to his more overt emphasis on the evils of hereditary class privilege, Barbosa implicitly racialized the political discourse by accusing Luís Muñoz Rivera of having been an accomplice and instrument of the

Spanish government, suggesting that victory for the Federales would be a return to rule by *los blancos o los de la otra banda.*

Unlike Muñoz Rivera, and despite his own *de facto* leadership, Barbosa refused to assume the presidency of the Republican Party. In like fashion, Barbosa never took on the directorship of the newspaper, *El Tiempo*, the Republican Party daily which he founded in 1907. This pattern of exerting power from "behind the scenes" would characterize Barbosa's entire career; [...]

Barbosa thus negotiated a fine line between a defensive "racial pride" and accommodation to the colonial status quo, both under Spain and the United States. This balancing act would result in a string of contradictions as he wrestled to speak as a Puerto Rican, as a black man, and as an accomplice of the United States colonial regime. Barbosa did indeed "stay in his place," in the sense that he maintained a non-confrontational stance throughout his life, but he was situated in a number of "places" which continually shifted and only rarely converged. Outspoken in his attacks against racial and class privileges while the Island was still under Spanish rule, Barbosa seems to have fallen victim to the same historical amnesia (albeit to a lesser degree) that would afflict other Puerto Ricans once under United States colonial rule. In a 1896 article, for example, Barbosa wrote of his "struggles" against "the Spanish Catholic Jesuits" and "the Yankee professors" who hindered the educational aspirations of "a son of the people" because he lacked "a false dossier of pure blood."[23] Less than ten years later, Barbosa would insist that "the color problem does not exist in Puerto Rico.... has never germinated in Puerto Rico," and recall the Spanish policy of "purity of blood" as "a mere formality" (Barbosa 1909: 33).

What would remain consistent in Barbosa's writings was a belief in privilege based on merit, not on "an accident of birth." Thus, under Spanish rule, Barbosa would assert his own demonstrated superiority over "those who are truly inferior" because they owe everything they possess "to the capricious luck of their name" (Barbosa 1909: 26). Years later he would claim that under United States tutelage, "...superiority is manifested, not in one's race, nor in the greater or lesser quantity of coloring material in the skin. Superiority depends on the quantity of gray matter, on the refinement of the cerebral circumvolutions, on education, on will, on moral preparation, on the environment.... essential factors for individual and collective superiority" (Barbosa 1920: 19–20).

En Nuestro Terreno: Barbosa on "Race"

The bulk of Barbosa's writings on race issues were originally published in the Republican Party newspaper *El Tiempo*, between 1915 and 1920, and correspond to specific and politically significant events surrounding the First World War. In 1917, the United States would confer citizenship on Puerto Ricans, a step in the direction advocated by Barbosa's Republican Party. Growing dissatisfaction on the Island was finding expression in a more militant labor movement; the Socialist Party, founded less than two years before, had easily garnered 12% of the vote in the 1917 elections, attracting many former members of the Republican Party. By 1920, it was apparent that the United States had no interest in fulfilling the political and economic aspirations of the Island's people. Increasing racial tensions in the United States— most notably the wholesale lynchings and riots which marked the aftermath of the war— had also made Puerto Rican membership in the Union extremely unlikely, and for many sectors, clearly undesirable.

In the series of articles written before 1917 Barbosa is primarily concerned with reassuring other Puerto Ricans—and particularly other Blacks—that they have nothing to fear from the United States, and that any danger of racism resides closer to home. Indeed, despite his frequent claims regarding the nonexistence of racism on the Island, the articles were invariably motivated by denigrating statements made about him by other Puerto Ricans and Barbosa actually offered numerous examples of his personal tribulations. He was usually careful, however, to direct attention away from *los americanos* and point the finger of any possible blame at individual Puerto Ricans. Thus in the articles published under the title *"En nuestro terreno"* [In Our Land], a direct reply to the many accusations launched against him as "a traitor" to his "race," Barbosa identifies racism as an internal problem, one that need not be imported because it already exists. Insisting that he had always been treated with respect and consideration by North American colonial administrators, Barbosa charges "certain Puerto Rican whites" with having conspired against him "because Barbosa was black." Letters, petitions, delegations and affidavits were all produced to destroy his reputation," [a]nd it was natives who engaged in such infamy. And it was white Puerto Ricans who thus tried to humiliate Barbosa." At the same time he argued that under statehood, the laws of Puerto Rico would be made by Puerto Ricans and they alone would be responsible for assuring that "race prejudice" not "become a problem." On race matters, Barbosa thus upholds the myth of racial equality while simultaneously holding the Island's "whites" and the masses of "quasi whites" explicitly accountable for whatever racial problem might exist.

For Barbosa, it is these pretenders to whiteness who pose a potential problem "for the race" and for the country as a whole. Seeing in the history of Blacks in the United States "an inspiration to men of color who must feel pride in the progress they have attained," Barbosa contrasts them to Blacks in Latin America, whom he accuses of being the real "race traitors":

...In the countries of South America, in the Antilles, and even in Europe, people of black blood have won high distinction, both political and civic, and have shone in the arts and literature. But they have moved in an environment of tolerance that has accepted them as equals, and once they have risen they have ceased being exponents of the African race and gone on to occupy a position of high distinction in the proclaiming of the great Latin culture, confusing themselves within the heterogeneity that is called *Latin civilization*. Transforming their descendency, through amalgamation, through crossing, they have succeeded in being classified as of the white race, and in thus they cannot be presented as exponents of the advancements and progress of the African race. (1937: 12—emphasis in original)

In a surprising twist, Barbosa actually finds cause for celebrating racism "because it gives blacks the opportunity to win in the battle, and demonstrate that, face to face, against a white race...[they] have advanced in all the spheres of life" (1927, 21). In a stance that attempts to accommodate local national integrity against the perceived threat of incorporation into an openly racist society, Barbosa insists that, in the United States, any obstacles to black advancement, any violation of the Constitution, has been carried out by the individual states and not by the federal government. Ironically, "state's rights," traditionally utilized by the South to maintain Jim Crow segregation, is invoked by Barbosa as a guarantee against Jim Crow segregation.

Never disputing the superiority of "legitimate whites," Barbosa instead appeals to the finer instincts, culture and refinement of Island "whites," calling for a higher moral position against those "dwarfs, upstarts of the white race, fresh from ethnic evolution, white of skin, dark of mind, shameful descendants of that race they scorn." The "genuine, direct representatives of the [white] race...." are above the pettiness bred by feelings of inferiority and "...give faith to their purity [of blood] in their distinguished manners, their respect and high regard for other classes." The "ignorant masses," who, fueled by the "envy of inferiority" deride Blacks and attempt to "confuse" themselves with "pure whites," are the real problem. In an accommodationist mode reminiscent of the North American black leader Booker T. Washington's 1895 Atlanta Speech (1994), Barbosa assures his readers of his belief in the separation of public and private life. Subscribing to a "stay in your place" bootstrap mentality of individual "improvement" that will ultimately prove one's worth to "legitimate whites", Barbosa is careful to stress that in his view "social mingling" is neither appropriate nor desirable. Indeed, he points to this willingness of Blacks to "stay in their place" as the reason for Puerto Rico not having a race problem:

Since there is *no color problem* in political life, or in public life, and since the colored element has never attempted to cross or erase the social line, the color problem does not exist in Puerto Rico. (1937: 31–32—emphasis in original)

Barbosa thus presents us with contradictory messages: On the one hand, he praises black people in the United States for having achieved as a "race," going so far as to see racism against them as ultimately being no more than a challenge, an opportunity to struggle and overcome obstacles. Simultaneously, Barbosa warns Blacks in Puerto Rico against any such race-based approach to equality. The color problem will not exist in Puerto Rico "...if the colored element manages to avoid, by all possible means, any race struggle; any linking of their rights to questions of race; or demands for benevolence for racial reasons, or consider as a favor the acts of justice made to colored men" (Barbosa 1937: 31–32).

Consistent with his elitist class perspective, Barbosa is convinced that, in the final analysis "class" will prevail and that having demonstrated their intelligence, cultural refinement and ability, Blacks will be recognized as equal by similarly intelligent, cultured and able whites. He cautions Puerto Rican youth, and especially those "of color" who study in the United States, not to become tainted by the prejudices that will surround them there. He seeks assurance that such ideas not be imported into the Island, arguing that, for the good of the Fatherland, "they should accept all that is good about that country and reject all that is bad." Ultimately, though, there is no need to fear that foreign ideas will take root in a Puerto Rico which has never known a race problem.

Thus, the men of color of Puerto Rico can remain calm and satisfied under the new sovereign because the Americans cannot, even if they tried, act against that element, nor will it be possible to import the color problem as long as the Puerto Ricans, by their expressed will, do not permit it (Barbosa 1937: 38).

The series of six articles published by Barbosa in 1919 on "the problem of race in the United States" reflects new concerns. Most evidently, they are a reaction to the growing labor militancy on the Island. But Barbosa was also writing in the aftermath of the Congressional debates in 1916 regarding the extension of citizenship to Puerto Ricans, sessions which left no doubt as to the low esteem in which the Islanders were held. The more sympathetic congressmen argued that the majority of Puerto Ricans were white and therefore deserving of citizenship. More common though, were the sentiments of Representative Joseph G. Cannon who asserted that "really 75 to 80 percent of the population...was pure African or had an African strain in their blood," and that given this inferior foundation there was little that could be expected by way of capacity for self-rule (quoted in Jiménez-

Muñoz 1993: 89). For a black man who had himself argued that the "masses" of Puerto Ricans were "quasi-whites," Barbosa found little space for maneuvering in the racially loaded debates. He could hardly assert his own "Africaness" when even a "strain" of it was cited as a deficiency, nor could he, in a climate that posed the redemptive powers of "whiteness" as the only avenue toward self-determination, refute claims to the "whiteness" of Puerto Ricans.

For many Puerto Ricans the First World War offered an opportunity to demonstrate their mettle to their colonizers, whether as proof of capacity for self-rule or of worthiness for equal incorporation into the United States. More difficult to defend was the drafting of Puerto Ricans into the segregated United States Army. The initial plan to ship Puerto Ricans to segregated training camps in the United States was successfully challenged by the Island's Republican Party. After some conflict with members of the Union Party who argued for segregated camps in Puerto Rico, Barbosa proposed his usual hands-off solution: two training camps-one for whites and one for coloreds—and allow the men themselves to select their camp. While his proposal resolved the immediate problem, it also made manifest both the racism among Puerto Ricans and the ability of the United States to impose their "race problem" on the Island.

Barbosa's writings offer ample evidence of his comprehensive knowledge of United States racial history as well as current events. Defending a broad spectrum of black leadership, which encompassed both Booker T. Washington and W.E.B. DuBois, he wrote sympathetically about the community's historic struggles for racial dignity and equal rights, and expressed confidence in their eventual success. At times explicitly identifying as a member of "the African race," Barbosa was careful also to establish distinctions between the conditions in the United States and those in Puerto Rico. Ultimately, the situation in the United States was one which Puerto Ricans should follow as "mere spectators, even when we become part of the American nation" (Barbosa 1937: 106).

[...]

Returning to his earlier attack on the color consciousness of the "masses" who have pretensions to whiteness, while continuing to deny the existence of any "race" problem, Barbosa is caught in the contradiction and finally falls back on an evolutionary argument, citing widespread racial mixture as the surest path to resolving any problem that might exist.

The race problem does not exist here.

That problem is resolving itself through the evolution of the
black race.

Here, the black race has been mixing with the other races;
and today every man of color in Puerto Rico is a conglomerate
of *blue blood, Indian blood, and African blood* and through
evolution, depending on the predominance of one of those
parts, and the fading of pigment, Blacks have evolved; from
black to mixed, *mulato* or white.

And the black Black continues to disappear.
And evolution will continue, and the problem will be resolved.
(1937: 142—emphasis in original)

Operating within the confines of a colonial and racist structure, Barbosa
could ultimately not sustain his posture as a "race man" without endangering his
legitimacy as a Puerto Rican. As an annexationist, for him to insist on the prevalence
of racism on the Island would be to fall victim, once again, to accusations of having
become a *piti-yanki*, a tool of alien domination intent on creating problems where
none exists."[24] Instead he succumbed to the pressures of an ideology that left him,
and all those who had not sufficiently "evolved," silenced and, increasingly, invisible.

Defining "el pueblo": From Barbosa to Tomás Blanco

[...]

Like Barbosa before him, Blanco sets up the United States as the benchmark for
racism. Like Barbosa, Blanco concludes that racism does not exist in Puerto Rico.
While Barbosa left open the possibility of its existence, Blanco is convinced that
the very nature of Spanish culture makes its existence untenable. To support his
position he offers examples that include the lack of correlation between racial terms
in the two countries; the more humane treatment of enslaved Africans and their
descendants under Spain; and the absence of *de jure* discrimination.

Like subsequent commentators on "race relations" in Puerto Rico, Blanco
focuses on slavery, even while emphasizing that Puerto Rico had a relatively small
enslaved population. Absent from his discussion is the situation of those (classified)
free Blacks and *pardos* who made up the majority of the population throughout the

Island's first 350 years. Instead, Blackness and slavery are strictly correlated; if all the Blacks were slaves and there were few slaves, then there were few Blacks.

His discussion on the contemporary manifestations of racism follows the same track. Jim Crow, anti-miscegenation laws, and lynchings are contrasted to the rampant miscegenation and social fraternization which he defines as the rule in Puerto Rico, acknowledging only the isolated incidence always attributable to North American influence—of racial discrimination. Echoing Barbosa, Blanco dismisses these incidences as the acts of ignorant individuals, and blames racist practices on "pretenders to whiteness." Such practices, according to him, are "foolishness" (ñoñerías) engaged in by "persons with certain doubts about their own whiteness" (Blanco 1985: 126). More importantly, any "ill-feeling" that might exist within certain social classes in Puerto Rico is "much more comical, but incomparably less bestial" than the racism of the United States. Consistent with Blanco's tendency to blame the "Other," he also singles out Puerto Rican women, with their "social scruples," as more inclined to practice racism than are men" (1985: 129).

For much of his essay, Blanco insists on the significance of miscegenation both as a cultural heritage of racial equality and as a form of immunity against racism. But he also argues for the essential "whiteness" of Puerto Ricans, taking umbrage at the North American suggestion that "Puerto Ricans are black" and that even those of Spanish genealogy are not really "white." [...]

[...]

Blanco's essay would become the canon on "race relations" in Puerto Rico. Future writers would report on the correlation between class position and color, the personal "prejudices" of certain "individuals" and the negative stereotypes associated with Blackness—and yet insist on the absence of "real" racism on an Island that was "whiter" than any other in the Caribbean, and getting "whiter" by the year. Even among those who acknowledged the discrimination experienced by black Puerto Ricans and professed sympathy for their plight, we find observations such as those expressed by two social scientists at the University of Puerto Rico, who analyzed census data for the period 1860-1935, and concluded that "the colored race will have finally disappeared from Puerto Rico in a period of 75 to 100 more years" (Colombán Rosario and Carrión 1940: 141). The noted linguist Manuel Álvarez Nazario seems particularly wedded to the Blanco construct, prefacing his oft-cited study of African influences in Puerto Rican Spanish with a lengthy disclaimer as to their significance. Álvarez Nazario establishes the "Spanish foundations" of Puerto

Rican culture, and the "ideal fraternization of the races," to explain "the minor quantitative and qualitative importance of words of African or Afro-American roots in the Hispanic-Puerto Rican vocabulary" (Álvarez Nazario 1974: 229). [...]

Discovering Zenón and the Consequences

The ideas postulated by Barbosa and Blanco were not seriously challenged until the early 1970s when the Civil Rights and Black Power movements made many of the fundamental premises of the Puerto Rican racial discourse no longer tenable. With the collapse of de jure segregation in the southern United States, Puerto Ricans could no longer point to lynchings and Jim Crow as characteristic of the "authentic" form of racism. Even more significant was the impact of the Black Power movement, with its emphasis on racial pride and an "in your face" militancy that proclaimed the legitimate right to protest assaults on black dignity.

One of the first serious challenges to the notion of harmonious "race relations" on the Island appeared in 1974, with the publication of Isabelo Zenón Cruz's two-volume study, *Narciso descubre su trasero: El negro en la cultura puertorriqueña*. Beginning with its provocative title, Zenón's book was a stunning indictment of racism in Puerto Rico, a compendium of historical facts, anecdotal accounts, and ironic commentary on a broad range of topics (theory, politics, education, sports, religion, literature, language, folklore and the arts) which seemingly left little room for rebuttal. A university professor of Spanish literature, Zenón was, like Barbosa, an educated and accomplished black man *"del pueblo"* who was influenced by the ideas of his day. Where Barbosa cited Booker T. Washington and W. E.B. DuBois, Zenón would look to Frantz Fanon and Eldridge Cleaver for inspiration and guidance.

Zenón not only documented a long list of abuses perpetrated against Blacks. collectively and individually—he named names—citing the Island intellectuals, the University of Puerto Rico, each of the Island's major political parties, and the Left, generally, as guilty of repeated acts of discrimination and blatant racism. His intent was no less than to demonstrate that "the black Puerto Rican has always been a second-class Puerto Rican," victim of a "repugnant alienation" that has been "constant, systematic, and all-encompassing" (Zenón 1974: 24). Arguing that within the context of a racist society race assumes primary significance for Blacks, Zenón simultaneously insisted on the Puerto Ricanness of the Island's black population and rejected any notion of *"la gran familia puertorriqueña"* that denied this integral membership in the national whole:[...]

[...]

What the "visibly" black man or women "experiences" is racism, and it makes him or her "invisible" as a Puerto Rican. For the black Puerto Ricans who have periodically dared to dispute the fictional image of the homogeneous and harmonious *gran familia* construct, that experience with racism has included further exclusion. So-called racial mixture, far from eliminating racism, has made invisible those whose faces still say "Africa," and thus made them complicit, for the sake of "the family," in their continued subordination. In the race toward "whiteness," black Puerto Ricans have been denied full and dignified membership in *la familia*, their presence—as so concisely portrayed in Fortunato Vizcarrondo's (1976) ¿Y *tu agüela 'onde ehtá?*—confined to the kitchen when company comes.

CHAPTER 2

Puerto Rico: The Pleasures and Traumas of Race

By Alan West-Durán

Puerto Rico's racial history is centuries old, sometimes troubled, always intricately layered, plagued by misunderstandings and denials, laced with insights, and just plain vexing. In what follows we will examine some of those baffling complexities through some canonical works of literature: *La cuarterona* by Alejandro Tapia y Rivera, "Mulata-Antilla" by Luis Palés Matos, *Maldito amor* by Rosario Ferré, "Negrito" by Tato Laviera, Edgardo Rodríguez Juliá's *El entierro de Cortijo*, and Mayra Santos Febre's short story "Marina." [...]

This [chapter] addresses only six authors spanning the last one hundred thirty years, and so it would be misleading to think that what follows is either exhaustive or "representative." Each work or author has something important to say about race and identity in the construction of Puerto Rican national consciousness, and they have been chosen because as writers their views are not only steeped in history, but also are engagingly nuanced with regard to the island's racial plight.

In 1937, Tomás Blanco, one of the island's seminal writers and thinkers, wrote the following: "Compared to the most intense explosions of that virulent behavior, our racial prejudice is the innocent game of a child" (Blanco 1985: 103). Blanco was contrasting Puerto Rico with the southern United States, and the comparison made several references to lynchings, segregation, and Jim Crow. Blanco's criticisms are all true with regard to his analysis of the U.S., but when looking homeward, his critical perspective is conspicuously absent. During most of his essay, "Racial Prejudice in Puerto Rico," he offers a benign (and inaccurate) racial history of the island, drawing a portrait suffused with Hispano-Catholic compassion, if not condescension. Two years earlier, in a classic essay, "Elogio de la plena," Blanco had written: "We have abundant black blood in us, and this should not make us feel ashamed; but, in honoring the truth, we cannot be classified as a black people" (Blanco 1975: 1004). The inconsistencies and racism of Blanco's insights have not held up well, even though his views are still echoed by some.[1]

Originally published in *CENTRO: Journal of the Center for Puerto Rican Studies* 17(1): 47–69, 2005.

Thirty-seven years later Isabelo Zenón Cruz spoke of the hypocrisy of the expression *negro puertorriqueño*, where Puerto Rican has become an adjective. Why is a black Puerto Rican identified as black before he is considered Puerto Rican, he sarcastically asks in his monumental two-volume study *Narciso descubre su trasero*. Zenón Cruz's painstaking analysis, more than 700 pages long, of historical documents, poems, literature, jokes, religion, lyrics to songs, and popular culture is a landmark study that perhaps not so curiously has been out of print for more than two decades.

Not long after Zenón, writer José Luis González stated in 1979 that Puerto Rico was basically an Afro-Caribbean nation in *El país de cuatro pisos*. Using a architectural metaphor, he said the first and foundational floor of the island edifice was laid down by black slaves, and that subsequent floors (Spanish, European, and North American) have elaborated on, changed, or transformed these African origins. Gonzalez's essay engendered substantial debate and controversy, and to date it still remains—whatever its flaws—a crucial reference in the intellectual discourse on race and identity.

These writers reflect the tensions and contradictions in examining the racial dimensions of Puerto Rican identity, and could be broadly described as Hispanicist (with racist overtones), anti-racist, and Afrocentric. Most *boricuas* would claim a mixed-raced heritage in a cultural sense, but a more whitened definition in a strictly racial sense. [...] [W]hiteness is still considered the norm, as will be argued further on [...].

What Blanco, Zenón, González, and Duany address, directly or indirectly, is a complex racial history that is both local and yet intersects with the racial dynamics of two imperial powers: Spain (1493–1898) and the United States (1898 to the present). [...]

[...]

Mulatas, madness and miscege(nation)
By the mid-1860s, it was clear that slavery's days were numbered. The play *La cuarterona* (1867), by Alejandro Tapia y Rivera (1826–1882), seems simultaneously to belie that reality and prophesy its demise. The play deals with a romance between an upper class white male and a quadroon servant, revealing the human, psychological, and emotional destructiveness of racism and slavery. Because of censorship Tapia placed the action in Havana.

Arguably the best play of nineteenth-century Puerto Rico, Tapia's work, which in English would read "The Quadroon" (or, more accurately, "Julia, The Quadroon"), is a complex and emblematic portrait of Puerto Rico's tangled social, racial, and sexual politics under Spanish colonialism in the waning years of slavery.

Tapia eclectically places lyrical flights of romanticism within a realist dramaturgy, which keeps the work from becoming overly melodramatic. The author wastes no time in presenting the amorous problems unleashed by racial injustice. The first scene is between Carlos, a young, white aristocrat, and Jorge, his servant, a black slave. Carlos has recently returned from France, and they speak about Julia, the quadroon, whom Carlos is in love with. Julia is not a slave. He does not admit this love to the slave, but instead pumps him for information about Julia's behavior in his absence. Jorge, the ever-obedient slave, tells his master about Julia's tears and her emotional volatility. Despite the stereotypical submissiveness of Jorge, Tapia has skillfully set up a racial and social triangle that will later be echoed by an amorous triangle as well. Interestingly, Jorge's information about his master comes by way of Julia, a route analogous to the way Julia's information is provided to Carlos through Jorge. This is understandable since Carlos has been physically absent, and a first reminder that absence and lack are important structural and symbolic elements of the play.

Jorge exits and Carlos's ensuing short monologue reveals much of what will transpire in the play. He says that Julia loves him, but quickly adds that this is a "disparate, una locura" (nonsense, foolishness, madness). He imagines, however, Julia's reaction, claiming that she will only see him as a childhood companion or "brother," that she does not know his love, know his heart, and that she is oblivious to the fact that he is "above certain vile concerns." Absence has made him see her as "the image of my reveries," "the star of my destiny," and also as a "sorceress." But again he gives in to despair as he claims Julia will only see an abyss between them, one that he is willing to leap across. Then Carlos speculates about his mother's views: although she raised Julia as her own, the haughty countess will see Julia as just a "poor mestiza." The monologue ends with a return to the theme of madness, a madness that begins to plot his misfortune.

Tapia sets up one of the oppositions that will define the play: the tension between sense and non-sense, madness and reason, whim and will, which not only have a personal, but social, racial, and ethical dimensions as well. Carlos's love for Julia is seen by his mother (the Countess) and even by Julia as crazy, irrational, and foolish. One of the most often used words in their arguments is *juicio*, which has rich associations in Spanish: sense, commonsense, judgment, sanity, discernment, and trial, in the strict legal sense. All of these meanings will crop up at different moments, during Carlos's and Julia's trials and tribulations. But Tapia constructs his play to help us reconsider and reverse the meanings of the terms as well, where, of course, *prejuicio* (prejudice, pre-judgment) plays an important role; and where the racial prejudices and fears of his mother, his future and imposed fiancée (Emilia), and father-in-law (Don Críspulo) are made to be seen as irrational, and mean-spirited. This is skillfully synthesized in a moment when Carlos, saying he will protect Julia, invokes the law, but quickly corrects himself and says justice: "La ley...digo mal: la justicia...." What seems "rational" as stated by the law is seen as unjust by those who oppose racism and slavery.

Despite his antipathy towards racism and his altruism, Carlos's worldview is still class-bound and not entirely free of an implicit racial superiority. Indeed, Carlos's whiteness is so ingrained, so "natural," and so transparent that he can't see how whiteness implies dominance, thereby letting him avoid asking some difficult questions. Carlos's mother is a countess, but they belong to an aristocracy in ruins. We find out at the end of the Act I that a central reason for his mother's interest in her son's betrothal to Emilia is her father's wealth. Because of their debts, their last sugar mill will be sold or auctioned off, and by marrying Don Crispulo's daughter they can stave off financial ruin. Don Crispulo is a nouveau riche, and would benefit socially from his daughter marrying into the aristocracy.

Carlos's aristocratic background is even belied in his early monologue mentioned earlier. He says he is "above certain vile concerns." Those vile concerns are not only avarice, but social appearances, and racial prejudice. On several occasions he suggests to Julia that they go and live in another country, free of obsessions related to color and race. A true child of the Enlightenment, but imbued with the quintessential Romantic ethos, Carlos, is physically above the fray. Epistemologically he embraces the objectivity that stands outside the subject-object relationship, the value-free standpoint, the "view from nowhere." By believing himself to be above the fray, he will clash with not only Julia, but those around him.

Julia reminds him that they are from two different worlds, especially in a country like Cuba (read Puerto Rico). She is much more grounded in seeing and living both racial and class difference. She has neither the physical mobility (class position) of Carlos, and epistemologically she embodies a situated knowledge, embedded in social, spatial, political, and historical relationships (Code 1993: 32–3). In opposition to Carlos, who often refers to Julia in celestial or incorporeal terms (star, angel, image, dream), Julia's imagery is more concrete and spatial (abyss, body, country, and house are examples).

How does Julia see herself, her condition? Her words are telling, reflecting a knowledge of racial positioning embedded in a moral-religious discourse. "A stain [stigma] that must be very visible, because everyone sees it, everyone rubs it in my face. When everyone says it to me! ...And yet, this is not the stain of crime: I've had it since my first moment, I was born with it ...Ah! If I could only erase it! They say I'm beautiful...ha...ha...ha! How can I be with this stain? This is my original sin, but without redemption, without redemption!" (Tapia 1993: 138). It would be difficult to find a more apt illustration of W.E.B. Du Bois's concept of "double consciousness... of always looking at one's self through the eyes of others," of the turmoil in living as "two souls, two thoughts, two unreconciled strivings; two warring ideals in one dark body" (Du Bois 1999: 11).

Julia's words admirably capture Foucault's term of bio-power, an intersection of the religious, sexual, and socio-racial gazes that underpin the visibility of power, as well as the power of visibility. Although Julia is free, unlike Jorge, who is still a slave, her existence is still severely circumscribed (her mother, a mulata, was a slave, her father white). It will eventually cost her her life.

This bio-power is synthesized in the figure of Don Críspulo. At the very end of the play Jorge, the slave, provides important information: Julia is the offspring of none other than Don Críspulo. Plotwise this might seem pat or predictable, but its effect is devastating: the social, economic, personal, and erotic dimensions of racism all converge on this character, thereby making Tapia's critique multidimensional. Don Críspulo's power (economic, male, and white) and desire have unleashed their destructiveness on Julia's life, on Carlos's dreams of happiness and Emilia's independence, on the Condesa's hopes for financial relief, and has even turned on his own yearning for social respectability.

The strength of Tapia's play is in how it attacks slavery in its widest repercussions, since after all Julia (and not Jorge) is the pivotal character, along with Carlos, of course. Tapia's critique overlaps with that of abolitionists like Segundo Ruiz Belvis, José Julián Acosta, and Francisco Mariano Quiñones, who outlined the ripple effects of slavery, of how it pervades a society even when most of its members are "free" [...]

Still, Tapia's play could be criticized for being too indirect, as well as somewhat fatalistic. Carlos indeed suffers, but unlike Julia he does not die. And while the last line of the play has the slave Jorge utter "God will deliver justice!", Tapia's reformism is what prevails, one that dovetails with a fairly common occurrence in Caribbean and U.S. literature of the nineteenth century: the tragic mulatta figure, most notably depicted in works like Cecilia Valdés (Villaverde) or Clotel, by William Wells Brown, a former slave. This tragic figure, ambiguous, was seen as the epitome of sensuality, a social climber, a symbol of the frustrations and aspirations of a racially divided society, and a visual reminder of miscegenation (not to mention an undercurrent of sexual violence). The mulatto, more often the mulatta, could be interpreted in either positive or negative ways: as a symbol of mestizaje, a new national subject, or as someone who combined the worst of both races, or in the best of cases as someone who was neither one thing (white) or another (black), a being who wavered in his/her search for self-definition.

[...]

Hispanophilia and mulata on display, or How to wiggle your flag in search of the lost m(other)

In 1898 Puerto Rico became a U.S. colony when the Spanish-Cuban-American War ended. Puerto Ricans quickly became aware of U.S. racial attitudes, which they found harsh and polarized. Yet at the same time the size and dynamism of the U.S. economy provided jobs to many dark-skinned Puerto Ricans, either on the island or to those who emigrated. Under the U.S., Puerto Rico's sugar economy expanded again, with absentee owners buying the land of many small local producers. The U.S. had not satisfactorily resolved issues of autonomy and citizenship, a failing that was deeply resented by Puerto Ricans. Finally, the U.S. unilaterally imposed citizenship in the 1917 Jones Act. But resentment did not recede since governors (the supreme executive official) were still picked by the U.S., and English was imposed as the official language in the school system. Successfully resisted, English was eventually eliminated in 1930, and represents an important example of Puerto Rican linguistic and cultural sovereignty in resisting U.S. colonialism. This resentment flared up during WWI, when Puerto Ricans who considered themselves white within the broader island definition of race were placed in segregated Negro units of the U.S. army. To many Puerto Ricans this was an outrage; the U.S. solution was to create a "Puerto Rican white" category, viewed by many islanders as unsatisfactory.

Even a revolutionary nationalist like Pedro Albizu Campos (1891–1965), jailed several times for his views and actions calling for the violent overthrow of the island's colonial system, did not give racial issues their due. Albizu, in a famous speech from October 12, 1933, speaks proudly of the fact that he had black blood (as well as Indian and Spanish) in his veins and vehemently criticized the racial realities of the U.S. as being barbaric (Albizu Campos 1972: 191–218). However, he ultimately saw race as divisive to his political goals and subsumed race under the overarching concept of Puerto Rican culture. Albizu shared a point in common with intellectuals of the Thirties Generation, such as Tomás Blanco (1900–1975) and Antonio S. Pedreira (1899–1939): in trying to counteract U.S. cultural and ideological influence in Puerto Rico, they fell back on an acritical and ahistorical Hispanophilia, which had a strong racial (and anti-black) undercurrent.[2]

One of the few intellectuals who resisted that Hispanophilia was poet Luis Palés Matos (1898–1959). Palés was born in Guayama, an area historically populated by Puerto Ricans of African descent. Although his poetry was thematically wide-ranging, it is his Afro-Antillean poetry that earned his fame, particularly his *Tuntún de pasa y grifería* [Kinky-haired and carousing drum beat], written between 1925 and 1937. Intensely rhythmic, onomatopoeic, playful, and sensual, Pales's poetry explored the cultural, religious, historical, and sexual dimensions of Puerto Rico's African identity. For the first time a publicly known figure not only pointed out but celebrated African contributions to the island's language, music, food, sports, and social behavior. Reworking a phrase by Jung, Palés stated in an interview: "...[T]he Antillean is a Spaniard with the mores and ethos of a mulatto and the soul of a black" (Palés Matos 1978: 216). Anticipating a heated response, Palés ends by saying, "This definition will no doubt cause an uproar among many. But neither Spaniard nor black will protest it" (Palés Matos 1978: 216). Despite the bold phrase, Pales's words belie a Eurocentric bias: why is the Antillean (read Puerto Rican, Cuban, Dominican) a Spaniard with mores and moves of a mulatto and not the other way?

Nowadays, it is difficult to imagine how "scandalous" *Tuntún de pasa y grifería* was when it was first published, notwithstanding the positive reviews from the likes of Tomás Blanco, Federico de Onís, and Margot Arce. Actually, Pales's *poemas negros* were being criticized since at least 1932, and the criticisms ranged from exoticism, primitivism, and romanticism, to stereotyping and evasion. [...] [T]here are moments (and not only a few) in his poetry where the irony or the implied reversal of stereotypes continue to reinforce black stereotypes. Still, Palés's Afro-Antillean verses are complex; to dismiss them entirely would be lose sight of their critical edge. However, to claim that his irony freed him from racist stereotypes would be naïve, even allowing for the mitigating circumstances of the time. After all, the likes of Nicolás Guillén, Claude McKay, Langston Hughes, and others of the Harlem Renaissance were writing with a *negrista* ethos that avoided or openly combated such stereotypes.

To those who define patriotism platonically (and white-hued), Palés irreverently conjoined nationalism with eroticism, also unequivocally stating that *mulatez* was positive. [...] Of course Palés offers a symbolic identification with the island's (at that point) long ignored African-ness; but at the same time he seems to draw a more radical conclusion: that the national being includes the Other (blackness), and not only as a social-racial construct, but both as national pleasure and enjoyment (jouissance).

[...]

Palés captures beautifully this double dimension of what can't be articulated and the enjoyment-in-sense of ideology in a poem like "Mulata-Antilla." The beginning stanzas are an erotic-celebratory (albeit sexist) reconstruction of the mulata. In the first stanza, Palés makes one of his most common associations of the mulata with honey (miel o melaza), as well as using marine imagery (associations with Venus). In the second, the author likens himself to a boat traversing the mulata-antilla's curves (or coast lines). In the third music is evoked along with the smells of the islands: lime, tobacco, and pineapple. The fourth stanza is both a summing up and a transition that again evokes not only fruit and song, but also the presence of tourists. The fifth lovingly links the joining of two races (African and European), celebrating mestizaje, and then spawns a series of analogies between the mulata and the biblical Song of Songs. The final stanza invokes several of the Caribbean islands "...all united/ dreaming, suffering, and struggling/against plagues, cyclones, and greed" and ends with a metaphor of the mulata as "freedom singing in my Antilles" (Palés Matos 1978: 173).

Much has been written about the image of the mulata in Caribbean literature, popular music and culture, rightly criticizing its sexism and racism.[3] For some critics, mestizaje or mulatez have been used as symbols of racial democracy in all of Latin America, often to sidestep or deny the existence of racism. Here Palés is treading on thin, and, ultimately, indefensible ground. This can be seen in the use of nature (earth, sea, cyclones, flowers), food (milk, honey, sugar, coconut, etc.), and animal imagery (cats, horses), all used to enhance the mulata's sensuality, "tastiness," and sexuality. Even when Pales in the fourth stanza ostensibly uses the word *catinga* (a word to denote the strong, read negative odor of either indigenous people or Africans) in a positive sense, one cannot help but wonder if he is not resurrecting racial stereotypes. So, despite Pales's analogy of the mulata and freedom, the mulata as sexual object [...] is still present in the poem, although it is does not exhaust the poem's meaning. Indeed, the mulata-islands who are as one "dreaming, suffering, and striving/against plagues, hurricanes and greed" become the "freedom singing in the Antilles" (Palés Matos 1978: 173). This ending is a remarkable transformation, since until then the poem had restrained from any mention of freedom and liberation.[4]

Palés mocks white fears of the racial Other through sexuality, biblical references, and an analogy to freedom, and ultimately says the "Other" is us. And yet the sexualization and carnivalization of that fear seem to indicate that there is a social, cultural, and even spatial distance as well. [...]

The Puerto Rican (or Caribbean) social fantasy of the mulata is part of a cultural memory (different from merely personal memory or history). [...]

The mulata fantasy is utopian because it wants to present her as national symbol, as an emblem of conciliation, a visual token that ignores all the symptoms of a divided society (race, class, and gender). However, there is instability in her meaning, in her image. Her eroticization presents a dilemma by confusing pleasure (located on her body) and desire (atopic, proliferative), between pleasure and enjoyment (*jouissance*). [...]

Something similar happens racially: in not embracing blackness (jouissance) completely, a more whitened (pleasure) version of blackness is presented: mulatez (pleasure masquerading as enjoyment). Mulatez is a way of keeping enjoyment under the law, under the pleasure principle, under Whiteness. And yet mulatez is always a reminder of how pleasure gave way to jouissance, of the Other, of the presence of trauma (miscegenation as rape), of the return of the wound that we have refused to heal. (It's germane to recall that in Puerto Rico miscegenation is viewed as a whitening process.)

The compromise formation evades or circles the trauma of slavery, oppression, sexual violence, and turns it into an emblem of pleasure. [...]

Revenge of the mulatas: Patriarchy's myths exposed
Rosario Ferré's *Maldito amor* (1986) examines both the gender, sexual, and racial underpinnings of this national enjoyment. Ostensibly the story of a great national (and local) hero, Don Ubaldino, as told by a narrator, Don Hermenegildo Martínez (the town notary and lawyer), Ferré overturns the narrative with successive revelations by the women characters (Titina, Laura, Gloria), ultimately debunking the "founding father." Gloria Campubrí is a "traffic-stopping" mulata nurse brought to the De la Valle plantation to care for the aged and dying Ubaldino. One son, Arístedes, carries on an affair with her, and wants to marry her, but his mother (Laura) prohibits their union, and instead marries Gloria off to her other son Nicolás, whom the brother claims is gay. The plan was that after Ubaldino died, the marriage would be annulled, and Gloria would leave, "with proper compensation." But Nicolás, after getting Gloria pregnant, dies in a suspicious accident six months after the wedding. Gloria leaves, and eventually becomes a prostitute in the bars of Guamaní, the mythical town recreated by Ferré in this short novel.

Though Ferré's narrative focuses heavily on patriarchy and gender inequalities (and to a lesser degree homophobia), the racial dimensions are not lost on the reader. Again, there is a mulata figure who disrupts the racial, sexual, and social tranquility of an elite family, obsessed with their pedigree and social standing, as well as their economic power, which has been threatened by U.S. firms who are gobbling up land and sugar refineries as the new colonial power on the island. One of the interesting details revealed late in the novel by Laura is that the grandfather of her children was also black. The so-called "purity" and "reputation" of the family was a myth, and its final debunking (which ends the novel) encompasses the words of Gloria herself, speaking to Titina Rivera, the daughter of a freed slave. She and her brother Nestor had lived in a little house in the backyard of the family home, and they had hoped to inherit it after living there for forty years. Ubaldino has died, but his children, Arístedes and his sisters, will not let them inherit the little house either. It is a stinging finale about pernicious racism, all the more poignant since it ends with the words to "Maldito Amor" by the mulatto composer Juan Morel Campos, the island's greatest composer of the nineteenth century. Ferré takes on the "tragic mulata figure" head on, and although she has suffered greatly at the hands of the de la Valle family, her "authorial voice" at the end of the narrative (as well as doña Laura's wish for her to be the sole inheritor of the family), ultimately shifts the his/her-story being told. Gender-wise and racially, Ferré seems to suggest that Caribbean national narratives, instead of focusing on "founding fathers," need to tell the story of its vast majorities: the mulatos *and mulatas*, the daughters and sons.

[...]

Whitening and racial self-perception: *Mulattoes and blacks disappear*

At the beginning of the twentieth century Puerto Rico still perceived itself as whitening. [...] Perceptually, Puerto Ricans who saw themselves as mulattoes at one point became whites, and those who previously identified themselves as blacks became mulattoes. [...]

These contrasting perceptions reflect the radically different worlds of racial categorization used as reference points by U.S. observers compared to Puerto Rican subjectivity. In Puerto Rico's own racial history under Spanish colonialism, miscegenation was viewed as a whitening, not a darkening, process. Also, Puerto Ricans continued to resist the imposition of U.S. racial classifications. Indeed, many dark-skinned Puerto Ricans were often identified as African-Americans, a label they rejected not only for racial reasons, but also out of nationalism and culture. It is not that Puerto Ricans are not race conscious, but cultural belonging supersedes it, a common enough attitude throughout the Caribbean. Moreover, the uniqueness of the island's history often makes racial self-definition an expression of resistance to U.S. colonialism. Puerto Ricans in the U.S., when asked what they are, respond that they are Puerto Ricans, not black or white. [...]

These complexities are eloquently described in Piri Thomas's celebrated *Down These Mean Streets* (1967) or in Tato Laviera's poem "Negrito." Interestingly, many black and mulatto Puerto Rican writers born or raised from infancy in the U.S. have taken on issues of race in their literature: aside from Thomas and Laviera, there is Nicholasa Mohr, Ed Vega, Louis Reyes Rivera, Esmeralda Santiago, and Jack Agüeros. The shocking experience of moving through two worlds of race— one nuanced and complex, the other cruelly absolute—stimulates a struggle often expressed through art or political activism.

In Laviera's "Negrito," a young, dark-skinned Puerto Rican boy has just moved to New York and converses with his aunt. The aunt tells him "No te juntes con los prietos, negrito" (Don't hang out with black folks, negrito) (Laviera 1985: 41). He says to his aunt that he is as dark as the black folks she has warned him about. She keeps insisting on his whiteness, which only brings on sadness and confusion to the young boy. Laviera, who admits the poem is autobiographical, keenly underlines the different perceptions of race between the U.S. and Puerto Rico, beginning with the title of the poem. "Negrito" can literally refer to a small black boy, who is the subject of the poem. But negrito and negrita have other connotations as well: they can be expressions of affection to a friend, family member, or loved one, regardless of their race. Pedro Pietri in *Puerto Rican Obituary* says it means honey. So the young boy's aunt is also using a term of affection as well, understandable with a family member. But her trying to explain the U.S. color line underscores two things. First, she is trying to enforce the Puerto Rican insistence on cultural and national identity over racial identity. Second, although her nephew is phenotypically similar to African-Americans, she is aware of what being black means in the U.S. as com-pared to Puerto Rico. Not surprisingly, the young boy of the poem is perplexed: "new york waved hi/and said to him 'confusion'" (Laviera 1985: 41).

In situating himself between two worlds Laviera's poem not only expresses the confusion and disappointment of the young boy in the poem, but also a coming to awareness of his Afro-Puerto Rican heritage. (Curiously the two worlds are not echoed linguistically, and unlike many of his poems, "Negrito" is entirely in Spanish.) Laviera, instead of heeding the aunt's words, has chosen to affirm his Afroboricua heritage (and its links to a greater Afrodiasporic dialogue), be it through the use of certain rhythmic structures, themes, or drawing on street vernaculars. In an interview, Laviera admits that half of his poetry readings are for black constituencies (Hernández 1997: 81).

The fact that many Puerto Ricans are living in places like New York, in close physical proximity with African-Americans and other peoples from the Caribbean, has resulted in drawing boricuas into the orbit of other African-based cultures. In dress and language, many Puerto Ricans show the influences of U.S. African-Americans and many identify with hip-hop culture. There are Puerto Rican rappers (like Big Pun, Rick Rodríguez, Anthony Boston, Charlie Chase, Tony Touch, Angie Martínez) who sing in English and/or Spanish, and many others who are graffiti artists, like the legendary Lee Quiñones. This does not include the extraordinary boricua presence in the evolution of break dancing (Rock Steady Crew, The Furious

Rockers, The New York City Breakers and others). This intercultural effervescence is happening on the island as well, with rappers such as Vico C, Lisa M, Francheska, Ruben DJ, Welmo, and Tego Calderón.[5] What is particularly interesting about island rappers is that they invoke and celebrate island culture, but no longer buy into the portrait of Puerto Rico as a big, happy multiracial family (Calderón 2002).[6]

Cortijo, salsa, and afroboricua pride: Mulattoes own the streets

Since the 1960s there has been greater awareness and debate of racial issues, and increasing pride in being *Afroboricua* (Afro-Puerto Rican). The new self-esteem came through music, not literature. One of the turning points in that new consciousness was the work of bandleader Rafael Cortijo (1928–1982) and singer Ismael Rivera (1931–1987), who teamed up in the mid-fifties to create some of the island's greatest music, based on the traditions of bomba and plena, both Afro-Puerto Rican musical traditions. Cortijo's sound became known internationally, just as before him the songs of Rafael Hernández (1893–1965) were greatly admired throughout all Latin America and the Caribbean. (One could argue that Rivera's version of Tite Curet Alonso's "Mi gente negra" did more for shaping a positive image of Afroboricua pride than all of Pales Matos's poems.) Cortijo's music (along with Afro-Cuban musical traditions) formed the basis of salsa, a hybrid genre that grew out of the urban experience of many Afro-Puerto Ricans in New York City and dealt with themes of poverty, racism, social violence, education, and drugs. It was equally a period of great community mobilizations, the creation of the Young Lords, and the Nuyorican Poets Café. The experience of American-style racism gave many boricuas a new sense of their Afroboricua roots, which had they stayed on the island might have taken more time to coalesce.

All these issues suffuse *El entierro de Cortijo* (1983) by Edgardo Rodríguez Juliá, a highly charged, humorous, hard-hitting chronicle of Cortijo's funeral, which took place on November 6, 1982. Held at the Luis Lloréns Torres housing project, the chronicle plays with the notion of death as the great equalizer that cuts through all the divisions (class, race, gender) within Puerto Rican society. Although a thorough analysis of this book is not possible here, there are some points worth mentioning.

Rodríguez Juliá's chronicle reflects the shift in Puerto Rican popular culture towards Afro-Puerto Rican and working class expressions, notably analyzed by the likes of Juan Flores, José Luis González, Ángel Quintero Rivera, and Jorge Duany in the seventies and eighties and a host of scholars since the nineties (Frances Aparicio, Ruth Glasser, Edgardo Díaz Díaz).

In part this reflects the importance of two authors who polemically brought issues of race to the forefront: Isabelo Zenón Cruz (1939–2002) and José Luis González

(1926–1996). Zenón's exhaustive 1974 two-volume study, *Narciso descubre su trasero* [Narcissus Discovers his Backside], is subtitled "The Black in Puerto Rican Culture." Although the author draws heavily on literature and the arts, Zenón's book includes much historical, political, and educational material, even government reports. His work was controversial because it attacked much of the hypocrisy around race on the island, drawing on unexamined assumptions from popular culture, such as jokes, sayings, and proverbs, to prove his point. Zenón spares no one in his meticulously documented study.

González's 1979 essay was first published in Puerto Rico in 1980. Although the "Four Storeyed-Country" has been criticized both for what it says (or does not say), the essay brought the discussion of the country's African roots to the fore.[7] Most importantly, after Zenón and González, it was impossible for intellectuals, historians, and literary scholars to ignore racism and its insidious consequences.

Secondly, *El entierro de Cortijo* shows how racial discrimination is now indirectly expressed through concern about crime. The author, from the beginning, shows apprehension, knowing that he is a middle-class and white, in a neighborhood where most are dark-skinned and poor. He even mentions a street that divides Lloréns Torres (described as lumpen) from the next neighborhood, Villa Palmeras, which is working-class and also the site where the chronicle ends. The crime is real enough (the island has high murder and armed robbery figures), but it has been racialized, with black and darker-skinned mulattoes suffering the brunt of arrests, even though the police do not keep statistics on race (Santiago-Valles 1995).

To his credit, Rodríguez Juliá never claims to be merely an observer, but acknowledges that he is situated socially and racially, although he clearly is an "outsider" in that particular neighborhood. [...]

Perhaps the greatest achievement of Rodríguez Juliá's chronicle is his capture of the ever inventive and multiform colloquial Spanish spoken in Puerto Rico. Through certain words or verbal rhythms, the author reveals an extremely complex portrait of Puerto Rico, especially issues of race, class, and gender.

Since he is a writer and not a sociologist or politician, Rodríguez Juliá offers no neat, tidy, and consoling summations. He debunks the patriarchal myth of the great Puerto Rican family, constantly invoked by politicians and pundits; and shows how the old class order is being overturned, exemplified in how the burial turns into a street party, to the alarm of some. Although he knows the old ways were often repugnantly racist and classist, the emerging situation can be confusing, disruptive, and disorienting, [...].

Rodríguez Juliá's *crónica*, despite the obvious focus on Cortijo's life and work, seems to have as a historical soundtrack two landmark songs, one Puerto Rican, another

Cuban. Both songs are steeped in Afro-Caribbean working class culture: "Los entierros de mi gente pobre" by Tite Curet Alonso (made famous by singer Cheo Feliciano) and "Los funerales del Papá Montero" by Enrique Byron and Manuel Corona. [In t]he first, written by the recently deceased great Afro-Puerto Rican composer, Rodríguez Juliá seems to have appropriated the spirit, authenticity, and humility of lower class life in the island, where funerals are genuine outpourings of grief thankfully bereft of hypocrisy. In the latter, we find the kind of raucous and irreverent humor from the guaracha tradition that can turn even a funeral into a celebration.

But even more remarkably, Rodríguez Juliá's book seems to exemplify central tenets of Yoruba philosophy, where character, coolness, and beauty are intimately intertwined within a context of post-WWII social mobility, and later post-muñocista Puerto Rico. This might seem a contradictory assertion given the excessive, almost chaotic denouement of the funeral, but the deeper forces brought to the fore are those that emphasize generosity and the surfacing of a beauty that is neither too beautiful nor too ugly, of capturing a certain *aché* that suffuses the text between the lines (Thompson 1993: 3–18).

Black and proud: In your face (and nose)

Mayra Santos Febres, a fiction writer, helped form the Union of Afro-Puerto Rican Women along with Ana Rivera, Rayda Cotto, Celia M. Romano, and Marie Ramos Rosado. Her book *Pez de vidrio* won the 1994 Letras de Oro award, and was published in Puerto Rico in 1996. One story from this book, "Marina y su olor" [Marina and her odors], openly confronts a racist stereotype with humor and poetic flair.

Marina, now forty-nine years old, narrates her experiences growing up. The story focuses on Marina's odors in a kind of fairy tale of retribution. As a girl she helps out by cooking in her parents' small eatery. From eight to thirteen her smells were "spicy, salty, and sweet." At thirteen she began to smell like the sea; her fragrances began to attract and bewitch the male customers. Concerned, her mother sends her as cook and servant to a family, under the watchful eye of Georgina Velázquez, described as "white, pious, and a vulgar rich person." First, she began to conjure up food smells as she would mentally prepare menus for the next day, but eventually she began to experiment with the smells of emotions (sadness, solitude, desire). Marina rebuffs the advances of Hipólito, Georgina's son, who would spend his nights bedding young mulatas, enamored of dark flesh. At age fifteen Marina begins to take notice of boys and falls in love with Eladio Salamán, who is black like her. But both Georgina and her parents find out and she is kept from seeing him. Georgina insults her, saying "You're a bad woman, a slut, indecent, a stinking black, you stink!" (Santos Febres 1996: 48). One day, using her ability to create smells and gauging the direction of the wind, she is able to bring Eladio to her, and they begin kissing each other joyfully. Her bliss is short-lived since she is discovered by Hipólito. He offers not to tell her employer if he can suck her breasts. Marina becomes so incensed that she gives off a powerful smell that literally knocks Hipólito out. Then she proceeds to deal with Georgina, "fumigating her room with an aroma of desperate melancholy (which she had picked up from her father)" (Santos Febres: 50). The rest of the house was left with an odor so disorienting that no one in the town ever visited the Velázquez house again. Triumphantly, Marina leaves the house uttering: "There! So you can now say that blacks stink!" (Santos Febres 1996: 50).

Santos Febres has taken a persistent racist stereotype about smell and turned it around, almost as if to say "You want to raise a stink? I'll show what raising a stink is!" Of all the five senses, smell is seen as the lowliest, the most "animal." Sniffing is an activity we associate with animals (dogs, cats). This animality is also linked to racist stereotypes of lack of intelligence, hyper-sexuality, and moral turpitude. Rodríguez Juliá, in his *El entierro de Cortijo*, talks about a characteristic island trait, *husmear*. Literally, of course, it means to sniff, but in a more social context it means to size up, find out things, to be curious in an almost gossipy way. Santos Febres seems to be *husmeando* into the heart of racial attitudes on the island [...]Marina is able to take that "animalness" and make it a weapon of self-defense. Odor is linked to notions of power as when expressed in phrases like "the lower classes don't wash, they smell," or Thomas Jefferson's remark that "blacks have a strong, disagreeable odor," or male jokes about women's genitalia. All these notions of odor undergird sexism, racism, and classism. In Marina's case, her odors have a symbolic resonance with class, race, and gender (Synnott 1993: 194–9).

Odor also has strong moral connotations as well. Witness how we describe suspicious, illegal or immoral behavior in terms of words and phrases such as "foul," "it stinks," and "it's fishy." The story begins with the sexual connotations of odor, then goes on to link it to food, and, later, the emotions. Only at the end do we see Marina's odors fighting against racism and advancing her autonomy as a woman. The emotional link is crucial. It is her love for Eladio that sets off positive emotions, and equally affects the way she cooks (and smells). When she is prohibited from seeing Eladio her sadness makes the food taste different (shrimps taste like pork chops) or is negative (they all throw up). At the end of the story, the smells take on an ethical dimension: they ensure she does not suffer from the predatory sexuality of Hipólito, or the racism (with class and gender overtones) of Georgina. Marina's fumigating refusal has the whiff of justice: she escapes the house, and the lingering odors keep away visitors (the family has been isolated from the community).

[...] Georgina clearly saw Marina in terms of that excess of enjoyment: her smells (body and food), her sexuality, her autonomy as human and social subject. She was punished for that: she was prohibited from seeing Eladio, and her salary was cut. These events make the ending all the more gratifying and ironic: if previously Georgina had made Marina into the "other" (racially, socially, sexually), it is now Georgina who will be the "other" (shunned by her community).

Conclusion: Still conflicted, still struggling

Though Puerto Rico has long been called a racial democracy, the whitest of the Spanish-speaking islands, a country free of prejudice, these claims are no longer voiced with the same self-assuredness as before. Even its best minds have found race an elusive topic, but as the previous literary examples discussed show, many of these myths are unsustainable and are being debunked or confronted by its artists, writers, and musicians.

Although the new racial awareness of the last decades has been transformative and has revealed a greater complexity in defining national (and racial) identity, the political and economic elites of the country are still mostly white or light-skinned mulattoes. Puerto Rico's racial dynamics show both great nuance and fluidity, and at the same time a certain avoidance or denial. The major political and social issues still are expressed in terms of either nation (political status) or class (economic opportunity) or education (social mobility) or negotiation of public space (crime). Despite pervasive and subtle forms of racial prejudice and discrimination, the country is ever more aware of its changing and evolving Afro-Caribbean identity and culture, which it also increasingly celebrates. Its writers, artists, musicians, and rappers are in the forefront of both the critique of racism and the celebration of the island's Afroboricua roots. But the more subtle forms of discrimination, much like what happens in the U.S., are still pervasive (limited access to housing, poor educational opportunities, limited bank loans, poorer health); the racial self-perception is increasingly whitened, and then there is the persistence of the myth of the mestizaje. All these factors point to the fact that Puerto Rico still needs to examine its racial inequities with greater insight, creativity, and honesty.

[...]

CHAPTER 3

AfroPuerto Rican Cultural Studies: Beyond *cultura negroide* and *antillanismo*

By Juan A. Giusti Cordero

Approaches to the historical experience of Puerto Ricans of color have been overwhelmed by the urgency of confronting racism, against recurrent claims that Puerto Ricans uniformly practice "racial democracy."[1] The debate on racial prejudice in Puerto Rico has experienced "a profound repression" (Díaz-Quiñones 1993: 59). Racism in Puerto Rico is "silken or rough" (Zenón 1991: iii)[2] and it is often subtler and more complex, but no less toxic especially among the upper strata—than in the U.S.[3] Much remains to be said about racism in Puerto Rico, with regard to its almost perverse semantic richness and strategic ambiguity, and to its prime location in matters of Puerto Rican national identity (Godreau 1995).[4] Yet phenotypical boundaries among Puerto Ricans are part of the larger whole that is the historical experience of Puerto Ricans of color (Aponte 1995).

[...]

National culture and cultural context

[...] The Puerto Rican understandings of race is condensed in the saying *"El que no tiene dinga, tiene mandinga."*[5] This refrain simultaneously recognizes the deep African dimensions of Puerto Rico while waving aside (or, perhaps, laughing away) further discussion. Whatever we may make of it, this intense ambiguity about race sets Puerto Rico apart from the U.S. and constitutes a dimension of its national culture.

[...]

[...] Perhaps it will be useful, in this regard, to consider the cultural and political projects of *cultura negroide and antillanismo*—the two major AfroPuerto Rican

Originally published in *CENTRO: Journal of the Center for Puerto Rican Studies* 8(1&2): 57–77, 1996.

movements in the twentieth century—as permeable cultural and sociohistorical practices, spaces and contexts.

Cultura negroide

[...] Concepts such as syncretism, transculturation, and creolization seek to grasp th[e] dynamism [in the cultural contexts in Puerto Rico]. Attempts to isolate, within Puerto Rican culture, a bedrock of *hispanidad*[6] are as futile as those that would elaborate a Taíno nation or an African essence. However, AfroPuerto Rican culture has been especially prone to treatment as a discrete though subordinate field; and this was done earliest in the paradigm of *cultura negroide* (or *afro-negroide*), a name that I employ somewhat arbitrarily to designate the first epoch of public AfroPuerto Rican cultural expression in [the twentieth] century.

The term *"cultura negroide"* is evidently loaded. *"Cultura"* by itself throws up fences, whereas *"negroide"* focuses attention too narrowly on color.[7] Moreover, the *"—oide"* ending infuses *negroide* with a sense of artificiality and inferiority, the nearest equivalent occurs in science fiction, when a writer addressed the difference between being "human" and being "humanoid." But the term *"cultura negroide,"* and especially *poesía negroide*, was current in Puerto Rico already in the 1930s. As in other representations of "Africanism" in the Americas in the first half of the twentieth century (Herskovits 1960), including the thrust of *Négritude* and Haitian *Indigénisme*, Puerto Rico's *cultura negroide* sought in Puerto Rico relatively "pure," "African" patterns and traits surviving among people of African descent, though perhaps the larger frame of reference was not Africa but something closer: blackness, lo *negroide*, and geographically, an impressionistic Caribbean. Blackness, whatever it was or deemed to be, was at the root of lo *negroide*; the exclusively African, rather than Indian or folk-European pedigree of many traits, in particular the determination of their specific origins and meaning in given zones within the continent tended to require further research.

It was in literature, and especially in poetry, that *cultura negroide* attained its most explicit articulation. The two leading poets are Luis Palés Matos and Fortunato Vizcarrondo. Both men wrote most of their *negroide* poetry in the 1920s and 1930s, Palés was the earlier of the two to publish. Both authors, I should note, might have taken issue with the terms *"cultura"* and *"negroide"*: Palés used the additives *"afro-antillana"* and *"antillana"* to describe his poetry at a time when the term *"afrocubanismo"* was current in Cuba. Yet the work of Palés, even more than Vizcarrondo, is at the center of popular definitions of *poesía negroide*. Palés' poetry is full of onomatopoeic plays on word sounds, e.g., of Caribbean and African geography, and of AfroPuerto Rican words. Most of Vizcarrondo's poetry, on the other hand, fully depend on AfroPuerto Rican speech.

[...]

The main *negroide* traits include sensuality (*sandunguería, sabrosura*), indeed a heightened experience and deployment of all the senses, directly corresponding to a deemphasis on the rational, and an appeal to the "primitive"; festiveness (*bachata*) to the point of self-conscious primitiveness; sensual and fluid body movement; upbeat music and rhythm, especially on hand drums; enchantment with the coastal landscape; idealization of the traditional, rustic lifestyle of the *negros de la costa*.

[...]

Cultura negroide is also significant for its celebration of black and sometimes mulatto beauty (see Vizcarrondo 1976b), though often caricaturing "primitive" sensuality. Its cultural representations raise issues of race, gender, and class that require closer discussion, as it was women, and especially black women from the working classes, who were deemed to be most erotic, and whose persona was entirely eroticized see (Palés Matos 1993; Vizcarrondo 1976a).

Finally, there is also in *cultura negroide* social and political comment from a democratic perspective, made with deft irony and razor-sharp imagery. In Vizcarrondo's poetry there is a series of eighteen such poems. By far the best known of these is *"¿Y tu agüela a'onde ejtá?"* The current of social and political comment, almost entirely absent from Palés Matos' work, was important in *poesía negroide*. [...] Partly because Palés did not practice that subgenre, it is not usually seen as part and parcel of the definition of *cultura negroide*, or as a social manifesto of far broader import.

In the explicitly racist conceptions of the period, it is important to note, there were only certain fields of expression open to *negroide* poetry; even though a "black" poet like Vizcarrondo could write "white" poetry—this is, after all Puerto Rico—the literary canons demanded that the themes of one and another genre remain distinct. [...]

In a preface to the second edition of Vizcarrondo's *Dinga y mandinga*, of all places, we find a brazen distinction between "white" and "black" poetry. "White" poetry is classically spiritual, "black" poetry a coarse portrayal of the *costumbres de negros*, defunct or nearly so. Black poetry-- and this happens in every poem of the *negroide* genre that I know, by different authors"—is not "inspired in beauty in any of its manifestations" (Martínez Acosta 1976: xxv). In this reading, *negroide* poetry is mindless and heartless, purely physical, indeed metabolic.

[...]

[...] In any event, in music and dance lo *afro-puertorriqueño* gained a preeminence, and more genuine expression, that it was denied in literature. While the musical boundaries of *cultura negroide* are subject to debate when viewed as a broad cultural movement or epoch, clearly the *negroide* in the early twentieth century broke with the boundaries imposed on it in slave times as "black music," and indirectly spawned the *plena*—simultaneously, of course, as music and dance—which also developed in the early years of the century.

The *plena* also expressed a more critical understanding of social class and everyday life than did *poesía negroide*. From the time of its origins in Ponce, the working-class currents that shaped the *plena* were evident, during a period of intense internal migration and social transformation.

[...]

The *plena* reached commercial success with Canario (Manuel Jiménez) in the 1930s, both in Puerto Rico and in New York, as Puerto Rican music (Flores 1992: 89; Glasser 1995). Rafael Hernández, a mulatto, also wrote a number of "afro" pieces, both *plenas* and rumbas. César Concepción, also a mulatto, led the best known big band that featured the *plena*. These were, in a sense, the mulatto and musical dimensions of *cultura negroide*.[8]

Indeed, several of Vizcarrondo's poems were musicalized as *plenas*, especially the anthemic *"¿Y tu agüela a'onde ejtá?"* This poem is, significantly, Vizcarrondo's strongest social comment; hence it was especially congenial to the *plena* tradition, forming a natural point for *plena* and *poesía negroide* to intersect. The subject, racial identity vs. family loyalties, was fundamental.

[...]

Cuisine—the sense of taste, metaphorized as *el sabor*—is also crucial in *cultura negroide*, as in Puerto Rican culture generally. And cuisine is an integral part of a selective, bucolic view of the coastal life of *los negros*. Eating AfroPuerto Rican food in the rustic restaurants of Loíza Aldea complete with straw huts (*bohíos*) and coconut-shell open hearths (*burenes, fogones*) is representative of a country existence. This was increasingly common through the 1930s and 1940s, when going for a drive "in the country" outside San Juan became popular. *Loíza Aldea* could also be a discreet place to pursue an affair.

Then since the 1970s the pursuit of *comida negroide*, as it were—or *comida típica* as it is more frequently called—continued more massively in the legendary roadside *friquitines* (kiosks) of the "wild" littoral of Piñones between San Juan and Loíza, which itself was regarded as a large-scale lovers' lane. Eating "typical" fare at a rustic, not very clean wooden kiosk made of assorted planks, the food fried in a large cauldron heated by burning coconut husks and firewood and washed down with coconut water (which the *loiceños* used to discard) became an act of affirmation of difference, of culture and identity.

[...]

Despite the considerable gains that the perspective of *cultura negroide* represented, it tended to racialize AfroPuerto Rican culture, robbing it of its historical depth and complexity (of which almost little was known, or studied). To Palés, who was the leading thinker and poet of *cultura negroide*, AfroPuerto Rican culture always remained "the other."

Palés separated *lo negro* from the Puerto Rican. He segregated him at the very moment in which he saw him "mixed" with "us." He denied *lo negro* by pretending, as he said, that he "lives physically and spiritually with us." He rose above the predominant prejudice of the time by conceiving a culturally mulatto Puerto Rico, but as a product of his milieu, he remained subject to the prejudices of his contemporaries (Zenón 1974–75: 47).

[...]

Cultura negroide also spatialized lo *afropuertorriqueño* in ways that connect with the notion of cultural context but which reify this notion. In *cultura negroide*, the town of Loíza-"Loíza Aldea" as it came to be called in this century—became the symbol and practically the only recognized locus of AfroPuerto Rican culture. *"Allá en Loíza es que están los negros," cultura negroide* seemed to say. Anthropologists agreed: noting the existence of "significant concentrations of persons of prevailingly negroid phenotype" in Loíza, Mintz identified proportion of blacks as the greatest in Puerto Rico—at more than 50 percent (Mintz 1966: 419).

Lo *negroide* in Loíza was crowned by the *annual fiestas de Santiago*, the best-known and most closely studied single aspect of AfroPuerto Rican culture.[9] The tradition of such salience in Loíza and Puerto Rico generally [was such] that it migrated to New York, where they are a major event in the Puerto Rican community.

Antillanismo

The terms *"antillanismo"* and *"afroantillanismo"* have been far longer in use in Puerto Rico than might seem, and at least since Palés Matos used them in 1932 (Negrón Muñoz 1973). But these terms are more aptly used to denominate the intellectual and artistic currents that succeeded *cultura negroide* in the 1960s. Expressed in literature, salsa music, historiography, drama and elsewhere, *antillanismo* tends to distance itself from *cultura negroide*, but rarely explicitly; it is actually quite close to *cultura negroide* in spirit. *Antillanismo* has been far more influential than *cultura negroide*, and has been a prevailing cultural influence among Puerto Rican intellectuals and artists of the younger generations over the last two decades: it is as close to a Zeitgeist as we may come in contemporary Puerto Rico. Moreover, *antillanismo* has largely defined the discussion on AfroPuerto Rican culture and history over the last two decades.

[...]

Crucially, however, *antillanismo* no longer views black culture in Puerto Rico as essentially distinct, but as a—or the—major component of Puerto Rican national culture—its hardest edge, as it were. This approach, which can be seen as "integrationist" but is in fact far more than that, coexists uneasily with *antillanismo* in a sense that the African dimension remains distinct, and with the result that it is an unending source of exoticism.

In regard to *cultura negroide*, *antillanismo* enriches perspectives on AfroPuerto Rican culture in interesting ways: *Antillanismo* authors have been exceedingly prolific, with an enormous number of works especially in music and literature, specifically short stories and novels. Poetry does not have in *antillanismo* the prominence that it gained in *cultura negroide*, and *antillanismo* in good measure has simply incorporated that legacy. [...]

The Puerto Rican community in the U.S., especially through salsa music, was extremely important in the development of *antillanismo*, to an even greater degree than was the case of the *plena* in the 1920s and 1930s. The early music of Willie Colón which explicitly demonstrated an African accent in such songs as *"Che Che Colé,"* and *"Ghana'é,"* sung in modified *negroide* beat by Héctor Lavoe of Ponce and New York, became lasting anthems for a generation of Puerto Ricans. In *"Che Che Colé,"* Lavoe sang: *"Vamos todos a bailar/este ritmo africano"*; in *" Ghana'é,"* references to Africa were evident in the title itself. These songs, and others of the early and mid-1970s (e.g. Cuban Celia Cruz's *"Químbara"*; Rubén Blades/Willie Colón's *"Canto Abacuá"*), stand out as remarkable tributes and bridges to Palés Matos himself, complete with fanciful "African" names and sound plays. Musically, the relationship between salsa rhythms and the *plena* rhythms of Cortijo, Ismael Rivera, and Tite Curet Alonso remains problematic.

Antillanismo holds Africa more explicitly, if still too vaguely and romantically, in its frame of reference. The African dimensions presented tend to be artificially bounded, pushed toward an exotic, colorful niche almost indistinguishable from the earlier *cultura negroide* approach. We are not confronted with the African presence as a dimension constitutive of a heterogeneous Puerto Rican social culture as a whole. [...]

[...]

At the same time, and to its credit, *antillanismo* also fixed its sights squarely on "mulatto culture," *la mulatez*, as a vital component. [...]

The AfroPuerto Rican tradition—for instance, *the fiestas de Santiago*—is now viewed as being, at least in part, more historically as an expression of cultural and political resistance, connected to traditions of slave resistance and *cimarronaje* (Ungerleider 1992).

[...] *Antillanismo* is more explicitly historical than *cultura negroide*. When Ana Lydia Vega writes of *historicidio* as the historical near-obsession of the writers of her generation, she is most specifically referring to the *antillanista* writers (Vega 1995). The major manifesto of *antillanismo*, *País de cuatro pisos*, is more historical than literary in character.

[...] *Antillanismo* has broader spatial parameters than *cultura negroide*. For the latter, the relevant space was strictly Loíza Aldea, with some reference to Guayama (Palés birthplace); few other images were offered. *Antillanismo* not only set forth Puerto Rico's coast in general as the relevant space; it also identified an counterspace, the highlands (*altura*) as the rival of the coast. The *altura*, since 1910 the heartland of Puerto Rican cultural nationalism, was now viewed by *antillanismo* as a conservative, white, overbearing pseudo-redoubt of Puerto Rican national culture. Puerto Rico's coastal dimension, the *antillanistas* insisted, needs reevaluation over and above the *altura* as a vital historical and cultural space.[10] Finally, *antillanismo* has identified more closely with the Caribbean region than has *cultura negroide*. While other Caribbean islands, like parts of Africa, appear rather fleetingly in the poetry of Palés, now Puerto Rican *antillanista*s are setting short stories and novels in other Caribbean islands, with an overriding focus on those island's African dimensions.

Locally, for *antillanismo* perhaps the main icon is no longer the Loíza Aldea of *cultura negroide*, but rather Piñones. Piñones is also in Loíza, but it is more rural and is at the same time closer to San Juan. Medianía, or at least the areas of Medianía that are more accessible to outsiders, is perhaps too urban, too evidently poor, and decidedly unbucolic in terms of the current ecological *mentalité*. Piñones, however—always San Juan's favorite "lovers' lane"—has "wild" beaches hard by the coastal highway and thus readily available to our automobile culture. The area consists of old communities, large *cocales*, fritter stands *(friquitines, negocitos, kioskos)* and large unbuilt space close to San Juan. The struggles of its communities against eviction, and later against hotel and residential construction, are also part of the area's allure of independence.

A 1991 essay by Rodríguez Juliá, *"Piñones, Una crónica"* (1991), locates Piñones in contemporary Puerto Rico". This essay, which chronicles a drive through Piñones, attempts to evoke a sense of place and of memory. Rodríguez Juliá is also mindful of changes in the Piñones landscape, especially in terms of restaurants and food stands that lent the area its particular mood and character. Yet the chronicle remains quite oblivious to the *piñoneros* themselves (except, on one occasion, as African characters straight out of *negroide* poetry). In all, Piñones here seems to remain a passive stage for outsiders' jaunts and reveries, with little more than a recent past.

Another, and perhaps more representative, text on Piñones is by Coqui Santaliz, a well-known journalist and writer. The article, titled *"Divina herencia en Vacía Talega"* (Divine Heritage in Vacía Talega), begins:

> Oh Piñones, who does not have you in some nook of memories robbed from the impositions of time. Ah, Piñones-Vacía Talega, without time (sin tiempo). An alcapurria (crabmeat fritter) crossing the distances of the city. Our Afro-Caribbean [afroantillana] heritage in each maroon look of dignity [en cada mirada cimarrona de dignidad] An idealized world that we thought would never end. The enclosed beach coves [pocitas] of my childhood; the little roads of interminable holes of that beach that was indeed ours. For everyone a spot [...] Always a hideaway to escape metropolitically [metropolitanamente] from the pollution of body and soul. (1988: 12–13)

There are evident continuities between *cultura negroide*'s Loíza Aldea and the Loíza and Piñones of *antillanismo*. In both, there is a reaffirmation of an AfroPuerto Rican space as a "hard-core" Puerto Rican space. Luis Rafael Sánchez's bittersweet story of emigration *"La guagua aérea"* (The air bus) comes to mind. One of the passengers on a San Juan—New York flight remarks, in a moving evocation of Piñones (...and Cortijo):

> I cannot live in Puerto Rico because there's no life for me there, so I'll bring it with me bit by bit; in this trip, four crabs from Vacía Talega, in the trip before, a fighting cock, in my next, all of Cortijo's records. (1987: 22)

Other Puerto Rican emigrants did not carry crabs in their suitcases, but perhaps went even further, renaming the old and spirited Puerto Rican community in the Lower East Side Loisaida and celebrating the *fiestas de Santiago*. Whatever the real changes in the Loíza coast, it remains a forceful presence in the Puerto Rican imagination.

Yet this vital identity at once AfroPuerto Rican and Puerto Rican remains entangled in *antillanismo*, and in contemporary Puerto Rican culture in general, with an iconization that suggests a backyard "Orientalism"[11] imposed on the AfroPuerto Rican heritage. Perhaps the iconization is cognizant of the specificity of that tradition, but it is rather self-centered all the same.

Zenón, González, Rodríguez Juliá, Ferré

[...] In 1974, Isabelo Zenón published the first (and more important) volume of his pathbreaking *Narciso descubre su trasero*;[12] the leading critique of racism in Puerto Rican culture, particularly in literature and language. Zenón stressed not only the denial of the *puertorriqueñidad* of Puerto Ricans of color but also the denial by black and mulatto Puerto Ricans of *lo negro*. The distance between *negro* and *africano* in *Narciso* seems, however, immense, almost unbridgeable (Zenón 1974–75: 45–46). The absence of a sustained claim to a radical AfroPuerto Rican distinctiveness is precisely what places Narciso outside *cultura negroide*, and Zenón virtually denounces *cultura negroide* at several points in his book.

However, in its insistence on the integral belonging of AfroPuerto Rican culture in Puerto Rican culture, Zenón established a key theme of *antillanismo*. Zenón viewed Puerto Rican culture as tripartite composed of Taíno, African and Spanish influences.[13] The boundaries between the three components are strictly phenotypical; Zenón's message is that all are responsible for forming Puerto Rican culture. (Zenón's advocacy of Puerto Rican independence and his allegiance to an embattled Puerto Rican national culture go far to explain this perspective.[14])

Zenón did not tackle in *Narciso* the vexing question of an AfroPuerto Rican cultural context and was quick to label *cultura negroide* as racist. His investigation of the nexus between Africa and Puerto Rico, e.g., the differences and connections between *africano* and *negro* or on the cultural roots of Puerto Rican folk religious practices such as *santiguo* or *espirituao*, are literally self-effacing.

Zenón takes up the matter of the *africano* versus the *negro* only in a footnote. There he relies largely on the authority of Roger Bastide, who himself appeals to specialists on the anglophone Caribbean. The quotes from Bastide are left without comment.[15] In becoming *negro*, according to Bastide, the *africano* disappeared: slavery was too brutal and longlasting. Bastide and Zenón do not take note of the historical particularities of Puerto Rico and the hispanophone Caribbean, where slavery was truly strong only in some regions, during some decades of the nineteenth century. In other regions, an old, creole, peasant, free black-mulatto-white population contextualized slavery in ways very different from the anglophone Caribbean. Thus Zenón's cryptic comment that the contribution of el negro to Puerto Rican culture is far vaster than that *el africano*, and that the contributions *el negro* have been essentially a matter not of groups, but of individuals, strikes me as simplistic. [...]

Zenón's perspective on "black" religious culture is more complex. [...]Zenón is especially concerned to counter racist dismissal of supposedly "black" practices. However, Zenón equally recognizes that it is also racist to dismiss the African cultural legacy in Puerto Rico as irrelevant. Thus he concludes that more reflection on this matter is necessary (Zenón 1974–75: 208). [...]

[...]

A second major work of *antillanismo* is a historical-cultural essay, José Luis González's *El país de cuatro pisos* (1980).[16] González, who had originally criticized Zenón's book as simplistic, by 1980 provoked debates at least as strong as those unleashed by *Narciso* six years before. González broke both with Zenón's tripartite cultural and racial schema to argue that Puerto Rican culture and history has been fundamentally African and Afro-Caribbean since the sixteenth century. Indeed, González argued, the first and presumably "truest" Puerto Rican were black, indeed "African." [...]

However, González's essay was read as a devastating attack on hispanophilia and its class correlate, the collapsed Puerto Rican national bourgeoisie. It is a sign of the intellectual tone of Puerto Rico that the specific implications of *País de cuatro pisos* for the discussion of AfroPuerto Rican culture went largely unheeded. *País de cuatro pisos* remained a major point of reference through the renewed hispanophilia of the late 1980s [...].

The most ambitious and influential *antillanista* author in Puerto Rico today is Edgardo Rodríguez Juliá. He was already a recognized writer when he published his first widely read work on a AfroPuerto Rican theme, *El entierro de Cortijo* (1983). *El entierro* is about the mass wake and burial in 1983 of Rafael Cortijo, the *plena* musician who was probably Puerto Rico's greatest percussionist and band leader in this century.

In *El entierro*, Rodríguez Juliá reproduces photographic detail actual and historical images of Cortijo's Cangrejos (Santurce) milieu, which historically has been closely linked with Loíza. A sense of the deep historicity and wide-ranging ramifications of AfroPuerto Rican culture permeates the work [...]. Rodríguez Juliá, however, brings the locale full speed into an urban-present-with-a-past, and the work is far more open to contradiction, including class contradiction, [...].

[...] [I]n exploring "black" identity Rodríguez Juliá recognized he was probing deep into his own. Nonetheless, the ethnographic spirit—for better and for worse—is fully with Rodríguez Juliá as he makes his way through the crowd in Cortijo's burial, where the writer captures a myriad of social types expressive of contemporary Puerto Rican popular identity: "To define is easy, but how difficult it is to describe!"[17] After *El entierro*, Rodríguez Juliá published a historical novel set in the 1790s about a maroon utopia in the mangrove country outside San Juan, entitled *La noche oscura del Niño Avilés* (1985).

While Rodríguez Juliá's genuine interest in history, and its connections with contemporary reality, has broken new ground in Puerto Rican literature, his approaches to AfroPuerto Rican history does not sufficiently register complexity and ambiguity. Rodríguez Juliá too quickly accepts stark dichotomies—highlands vs. coast, black-mulatto vs. *jíbaro*, peasant vs. proletarian, rural vs. urban—for Puerto Rican history, sharply distinct worlds populated since the nineteenth century by white highland peasants and black coastal proletarians. More generally, Rodríguez Juliá casts AfroPuerto Ricans as slaves, rebels, or maroons.

Perhaps this is why Rodríguez Juliá ultimately despairs of the possibilities even of his own field of literature: in order to attain a critical, historical understanding, he avers, writers must turn outside their field and to music. He perceives the intent of *antillanismo* to be "clear in music, more than in literature." While literature provides "sketches" at best, music offers "truly the chronicle of those new values, of those new ways of seeing reality". This is perhaps why he was at his best in his first widely known work, the brief chronicle *El entierro de Cortjjo* (1983).

New values or old? In her [...] *House on the Lagoon*, Rosario Ferré vindicates the role of literature with a summa of sorts of the *antillanista* literary tradition; it is a masterful achievement that may signal the dusk of that canon (Ortega 1991: 144). In a steady stream of writings since the 1970s, Ferré has interwoven ethnic-racial conflict with two dimensions that had been eclipsed in *antillanismo* especially in the works of Zenón and González: class and gender. [...]

But instead of "the world of *plena* culture" that appears elsewhere in her work (Flores 1992: 101), *House on the Lagoon* is governed by the clash of two telluric worlds—Africa and Spain—which are both seen as permanent essences. Angolan sorcerers and *conquistadores* from Extremadura battle it out in a metaphoric space that combines González's architectural metaphor—the house—with Rodríguez Juliá's mangrove geography—the lagoon. Unlike other *antillanista* works, here *antillanismo* has fully seen, and depicts the enemy...and it is Spain.

In *House on the Lagoon*, [...] as in *País de cuatro pisos*, a generalized black Africa is the surrogate for Puerto Rican popular culture. Ferré expresses *lo africano* with a purity that mimics the exoticism that has afflicted *antillanismo* and *cultura negroide*.

Ferré's nearly *palesiano* exoticism is especially sustained in her depiction of the African religious culture of Petra Avilés and her family, a devotion that the author exclusively on the cult of Eleggua. As depicted in *House*, the Avilés' belief in Eleggua is a piece of an intense and unperturbed *africanía*, [...]

[...] Ferré addresses AfroPuerto Rican folk religion with a schematism that echoes, again, "*País de cuatro pisos*": *lo africano* is the first "story" and to *lo español* and, to a lesser degree, other European "presences" are the second "story."

[...]

The distance we have traveled from *cultura negroide* is clear: the African dimension is no longer an exotic, subordinate "other," but a distinct, central, constitutive component of Puerto Rican culture. [...]

Despite its immense critical importance, the *antillanista* perspective remains cramped on several counts: first [...] there is the unilateral emphasis on ethnic and racial typing and the indifference to social class dimensions. Indeed, *antillanismo* collapses race and culture and class, considerably complicating any understanding of race and culture and leading straight into facile romanticism. There is also a perceptible impatience in much of *antillanismo*, which is fundamentally literary in scope, vis-á-vis history, including historical research and rethinking, as well as with regard to critical social science approaches. Third, one senses in *antillanismo* an ultimate failure to see Puerto Rico in the Caribbean context and beyond: despite flourishes of Caribbean reference, the frame of mind remains decidedly insularist.

The superficial and reified aspects of *antillanismo* do not exist in isolation, and need to be viewed in light of the preceding tradition of *cultura negroide*. Indeed, in important ways, antillanismo is a retooled and more imaginative *cultura negroide*— certainly more historical and more political and certainly more wide-ranging than *cultura negroide*, but still too close to the latter. In its historical vision, *antillanismo* seems still to lack the conceptual approaches and the historical understanding needed to reappraise Puerto Rican popular culture in the thick of its social relations. Like *cultura negroide*, *antillanismo* tends to focus too exclusively on the experience of "blacks," who are constructed rather abstractly as a stable, phenotypically-defined group that has remained basically homogeneous throughout.

Negroidismo stressed festive aspects, while *antillanismo* pointed at least as much to historical racism and oppression and to cultural aggression. Both approaches thus neglected the experience of a large and very diverse population of blacks and mulattos during the era of slavery and afterward. Accordingly, historical studies in the *antillanista* vein tended to seek the black experience either under slavery and immediately after emancipation, or in the history of San Juan and other coastal cities during the nineteenth and twentieth centuries. These are important fields: but almost nothing has been said about the agrarian experiences of AfroPuerto Ricans two or three generations out of slavery in the first decades of the twentieth century.

In sum, much of Puerto Rico's social history has been absent from all sides of the discussions on AfroPuerto Rican culture. To a large extent, neglect of the sociohistorical dimensions of culture has also marked Afro-Caribbean studies generally [...].

Conclusion: Rethinking AfroPuerto Rican culture

Cultura negroide was the first broad cultural current to focus on the specific cultural expression of Puerto Rican blacks and mulattos. *Cultura negroide* was an important step forward insofar as it pointed to the specificity of AfroPuerto Rican culture, for it made aspects of AfroPuerto Rican culture better known and in some ways dignified the island's African legacy. However, *cultura negroide* constructed AfroPuerto Rican culture Eurocentrically, as unique, primitive, erotic, and irrational.[18]

Antillanismo began in 1960s in conjunction with the protest culture and a renewed independence and labor movement, took *cultura negroide* forward. *Antillanismo* strongly developed themes already in *cultura negroide*, if not necessarily in Palés Matos' poetry; primarily a denunciation of racism in particular and of social injustice in general. The poetry of Vizcarrondo is an especially important, albeit neglected bridge between *cultura negroide* and *antillanismo* in this regard. The broad Caribbean scope of *antillanismo* and the turn toward Africa are clearly indebted to Palés.

In other ways, *antillanismo* moved ahead—of special importance are its broad social critique, strong antiracism, alertness to mulatto culture and to hybridity, openness to class dimensions, a systematic interest in social history, a more explicit sense of Africa, and a sense of the interaction between the different artistic and scholarly components that make it up. Crucially, *antillanismo* views the AfroPuerto Rican presence not as a distinct essence, but as a major component of Puerto Rican national culture. These directions begin to break with the premises *antillanismo* itself.

Yet the dominant currents of *antillanista* cultural expression, even in its most recent and impressive creations, continue to harbor strong continuities with *cultura negroide* and a tendency merely to hallow refurbished *negroide* icons: eroticism and primitiveness still seem to carry the day. One senses that there are many possibilities beyond *antillanismo* that would do more than stand in the shadow of, or invert the presuppositions behind, both *antillanismo* and *cultura negroide*.

[...]

But the poetry of Palés and Vizcarrondo does not tell—and probably could not tell—the whole story. Palés and Vizcarrondo, [...] resorted to explanations based largely on "isolation. The work of the young critical poets, who focus perhaps too narrowly on general issues of racial and class oppression, also cast aside the important historical issues that the *negroide* writers touched on. We need to look closely not only at phenotypical race, or at a culture directly inferred from race, but at culture actively entwined with social relations.

[...] We need to look closely at the various social groups that shaped and were shaped by AfroPuerto Rican tradition. We need, in short, a more concrete and historical sense of *afropuertorriqueña* culture.

In this effort, AfroPuerto Rican cultural studies also need to explore works far beyond Puerto Rico where similar issues are being raised, including the wealth of work on Afro-Caribbean and African-American culture in general. Indifference to U.S. African-American culture is especially glaring, while Africa remains virtually unknown. Of course, the problem has been reciprocal: Afro-Caribbean and African-American studies have displayed remarkable ignorance of Puerto Rico's specific social history. In historical analysis, it seems as if we are forced to choose between being classified as yet another Sugar Island peopled by slave masses and being evicted from the Caribbean region.

Among Puerto Ricans, the racialization of cultural discussion has blocked discussion of AfroPuerto Rican history and culture. A necessary affirmation of human universality, perhaps because made abstractly, has proved cooptable through the parading of disembodied folklore that "all" can share equally. [...]

Moreover, race and culture are not the only relevant dimensions; we cannot say that they are more fundamental. Concurrent, competing identities, often denied and suppressed, exist in terms of gender, sexual preference, class, ideology, nation, generation, and many other dimensions of personal and social experience that are quite impossible to conjoin neatly. All these identities are typically both multiple and overlapping. Both *cultura negroide* and *antillanismo* recognized this multiplicity, even if to an extent that seems insufficient today.

[...]

CHAPTER 4

Nanas negras: The Silenced Women in Rosario Ferré and Olga Nolla

By Mary Ann Gosser-Esquilín

In 1980, Puerto Rican author and critic José Luis González published "El país de cuatro pisos" ("The Four-Storeyed Country"), an essay that marks a crucial moment in Puerto Rican letters. González uses the analogy of a house to present a Puerto Rico that is racially and economically constituted of four "floors." These have interacted and come into conflict since Puerto Rico was inserted into the vortex of the Western world's historical and racial constructs. Puerto Rican society has kept its Afro-Caribbean elements in a metaphorical basement, whereas González forcefully places them on the first floor of the nation/house. [...] Nevertheless, Puerto Rico's racial tensions continue, as contemporary works of fiction clearly demonstrate. [...]

In Puerto Rican literature, traditionally and usually, the Black characters in fiction function as the backdrop or, to use González's metaphor, the lower floor of a four-storeyed country. Puerto Rican women writers bring gender issues to the foreground; yet, in spite of that, black women characters remain somewhat marginalized. Rosario Ferré's *The House on the Lagoon* (1995) and Olga Nolla's *El manuscrito de Miramar* (1998) serve as a departure for our exploration of the still partially silenced voices of black women in contemporary Puerto Rican fiction. The study of black women through historical and social lenses will allow us to review how race and gender play a significant role in the political and economic power struggles in present-day Puerto Rican society.

A mythical reconstruction of Puerto Rican history pretends that Puerto Ricans are the seamless result of a perfect blending of the Taíno, the African, and, above all else, the European (Spanish) "races." On March 23, 1924, the influential editor and contributor of the *Boletín histórico de Puerto Rico*, Dr. Cayetano Coll y Toste, responds to a question on the origins of the jíbaro by using "historical evidence" (all of it recorded by whites). The *jíbaro* results from the mixing of the Spanish and the native populations in the mountains. Spanish and blacks mixed on the coastal plains, and therefore, he

Originally published in *CENTRO: Journal of the Center for Puerto Rican Studies* 14(2): 48–63, 2002.

claims that in five or ten centuries "no se encontrará un tipo genuinamente negro en toda la isla" (158). Other Puerto Rican authors have also been preoccupied with racial issues. Part of the emphasis of the earlier *Negrismo* movement in Puerto Rico, associated to white poet Luis Palés Matos, was to bring to the foreground the "blackness" present in Puerto Rican culture. His poetry brought recognition to some of the contributions the descendants of slaves had made to Puerto Rican culture. As explored by Palés Matos, these contributions tend to be limited to elements of popular culture such as music and food. The Afro-Caribbean characters and, especially, the black and mulatto women remained exotic, sexual, sensual, and Other.

[...]

[F]or women of African descent, the stereotypical perception is that they are capable of bringing out the most intense of sexual passions in those who cross their paths. The Afro-Caribbean woman, [...], tends to be associated with the arousal of unbridled sexuality. The mulatta especially is considered passion incarnate, and so the language used to describe her tends to reflect this vision of her. [...]

In contemporary fiction, especially that done by Puerto Rican women writers such as Rosario Ferré and Olga Nolla, among others, race and gender issues are being presented and negotiated in a more complex manner. [...] [A]lthough the representation of Afro-Caribbean women is still not perfect, critical investigations into the discriminating and biased mores of Puerto Rican society have begun in earnest.

The older, female characters, for the most part, remain as nannies, housekeepers, or cooks or a combination of these. Nevertheless, changes in their presentation or in the voice they are given have occurred. In the case of Ferré's novel, they are given speaking parts and significant roles to play within the plot. As for the younger generation of mulattas (such as Coral and Perla Ustariz in Ferré's novel), these are more educated and professional women who are not afraid to speak their minds. Even so, many continue to be the object of marginalization, hence their novelistic fate reflects the racism and prejudice that are still pervasive in Puerto Rican society. The characters can only fight against discrimination if they are educated and given the opportunity to succeed. The mulatta, especially, still exudes sexuality, and the male characters are physically attracted to her, even when she is an educated woman.

Women novelists such as Ferré and Nolla attempt to incorporate as many women of color as they can and try to explore their backgrounds and examine their historical silencing and ill treatment at the hands of a racist elite. Ferré and Nolla offer renewed efforts when looking at the plight of these women of color with new eyes, but nonetheless, the characters are still part of a society that discriminates against people based on their gender and race. What remains to be seen is how much more significant their roles will be in future narratives as Puerto Rican society continues to evolve. Afro-Puerto Rican women writers such as Mayra Santos Febres positively impact the Puerto Rican literary milieu. Her work renews attempts to bring to the foreground the multiple and varied contributions of Afro-Puerto Ricans and not just limit the presentation to the popular elements of Puerto Rican culture.

In some instances, the black female or mulatta characters themselves denounce the racial as well as the gender discriminations they face. In Ferré's novel, *The House on the Lagoon,* the well-to-do, white, Puerto Rican female writer protagonist, Isabel Monfort de Mendizábal, gives voice to Petra Avilés (the rarely heard black servant or nanny) and some of her descendants and also to the mulatta Ermelinda Quiñones (a dressmaker) and her descendants. Olga Nolla's *El manuscrito de Miramar* gives voice to a black nanny in a separate chapter (#13) in the reconstructed first-person narrative done by María Isabel Gómez-Sabater, daughter of Sonia the author of the original manuscript.

The crucial role that Afro-Puerto Rican women have played in the construction of the nation is highlighted. However, their presence in the text remains problematic precisely because they still represent what is going on in contemporary Puerto Rican society, namely, that they have some more opportunities and a voice, but one that is in a separate space, either in the basement or the kitchen of the house or above the garage or in a separate chapter, and at times isolated from the rest of the characters. This is partly due to the fact that they belong to the realm of oral tradition. They are not the ones writing their history, and although present, are still marginalized within the official discourse oftentimes controlled by the whites writing history.

Recalling González's analogy, the Afro-Puerto Rican women are the foundational first floor, and as such are strong but remain underneath the other floors. Their role in the narrative helps to support the protagonists, and, as will be seen, they play a significant role in the development of the plot, and by extension the development of the nation/house. These often silent characters are present and ready to help the protagonists, even when these protagonists may not have given them much thought at first. In fact, in both novels, an earlier erasure or whitening of the Afro-Puerto Rican women's pages turns out to be an important part of the text in a writing exercise that may be described as palimpsestic. They—both the Afro-Puerto Rican women and their pages—are being written over in a different light by the writer/protagonists once their significance is established and re-appreciated by the white writer/protagonists of the novels.

[...]

In María Isabel's case, she is the one who recognizes Toñita, the black nanny at her mother's funeral. When Toñita's stream of consciousness is presented in the inauspicious thirteenth chapter, she points out the race, gender, and class divides. It is as if the novel were signaling what bad luck it is to be born female and dark in Puerto Rico. [...] What is fascinating is to see her accept it as if it were natural, as if these divides were to be expected and respected. Like Petra, she belongs to a different generation of women of color who did not feel the need to be raising their voices and expressing how they felt and lived the racism they experienced, because it was taken for granted. Toñita does not have a full name, just a nickname (for Antonia) in its diminutive form. As such, it serves as a marker of her quasi-invisibility or her status as a child being treated in a condescending and patronizing way. The fact that she does not have a last name signals her seemingly transitory condition and marginality vis-à-vis the well-to-do characters in the novel.

In "The Four-Storeyed Country," González divides the racial and economic development of Puerto Rico into four distinct moments. The first Puerto Ricans, he states, were black Puerto Ricans in the sense that these were "*criollos*," meaning they were born in the new country from African slaves. He makes a strong case for this bold assertion, for even when Spaniards had children on the island, they nonetheless considered themselves as nothing else but Spaniards with the possibility of going back "home" to Spain, *la Madre Patria*. The Africans, who could only aspire to return to Guinea (the afterlife), had no home to return to as far as the Spanish authorities were concerned. They, together with the Spaniards and the Taínos, constitute the first floor of the Puerto Rican nation/house. The African group remains the most silenced and hidden of the three.

In González's essay, gender was never an issue, whereas in these novels, gender is at the core of the narratives. Ferré's novel has as its center a female voice: Isabel, a white, well-to-do Puerto Rican woman writer. Isabel's novel is written and rewritten by the characters as they interact with her and unveil unpleasant traits of Puerto Rican society (racism, *machismo*, classism). Isabel's interactions with her husband, Quintín, and the Afro-Caribbean servant, Petra Avilés, contribute to the unveiling of racism as practiced among the elite. Yet the exchanges are revisited because a woman is now compiling and telling the story. Petra and her extended family literally occupy that foundational space, the cellar of the multiple reincarnations of the house on the lagoon. Or they live at Lucumí beach, the mangroves, or the Las Minas slum. These are all "black" spaces in Ferré's novel, separate and distinct from the above-the-ground floors of the house. Yet without them the house would not run smoothly. These background characters allow the likes of Isabel (and in Nolla's novel, Sonia and María Isabel) to achieve their goals as creative and outspoken women.

[...]

In Puerto Rico, these characters belonging to the well-to-do ruling families never sensed there was any segregation or discrimination. As part of the Puerto Rican elite on the island, they were "whites" in spite of not being "white" by United States' standards. Hence there exists a need to emphasize the Spanish heritage, which, because it is European, is believed to be superior to that of the United States. This reinterpretation of the Puerto Rican racial and cultural past is carried out at the expense of the contributions the descendants of Africans have made. These contributions, not only to Puerto Rico's miscegenation but also to its music, food, art, and culture, are deemed inferior by this elite because they are not European. For blacks and poor whites, to go back to these Hispanic roots as they were understood and prescribed by the elite was actually a step backwards into the Spanish era of colonization. Upon realizing that their olive-colored skins cause suspicion, Puerto Ricans belonging to the elite embrace the English language more ardently and play the part of Caucasian-Americans.

[...]

In *The House*, the characters are very much torn by this issue as they struggle and cope with racial discrimination in various ways. Overall, the patriotic quest to define what it is to be Puerto Rican is pinned by Isabel on the figure of the *jíbaro*. He (and it is frequently a he) is usually represented as a poor, light-skinned inhabitant of the mountains who has adopted some of the African ways of life in terms of language and food. At the same time, he is a survivor, and as such, he is exalted. [...] Isabel's family descends from the coffee growers of the mountains. Her narrative perpetrates accepted perceptions and serves to oppose her family to the coastal *nouveaux riches* exemplified by the Mendizábal side. For example, when she speaks of her cousin Margarita's skin color, Isabel explains that her "skin wasn't white. It was more the color of sandalwood, as is often the case with the people from the mountains" (306). By synthesizing the African elements into this one romantic and melancholy figure, there is an erasure of African elements and a "whitening" of them. The professional and intellectual elite of the '50s through the '80s seems to have won the racial battle by way of acculturation to the Spanish heritage.

[...]

The "white" family that Isabel examines is marked by the, at times, forced interactions among the island's various racial, social, and class groups. Eventually, by legal marriage or by rape, the races come together. The Mendizábal blood is forever mixed with that of the Avilés lineage. On the genealogical chart proposed by the author before we even begin to read the novel, the Buenaventura bloodline runs parallel to that of the Avilés matriarchal family, and finally the two intersect through Carmelina's rape. The patriarch of the black family, Bernabé Avilés, is a "negro bozal"; the epithet carries the meaning that he was born in Africa and brought as a slave to the island. He speaks a Bantu language and organizes a slave revolt that fails. Instead of being executed, he is brought to the plaza and [his tongue is cut off.]

[...]

The scene is symbolic of the silencing of the blacks trying to rebel against their fate. Petra, his granddaughter, is the cook and maid of the Mendizábal family. She and her family live in the cellar of the house on the lagoon, close to the mangrove and the land crabs that crawl around and about. As a medicine woman from Guayama, as well as a transmitter of Afro-Puerto Rican traditions, she cooks a combination of Spanish dishes and the inherited fare of the African slaves. Her devotion is to Elegguá, her favorite saint—an important figure who will eventually save the manuscript we are reading. However, most of the time she remains silent, in the background of the house and the plot of the manuscript.

Another character and her descendants of color are not present on that genealogy page of the Mendizábals and the Avilés: Doña Ermelinda Quiñones, a mulatta and famous dressmaker from Ponce. After defending her for protesting over the dire pay of needleworkers, the white lawyer Don Bolívar Márquez makes her his mistress. In spite of this twist from fate, she remains a triply dangerous character because she is 1) a woman, 2) a mulatta, and 3) an outspoken advocate for the creation of unions to protect the needleworkers, all women and of mostly poor and mixed origins. A smart woman, whose spirit was somewhat broken after her jail arrest, she reincarnates in the courageous nature of her two granddaughters, Coral and Perla Ustariz. In the novel, Ermelinda is described as "very good looking—tall and willowy, with fine features. Her eyes were the color of molasses and her skin was a light cinnamon. Her only drawback was the mat of corkscrew curls that grew on top of her head, so wild and thick and spirited there was no way to comb them into a civilized hairdo. For this reason, ever since she turned fifteen, Ermelinda wore a red turban tied around her head" (219). The key word is "drawback," signifying that to be deprived of straight hair is a curse to any woman, and that she better not dare to mingle with the "white," well-to-do Puerto Rican society, where she could have perhaps otherwise pass as white. The use of the term "drawback" also signals the underlying prejudices that Isabel covertly espouses.

At first, Ignacio, Quintín's brother, courts Esmeralda, her daughter, but the Mendizábal clan forbids the interaction. Because Ignacio commits suicide, the color lines are not crossed, and the family can maintain its "official" purity of blood. The omission of the Quiñones genealogy represents another erasure of Afro-Caribbean women, because although they do not marry into the Mendizábal family, Ermelinda's descendants are courted by two generations of Mendizábal men.

The racial prejudice against the Quiñones women crops up again when Manuel, one of Isabel and Quintín's sons, wants to marry Coral, a redhead with light gold skin. Willie (Isabel and Quintín's adopted son) dates her sister, Perla. Quintín's racism clearly comes out in the open when Manuel asks him for his permission and his blessing to marry Coral. After making an incision on the tip of one of his fingers and letting blood out, he explains [...] The "pure" white Mendizábal bloodline cannot be officially or legally tainted.

[...]

These figures are brought to the foreground by Isabel, a white upper-class educated woman who is trying to revive her family's history along with Puerto Rican history, and there is no denying that the racial and gender issues constitute important elements. For the most part, the black characters remain in the background or the cellar; their mulatto descendants are no longer exclusively nannies, but mostly professionals (journalist, social worker, painter) who because of their education and money have begun to cross the color line. In the eyes of some old, entrenched racists, for example Quintín, they are blacks or descendants of blacks, and there is not much else to discuss. A man of his stature and race may satisfy his sexual urges with them— he sees these women only as objects—but [would] never legalize such a union. Crossing the color line is a clandestine and quiet or private activity and should not be recorded for posterity, not even in fiction, as Isabel does. According to Quintín, Isabel is "tainting" family history as well as Puerto Rican history *with feminist prejudices* (108).[1] Her views on his family's racial prejudices are just as damning. As for Isabel, she tries to walk the fine color line, yet her racial and gender prejudices do come through. It will be up to the next generation, Willie and Manuel, to effect changes—one through the arts and the other through armed conflict. As we shall see, similar phenomena related to race and gender appear in Nolla's novel.

Olga Nolla's novel, *El manuscrito de Miramar*, takes us into the year 2025 and into the life of a professional woman, María Isabel a medical doctor in the U.S., who is trying to reconstruct her mother's life (Sonia) as well as that of her island based on a manuscript found in their demolished childhood house years after her mother's death. Sonia had decided to write the story of her affair with her University of Puerto Rico Caribbean History Professor, Don Enrique Suárez Castillo. His knowledge and his nationalist inclinations had swayed her. The novel, once again, is an attempt to reconstruct Puerto Rican history as seen through gendered lenses. The author incorporates a chapter in the voice of the family's black nanny, and some of the same stereotypes seen in Ferré are reinforced.

First of all, the chapter (#13 out of 16) comes toward the end of the novel. The character is only presented as Toñita (a diminutive nickname with no last name and not even the "doña" which is reserved for Sonia). In great awe of this family, she feels compelled to attend doña Sonia's funeral upon reading the obituary in the local papers. In other words, even though she served the family faithfully for many years, no one remembers to contact her. At the beginning of the novel she is a background presence, taking care of the children so that the white, upper-class woman can attend classes at the university and also indulge in having a torrid love affair. Then, Toñita is excised from the text, until she reappears at the funeral.

In that chapter, the reader learns why Toñita disappears. Her narrative explains that upon finding out that she was pregnant and unmarried, doña Sonia condescendingly asks her if she knows who the father is and if they were planning on getting married. Toñita will be allowed to work for the family until the end of the month. In this instance we recall [...] how the black woman is represented as promiscuous and careless with her sexuality. Ironically, the questioning comes from Sonia, a married woman who studies biology, uses contraceptive methods, yet has had an extramarital affair, has gotten pregnant, and does not know who the father is. As an upper-class, white woman with economic means and contacts, she eventually undergoes an abortion, and then goes on a romantic trip to Italy to forget the traumatic experience and turn a new leaf.

Sonia insists on meeting Toñita's future husband and grills him with questions. Sonia does not ask what Toñita wants or needs. For Toñita, an abortion is not an option. Sonia's prejudicial attitude is very marked: out-of-wedlock sexual relations among people of color cannot be condoned. That sexuality must be curtailed because it is dangerous and could bring the demise of fine Puerto Rican society as doña Sonia knows it. The harshness of the text decries a racial and class gap that does not allow female solidarity to bridge it. When addressing both Toñita and Juanito (also a diminutive and no last name), Sonia dictates their future. [...]

Sonia silences Toñita and imposes public and accepted white, bourgeois values upon her children's *nana*, while in her own private circle, these values are but a façade. Nonetheless, Toñita feels she owes the *señora* a big debt and comes to the funeral, even though "una pobre prieta como yo parece una cucaracha en baile de gallinas" (166). When speaking of doña Sonia's children, María Isabel and Antonio, she refers to them as "mis dos niños blancos" (167). As mentioned earlier, don Felipe (Sonia's husband) does not really recognize her: she had merely been one of the many hard-working shadows in his household. Servants had their living quarters above the garage, separate from the rest of the house (*juntos pero no revueltos*). However, Toñita is quick to point out that at least one of her daughters (we assume mulatta) has fared differently: "Pero mis hijas están bien; una de ellas estudió enfermería y trabaja en el hospital Regional de Carolina; es la que todavía vive conmigo" (169). Ironically, she is a nurse, whereas María Isabel is a doctor (class and race have certainly played a role in their respective fates). Toñita's daughters have been limited by their economic means, which in turn have been affected by the color of their skin and their social class.

Toñita, like Petra portrayed as a preserver of Puerto Rican culture, is the one who directly asks Antonio, who lives in the U.S., "¿por qué no vuelves a vivir acá?" (173); to which he answers that he has grown used to living in the United States, and earns more money there. The question is, had he been a dark-skinned Puerto Rican of the lower economic class, would he have done so well in America? Toñita finds him "guapísimo" (173), probably because he is white. From this comment, the reader infers that her notion of beauty has also been molded by that of the economically dominant "white" culture. Yet in her own modest way, Toñita is the only one who realizes that if Puerto Ricans move out of the island, culture and what it means to be Puerto Rican could be lost. Nolla's ironic narrative *clin d'oeil* becomes evident in the names chosen for these two diametrically opposed characters: one, a white, well-to-do male; the other, a black, lower-class woman. Antonio's chapter follows Toñita's—hers serves as the foundation for his. Throughout the novel, he preserves his entire name that happens to be the same as Toñita's (Antonia), but in the masculine version. In an oblique way, he renders tribute to Toñita's African ancestry as he recalls the beauty, strength, and sweetness of the wife of the President of Nigeria and is reminded of his *nana*. But he undermines the tribute when he adds "Me recordó a Toñita, eso creo" [(186) my emphasis], and the only actions he immediately remembers her by are that she bathed and dressed him.

This short chapter in *El manuscrito* is an effort at giving a voice to a black woman, a character who does not get many opportunities to express herself. Her character has adopted the upper white classes' worldview and does not question it. In many instances, she is representative of a group who acknowledges being different, yet has not figured out that these differences are important and integral parts of Puerto Rican culture. More importantly, it allows us to examine the pivotal yet forgotten role that the *nanas negras* have played throughout our history: as some of the humblest and most exploited members of our society, they have provided the basic care of many well-to-do white children. They have often been the first tangible contact with a part of Puerto Rican culture (i.e., Afro-Caribbean) that the younger generation of upper-class whites may not have otherwise received.

In these two novels, the mulatta descendants of the *nanas negras* have slowly begun to make their mark by participating more fully in many facets of Puerto Rican life, especially at the professional level. Besides, the daughters and granddaughters of the *nanas negras* have a firm footing in the house's foundation while slowly but surely climbing the convoluted stairs that lead to other parts of the nation/house that constitute Puerto Rico. These floors, or the stairs leading to them, are not always easy to discern because of our history of silencing the offspring of miscegenation. Rosario Ferré and Olga Nolla have dared to tackle such a complex issue in their novels. Their writing protagonists all write from the inside of houses that keep being modified as their writings are also transformed by events surrounding them. The scaffolding supporting the nation/house/novels is built around issues of gender and race. While the white, well-to-do female writers can tell and fashion their own stories, the same is not entirely true of the Afro-Caribbean women in the texts. Their stories are still being written by others, and even when they have a voice (as in Toñita's case), they are told how to act. The Afro-Caribbean markers are still associated with popular culture—in Petra's case, through food and beliefs; in Toñita's case, through a brief glimpse at her language [e.g., "estoy preñá" (165)]. The *nanas negras* are still in separate quarters that are different from those of the white protagonists who consider those spaces as distinct and separate.

While fending off *machista* views on gender issues, the novelists deal with ingrained racial issues. Even though these are not resolved, there is an attempt to address them and bring them to the forefront through gendered lenses. Afro-Caribbean women, in spite of all of the maginalizations, are present in the novels in entire segments through the prism, of course, of their white *métrices en scène*.

Their voices are not completely lost because the reader is not entirely focused on the voluptuousness of their bodies or the sensuality they exude while "walking in a certain kind of way." By writing them into the texts, the authors address some of the erasure and the silencing to which Afro-Caribbean women have been subject for so long in a house/nation also built through their efforts.

CHAPTER 5

Brothels, Hell and Puerto Rican Bodies: Sex, Race, and Other Cultural Politics in 21st Century Artistic Representations

By Hilda Lloréns

[...]

Sex. Race. Gender. Nation. Religion. Faith. Family. Power. Love. Truth. Desire. Failure. Success. Death. Each is a significant discursive notion used to describe encounters between bodies. At the center of this analysis are both real and fictional Puerto Rican bodies. In this [chapter] I offer a cultural analysis of Mayra Santos-Febres' novel *Nuestra Señora de la Noche/Our Lady of the Night* (2006) [...] Santos-Febres' novel is a contestatory narrative written from the embodied experience of a black woman. [...] *Nuestra Señora de la Noche* deploys black sex as a conduit to power. [...]

Nuestra Señora de La Noche/Our Lady of the Night
There is a Brazilian adage that says, "A white woman to marry, a mulata to fornicate, a black woman to cook" (Caldwell 2004: 21). In *Nuestra Señora de La Noche (Our Lady of The Night)*, (2006) Santos-Febres echoes this Brazilian adage. The novel is a nuanced narrative play set on a stage of themes found in Puerto Rican reality. All of these themes merit a careful reading. Here, however I limit my reading to some instances pertaining mainly to race, gender, religion, and nation. I should note that my analysis does not follow a linear progression through the novel; rather, I discuss themes within the work that I found particularly riveting.[...]

I refer to the novel as a "play" to denote its performative character. One of the more interesting aspects of this fictional text lies in its sharp border-crossings. Santos-Febres' now iconic performative language and rhetoric turns, which she collides

Originally published in *CENTRO: Journal of the Center for Puerto Rican Studies* 20(1): 192–217, 2008.

against everyday vernacular language, produces a profoundly Puerto Rican narrative. [...] This novel, a "historical fiction,"[1] takes the reader to Puerto Rico, and specifically to the Ponce of the first half of the twentieth century. It tells an intricate tale of the lives of an entire town's people. The lives that populate the text intersect around the main character Isabel Luberza Oppenheimer.

The novel's first scene takes us to a nervous Isabel, *La Negra Luberza*, as she transgresses, literally crossing the invisible racial divide between her (the black) and the white Ponce elite. Clad in fine clothing and jewels, Isabel makes her way into a Cruz Roja (Red Cross) charity event while looking directly onto a mass of elite men and their wives. These same powerful men are often clients at her place of business: Elizabeth's Dancing Place. Even when she is nervous, Isabel doesn't betray herself, walking assuredly, almost in penetrative stride, into Ponce's white domain. Her knowledge of the men's sexual indiscretions is her biggest weapon. Since she has amassed a great deal of personal knowledge about the men and women at the event, she is indeed quite a powerful woman.

Describing Elizabeth's Dancing Place, Santos-Febres writes:

> *Era otra dimensión, distinta y alegre; parecida a los carnavales...Pero no. Era otra la alegría del Elizabeth's. (2006: 33–4)*
> *[It was another dimension, different, happy; similar to carnivals...But no. It was another kind of happiness at Elizabeth's—all translations from the Spanish by author.]*

[...] [C]arnival is a moment when societal boundaries of normalcy temporarily collapse. Resulting from the Carnival's sanctioned status, its marked beginning and ending, the carnivalesque as metaphor is constrained. The social dimension at Elizabeth's is of another, on-going kind of metaphor. Elizabeth's Dancing Place comprises a dimension that exists during the revelry and long after the carnival is over. In this framework the satisfaction sexual desires has turned into a consumer product in high demand.

[...]

Skin color, hue, and tone

Enter Isabel Luberza Oppenheimer, *La Negra Luberza*, darkest among the dark.

> *Su piel era azul, azul pantera, azul sombra de ojo hambriento...Su pelo corto, tieso, enmarcaba un rostro de labios carnosos, de nariz diminuta como botón de mu-*

ñeca, con mentón duro, más bien cuadrado. Tenía la piel tan tersa que era difícil
creerla piel. Su cuerpo inquietaba con una cintura minimísima, con unas caderas
anchas y pechos mullidos, firmes, sobre el escote pronunciado que anunciaba
aquel brillo azul de piel...Nada. Sabía, además, que su piel era una provocación y
que bastaba mirarla para impresionar a cualquiera. (Santos-Febres 2006: 35)
[Her skin was blue, panther blue, shadow blue of hungry eye...Her hair short,
tense, framing a face with meaty lips, a tiny nose like a doll's button, with a hard
profile, better yet, a square profile. Her skin was so terse that it was difficult to
believe that it was skin. Her body was disquieting with a minimal waist and wide
hips, small breasts, firm, over the very revealing low-cut top that announced that
blue shine in her skin...Nothing. She knew, more over, that her skin was a provo-
cation and that one look was enough to impress anyone.]

[...] Santos-Febres' novel is an archetypal tale about the life of one black woman determined to survive and rise above the humiliation caused by racial and class oppression. Operating throughout the novel is the virgin/whore binary and its constitutive lived notions. The identities of female Saint and Prostitute are both ultimately forged by male sexual projections and desires. The main character, the madam, is not just any black woman, she is *"una negra, negra/*a black black" woman, as dark-skinned people are often described in Puerto Rican vernacular. The double is used to emphasize or signify how dark a person's skin color is (*"negro, negro, negro"* means that the person skin is even darker). In a racial democracy where discursive strategies are used to whiten everyone, the darkest person has very little room to assert a non-black identity.

In the racialized imagination, a mythic power has been assigned to the darkest of the skins. A few examples of this diasporic mythical construction range from Alex Hayle's Kunta Kinte in *Roots* (1976), to Maryse Conde's I, *Tituba, Black Witch of Salem* (1994), to the character Nunu in the film *Sankofa* (1993), to Whoopi Goldberg as Oda Mae Brown in *Ghost* (1990). Certainly, the broad-bosomed mammies and faithful servants who have been deployed in television, cinema, and advertising (e.g. Aunt Jemima), are usually dark-skinned. This dark skin works as signifier of a more pure connection to Africa, of a closeness to a pre-enslavement past, to primitivism, strength, and animal sexuality. Dark-skinned individuals are also believed to have extra-human powers, particularly in communicating with the spirits, the ancestors, witchcraft, and the beyond. They are also cast aside and are never really seen or deployed as beautiful.

Embedded in subtle aspects of skin color, hue and tone are cultural ideas about a body's race, hence its social-cultural belongings and boundaries. While still using the white/black binary as extreme versions in the population, the in-betweens play a role in everyday practices of racializing. In Puerto Rico, similar to other racial democracies' racial categorizing, racism, inclusion, and exclusion are highly contextual and also formulaic. Adding together or subtracting a series of bodily racial signifiers, skin color, hair, nose, lips, ass, more recently breasts, and body fat, a person arrives at one of many possible racial/phenotypical categories, which carry with it broader social implications.

National racial signifiers and anxieties are mapped onto the body. Echoing José Vasconcelos (1997) Santos-Febres writes:

Sus pieles eran como un arco iris de madera tostada... Algunas pieles eran muy claras, tan claras como la suya, pero acusaban otra hechura contra el hueso. Los cabellos se presentaban tan variados como las pieles. Mechas lacias, muy oscuras, otras onduladas y duras como cepillo, rizos sueltos de un color sorpresivamente cobrizo y otros con rizo apretados como malla de lijar. Los labios y los ojos acogían formas inesperadas, finos en una cara oscura como la brea, anchos contra pieles casi blancas, de pecas acompañando una pasa roja y unos ojos verdosos como de gato agazapado, como los de los hombres Fornarís. (Santos-Febres 2006: 119–20)

[Their skins were like a rainbow of toasted wood...Some skins were very fair, as fair as his, but they betrayed another something against the bone. Their hair as varied as their skins. Straight hair, some dark, others wavy and hard like brush, curly loose hair the surprising color of copper and others with curly hair as tight as a scrubbing pad. The lips and eyes took on surprising shapes, fine features on a face as dark as tar, wide features in almost white skins, with freckles and a red kink and greenish stalking-cat eyes, like those of the Fornaris' men.]

Race is a bodily matter. It lives on/in the body, and it is deployed between bodies. [...] Using the body of Isabel Luberza Oppenheimer, Santos-Febres' takes the reader directly to "the meat," the flesh where race is enacted, lived, and reproduced. Reproduction is important because inherent in such a metaphor are mythologies about legitimacy versus illegitimacy—who are the legitimate sons and daughters of the nation? And who are not? The nation successfully reproduces itself, but power is bestowed upon some and not others.

[...]

Afro-christianity and the virgin/whore

Throughout the novel, there is a loud voice of a uniquely Puerto Rican Afro-Chris-tian tradition. What I am calling Afro-Christian traditions are practiced in Puerto Rico and much of the Caribbean. The *process* by which Afro-Christian formations occurred is referred to as syncretism. Syncretism explains the melding or fusing of two distinct traditions into one unique, completely different tradition. Much of the scholarship exploring Caribbean religions have identified *the processes* by which an Afro-Christian tradition was created, but more work is needed to explore what those traditions actually look like on/from the ground.[2] It is precisely in capturing and narrating Afro-Christian traditions that Santos-Febres' work is most compelling. Afro-Catholic and, at times, the more severe language and tone of Afro-Evangelical symbolism permeate the novel.

> *Eran tres los juanes que navegaban por el mar. Vino una tormeta de agua y viento. Viró la yola en la que navegaban; se estaban ahogando...La virgen se les apareció y los salvó a los tres, a Juan Odio, a Juan Indio, y a Juan Esclavo... (Santos-Febres 2006: 71–2)*

> *[It was the three Juans who were navigating the sea. A storm of water and wind came. It overturned their vessel; they were drowning...The Virgin appeared and saved the three of them, it saved Juan Hate, Juan Indian, and Juan Slave...]*

This variant of a prayer to La Caridad del Cobre, patron saint of Cuba, and pro-tector of fishers, mariners, and travelers[3], can also be read against the Institute of Puerto Rican Culture's canonical myth[4] that the three races—Indian, European, Af-rican— came together and gave birth to the Puerto Rican. The play with a uniquely Afro-Christian prayer also traces generative claims to the island's sea and land. The sea signifies Yemayá, the sea goddess and universal mother—and also alludes to re-production. The sea brings the reader back to the realities of living on an island. La Caridad del Cobre is also Oshún, the goddess of sex and love. A dark-skinned lover, she is in charge of pleasuring the world. Here is an evocation to Santos-Febres' char-acters Sirena Selena (2000) and, now, Isabel Luberza Oppenheimer: the triple mar-ginal (black, transexual, prostitute and black, woman, prostitute, respectively), and the owners and givers of sexual pleasure.

At other times, Isabel, La Negra Luberza, is deployed as Yemayá, the mother of all the women at Elizabeth's. Like Yemayá, at times she embodies the benevolent mother who also has the capacity of turning into a violent Yemayá Oggutte.

[...]
She is both mother and protector of the women "without history," and without family as well. She offers the women at Elizabeth's—both from nearby, in *el campo* (the country) and from far away (Panama)—a place to call home. Santos-Febres' characters, again drawing parallels between Isabel and Selena, are deployed as motherless children.

Two women inhabit the body of Isabel/La Madama. The reader is able to detect two strong female narrative voices in the story; the mother who wants to birth a child, and the woman who has a child; these are the illegitimate mother and the legitimate mother, respectively. The white virgin, mother of the legitimate national son, and the black virgin Montserrat, keeper of the mixed-race son, stand in stark contrast against the whore. Isabel Luberza Oppenheimer is the black whore who gave birth to this illegitimate mixed-race son. She is the same woman who, by virtue of her blackness, was stamped as "sucia" (dirty) since childhood (Santos-Febres 2006: 61)

Geographic blackness

Geographic blackness describes the practice in Puerto Rico of assigning blackness to certain neighborhoods or towns. Notable examples of this practice include the neighborhood San Antón in Ponce, Yaurel in Arroyo and the entire town of Loíza. In local or national imaginary these are the specific locations where "black people live." This is a strategy to segregate and marginalize blackness from the national body. San Antón is a significant Afro-Puerto Rican space.[5] It is a marginal location at once feared and needed by the white elite. It functions as a satellite of the elite, where the laundresses, servants, house-cleaners and mammies, entertainers, prostitutes, and rum dealers dwell. There also dwells the menacing seed of rebellion. [...] An example of what I have elsewhere (Lloréns 2005) called "subversive blackness" is embodied in Demetrio Sterling's character. He is a political activist, a purveyor of knowledge and a seer of sorts.

> *Demetrio, Demetrio Sterling. 'Los blancos de pueblo no lo podían ver ni en pintura'... Huelgas, centros obreros. Allá su nombre sonaba a proscrito. Todo el mundo comentaba sus andanzas sindicales, su empate con Alonso Gual, el editor del periódico El Águila, otro negro parejero que insultaba de gratis los dueños de finca y taller, denunciándolos por cualquier cosa ante la opinión pública. (Santos-Febres 2006: 130)*

> [Demetrio. Demetrio Sterling. 'The town's whites could not even see him on paint.'... Strikes, workers' centers. Over there his named sounded forbidden. Ev-

eryone commented about his organizing, his connections to Alonso Gual, editor of El Águila newspaper, that other black troublemaker who freely insulted planta- tion and shop owners, accusing them for any little thing under public opinion.]

Blackness is subversive because in spite of attempts to deny it, erase it, silence and marginalize it from the national mythos, a black identity surfaces time and again in the lived bodies of Puerto Ricans, in everyday practices, cultural identity and his- tory. The well-documented, historic Puerto Rican discomfort regarding race, and blackness in particular, results from the fact that a black identity has never been suc- cessfully silenced or erased. Consequently, blackness seeps through any attempts to disregard it as a major part of the Puerto Rican national body. Through Sterling, Isa- bel encounters the work of Luisa Capetillo, a model of a "woman of means," indepen- dently charting her own destiny.

[...]

[...] Mayra Santos-Febres' novel inscribes Isabel Luberza Oppenheimer's name in early twentieth century Ponce.[6] We must name and evoke in order to remember. Santos-Febres also complicates what has been the glaring absence and marginal sta- tus of black women in Puerto Rican national imaginings and representations. Here the black woman, who has been naturalized as the most marginal, is brought to the center. Through her ownership of legal title to land a territorial claim to national belonging is made: "...podía decir que ella, Isabel Luberza Oppenheimer, poseía poco menos de tres cuerdas a orillas del río Portugués" [...she could say that she, Isabel Lu- berza Oppenheimer, possessed a little less than three acres at the shore of the Portu- gués river] (Santos-Febres 2006: 259). Isabel Luberza Oppenheimer is a culture hero. Even when Isabel is a culture hero, "a woman of means," the reader is made aware that money and class status might not truly transcend racial class/caste as it is often claimed in much of the Puerto Rican literature about race (see Lloréns 2005). In the style of a Fanonian interpellation and referring to color and social standing, Demetrio Sterling reminds Isabel: "Hay cosas que no las cambia el dinero" [There are things that money does not change] (Santos-Febres 2006: 131).

Conclusion

Mayra Santos-Febres' *Nuestra Señora de la Noche* brings to the fore the life of one black woman whose rise to power is also her demise. *La Negra Luberza*'s line of busi- ness reveals one aspect of how Puerto Rico's racial democracy works in post-emancipation society: racial equality is a myth. Yet Isabel Luberza Oppenheimer understood that the moment when [black] women stopped being the property of white men was the moment when women could sell sex, in the market economy model of capitalism, as a means of amassing power. The prostitute's role is to mediate the cracks of a system that uses silence and shame as a strategy to oppress everyone, but this oppression is particularly brutal for black men and women. La Madama and her girls confront the fundamental lack of freedom and entrapment in a global scheme encompassing racial, class, and national inequality. Mayra Santos-Febres tells an untold and ignored narrative about black women's lives in Puerto Rico. Perhaps it is a positive sign of the times when a woman, a black woman, is able to reclaim the agency that Luberza and the women who worked in her brothel were only fleetingly able to access during their lifetime.

[...]

Throughout this [chapter] I have explored the connections between art/cultural production and the wider cultural and sociopolitical universe within which these works were produced. I have paid particular attention to how official discourses about race, gender, sex, religion, language, and proper comportment are "messed with" in these artworks. I have done this to understand how embodied realities of race and gender inform works of art and how works of art, in turn, inform lived realities. As Maurice Berger reminds us, "Art is never value-free nor an independent source of values; to one extent or another, it always reflects the needs, politics, intellectual and aesthetic priorities, and tastes of the artist, the institutions that support and disseminate his or her work, and the social and cultural universe of which both are part" (1998: 11). The implications of art in revealing aspects of cultural and identity politics offers cultural workers the opportunity to engage with the cultural productions that work to inform, maintain, and sometimes create cultural and discursive practices. My intention here has been to promote experimentation, provocation, inspiration, and, most significantly, propose a widening of the field of discourse from which to draw cultural data in order to expose the complex interactivity between bodies, art and cultural practices.

SECTION II.
Racialization in Migration: Modes of Incorporation

CHAPTER 6

Afro-Puerto Rican Radicalism in the United States: Reflections on the Political Trajectories of Arturo Schomburg and Jesús Colón

By Winston James

They were both black and Puerto Rican, both in their youth burned with the fire of Puerto Rican nationalism, both migrated to the United States as young men, and both settled, lived and died in New York City. Yet Arturo Schomburg (1874–1938) and Jesús Colón (1901–1974) are seldom mentioned in the same breath. Each is known, it is fair to say, by a different set of people, with different political and intellectual interests; they made different friendships and associations, and were driven, eventually, by different passions. It is true that Schomburg and Colón were different generations, but that hardly accounts for the striking difference in their political evolution, and in the perception and remembrance of them. The fact is that, despite similar points of political origin, they followed radically divergent political paths, were absorbed by different objectives, and had dissimilar destinations. Schomburg died an ardent Pan-Africanist, with definite black nationalist sympathies wedded to the struggles and aspirations of Afro-America. Colón died a socialist and Puerto Rican nationalist, with no time for black nationalism. How do we account for the marked difference in the political trajectory of these two men? How does one explain their political evolution against the historical background of the Hispanic Caribbean and the Puerto Rican society from which they both came? How did America and the articulation of race in American society conditioned their political evolution? These are some of the key questions I hope to address in this essay.

One thing is clear from the outset: Arturo Schomburg, not Jesús Colón, was the Puerto Rican political aberration. For one of the most striking patterns that emerges from the examination of the Caribbean experience in the United States in the first half of the century is that among black radicals from the Hispanic Caribbean there was

Originally published in *CENTRO: Journal of the Center for Puerto Rican Studies* 8(1&2): 92–127, 1996.

relative indifference, if not aversion, to black nationalism. Such a position contrasted sharply with a noticeable attraction to an unhyphenated socialism. Arturo Schomburg's sympathy for black nationalism, his profound interest and pioneering work in the history of peoples of African descent, was not shared by his black Puerto Rican compatriots in New York City in the 1920s and 1930s. And Schomburg's anomalous situation cannot be explained without understanding the specificity of race in the Hispanic, as well as in the non-Hispanic, Caribbean. Puerto Rico could not have produced a Marcus Garvey, the Jamaican-born founder of the black nationalist Universal Negro Improvement Association, and Jamaica, by the same token, could not have produced a Jesús Colón. Differences in the ways that race operated hold the key to explaining this pattern. There is thus a need to outline and analyze, if only briefly, these important but rarely examined intra-Caribbean differences that, it should he noted, carry over into the diaspora in America. And as will be argued, Schomburg's peculiar political evolution cannot be accounted for outside of these intra-Caribbean variations.

Up to about 1800 the Hispanic Caribbean islands were colonies in which a comparatively large number of Europeans decided to live, or ended up living, on a permanent basis. In comparison to the northern European colonies, landholdings were small, even though the land-population ratio was large. After the center of gravity of Spanish America shifted to the gold and silver riches of Mexico and Peru in the early sixteenth century, the islands became relatively underexploited. Their links to the expanding capitalist world economy were not as strong as it was to be for the Caribbean colonies that Britain, France, and Holland acquired in the seventeenth century. [...] Subsistence farming and ranching became the mainstay of the islands. Cuba, Puerto Rico, and Santo Domingo, from the earliest days of settlement had African slaves, but the percentage of the black population that was free was consistently higher than that which obtained in the non-Hispanic colonies of the New World.

With capitalism far more developed than in Spain, over the centuries Britain, France and Holland had the economic and political infrastructure to exploit their Caribbean possessions far more systematically and intensively than Spain ever did. [...] The islands, previously the center of Spanish colonial attention in the New World, were, by the mid-sixteenth century, of minor, if any, intrinsic value to Spain, functioning as handmaidens to the mainland colonies—as re-fueling stations and garrisons, aiding the protection of convoys on their way to Spain laden with American gold and silver.

[...]

Outside of Havana and western Cuba, from the mid-sixteenth to the eighteenth century, Spain's insular possessions languished, the region turning in upon itself and into a colonial backwater; they lacked the gold and silver that held Spain's attention on the mainland. It was in this context of relative neglect that the northern European powers were able, by the early seventeenth century, to pluck away, one by one, a number of islands from the Spanish imperial body politic.

Spain's imperial malaise and neglect of the islands—as well as its effective abandonment of eastern Cuba in the late sixteenth century—provided local opportunity for those who lived in them. For one thing, imperial nonchalance provided a level of de facto autonomy for the inhabitants that they otherwise would not have enjoyed. The development of a substantial (relative to the slave population), black peasantry in the sixteenth right up to the eighteenth century cannot be explained outside of this wider context. It was also such circumstances that facilitated the growth and reproduction of a large (compared to the slave population), white, small-holding, settler population in the Spanish islands. Along with these developments occurred a level of interaction between the black and white population that was prolonged and unparalleled in the New World.

By the late eighteenth century, however, the noisy march of European capitalism had disturbed the rustic somnolence of the Spanish Caribbean. Starting with Cuba, the slave trade dramatically expanded, gigantic plantations were laid out and established, and the smallholding peasantry found it increasingly difficult to maintain its cherished independence. For the enslaved Africans, the acquisition of manumission became more difficult as their labor became more valuable. In short, Spain's Caribbean possessions became progressively more like the northern European colonies as sugar became the crop of choice.

The metamorphosis of the Spanish Caribbean rapidly accelerated after revolution broke out in Saint Domingue, the richest sugar colony in the New World, in 1791. The Haitian slaves punched a massive hole in the world sugar market. Almost 80,000 tons of sugars were produced on the eve of revolution in 1791. But, with the destruction wrought by a devastating war and with a new and fiercely independent peasantry shunning the diabolical plantation system, Haiti produced only 8 tons of sugar in 1836 (Knight 1990). The *hacendados* in the islands, like their counterparts elsewhere, took advantage of this unprecedented and unique opportunity. And so the sugar revolution, which first broke out in the British possessions in the seventeenth century, belatedly took hold of the Hispanic territories, spreading from Cuba in the middle of the eighteenth, moving, to Puerto Rico and on to the Dominican Republic in the nineteenth and early twentieth century (Moreno Fraginals et al. 1985, Moreno Fraginals 1964, Knight 1970, Scott 1985, Mintz 1974a, Lewis 1963, Scarano 1984, Dietz 1986, Hoetink 1982). But even during the nineteenth century, during the din and turmoil of King Sugar ascending his throne, dripping with the blood of Africans, the Hispanic territories displayed distinct characteristics vis-à-vis the non-Hispanic areas, carried over from their classic, and relatively prolonged, settler period. [...]

The dissimilar political economy that shaped the two areas of the Caribbean profoundly affected their demographic and ethnic patterns which, in turn, significantly influenced the articulation of race and color. In this respect, one key difference is that whites made up a much larger proportion of the population of the Hispanic Caribbean relative to the proportion found in the non-Hispanic Caribbean. It is true that racial definitions of "white" tend to be more elastic in the Hispanic compared to the non-Hispanic Caribbean, but, even by the most restrictive criteria, the Hispanic areas of the archipelago have always had a relatively high proportion of white people among their inhabitants. Thus, while the Hispanic Caribbean, with the exception of the Dominican Republic, had, for instance in the nineteenth century, approximately half of its population designated as "white," the non-Hispanic Caribbean, typically, had less than 10 percent so defined (Knight 1990; Hoetink 1970, 1982; Moya Pons 1985).

Prior to the abolition of slavery, the Hispanic Caribbean had a proportionately larger free non-white population compared to that in the non-Hispanic territories. The rate of manumission was much higher in the former area. Thus, on the eve of abolition in 1834, less than twelve out of every hundred non-white Jamaicans, and only seven out of a hundred non-white Barbadians, were free; all the others were enslaved. By contrast, almost sixty percent of non-white Cubans were free in 1880, six years before abolition, and ninety percent of their Puerto Rican counterparts were free by the time of abolition in 1873 This distribution of black freedom in the archipelago was not an aberration of the nineteenth century. It was a secular trend. In 1773 less than one percent (0.7 percent), of black and mulatto Barbadians were free, 534 out of 69,082. Their Jamaican counterparts hardly fared better, 2.3 percent being legally free, 4,500 out of 197,300, in 1775. In the same year, 41 percent of non-white Cubans (30,847 out of 75,180), and a stunning 82.2 percent of their Puerto Rican brothers and sisters were free (Handler 1974; Hall 1974; Kiple 1976; Díaz Soler 1981; Cohen and Greene 1974; Elisabeth 1974; Hall 1974; Hoetink 1974 Hall 1992). Why the massive differential between British and Spanish territories? As a number of scholars have argued, this was largely due to the relative economic backwardness of the Spanish possessions and of Spain itself; and was rather less a product, as some had previously suggested, of supposedly benign cultural characteristics of Spanish colonialism in the region. After all, as sugar became king in the nineteenth-century, it was in Cuba, under the same Catholic Spanish colonial rule, that the rate and ease with which the slaves acquired their manumission diminished, while the slave trade dramatically expanded. Unable to mobilize the resources to import anywhere near as many African slaves as they claimed they needed, the Puerto Rican *hacendados* in the nineteenth century, in a desperate bid to solve the labor "scarcity" problem, subordinated peasants and workers, black and white alike, to the rule of capital through extraordinarily coercive legislation.

[...]

The black and white peasantry underwent some of the same travails in the Hispanic Caribbean. [...] Adversity often bonded the oppressed, joining black and white together. Because of these historical patterns, blackness was therefore not as profoundly associated with subordination in the Hispanic as it was in the non-Hispanic areas of the archipelago (Hoetink 1985; Lewis 1963; Mintz 1974a). The occupational distance between the black and mulatto in the Hispanic Caribbean was less than it was in the non-Hispanic Caribbean. In 1872, the year before abolition, it was estimated that 35 percent of Puerto Rican slaves were mulatto or mestizo; indeed, 1.5 percent were described as "white." In 1832, two years before abolition, 14 percent of Barbadian and 10 percent of Jamaican slaves were colored; none was designated as "white" (Nistal-Moret 1985; Higman 1984, 1976).

The distinct pattern of interaction between black and white contributed to the growth of a relatively large colored population in the Hispanic compared to that in the non-Hispanic Caribbean (Greene and Cohen 1974). The sexual relations between black and white in the Hispanic Caribbean, and Puerto Rico in particular, were less marked by the profound imbalance of power that characterized such relations in the non-Hispanic Caribbean, especially in Jamaica and St. Domingue. While in Puerto Rico such cross-racial relations were often established between black and white workers and peasants, in Jamaica and St. Domingue they were generally ones between white masters or overseers and female slaves in their charge. In any case, the offspring of such unions were regarded as neither "black" nor "white"—they were a category *sui generis*. (This kind of formulation would come into sharp conflict with the fundamentally binary—"black"/"white"—distribution of the racialized population in the United States.)

The high level of interaction between black and white peasants and workers, and the many points at which their interests and fortunes converge, help to explain another outstanding feature of Hispanic Caribbean society: the high level of black mobilization and enthusiasm for nationalist projects. It is no accident that Oriente Province, the most eastern provience of Cuba, was the place that the support for the Ten Years' War and the independence struggle against Spain was greatest. [...] Oriente had a large black and colored free population who had exceptionally good access to land through ownership, renting or squatting. The small peasantry predominated there, black and white, with remarkably similar land tenure patterns. [...] It is in this environment that the encroachment of the Spanish government and the local *peninsulares* provoked joint revolt (Pérez 1986; Hoernel 1976; Pérez 1982; Scott 1985; Ferrer 1991; Robert 1992; Helg 1995). The free people of color (black and mixed-race) in Puerto Rico enjoyed even greater access to the land than did their counterparts in nineteenth-century Cuba. In 1860, six years before the revolt in the north-western town of Lares, they made up over 35 percent of the peasant farmers, 34 percent of proprietors and over 36 percent of the artisans of the island; the free colored population was estimated to make up 46 percent of Puerto Rico's free population at the time (Díaz Soler 1970; Jiménez de Waggenheim 1985; González 1980; Scarano 1984).

From *el grito de Lares*, Puerto Rico's nationalist insurrection in 1868, through the Ten Years War and Cuba's war of independence of the 1890s, right up to the victory of the Fidelistas in 1959, black people have not only been present, but have been prominent and distinguished fighters in the anti-colonial struggle. In Cuba's war against Spain, almost half of the fighters were black. Antonio Maceo, Cuba's "bronze titan" and his brother José, fell on the field of battle, as did countless other black Cubans. The sacrifices of war not only strengthen the bonds of fellowship between black and white patriots, it also reinforced the claims of citizenship and belonging (Fagen 1976; Foner 1977; Wolf 1975; Helg 1995). [...] In Puerto Rico, Ramón Emeterio Betances (1827-1898), a mulatto, is, as José Luis González put it, "recognized by all supporters of Puerto Rican independence as the Father of the Nation" (Gonzalez 1980). Arturo Schomburg and Jesús Colón were only two of a long and distinguished line of black or "colored" Puerto Rican nationalists: from Francisco Gonzalo "Pachín" Marín, Sotero Figueroa, Pedro Albizu Campos, right down to Felipe Luciano, Chairman of the Young Lords (migrant Puerto Rico's equivalent of the Black Panthers) in the early 1970s.

The British, French, Dutch and Danish Caribbean had no equivalent of the popular cross-racial nationalism that developed in Puerto Rico and Cuba in the nineteenth and early twentieth century. The white creole minority was too small and fearful of the black masses to break with London, Paris, Amsterdam or Copenhagen. The mulatto elite often harbored nationalist yearnings, at times hating the metropole, especially its arrogant European-born agents. But their contempt for and fear of the African masses was more powerful than any desire they may have had to sever links with the mother country. The masses, for their part, despised the mulattos, the white creoles as well as the European-born whites. Moreover, they always viewed the metropolitan center, and the monarchy in particular, as bulwarks against the tyranny of officialdom and the tender mercies of the local oligarchy who vigorously opposed their emancipation. In short, unlike the black and white *criollos* in the Spanish Caribbean—and for that matter, on the continent—no one was sufficiently desperate, or hated the colonial center enough to make a bid for independence, nor did they feel themselves powerful enough to succeed in such a venture. Britain and Spain in the nineteenth century were by no means military, political or economic equivalents.

At a number of levels, then, the Hispanic Caribbean, because of its historical and cultural experience, displays distinct differences with the non-Hispanic Caribbean in the perception and operation of race and color.

But throughout the Caribbean, Hispanic and non-Hispanic, there existed—nationalist collaboration notwithstanding—a hierarchy of race and color where the "whiter" and "lighter" are generally located at the top of the social pyramid, with the "darker" at the bottom. Caribbean societies were and are characterized, to a greater or lesser degree, by what the late Gordon Lewis has aptly dubbed a "multi-layered pigmentocracy" (Lewis 1969: 80, Lewis 1983). Despite this general pattern, individual "black" people could be found relatively high up the socio-economic ladder. And although after emancipation insidious practices of discrimination occurred, especially in the professions and in the colonial administration of the northern European possessions, no discriminatory legislation, explicitly based upon race, sat on the statute books of the islands (Dietz 1986; Thomas 1971; Wolf 1975). Social class, which overlapped considerably with race and color, was the primary mechanism of overt social stratification and ordering. It is true though that in the Hispanic Caribbean, and in Puerto Rico in particular, the degree of overlapping between race and class was not as exact as it was in the British and French territories. Thus in nineteenth and early twentieth century Puerto Rico, considerable collaboration between members of the working class and their organizations took place across racial lines. This was especially so among the *tabaqueros* and artisans, many of whom were black and colored. The United States Resident Commissioner, Henry Carroll, with evident surprise, reported at the turn of the century that of the eleven working class representatives who testified before him, nine were black, and all except one, could read and write, and all were decently clothed (Lewis 1963).

It is for these reasons that black Puerto Ricans, compared to Caribbean migrants from the non-Hispanic areas of the region, entered the United States with relatively low "race" or black consciousness. They seldom articulated their demands on the basis of race. They were not used to being mobilized on the basis of their blackness or their race, but on the basis of their class. And while racism in early twentieth-century America heightened the race consciousness of black migrants, in general, black Puerto Ricans responded differently. The characteristic behavior of this group of migrants has historically been to close ranks with fellow "Spanish" compatriots—"black" and "white" together—distinguishing themselves, deliberately or otherwise, from those classified as "Negroes" in the United States. Writing in 1925 of the black migrants from the Caribbean, the Jamaican radical and journalist W. A. Domingo observed that the "Spanish element has but little contact with the English-speaking majority. For the most part they keep to themselves and follow in the main certain occupational lines" (Domingo 1925: 342). [...] In *Harlem: Negro Metropolis*, his 1940 study, Claude McKay noted that the African American in Harlem "cannot comprehend the brown Puerto Rican rejecting the appellation 'Negro,' and preferring to remain Puerto Rican. He is resentful of what he considers to be the superior attitude of the Negroid Puerto Rican" (McKay 1940: 136).

There was an almost complete absence of involvement of this group of diaspora Africans in black nationalist politics during the heady days of the First World War and early 1920s. It is not insignificant that the Universal Negro Improvement Association (UNIA) branches in Cuba, Costa Rica, Panama, and elsewhere in Latin America were constituted with few exceptions of migrant workers from the non-Hispanic Caribbean and especially those from Jamaica. And in Cuba, where the UNIA had its largest organized contingent outside of the United States—no less than 52 branches at its peak—the Afro-Cubans would sometimes attend the meetings of the Garveyites, but seldom joined the organization. [...] Although Carlos Cooks (1913-1966), an important figure among Harlem's black nationalists from the 1930s to the 1960s, was born in the Dominican Republic, he was brought up in an English-speaking community of British Caribbean migrant laborers on the island. Both his parents, James Henry Cooks and Alice Cooks, had earlier migrated from neighboring St. Martin. They were staunch Garveyites, as many of these migrants were in the 1920s. As a child, young Carlos' father and uncle took him with them to UNIA meetings. Cooks came to the United States in 1929 (Harris et al 1992). Carlos Moore, the most outspoken and controversial black nationalist critic of some of the policies of postrevolutionary Cuba, was born in Oriente of British Caribbean parents (his father was Barbadian; his mother, Jamaican), within a milieu of English-speaking migrants who worked on Cuba's sugar plantations (Moore 1989).[1]

Thus, Arturo Schomburg, who migrated to New York in 1891, was, against such a background and pattern, conspicuous in Harlem in the 1920s for being a black Puerto Rican who actively supported and identified with black nationalist aspirations, and with the struggles of African Americans (Sinnette 1989). His life's project, was, in the vocabulary of the time, "the vindication of the Negro race." It was a counter struggle against racist ideology, characteristically entailing the assiduous documentation— in practice, at enormous personal cost—of the achievements of people of African descent, past and present, around the world. Schomburg dedicated himself to this lifelong struggle when, as a schoolboy in Puerto Rico, one of his teachers had told him that black people had no history, no heroes, no great moments. This cruel racist propaganda, inflicted on him as a child, appeared to have been the primary source of the fuel that drove his lifelong quest. But the fact that he belonged to a youth club in which the study of history was a key element also contributed to his mission. For in this club, "there was a tendency among the whites and near-whites to point with more pride to the achievements of their white ancestors, than the blacks seemed able to their ancestors." Young Schomburg noted this and decided to study up on the achievements of black Puerto Ricans, so that when his white associates began to tell of what history white Puerto Ricans had made, "he could talk equally as freely of the history black Puerto Ricans had made." According to Schomburg a kind of "historic rivalry" developed between the members of the club, and he found his researches extending to the Virgin Islands, Haiti, San Domingo, Cuba and the other islands of the Caribbean. When he came to the United States, he pursued his hobby more systematically and extensively and began to collect books on black people, their experience and, most notably, their achievements across space and time (Calvin 1927).

[...] Schomburg's passionate collecting of books, prints, manuscripts, and paintings by and related to Africans would continue to the end of his life. And in 1926 the Carnegie Corporation bought his collection of "over 10,000 books, manuscripts, newspapers, prints, and other materials" allegedly, at a fifth of its intrinsic value for the New York Public Library (Dodson 1986: 7; Rogers 1972: 449). The collection, accumulated by Schomburg over a period of thirty-five years, would form the nucleus of what became the Schomburg Center for Research in Black Culture. [...]

[...]

Jesús Colón (1901-1974), [...], arrived in New York in 1918. A committed socialist before he left Puerto Rico, he became involved in the struggles of Puerto Rican and Cuban cigarmakers—*tabaqueros*—in New York, was a member of the Socialist Party (and later, a Communist Party member), and fighter for Puerto Rican independence. From all the evidence, a charming, urbane and sensitive man, Colón was remarkably untouched by black nationalism. Schomburg's interest in black history and politics and his apparent drift away from the Puerto Rican struggle remained a mystery to Colón right up to the end of his life: "[S]omething happened whereby Arturo shifted his interest away from the Puerto Rican liberation movement and put all his energy into the [black] movement" (Sinette 1989: 23). Schomburg's behavior evidently raised eyebrows in the Puerto Rican community in New York. According to Bernardo Vega, another of his compatriots, when Schomburg moved "up to the neighborhood where North American Blacks lived," quite a few Puerto Ricans who knew him thought that he was "trying to deny his distant homeland" (Andreu Iglesias 1984: 195).

Vega might not have been as mystified as Colón was by Schomburg's behavior, but he nevertheless found it somewhat bizarre. In his discussion of Schomburg, he set up, no doubt unconsciously, an insidious and disturbing binary opposition between being "black" and being "Puerto Rican." Despite himself, the feeling is imparted that by having been interested in the African experience in the Americas, Schomburg had somehow diminished, if not deserted completely, his Puerto Ricanness. Significantly, Vega never described Colón—who was several shades darker than Schomburg—as "black," but Schomburg is so described. Colón was Puerto Rican, while Schomburg became black; Schomburg, apparently, could not have been black and Puerto Rican at the same time—Vega, at any rate, found it difficult to think of Schomburg as black *and* Puerto Rican. In what is, nonetheless, a generous and moving tribute to Schomburg, Vega concludes: "He came here as an emigrant and bequeathed a wealth of accomplishments to our countrymen [Puerto Ricans] and to North American blacks. What a magnificent example of solidarity among all oppressed peoples! (Andreu Iglesias 1984: 196) [...] I am inclined to believe that, as a fervent Pan-Africanist, Arturo Schomburg would prefer that his work be seen as an act of self- help, rather than one of solidarity. And this is so because he counted himself as a member of Africa's scattered children who also happened to have been born in Puerto Rico. Like his mentor, John Edward Bruce, he regarded oppressed people of African descent as belonging to one family. Schomburg used the first-person plural "We" when talking of people of African descent (Gilbert 1971; Piñeiro de Rivera 1989). Clearly, this dimension of Schomburg's thinking and political loyalties fell outside Bernado Vega's purview. That he found Schomburg so difficult to classify and conceptualize is not entirely Vega's fault; Schomburg was one of a rare breed of Puerto Ricans, if not a species of one.

The key to the singularity of Schomburg as a Puerto Rican black nationalist lies in his background. He was unusual in five important respects. First, Arturo's mother, Mary Joseph, was an *extranjera*, not a Puerto Rican. She was a black migrant worker from St. Croix, in the Virgin Islands, with strong family ties not only to St. Croix but also to the Danish-controlled sister island of St. Thomas. Second, Arturo's father was the son of a German immigrant and a Puerto Rican woman. Some sources claim, inaccurately, that Arturo's father was himself a German immigrant from Hamburg (Ortiz 1986; Sinette 1989). In any case, his father's side of the family not only had strong foreign connections, it also had strong northern European, non-Iberian roots;

such a background was hardly typical of nineteenth century Puerto Rican society. Schomburg, whose parents were unmarried, had little contact with his father. According to his son, Schomburg senior was a merchant who was born in Mayaguez, on the western end of the island. From the questionnaire that Schomburg answered in the 1930s for a study of the black family, it is evident that he knew very little about his father's side compared to his mother's side of his family.[2] Indeed, according to his biographer there is no evidence that Schomburg's father "recognized him as his son or supported either child or mother. Nothing suggests that Arturo was raised as an heir of the Schomburg family, a name well known in Puerto Rico" (Sinette 1989: 14).

Third, because of his parents' estrangement, Arturo was brought up by his mother and was thus substantially influenced by the culture of his mother's native land, the Virgin Islands. Moreover, fourth, Arturo during his boyhood spent time probably several years in the Virgin Islands, where he apparently lived with his mother's relatives and claimed to have attended St. Thomas College, a secondary school. There is, however, no record to corroborate his claim of having gone to St. Thomas College. Significantly, Schomburg—who was especially fond of his maternal grandfather, Nicholas Joseph, a butcher—clearly enjoyed life among his relatives and friends on St. Croix and St. Thomas. And evidently, he imbibed the culture of the Virgin Islands. [...] Fifth, unlike many Puerto Ricans and indeed, Hispanic Caribbeans at the time, Arturo Schomburg was not a Catholic, nominally or otherwise, but an Episcopalian; he adopted the religion of his mother and his maternal grandparents. All of his own children were brought up in the Protestant Episcopal Church. Schomburg, in marked contrast to the Puerto Rican and Cuban *tabaqueros* who migrated to the United States around the same time that he did, was profoundly religious. As discussed later, the *tabaqueros* were renowned for their atheistic and freethinking ways, linked to their political radicalism. [...]

[...]

[...] The extent to which Schomburg's religious belief contributed to his alienation from the Puerto Rican and Cuban revolutionary nationalists at the turn of the century is by no means clear, but it might have played a role. Certainly, if, as he claimed, his religiosity was as unchanging as the laws of mathematics, then he would have been uncomfortable all along with his comrades in Las Dos Antillas, militant rationalists and free-thinkers that they were. One similar, contemporaneous Afro-Cuban group in Tampa, Florida, made no secret of their views. Formed in 1900, they called themselves La Sociedad de Libre Pensadores de Martí-Maceo (Mormino and Pozzetta 1987). But as we will see, Schomburg's negative attitude toward the Communist Party of the United States and growing profession of religious faith did not make him a conservative.

Asked, in the questionnaire mentioned earlier who influenced him the most, Schomburg replied that it was his mother. He evidently loved and idealized her. She represented the "painstaking and faithful ideals of womanhood." To her son, Mary Joseph was "a loving mother of high and pure ideal" (Frazier 1939, questionnaire No. 2579).

In short, though he was born in Puerto Rico and, apparently, spent most of his childhood there, Arturo Schomburg was substantially shaped by the culture of the non-Hispanic and Anglophone Caribbean. Schomburg, astonishingly, discouraged his children from learning Spanish (Sinnette 1989; Ortiz 1986). Although he worked for years with Pura Belpré, a black Puerto Rican librarian, he never, reported one writer, spoke to her about their "shared heritage and mother tongue" (Ortiz 1986: 99). But, on reflection, given the evidence of Schomburg's formation, it is not surprising[,] for Schomburg had a dual heritage and mother tongue—one Hispanic, the other non-Hispanic. And it now appears that the non-Hispanic heritage was equally as strong as, if not stronger than the Hispanic one. For most of his life he used the Anglicized version of his first name, although he increasingly returned to Arturo toward the end of his life. Less than a year before he died, in one of his most despairing letters, brought on by his daily exposure to black Harlem's desperate plight during the Depression, Schomburg wrote to his close friend and confidante, the African-American journalist, Wendell P. Dabney: "You request me to practice moderation. I am sick and tired of the conditions that I see every night in Harlem. I am still dreaming," he confessed, "of going to the Virgin Islands and spending the remainder of my life in the calm and solicitude that can only be had in such a restful place."[3] There is no mention of Puerto Rico in the letter, let alone its consideration by Schomburg as a final resting place. After he broke with the Cuban and Puerto Rican nationalists around 1898, Schomburg maintained no close friendships within the Puerto Rican community. In marked contrast, he established, broadened and cultivated his closest friendships not only among African Americans, but also among fellow Afro-Caribbean migrants from the English-speaking Caribbean, including Hubert Harrison and Casper Holstein from the Virgin Islands.

Given such a background and orientation, it comes as no surprise that Schomburg's political trajectory in the United States bore remarkable similarity to that of Caribbean migrants from the non-Hispanic areas of the archipelago. But his disillusion with Cuban and Puerto Rican exile nationalist politics in America at the turn of the century (Ortiz 1986, Sinnete 1989), his painful experiences of Jim Crow segregation when he visited his children in the South, his membership and leading role in a black masonic lodge, his working in a job that was isolated from other Puerto Ricans, his befriending and being profoundly influenced by leading black nationalists of the day, especially John E. Bruce and Hubert Harrison, all contributed to the direction in which Schomburg's politics and worldview developed.

We should never forget, however, that Schomburg chose to withdraw from Puerto Rican and Cuban nationalist politics, chose to marry African-American women, chose to expend his energies on developing the black Prince Hall Lodge, chose the close association with black nationalists such as Bruce and Harrison, chose to live in the black San Juan Hill district of Manhattan at the turn of the century and, later, black Harlem, rather than live in one of New York's Puerto Rican neighborhoods. All of these choices become comprehensible only in the context of his formation before migrating to the United States. This is not to say that his early biography *determined* the pattern of his choices, but that it *predisposed* him to make the choices he made. After all, his immediate contemporaries and black Hispanic friends in New York, such as Rafael Serra (Cuba) and Sotero Figueroa (Puerto Rico) made different choices and followed a different, more orthodox, path (Andreu Iglesias 1984; Poyo 1989; Zenón Cruz 1974, 1975; Wolf 1975; Helg 1995). Schomburg's close friend, Claude McKay, noted that in appearance, Schomburg was like "an Andalusian gypsy, olive-complexioned and curly-haired, and he might easily have become merged in that considerable class of foreigners who exist on the fringe of the white world." But Schomburg, observed McKay, "*chose* to identify himself with the Aframerican (sic) group" (McKay 1940:140). Thus, to view Schomburg's political evolution in the United States as simply the product of his generational location and circumstances is to ignore the clear and concrete choices that he made in his life.

Schomburg's accomplishments, especially given his limited educational background, verged on the miraculous. He was in fact, despite his pretensions to the contrary, an autodidact. He was in 1892, co-founder and Secretary of Las Dos Antillas, a society of Cuban and Puerto Rican revolutionary nationalists, inspired by José Martí. He served as its Secretary up to 1896. Schomburg was struck by the double blow of Martí's and Antonio Maceo's death in combat in 1895 and 1896, respectively, during Cuba's war against Spain. His fellow *afroborinqueño*, the revolutionary poet "Pachín" Marín, also fell in Cuba's war of independence. The United States declared war against Spain in February 1898, and by July of the same year Spain had surrendered, ceding the Philippines and Guam, along with Cuba and Puerto Rico, to the Americans. The Puerto Rican and Cuban revolutionaries in New York quarreled among themselves, disagreeing on how to respond to the new and unforeseen circumstances. The Puerto Rican section of the Cuban Revolutionary Party dissolved itself in 1898. With a combination of disgust and disillusion, Schomburg ended his direct and deep involvement in Puerto Rican and Cuban nationalist politics, turning his attention almost exclusively to Afro-America.

[...]

Schomburg's forte was collecting and research, and it was in those areas that he excelled. As McKay delicately put it, he was not "typically literary." And his private taste in books was "inclined to the esoterically erotic." But, said McKay, Schomburg possessed "a bloodhound's nose in tracing any literary item about Negroes. He could not discourse like a scholar, but he could delve deep and bring up nuggets for a scholar which had baffled discovery" (McKay 1940: 141). The praise that Schomburg received from *cognoscenti,* such as that from his close friend, Dr. John Wesley Cromwell, former president of the American Negro Academy, was expansive. [...]

[...]

[...][O]ne of the most recurring descriptions of Schomburg by his contemporaries, albeit after his death, is the generosity with which he shared his knowledge. This sharing of knowledge came from a profound dual obligation that Schomburg felt he had to black people: on the one hand, an obligation to those who have gone before, remembering their struggle, dreams and accomplishment; and, on the other, an obligation to the next generation, the young, to reinforce and buttress them in a hostile social environment that professes their "racial" inferiority and often denies their very humanity, the humanity of people of African descent. Schomburg's project is often misconstrued. He was far less interested in persuading white people of black people's humanity and accomplishment than in convincing black people themselves of their own worth and historical stature as members of the human family. Schomburg tried to blast to pieces the centuries-old, granite accretion of black self-doubt and enforced amnesia, and sought the cultivation of a self-confident and historically informed people with the capacity to fight, precisely because they feel that they deserve better. He believed that, for people of African descent, being self-confident in the world and being historically informed went together. It is impossible for a black person to be at ease with him or herself in the world while believing the lies of Europe about black inferiority, African historylessness and lack of accomplishment.

These beliefs and ideas formed the driving force behind Schomburg's extraordinary and strenuous counter-hegemonic exertions.

[...]

In general, Jesús Colón had different dreams and nightmares and moved in different circles to Schomburg. His world was not that of *los negros Americanos,* nor was his preoccupation the fate of Afro-America. Colón had remained faithful to the world of the *tabaqueros*—in whose midst he was born—and faithful to the struggles of the Puerto Rican migrant community (especially in Brooklyn and in *El Barrio* in East Harlem), and faithful to Puerto Rican nationalism and international socialism.

Colón was born in 1901, in the dignified working class world of Puerto Rico's tobacco growers and cigarmakers in Cayey (Colón 1961; Andreu Iglesias 1984; Acosta-Belén and Sánchez-Korrol 1993). One of his earliest childhood memories is of hearing through his window at about ten every morning a clear, strong voice coming from the big cigar factory at the back of his house. He later discovered that the voice was that of *el lector*, the reader, who read to the one hundred and fifty cigarmakers as they bent over their desks, silently rolling tobacco leaves into neat cigars. [...] The cigarmakers were among the most literate and most highly educated groups of workers in Puerto Rico.

Interestingly, because of the tradition of *la lectura*, illiteracy was substantially uncoupled from ignorance. Even though some of the cigarmakers were unable to read and write, they were nonetheless highly informed and educated persons. [...]

[...]

Around the age of sixteen, Colón was elected by the whole student body of his school, to the editorship of the school magazine, ¡*Adelante! [Forward!]*).

It was in connection with ¡*Adelante!* that Colón revealed a crucial event in his political formation. While his school was being rebuilt in 1917, classrooms were temporarily located in makeshift wooden barracks elsewhere in the city. The students dubbed the new quarters "Barracones," which were located in a working class district called Puerto de Tierra, near the docks in San Juan.

During a dock workers' strike, the workers, their wives, and supporters held a demonstration to publicize their cause. Parades and public demonstrations had been outlawed by the authorities during the strike period. Jesús Colón and some four hundred students were enjoying their after-lunch break when the parade of striking dock workers was passing. Distracted by the noise, the students rushed to look, sticking their heads in the slats in the fence for a better view. As they watched the parade of workers and their wives marching down the street, they noticed about a dozen mounted policemen armed with carbines coming from the opposite direction. Undeterred, the marchers continued, "with slogans and union banners flying." Over forty years after the incident, Colón could still remember clearly what happened:

> As the mounted police saw the parade formation coming towards them, they lined up on their large, strong horses, into an impassable fortress from one side of the street to the other. There was a moment of suspense and indecision on the part of the workers—it might have been fifteen seconds or more. To us boys and girls, with our heads between the fence slats, these seconds of hesitancy were like an eternity. At last, taking two steps forward, one of the strikers holding a banner began to march forward and sang at the same time: Arriba los pobres del mundo/De pie los esclavos sin pan.
>
> He continued marching with head up toward the mounted police. The rest of the strikers with their wives and their sisters followed after him.
>
> The one in charge of the mounted platoon gave a signal, so imperceptible that nobody seemed to notice. The police moved as if by a spring, moving their carbines to their shoulders and taking aim. It was done rapidly, but coolly, calmly, dispassionately. It seems to me as if I can see them right now. Another almost imperceptible signal and all of them shot at the same time. The worker with the banner was the first to fall pierced by the police bullets.

Colón noticed a "strange thing" happening. Instead of intimidating the marchers, the shooting stiffened their resolve and "incensed them to a fury." The strikers and their supporters continued marching forward until "strikers, horses, women, children and police were in a whirling mass of fighting humanity." Women stabbed the underbelly of the police horses with long hat pins, causing them to dislodge their riders into the melee. "The strikers kept on pushing, singing and fighting the police," said Colón. [...]

[...]

A sixteen-year-old who witnessed the event reported it for ¡Adelante! In his article, entitled "Honest Struggle of Our Parents," he lamented: "Our dear fathers struggle for bread but they fall vanquished, covered with blood." He grew up to become the President of the Puerto Rican Confederation of Labor. "Nothing," said Colón, "in those schoolrooms of old Barracones has taught me as much as that encounter between the workers and the police that eventful day" (Colón 1961: 17-21).

Within a year of the incident, Colón, empty handed, walked up the gangway from San Juan dock onto the "S.S. Carolina" and stowed away to New York City. In his new abode, he continued what he had begun in his native Puerto Rico: he expanded his education, earning against the odds his high school diploma by attending night school in Brooklyn, and attended St. John's University for two years; he sustained and deepened his love affair with books, sparked by the *tabaqueros* in Cayey; he worked at the craft of writing and wrote for the working class and radical publications in New York and Puerto Rico: he became one of the most important organic intellectuals of exiled Puerto Rico[...]

Colón founded and led numerous cultural and political organizations among the Hispanic population. Included among these were the Alianza Obrera Puertor-riqueña, Ateneo Obrero Hispano, Sociedad Fraternal Cervantes, the latter being the Spanish-speaking section of the International Workers Order. A multi-ethnic and multi-racial order, the IWO was founded in 1930 by members of the Communist Party and Jewish radicals. [...] It played an active role in the formation of the Congress of Industrial Organizations and campaigned for the unemployed during the Depression years. By 1947, the IWO had almost 190,000 members. Colón by this time was in charge of thirty Spanish and Portuguese-speaking lodges affiliated to the IWO throughout the United States.[4] Colón joined the Communist Party in 1933—having, apparently years earlier, left the Socialist Party—and remained a loyal Party member up to his death forty years later. Between 1953 and 1968, he made three unsuccessful bids for public office in the New York State Assembly and New York City Council, the last for City Controller on the Communist Party ticket. Like many other radicals at the time, Colón was hauled up in front of the House Un-American Activities Committee; unlike many others, he was remarkably unfrightened by the McCarthyites. He was, instead, outraged by them. As his testimony shows, he was courageous and combative, dubbing the witchunters "the Un-Americans," symbolically turning the tables on his persecutors. A man of almost sixty at the time, he apparently escaped unpunished by the authorities (Colón 1959b, 1959c, 1993). The Cuban Revolution and the guerrilla movements in Latin America fueled his political ardor and optimism and brought him cheer during the autumn of his life.

Through the course of his life, Colón maintained an unusually straight political line of march: he was and remained an active socialist and an *independentista* from his early youth to the end of his days.

Given his background and experience, it is not surprising that Colón was a class man, not a race man, exercised more by issues of class than of ethnicity and race. Thus, of the two, the enigmatic and anomalous figure, is not Jesús Colón, the Puerto Rican black socialist, but Arturo Schomburg, the Puerto Rican with strong black nationalist sympathies. Schomburg, and not Colón, is the Puerto Rican aberration.

Thus, it is more extraneously than by its actual contents that one discovers that the author of the beautifully written, charming, generous, and wise—I have weighed my adjectives carefully—document, *A Puerto Rican in New York and Other Sketches*, was indeed black. The Puerto Ricans' "American hero," Colón accurately wrote in

1961, "was and still is Vito Marcantonio," the remarkable Italian-American radical Congressman from East Harlem who represented the district, almost without break, from 1934 to 1950 (Colón 1993: 200). While Schomburg bursting with excitement over the Black Star Line proclaimed: "Garvey is the man!" and that "Garvey, *veni, vidi, vici*," nowhere in Colón's writing do the words Marcus Garvey appear. Never once in his more than four hundred pieces of writings is the acronym UNIA to be seen; neither man nor organization was praised or condemned by Colón. It was as if Garvey had never lived and the Universal Negro Improvement Association had never been born. Arriving in New York in 1918 and living in the city right up to his death in 1974, it would have been impossible, even though he lived most of the time in Brooklyn, for Colón not to have heard of Garvey and the UNIA. He clearly had no interest in either.

Significantly, the Civil Rights Movement of the late 1950s and 1960s roused Colón to reflect publicly and more explicitly—about race and racism in the United States, in his native Puerto Rico and elsewhere. It was as if the movement, triggered by the arrest of Rosa Parks in December 1955, had given him permission to remember painful experiences, hitherto repressed, and had endowed him with the right to speak out more openly about racial oppression. "Little Things are Big" and "Hiawatha into Spanish," two of his most skillfully executed sketches, are at once under-stated and searing indictments of racism. They were both written during the heat of the Civil Rights Movement in 1956. It was also in 1956 that Colón first mentions Schomburg in writing, describing him as "a great Negro Puerto Rican," and "a great figure in the life of the 19th century Puerto Rican in New York" (Colón 1956d, 1956e, 1956c). In the following year, Colón encouraged his Puerto Rican compatriots to march on Washington on the Pilgrimage of Prayer, organized by A. Philip Randolph and the civil rights leadership. Colón attended the march, was deeply moved by it, and told his readers about the event. "Phrase Heard in a Bus," published in 1957, like "Hiawatha into Spanish," recalled incidents of racism that he had experienced and bottled up for forty years. The school desegregation struggles in Little Rock, Arkansas, also commanded a column in 1957 (Colón 1957b, 1957c, 1957d).

Colón, it should be said, did discuss, if only infrequently, racism in his writings of an earlier period. But the language he mobilized was that of anti-fascism rather than that of anti-racism. The analysis was unsatisfactory and crude. In fact, it is fair to say that although his understanding of the phenomenon of racism improved significantly over time, Colón, even in the 1950s and 1960s, never adequately came to grips with the complexity and embeddedness of racism in American society. This failure was not entirely Colón's; it was also that of the Communist Party of the United States, to which he belonged. Like the Communist Party, he never saw racism as anything other than the direct result of ruling class manipulation, and an expression of false consciousness on the part of white workers. [...]

[...]

Having conceptualized racism in such a manner, Colón, not surprisingly, was overly optimistic as to the extent to which socialists could provide the antidote. Education and exemplary deeds on the part of "progressives" was the remedy. Accordingly, he applauded and encouraged every act of class solidarity and human decency that countered racism. He was right to have done so, but he overestimated the effects of his civilized cheerleading and encouragement in the pages of *The Daily Worker* and The *Worker* (Colón 1956b, 1958a, 1957e, 1958a, 1958b, 1958c, 1958d). Colón was never comfortable when it came to talking about race. It is interesting that his column on the "The Negro in Puerto Rican History" was requested by his readers, not a subject he himself chose to write on. And although he had promised to write the following week on "The Negro in Puerto Rico Today," Colón's essay on the subject appeared, not a week, but four columns and over a month later (Colón 1960a, 1960b). [...]

Colón was at home talking class politics, the Cuban revolution, the Puerto Rican struggle and American imperialism in Latin America. He was out of his depth when it came to the madness of race in America. It was as if his mind was too cultivated and civilized, his instincts too decent, generous and human for him to have plumbed the depths of American racism. And he squared the circle of his analysis by crudely, and repeatedly, reducing race to class, and racism to bourgeois conspiracy—hence the notion of racism as capitalist poison.

But the emphasis of class and nationality over race by Colón and other Puerto Ricans in New York has substantially been a reflection of the greater salience of the former, class, compared to race within Puerto Rican society itself. And the discrimination that they experience as a group—partly on linguistic and cultural grounds— in the United States reinforces the salience of class and nationality (Handlin 1959, Colón 1956a, 1957a, 1958e, 1959a). The Spanish language itself cemented the bonds of national and ethnic identification over more narrowly racial identification. [...]

The Catholic religion provided a similar force of cohesion, though a far less powerful one than the Spanish language, among the Puerto Ricans, which transcended race and color. This is not to say that racism and colorism did not exist within the community. It did and does. Even Colón, that most sanguine of Puerto Rican voices, acknowledged its existence (Colón 1946, 1960b, 1993). What the centripetal and shepherding power of a common language and a common religion does in a hostile environment is to act as a countervailing force against the centrifuge of race, color, and difference within the group. Powerful though they were, the centripetal forces could not hold everyone. [...]

[...]

The cross-racial cohesion, which varied in strength over time, among working class Puerto Ricans at home and in exile, combined with a relatively low race consciousness, and a comparatively high level of educational attainment and class consciousness made it easier for them to work with white people in radical organizations such as the Socialist and Communist Parties in the United States. African Caribbeans in general—but in particular those from the Hispanic territories—because of their experience in the Caribbean were, clearly, not as prone to view white people with the degree of distrust and suspicion that African Americans were. We are relatively familiar with the names of Caribbeans such as Hubert Harrison, Wilfred Domingo, Cyril Briggs and Otto Huiswoud in discussions of black radicalism in early twentieth century America. Yet Jesús Colón, as early as 1918—the very year he arrived in the United States—was not only a member of the Socialist Party, but was a member of the first committee within the Party to be made up of Puerto Ricans (Andreu Iglesias 1984). [...]

Given his background and experience, it is perfectly rational and understandable that Colón adopted the political positions that he did. His was the trajectory of the radical Puerto Rican who happened to be black. Schomburg, through background, circumstances and choice, evolved in a different direction. He embraced African Americans with as much intensity as Colón lovingly clinged to his exiled Puerto Rico. Schomburg became a Pan-Africanist and worked vigorously to vindicate his disinherited and maligned race. He is remembered and revered by African Americans primarily for his most conspicuous, monumental and vibrant legacy, the Schomburg Center for the Study of Black Culture, at the New York Public Library in Harlem. And no history of the Harlem Renaissance is complete without the recognition of Schomburg's enormous contribution to that cultural and political flowering. In general, those who know about Schomburg know nothing of Colón. Colón is remembered by Puerto Rican New York, its radical intelligentsia and activists. Arturo Schomburg is hardly known in this, Colón's, world. And when known, he is hardly seen as a member of the Puerto Rican community, even on the minimal basis of descent. He is given over, as it were, to Afro-America, in which he sought his political and intellectual home. [...]

CHAPTER 7

Remembering Pura Belpré's Early Career at The 135th Street New York Public Library: Interracial Cooperation And Puerto Rican Settlement during The Harlem Renaissance

By Victoria Núñez

The history of New York City's ethnoscape includes encounters between established groups and new Puerto Rican migrants, encounters that were constituted through a series of interactions and interrelations that scholars and first-person accounts have characterized most commonly as racist.[1] However, a close look at one Puerto Rican woman's unusual experiences in New York, that of Pura Belpré, reveals that there were cooperative working relationships between Puerto Rican migrants and members of other ethnoracial groups as early as the 1920s. These working relationships contributed to the formation of Puerto Rican migrant communities and the development of migrant culture in New York. The present article adds to the existing historical narrative by offering more possibilities of understanding cross-racial relations between Puerto Rican migrants, U.S.-born Whites, and African Americans as they intersected in and around the 135th Street Branch of the New York Public Library (NYPL) in Central Harlem.

Much of this article recalls the early career of Pura Belpré, a Black Puerto Rican woman, who was among the most accomplished of her generation of Puerto Rican *pioneros*, but not a figure who is well remembered within Latino/a studies. But there are other protagonists of this story who also have been forgotten and are worthy of being remembered as significant to the formation of New York's Latino/a communities. First is the Puerto Rican community, possibly a predominantly Black Puerto Rican community, that lived in Central Harlem. Second is the library and its head librarian, Ernestine Rose. The library is present as public space in which interracial

Originally published in *CENTRO: Journal of the Center for Puerto Rican Studies* 21(1): 52–77, 2009.

cooperation and alliances could and did form. Viewed from this historical perspective, the library emerges as an institutional space that allowed individuals to resist unjust racial hierarchies, beyond better-recognized institutions of resistance such as progressive political parties and unions.[2]

Remembering examples of interracial cooperation can affect the narration of other historical examples as we continue to construct the history of Latinos in the northeastern United States. Interracial cooperation may not be as well remembered as racial violence and hostility because the hostility was more prevalent, but it is an important societal dynamic to recall for students and scholars of Puerto Rican history who are often in the position of interpreting the past based on incomplete information.

The brief biographical summary of Belpré's early work history I present illustrates my argument that Belpré encountered an opportunity structure in New York City, specifically Harlem, that was rare for the pre-civil rights era. [...] Earlier scholarship on Belpré's life has focused on her career after she left the 135th Street Branch. There has been no notice made that Belpré worked in Harlem during the Harlem Renaissance, nor that she was present at the same time the Schomburg archives were being established, nor that her tenure overlapped with that of Arturo Schomburg at the library.

At the 135th Street Branch Belpré encountered a unique series of opportunities, what I refer to as an opportunity structure. Those opportunities include being among the earliest staff people hired in an integrated library setting, working for a public library system so large that it established its own training school; attending this training school to professionalize; receiving encouragement to publish her stories; and having a paid job in the center of Harlem when writing and publishing in the Black diasporic community was very much on people's minds. [...]

Belpré's early career with the NYPL

Belpré arrived in New York City in 1920 as a part of the first wave of post-1898 migration from Puerto Rico. She was hired at the 135th Street Branch as the Spanish-speaking assistant in 1921, and her career at the branch spanned from 1921 to 1927 (Belpré n.d.[c]: 2). Belpré credits the library staff for having the foresight to reach out to a new Puerto Rican community that was establishing itself around the 135th Street Library in the 1920s. [...]

Neither Belpré nor her employer could have predicted the historical significance of this hire, as Belpré has become known as the first Puerto Rican to work for the New York Public Library, the first Puerto Rican librarian, and, given the concentration of Puerto Rican migrants in New York City, most probably the first Puerto Rican librarian in the continental States. [...] Working as a librarian was just one of her contributions as she was the author of eight books, a folklorist, storyteller and a puppeteer. [...]

Initially, Belpré worked in both the adult room and the children's room, but her work in the children's room became more compelling and central to her career. The kinds of work Belpré would have been involved in as a Spanish-speaking library assistant would have included re-shelving and organizing books, helping to translate for Spanish-speaking patrons and helping them to find books. [...]

Belpré, as a Puerto Rican who had grown up in a family with a storytelling tradition, was aware of Puerto Rican folkloric tales and, being in the environment of the library, she could have imagined the presence and the power of those stories for Puerto Rican and non-Puerto Rican children alike (n.d.[f]: 1, 2).

[...]

Belpré points out the nexus between her training as a librarian and as a writer in discussing her education in library school which she began in 1925, [...]. Belpré took her first storytelling course in library school from Mary Gould Davis. She wrote her first folk tale, "Perez and Martina" in Davis' class. It was from Davis that she needed to seek approval before beginning to tell unpublished stories in the library. [...]

[...]

The ways in which Belpré contributed to literacy practices in Puerto Rican communities were not limited to her work in children's librarianship, but this was certainly the base of her work. In a number of her unpublished documents, Belpré makes a special effort to recognize the NYPL's role in the promotion of literacy in Puerto Rican migrant communities, and she always names the individuals who played an important role in making this work happen.

[...]

[...] In her role as a librarian she was positioned as a mediator between Puerto Rican migrant communities and the broader U.S. society; and she demonstrated agency in defining and shaping this role to include oral storytelling and transforming the stories she knew (I hesitate to call them her stories) into written books and puppet plays. After she married at age 40, she quit her job at the library and dedicated herself in the second phase of her career to writing and publishing. When her husband died in 1960, she returned to the library. The third phase of her career began in the context of the war on poverty of the 1960s when she was recruited to work in the South Bronx where the largest concentration of Puerto Ricans was to be found. In the present, Belpré's work in the South Bronx is perhaps the best remembered period of her career, yet the first phase of her career contributes to the history of Puerto Rican women in the early twentieth century.

Identity and opportunity

Belpré's experiences at the library were undoubtedly shaped by her class, racial, and gender identity. Because Belpré achieved a high level of success as an early Puerto Rican migrant, she is arguably the most accomplished woman of the generation of los pioneros. I questioned whether some of her success in the U.S. could be attributed to social capital she was born into or developed in Puerto Rico. [...] There are hints of a middle class background that lacked a stable income. [...] Belpré's father worked as a building contractor which led the family to move to different parts of the island during Belpré's childhood as he sought work.

[...]

[...] Belpré graduated from Central High School in Santurce, an unusual achievement for a young woman of her era. Her enrollment in the University of Puerto Rico for one year in 1920 is a more definitive sign of middle class status. Her sister worked as a teacher in Puerto Rico for ten years before migrating to New York, another sign of the Belpré family's cultural capital (Belpré n.d.[c]). [...]

Belpré did not comment directly on her racial identity, so I address this topic somewhat speculatively. Photos of Belpré reveal her to be a Black woman, an identity she does not discuss. Whether she would have been viewed as a light-skinned black woman or a medium-complexioned woman is hard for me to judge after having seen her image in a video interview as well as numerous photos. Her graduation from Central High School in Santurce, Puerto Rico, may signal that she came of age in a racially integrated community in Puerto Rico, an island culture that suffered from social and economic segregation. Because Santurce was historically a community with a large Black population, there may have been positive role models and associations with Blackness in her community.[3]

Her racial identity within Harlem's Black community most probably would have been affected by whether she was judged as a light- or medium-skinned black woman as the "color line within the color line," was operative at this point according to a number of observers and commentators.[4] [...]

Belpré's silence on her Black identity is not surprising given the fact that Latinos have begun to comment on issues of race most commonly in the post-civil rights period. One caveat to this statement is Arturo Alfonso Schomburg, a Puerto Rican who was a generation older than Belpré and who oriented his entire work life around the exploration and explication of Black identity. Belpré did comment on the need for Spanish-speaking services and on stereotypes in Puerto Rican children's books. She commented more openly on her ethnic identity as a Puerto Rican rather than on her racial identity. Lacking her perspective on her racial identity, I can only surmise that Belpré's identity in New York was as a Black Puerto Rican, who developed closer connections to African Americans than might a white Puerto Rican. [...]

[...]

Remembering black Puerto Ricans in Harlem
The example of interracial cooperation I explore here occurred in parts of Harlem referred to either as Harlem, West Harlem, or Central Harlem. The Puerto Rican community in this area is a community whose existence has essentially been erased because it was small and didn't grow in size. East Harlem, understood as a separate neighborhood, has become associated as the heart of the New York Puerto Rican migrant community, but this was not the case in the 1920s. The existing historical record tells us of a small number of Puerto Ricans who lived in Central Harlem, notably, all of whom were Black. Understanding the setting of Harlem and recovering the memories we have of Black Puerto Ricans in Harlem in the 1920s is one new element in the story of Puerto Rican settlement in New York City that emerges in examining closely Belpré's early career.

We don't know where Belpré lived when she got her job, but we do know that a policeman first told her about this branch's location, which suggests she lived in the neighborhood around the library. Her records indicate she lived in Harlem in 1931 at 1884 7th Avenue between 114th and 115th (Belpré n.d.[e]). Belpré's marriage to an African American, Clarence Cameron White, speaks to the effects of living in a neighborhood with a Black diaspora in which relationships could and did build across ethnoracial identity lines. Her husband was a successful Harlem musician, and her marriage is surely one reason why she settled in Harlem for the later 40 years of her life.[5] They lived together at 409 Edgecombe Avenue between 153rd and 154th Street in Harlem (Apt. 11F).

There are no estimates of the number of Latinos/as or Puerto Ricans in Harlem in this period. According to census reports, the black population in Harlem in 1915 included African Americans and others, approximately 28 percent of the entire group, who were foreign-born including many from Caribbean islands, but others from Panama and Cuba

(Watkins-Owens 1996: 45). In the early 1920s, West and Central Harlem were associated with African American and Black Caribbean communities who constituted at least 50 percent of the population. By 1920 the neighborhood had already undergone major transitions from being a majority White neighborhood, with many Jewish residents, to a highly mixed neighborhood. A great deal has been written about Harlem in this era, but there is little mention of Latino/a residents or Puerto Rican migrants.

[...]

Pura Belpré's essays along with the aforementioned sources tell us that Puerto Ricans and other Latinos did not grow to occupy a significant presence in Harlem as the decade unfolded. [...] Black Latinos in Harlem emerge as significant in a racial incident, The Harlem Riot of 1935. The incident that provoked the riot took place between a store clerk and "a dark skinned Latino boy, Lino Rivera," identified as a Puerto Rican, on 125th Street, an area of Harlem in which Black community members were protesting employment discrimination in local stores (Lewis 1982; McKay 1935). The store clerk accused Rivera of shoplifting a knife, and the altercation that followed was rumored to be worse than it probably was, but riots followed. The riots reflected the anger over the rumored incident but also over broader economic injustices that were occurring during the Great Depression and were affecting Black Harlemites more severely.

[...]

The Harlem Renaissance as a backdrop to interracial cooperation

Part of what made Belpré's experiences as a Puerto Rican migrant so unique was the cultural milieu into which she entered at the library: the Harlem Renaissance. The 135th Street Branch gained importance in this period as it was located at the center of action. Writers, artists, and actors all used the library as a space for cultural activities. In an undated oral history interview, Belpré comments, "I did see the beginning of what came to be the Negro Renaissance because it really began there" (López n.d.). [...]

In a separate undated autobiographical statement, Belpré elaborates that her experience at the library was "most rewarding," because,

> It acquainted me with Black Culture, and I experienced the Black Renaissance of art and literature, and the upsurge of Poets, Novelists, Dramatists and Musicians (sic). I saw the beginning of the now Schomburg collection come into being. (n.d.[c]: 2)

[...]

Pura Belpré was one of the first people of color hired by [Ernestine] Rose, although Catherine Latimer Allen, an African American woman, was already working at the library when Belpré first visited the branch.

The library originally opened in 1905 through funding from Andrew Carnegie to serve the surrounding neighborhood that at the time was predominantly Jewish; a neighborhood that underwent a rapid transition to one where one half of the residents were Black by 1920 (Bontemps 1944: 1). Too big for its existing building, the library moved to its second location on 136th Street in 1941 and was renamed the Countee Cullen Branch in 1951 after Cullen's death, which is its official name in the present. [...]

The library was approaching one of its first moments of glory in the period when Belpré was present. [...]

During the Renaissance, the library sponsored readings and lectures by the important writers of the day, including Countee Cullen, Langston Hughes, and James Weldon Johnson; it sponsored annual art exhibitions as well as a community chorus.

[...]

Tibbets writes that the combined forces of the Renaissance and the library's own activities created a situation in which "demand for books on blacks far exceeded the available supply. Residents were caught up in the growing interest in black and African history and could not quench a relentless intellectual thirst" (1989: 26).

As a result, Rose organized a committee in December, 1924, including prominent African Americans and Blacks from other parts of the diaspora to oversee the development of its collection (the officers included Arturo Schomburg and James Weldon Johnson). This committee envisioned the development of a research collection on black culture that would include books, sculptures, and photographs and was formally named the Division of Negro Literature, History and Prints. [...]

The evidence presented here, that Rose integrated the staff she hired; that she formed a committee of community members to plan the creation of a special research collection; and finally, that she paid attention to the culture of the community as she attempted to knit the library into the community, all point to the conclusion that Rose did not work from a position of dominance in relation to the subordinated Black and Puerto Rican communities in which she was based. Rather, she sought to work as an ally.

The presence and influence of this library on Black communities and Black culture in New York has been extensive. Novelist Nella Larsen worked in the children's room from 1923–1925, which overlaps with the period in which Belpré worked in the children's room. [...] Larsen, a married woman, left the NYPL in 1926 to write and published *Quicksand* (1928) and *Passing* (1929) soon thereafter (Howes 2001: 228). Jacob Lawrence researched the Black migration at the library in 1940–41 while painting his masterful series, *The Migration of the Negro*. Other famous users include writers Langston Hughes and Richard Wright. Sidney Poitier, Harry Belafonte, and Alice Childress all were involved in the American Negro Theater that met in the basement of the library. Belpré and Schomburg's experiences tell us that the library also significantly impacted Black Puerto Ricans in New York, first by presenting a model to Belpré of active library involvement in community's cultural lives; and second by creating a home for information on the Black diaspora including Black Puerto Ricans.

Belpré and Rose: Women shaping the profession

In 1929, the NYPL transferred Belpré to work as an assistant to the children's librarian at the 115th Street Library in Harlem, where it was noted that the Puerto Rican community was growing (Hernández-Delgado 1992: 429). Belpré notes, "This truly became the Spanish branch, with a complete program for the children's room as well as for the adult department" (Belpré n.d.[c]: 2). Hernández-Delgado (1992) describes the 115th Street Branch as beginning to play a role in the Spanish-speaking community similar to that being played by the 135th Street Branch in the Black community.

Librarians at the 115th Street Branch organized many literary readings and outreach activities to migrant community organizations. [...] Belpré notes that they organized for the first time a Feast of the Three Kings at the library, and created a puppet theatre in which puppet shows were presented in Spanish and English (Belpré n.d.[c]: 3). An undated postcard addressed in Belpré's distinctive handwriting to Jesús Colón announces a lecture by famed Mexican artist Diego Rivera at the library. In the vicinity of the 115th Street Branch, Belpré supported a group of mothers in carrying out Spanish language storytelling and a teen reading group, both in the Milagrosa Church (Sánchez González 2001: 79). Through these activities we see the way a woman shaped the relationship between the NYPL and the new Puerto Rican community with the 135th Street Branch and its activities during the Harlem Renaissance. [...]. Belpré then transferred to the 110th Street Branch in East Harlem most probably because that had emerged as the center of the Puerto Rican migrant community. Adding together the years at the 135th Street and 115th Street Branches, Belpré worked for sixteen years in Harlem before arriving in East Harlem.

The woman on the other side of the working relationship I describe here, Ernestine Rose, presents an example of how a young woman shaped a profession that had few precedents. [...]. Originally from the town of Bridgehampton, Long Island (NY), Rose was among the earliest generation of professionally trained librarians, graduating from the New York State Library School in Albany in 1905.[6] Rose entered a young field; at the time, free, public neighborhood branches were being built for the first time in New York City.

In 1906, she began working for the NYPL and in 1908, she moved to a branch on the Lower East Side, one of the centers of new immigrant life in New York City at the turn of the century. It was there that she developed her work of positioning libraries to work with communities. [...] From one library serving immigrants, she moved to the Seward Park Branch, also on the Lower East Side, located in a Jewish immigrant neighborhood, a branch in which the whole staff studied Yiddish and Russian literature, "and staff meetings included book discussions and lectures from rabbis, educators, Jewish newspapermen, and other workers in the neighborhood" (Tibbets 1989: 15). Rose worked at the Seward Park Branch for two years; thus, she had significant experience in orienting library services to the community being served by the time she was hired as branch librarian at the library on 135th Street in 1920, a community predominantly composed of Jewish and Black residents.[7] She worked at the Harlem Branch for 22 years and also taught in New York City library schools.[8]

Belpré and Rose's work relationship transcended a positive employer/employee relationship because it was merely one example of Rose's work to integrate the library from the perspective of staffing and services offered to the community. [...]

[...]

[...] The example of interracial cooperation between Belpré and Rose was more than a positive, one-on-one experience because this relationship was not a completely unique case. A second example is the alliance that developed between Puerto Rican Arturo Alfonso Schomburg and the 135th Street Branch Library. The outcome of this work among allies is far better known than Belpré's work.

A Parallel Example of Interracial Cooperation at the Library

Afro-Puerto Rican Arturo Alfonso Schomburg (1874–1938) collected books and other printed material about people of African descent as a means of "disproving the myth of black racial inferiority" (Dodson 1989: i). An autodidact, he left school in Puerto Rico at an early age and arrived as a migrant in the U.S. with little formal education but with a thirst for knowledge. As a Black Puerto Rican migrant who encountered an opportunity structure that allowed him to enter a professional class in New York, Schomburg shared an experience similar to Belpré's at the library.

Rose persuaded the NYPL to acquire Schomburg's collection in 1926. [...] After Schomburg sold his collection, he continued his collecting activities, continued making donations to the library for which he did not receive payment, and served as an energetic volunteer and staff member to the library (Sinnette 1989). [...]

Rose hired Schomburg to curate the collection at the library from 1932 to 1938. The years in which Schomburg worked at the library were the later years of the Depression and funds were tight. Rose argued strongly to her supervisor in favor of finding funding to support Schomburg's work at the library, in spite of the financial limitations the library was experiencing (1937b).

Little effort has been made to connect Schomburg's experience and that of Pura Belpré at the 135th Street library. There is one handwritten line in one of Belpré's autobiographical documents, in which she states, "I met Arthur Schomburg, and often chatted in Spanish" (n.d.[c]: 2). To date, I have found no further description of how they interacted with each [other] during their overlapping tenure at the library. Schomburg's collection, as well as his long-term involvement with the library, clearly contributed to the library's ability to serve the multiple Black communities that were forming in early twentieth century Harlem: African American, West Indian, Puerto Rican and other Latino/a communities as well. All of these communities included large numbers of recent migrants. Schomburg's relationship with the library endured for more than ten years until his death. His efforts combined with the library staffs' made this branch a central resource for the Black community in New York; it was an Africana collection not rivaled in the United States.

Alternative perspectives on migrants' settlement experiences in New York
Constructing a historical narrative that interprets Belpré's experience in the early years of her migration to New York City is something that I and other cultural studies scholars are doing in the present. [...]

[...]

Rather than a story of discrimination that horrified newly arriving Puerto Rican migrants, my reading of Belpré's early work life is one that highlights the heterogeneity of Puerto Rican migrants' experiences. Although the vast majority of Puerto Rican migrants arrived in the U.S. and entered working class jobs, there were some who encountered and have left written record of unusual opportunities as is the case with Belpré and Schomburg. Recalling Pura Belpré also reminds the reader that she became the best published Puerto Rican author in the United States of her time. I have presented evidence that the library system encouraged Belpré to publish her stories, but it is undoubtedly true as well that the Harlem Renaissance and the rich literary activity at the 135th Street Branch inspired her as others who worked there were also inspired to write and publish. Librarians have led the way in recovering Belpré's legacy, but a wider reading of her experience can remind the public that Belpré was more than a librarian, and Puerto Ricans have a literary history that stretches back to the early decades of the twentieth century.

[...]

I began this article by stating that I would challenge the uniform characterization that Puerto Ricans faced discrimination, hostility, and ignorance as they arrived early in the 20th century. My intention is not to negate or question the many instances of discrimination that Puerto Ricans have faced; one hypothesis I have proposed here is that Black Puerto Ricans may have moved to Harlem precisely because they perceived it to be a safer haven (not completely safe) from the discrimination they faced in other city neighborhoods. Rather, I seek to raise the sensitivity that we as students and scholars must use in discerning who faced this discrimination, where and when.

Black Puerto Ricans in the pioneros generation did have different experiences than did other Puerto Rican migrants; their first person accounts testify to this, often referring to racism they experienced. To the extent that they settled in Harlem, they had a more significant experience of intermingling with African American and West Indian Black communities. Both Belpré and Schomburg married African Americans which demonstrates the significance of living in this Black diasporic community. To what degree Puerto Rican migrants settled around the library in the decade of the 1920s, as Ernestine Rose had predicted, is unclear. Belpré suggests that this Puerto Rican community did not develop in size, [...]. User records, names of school children who attended programs at the 135th Street Branch, readers' adviser guides, and other library records do not indicate any real number of patrons with Hispanic surnames.[9]

The existing evidence suggests that Ernestine Rose and the 135th Street Branch staff were successful at reaching out to diverse communities in multiple ways, creative beyond the vision of the day for libraries of any race or ethnicity. The study of this history can contribute to prejudice reduction as we see Rose and her integrated staff and community volunteers challenging the prejudice that dominated the era. Rose also required some level of approval from the administrative librarians around her, suggesting that there was some institutional collaboration that contributed to her work. Most notable is Anne Carroll Moore, Belpré's library school instructor. I do not want to under-credit Rose for the important role she played in this example of interracial cooperation. But beyond Rose as a librarian and public servant unusual for her time, is the fact that she was an employee of the NYPL, which could have stopped or defunded her neighborhood work at any point had they viewed it as inconsistent with its priorities or as objectionable. Yet other evidence raises questions as to the motive the NYPL may have had in allowing Rose to integrate the 135th Street Branch staff.

The interracial cooperation described here between Belpré, Rose, Schomburg, the community, and the library launched Belpré's professional work as a librarian and author in a historical moment when both occupations were unusual for Puerto Rican and Black women. As such, the working relationships described all represent examples of the library as an institutional space in which members of Harlem's community could resist the policies and protocols of Jim Crow America. By at least three accounts (Belpré, Rose's biographer, and Malone), Rose was not working in communities of color in a way that furthered the interests of the dominant White community; rather, she was countering the racial inequality of the historical period. Belpré, Rose and Schomburg crossed the racial lines that encircled racial and ethnic enclaves in New York City.

The existing literature on early Puerto Rican migration to New York emphasizes themes of community building, both social and political, within Latino migrant communities and many examples of racial discrimination. One overlooked theme is that of interracial cooperation and alliances that significantly assisted the advancement and settlement of migrant Puerto Rican communities. The history of interaction between Puerto Rican migrant communities and the public libraries of New York that Belpré recalls in her papers suggests that, over time, Puerto Rican and other Latino staff were successful in building bridges between Latino/a migrants and the public libraries, thereby encouraging reading and literacy development. My research into the nature of this bridge between the NYPL and Puerto Rican and Latino communities reveals that it was not constructed primarily during Belpré's years at the 135th Street Branch. However, the induction into librarianship that Belpré received at the branch positioned her well to carry out the work of reaching out to new migrant communities in the other neighborhood libraries in which she worked. Belpré's memories of her library career and the constant interest in her services throughout a fifty-year work history, attest to the bridge Belpré began building in the 1920s to Puerto Rican migrant communities.

CHAPTER 8

Resisting the Racial Binary? Puerto Ricans' Encounter with Race in Depression-Era New York City.

By Lorrin Thomas

One afternoon in March, 1935, sixteen-year-old Lino Rivera got caught stealing a penknife at a Kress five-and-dime store on 125th Street and Seventh Avenue, a few blocks from his home on Manhattan Avenue and 122nd Street. When the store's manager confronted Rivera and detained him, the boy resisted and allegedly bit the man on the hand. Someone called the police, and a crowd gathered outside and in the front of the store. After the manager decided to let the boy go instead of arresting him, a police officer escorted Rivera through the basement to the back exit on 124th Street. When Rivera disappeared with the officer into the basement of the store, a rumor spread through the crowd that he was being beaten; and when an ambulance drove up to the back entrance of the store and drove away empty—having been called, some accounts noted, because of the hand wound Rivera was supposed to have inflicted on his captor—some in the crowd said that the boy had in fact been beaten to death. Even skeptics began to concur with this rumor when the driver of a hearse coincidentally parked in front the store on 125th Street. The crowd consisted of shoppers in the neighborhood's busy commercial district as well as residents of central Harlem, who were almost entirely African American, and it dispersed for a time after police arrested the woman accused of inciting the disturbance. Several hours later, a group of protesters began an impromptu public meeting about the rumored violence against a black child, and as the police were trying to remove a speaker from his soap box stand and clear the sidewalk, someone threw a rock into the front window of the Kress store (Greenberg 1991: 3; Fogelson and Rubenstein 1969: 2–7). Thus began a full-scale riot in which several thousand Harlemites participated, an event that before long would symbolize the acute suffering and resentment of the country's most storied African-American community.

Originally published in *CENTRO: Journal of the Center for Puerto Rican Studies* 21(1): 5–35, 2009.

The Harlem riot of 1935 is amply cited in the history of African Americans' civil rights struggles in the twentieth century, but rarely have historians and other chroniclers written about or even mentioned the fact that the "Negro" or "black" boy whose arrest set off the famous riot was, in fact, Puerto Rican. [...] The overwhelming silence about Rivera's nationality raises some questions about the significance of historical actors' categorical identity. How much did it matter, in this case, that the riot's unwitting instigator was not actually part of the community of African Americans in Central Harlem but resided, instead, in the Puerto Rican barrio to the east? More important, how significant was it that Rivera was categorized by most observers as simply "Negro," when actually, his New York compatriots, described him in far more flexible terms as a *"puertorriqueño de color"*? Racial categories have a long and variable history in the Americas, and in the United States in particular they have served not just to order but to minimize the complexity of the nation's racial past.[1] People in the United States have acknowledged the fact of mixed African and European heritage to varying degrees, and have given different names to mixed race people through time—someone referred to as a "quadroon" in 1880 might have been called, more generally, "mulatto" in 1900, or "biracial" in 1980. But North Americans' enduring categorization of racial identities has been the division of the majority of people into a binary scheme based on the labels "black" and "white" (Nash 1995). Despite the mutability of these categories as they conform to shifting social landscapes over time, the discourse surrounding them makes them seem fixed and true; and they have allowed little room for the inclusion of groups that don't describe their members in binary racial terms. Puerto Ricans, forming the fastest-growing community of foreign migrants in New York in the late twenties and thirties, contended with racial categories by ambivalently rejecting the American schema and clinging diffidently to their island's own contradictory racial discourses (Thomas 2002).

This [chapter] examines Puerto Rican migrants' local engagements with racial ascription, exploring how a group of racially mixed Caribbean migrants confronted the particular boundaries of racism in the United States. I analyze the commentary and debates about race among a diverse but mostly elite set of activists who became preoccupied with their group's racial identity in New York by the early thirties. For everyone in the city, it was a moment of especially intense "racial formation," due in part to the pressures of a broken economy but also to the major changes in the Northern urban social landscape following the arrival of millions of Southern blacks, and the shutting down of European immigration. Racial categories had hardened anew in New York City by 1930, the year that the United States Census dropped its "mulatto" category (in Puerto Rico as well as in the United States), leaving only "white" and

"Negro" thereafter (Guterl 2001: 154–44; Lee 1993; Loveman 2007).[2] The critiques and complaints of many Puerto Ricans in this period betrayed a fear that a proscribed racial identity, forged by the limitations of the binary racial regime, would lead to a circumscribed political identity within the nation, a fear that as a group they would fail to attain the promises of American citizenship.

Acutely aware of racist power dynamics within their own island society, Puerto Rican migrants across the political spectrum talked about the pitfalls of "second-class citizenship," of being relegated to the inferior status of the Negro—"citizens without rights"—and excluded from many of the benefits and protections that white citizens expected, demanded, and got.[3] Puerto Ricans confronted a particular problem as they sought to avoid categorization as "Negro" in the United States: if they refused that label, how would they fit into the nation? What alternative identity would be available to them?

My other objective here is to consider the extent to which historical narratives are distorted and flattened by the crude structure of racial ideology in the United States, and the damage such distortions have caused to our understandings of the past. The neglected fact of Lino Rivera's national identity in the story of the Harlem riots—a fact deemed unimportant by the vast majority of chroniclers, including historians, even up to the present—represents only one of countless silences that mark the "hidden history" of Puerto Ricans in New York City, where their racial ambiguity added another layer of invisibility to a group already marginalized for its colonial identity in the nation. The exclusion of Lino Rivera's Puerto Rican-ness from the narrative of the Harlem riot also diminishes the complexity of that story itself, refashioning as purely "American" the backdrop of foreign-born and mixed-race as well as native black and white residents of Harlem.[...]

[...] Examining this detail of the riot, and the ways the different groups of Harlem residents interpreted it, corrects the narrative and returns to it a complexity that would have been familiar to many New Yorkers at that time—even if they were not inclined to make it part of the official story. It also reminds us to look closely at the kinds of details about cultural, regional, and national identity that are often ignored, by contemporary chroniclers as well as scholars, in conventional narratives about race.

Puerto Ricans and the Racial Binary in New York City

To a large extent, it was American lawmakers' perception of the "mongrel" Puerto Rican people, members of a mixed and "alien race," that had inspired many in the United States Congress to fight against offering them citizenship after the United States took control of the island in 1898, just two years after the *Plessy* decision. But over the course of a decade or so, Puerto Ricans came to look less belligerent, not to mention less darkly "savage," than the Filipino people whose legal relationship to the United States was also under debate. The pragmatists in Congress (many of them openly racist, their defense of Puerto Ricans' lesser savagery notwithstanding) argued that the America would have greater control over the island if the constitution "followed the flag," and they won out in 1917, conferring United States citizenship on a mixed race people already controlled by American law (Perea 2001: 159; Smith 2001: 379).[4]

There was already a small but lively community of Puerto Ricans in New York, many of them dissident immigrants drawn to the city's enclave of Antillean *tabaqueros*, Cuban and Puerto Rican independence fighters whose major sector of employment was cigar making. [...] With citizenship suddenly in hand, thousands more Puerto Ricans also followed the economic boom inspired by World War I, alighting in New York City alongside the largest urban population of African Americans, many of whom had fled the stagnating South for the industrial North (Rosenwaike 1972: 121; Greenberg 1991: 13; Sánchez Korrol 1994: 58–60). Side by side, these two groups of largely impoverished migrants took up residence in the city that was experiencing, more than any other place, the social and political impact of restrictionist immigration policies that had radically reduced the number of European immigrants entering the United States by 1925. Native whites, who had reviled New York's poor Russian, Italian, and Eastern European transplants—at first seen as too "swarthy" and uncouth to be considered white—now readily adapted their old racisms to target the growing communities of darker-skinned newcomers from the south.

Puerto Ricans fit uneasily in this unstable social terrain. Rejected by the increasingly white-seeming ethnics as not white; suspicious, themselves, of the Negro racial identity reflexively imposed on them by white society; and seen by African Americans as "Spanish"—or, at least, distinctly foreign—more than black, Puerto Ricans began to perceive the degree to which the intense and distinctive racisms of the United States would shape their experience as Americans. Racism was, of course, an old and persistent problem, not only for African Americans in New York but also for migrants from Asia, Africa, Latin America, and the Caribbean. But New York during the depression years witnessed key changes in race relations, not only because of the exploding populations of African Americans and Puerto Ricans. The economic pressures of the depression also intensified social hierarchies, and thus do the 1930s provide an exceptionally clear glimpse of a society in the midst of "racial formation" (Winant 2001: 21).

In the 1920s, the community of thirty thousand or so Puerto Rican migrants was dominated numerically by a skilled working class and culturally by a small Hispanicized professional elite, some of whom coped with their concerns about North

American racism by "passing" for Spanish.[5] During the Depression, though, as their foreignness and their inscrutable racial origins hindered them in their competition with other New Yorkers for jobs and a growing array of welfare funds, and as their increasing numbers inspired intensifying prejudice on the part of whites, racial identity became a subject of intensely concerned debate within the Puerto Rican community. The new preoccupation with their ascribed racial identity was not limited to the light-skinned elite, including many nationalist activists, who felt they had the most to lose. Socialist internationalists and communist racial egalitarians participated in newspaper debates and public forums as well, worrying over the fact that the group was perceived not just as immigrants, but as "Negro" colonial transplants vying for a place in the metropole. To an extent, Puerto Ricans were confronting a problem that was common to many other immigrant groups. Mexican, Chinese, and Irish immigrants, among others, had been called "niggers" and faced violence, segregation, and discrimination that varied somewhat by place and time, but that delineated forcibly the distance between themselves and "native" white Americans. For those who were far less likely to find "whiteness" within their reach, as the Irish and other European immigrants eventually did, a slippery divide between "black" to not-quite-white would define their social identity and limit their prospects of achieving social equality.[6]

Puerto Ricans had been taking the measure of that divide, with increasing anxiety, since the early thirties. So when the Harlem riot exploded right alongside the largest Puerto Rican barrio in the city, it begged a kind of reckoning: Were the Negroes' problems Puerto Ricans' problems too? Many Puerto Ricans (and African Americans too) in the thirties tried to find some way to answer "No" to that question, as the discussion that follows will show. In that case, then, did it even matter that the riot's spark was a conflict involving a Puerto Rican boy? It did indeed matter. It mattered first as evidence of the contemporary invisibility of Puerto Ricans and other non-native "colored" people in New York, a fact that most white and black New Yorkers preferred to ignore—and one that many Puerto Ricans themselves sought to rectify at different points, but not by inserting themselves into "black American" dramas of city life.

The other reason that Lino Rivera's role in the riot matters is the historical and historiographic result of the first point: returning him to his place in the narrative helps fill in the silences that make the story of the Harlem riot not simply more accurate, but more accurately complicated. This richer version of the story of the riot has resonances that help us to interpret both a larger urban past that is more racially complex than many histories admit, and a present whose racial heterogeneity is hardly new (Trouillot 1995; James 1998; Hoffnung-Garskof 2001). Lino Rivera's place in the riot, even as it was being rubbed out of the story, inspired at least some discussion of where Puerto Ricans fit into the hardscrabble terrain of New York in the thirties.

[...]

While it was immediately clear that the Kress Store incident had struck a nerve with black Harlemites who saw an opportunity to publicize the suffering of their community, city officials and reporters took seriously rumors that the riots had been encouraged by external agitators with a political agenda. A group of mostly white Communists called the Young Liberators looked most suspicious to investigators, since members had been spied distributing incendiary leaflets as the rioting began: "Child Brutally Beaten Woman Attacked By BOSS and COPS = Child near DEATH" and "WORKERS! NEGRO AND WHITE Protest Against this Lynch Attack of Innocent Negro People," they trumpeted. With this evidence, many of the New York dailies pointed to the Communists as the primary instigators of the riot. A year later, though, writers of the Mayor's Committee final report disagreed, maintaining that it was simply residents' resentment over local conditions that had fanned the flames of protest in Harlem (Fogelson and Rubenstein 1969: 10–1).[7] Whatever role the Young Liberators played in the riots, their flyers certainly sensationalized racial tensions in Harlem, simultaneously trading on fears of black-white conflict and promoting black-white unity. And in doing so, they used Rivera as the symbolic "Negro" who was the innocent victim of "this Lynch Attack."[8] The *Amsterdam News*, New York's largest African-American daily, also failed to identify Rivera as Puerto Rican, referring to him instead as a "young Negro boy." Claude McKay was one of the very few contemporary chroniclers to specify that Rivera was Puerto Rican. McKay's sensitivity to nationality alongside race is not surprising, since West Indian-born residents of Harlem generally took pains to distinguish themselves from American-born blacks (Waters 1999; Reid 1970). [...] Perhaps African Americans elided the difference between an American Negro (or "colored boy") and a *"negro"* Puerto Rican to provide coherence in the narrative of the causes of the riot: to focus on Rivera's Puerto Rican identity would have diluted black Harlemites' message about racism and its effect on conditions in their neighborhood.

On the other hand, African Americans, and white observers too, seem to have viewed the riot's participants through their own binary racial lens. Many may well have known that Rivera was Puerto Rican, but the only social fact that really mattered was that he was colored, and if he was colored, he may as well be called "Negro." To whatever extent Puerto Ricans took part in the riot, they remained a more or less invisible presence in all of its coverage by the citywide dailies. The New York *Herald Tribune* did note in its front-page article that "a Puerto Rican youth [was] the cause," and the Brooklyn *Daily Eagle*—whose headline warned of a "race war"—even preceded its introduction of the "Porto Rican" Lino Rivera with the assertion that he was "almost forgotten in the hullabaloo." The New York *Sun*, on the other hand, which printed a photograph of him standing with an African-American police Lieutenant, ran an article subtitled, "Negro boy admits he was not beaten in store." The first *New York Times* report referred only to a "16 year old Negro boy" whose shoplifting precipitated the riot; a subsequent article pictured Rivera and gave his name, but commented no further on his role.[9]

New York's Spanish language daily *La Prensa*—headed in the 1920s and '30s by a Spaniard, José Comprubí, and frequently criticized by working class Puerto Ricans as a mouthpiece of the elite—more carefully noted the distinction between the rigid North American social category "Negro" and the more descriptive Spanish term *"negro,"* which referred to phenotype but did not necessarily represent a rigid social category.[10] *La Prensa* reporters implied that the "disturbances" were attributable only to *"gente de color, americana,"* and reported that most of the protesting and looting activity actually took place in central Harlem, several blocks west of the East Harlem barrio where most Spanish-speakers lived and shopped. Such elision between description and category in Spanish was characteristic of the way Puerto Ricans (and many other Latin Americans) talked about race; sociologist Maxine Gordon reported that in Puerto Rico in the forties, the racial vernacular was still peppered with a half dozen terms for different kinds of brown skin. It was a deceptively "flexible" system, according to historian Miriam Jiménez Román (1996: 10), one that allowed the existence of multiple contradictions. Puerto Ricans could uphold "the institutionally sanctioned and popularly reinforced belief in distinct races with identifiable, essential traits" alongside "a corresponding notion of a 'multiracial' society whose citizens enjoy harmonious relations," while propounding the notion of *"'la gran familia puertorriqueña,'* a 'race' of *mestizos* that shares a common culture, language and history"—but tended to minimize its African heritage (Gordon 1949: 294–301).[11]

[...]

If the African American press and city officials in New York agreed that the causes of the Harlem riot were rooted in the problems of Negroes, not Puerto Ricans, many middle-class Puerto Rican and Hispanic residents were happy to support that perspective. *La Prensa* reported on the rioting in central Harlem in distancing tones, calling the incident "race riots" among the "colored elements of that neighborhood." Here the editors were using the term "colored" in a North American sense, meaning Negro. The editorial printed two days after the riot offered an explicit warning about the dangers of Puerto Ricans' being implicated in the riots. "The fact that it was a Puerto Rican boy who was the excuse for the noisy disturbances and clashes with the police, could serve as the basis for a new, negative interpretation of...the Hispanic community here," wrote the editors. They described the "colored" sections of Harlem as characterized by "intense political activity" and "bizarre cults."[12] On the other hand, "entirely separate from this is the Spanish-speaking group of the neighborhood, with distinct problems, absolutely different interests, and ethnic characteristics that disassociate Hispanics from their colored American neighbors." The editorial ended with a warning that "events and situations created by the other half of the district, not Hispanics"—not only the riot, but also, for instance, the illegal numbers game—threatened to exacerbate the preexisting antipathy of "the authorities" towards Hispanics. The editors admonished their readers: "You must not ignore the fact that, once again, the discredit and unwanted notoriety generated by non-Hispanic Harlem, falls upon our part of the neighborhood."[13]

[...]

Challenging the Racial Binary, Part I

The threat of being marked by an "unwanted notoriety" was something that Puerto Ricans in New York, the migrant elite in particular, had been worrying over since the beginning of the decade. Behind *La Prensa*'s assertions of separateness from African Americans in the wake of the riots lay a specific, political concern expressed by the elite *colonia* members: If Puerto Ricans [were] landing on the "black" side of the racial line in the US, how could they capitalize on their citizenship, the benefits of which clearly were limited to whites? Their first call to alarm came late in 1930, when the *New York American* printed an article on "Newcomers in the Slums of East Harlem." The article referred to migrants as "wretched" and "the lowest grade of labor"—"lower than the colored worker."[14] María Más Pozo, a Nationalist activist and frequent contributor to *La Prensa*'s letters column, attacked the *New York American* article with venom. "It is time to think long and hard about the situation of my compatriots in this country," she said. She continued,

The Puerto Rican must not be seen as worse than the native blacks of this country. We do not want a North American citizenship that humiliates us, depriving us of our dignity, after having been stripped, in the name of humanity, of our blessed land. We want to be pure Puerto Ricans, only proud of single race; that which mixed her white blood with the passionate blood of the indian.[15]

[...] A number of similar letters followed in *La Prensa*'s "*de nuestros lectores*" section, including one from East Harlem resident Fernando Arjona López, a self-identified *independentista* who railed against the "humiliation" of "comparing us with black Americans...putting us in a debased sphere"—one of the many insults of U.S. colonialism.[16]

Only a single reader criticized both the *New York American* article and the commentators who failed to challenge the hierarchy in which Puerto Ricans fell beneath Negroes and Chinese immigrants. Introduced by *La Prensa*'s editors as "a Puerto Rican of the black race," Gabriel Rivera also protested "*los insultos de los yanquis*," but questioned other readers' outrage over being categorized with black Americans:

I don't see the motivation to feel so profoundly injured because they see us as black Americans; since...I wouldn't want to be seen as a white Texan or Georgian, either; because...I am filled with contempt and disgust by the white man for his savage and heretical instinct, which the lynchings in the Southern states have shown us so recently.[17]

Rivera's reference to "the lynchings in the Southern states" would not have surprised *La Prensa*'s readers in 1931, since the rise in racial violence in the South during the twenties was covered regularly in *La Prensa*.[18] More surprising, given the dominance of the slippery discourse of *mestizaje* in Puerto Rico—a discourse with a blind spot regarding the African component of the mestizo—was the way Rivera took Más Pozo to task for her definition of Puerto Rican peoplehood: "What would my countrywoman do with black-blooded *Boricuas*..., whose blood is mixed as much as white blood is mixed with indian?"

[...]

The several letter writers who followed Más Pozo's lead in decrying Puerto Ricans' social debasement argued for maximizing distance between the Puerto Rican and the American Negro.

Several years after the initial reaction to the *New York American* article, and a year before the explosion of rioting in Harlem in 1935, another sensationalist piece on Puerto Rico appeared in the American popular media. The controversy this time centered on the photographs of dark-skinned peasants for an article on Puerto Rico in the nationally circulating *Literary Digest*, just the kind of snapshot of her country that María Más Pozo was afraid of. [...]

This time the debate about the dilemmas of Puerto Ricans' racial identity in the United States played out differently. [...]

[...]

"We are what we are," said another reader. "They can spoil our language, impose their education on us, but they cannot take away our color."[19] In all of these 1934 letters, "our color"—to whatever extent North Americans viewed it as "black"— figured as a distinct source of pride for Puerto Ricans.

[...] Were outspoken Puerto Rican migrants beginning to embrace a political strategy of demanding rights as "underdogs," aligning them more closely with African Americans? The growing number of working class Puerto Ricans would have been hearing—and perhaps begun to agree with—the rising chorus of black activists in Harlem who were framing blackness as a political issue and demanding expanded civil rights, many of them influenced by Communist party discourse on race in the thirties and events like the Angelo Herndon case and, later, the trial of the Scottsboro boys. The more progressive letter writers in 1934 were willing to make peace with the idea that Americans might "see us as black." They also tended to give less credence to the rigid divisions required by racial ideology in the United States: "We are what we are...they cannot take away our color."[20] This assertion could have been interpreted readily in terms of the distinctly *non*-African "gran familia puertorriqueña," what María Más Pozo referred to as "pure Puerto Ricans, only proud of a single race." But in the context of the series of letters criticizing Álvarez for his anti-black racism, it actually represented a challenge to that discourse—as well as a challenge to the North American racial binary.[21]

In a similar vein of racial justice, one *La Prensa* reader wrote to the editor after the 1935 riots with a passionate critique of the conditions created in Harlem by the "*explotadores capitalistas.*" Libertad Narváez lived near the area of the rioting, outside of the boundary of El Barrio, and expressed deep sympathy with the plight and the grievances of the rioters:

Thousands of black workers, most of them unemployed...took to the
streets of Harlem with the sounds of protest against the miserly aid dis-
tributed by the "Relief" Administration, and the discriminatory...treat-
ment by officials of this agency of which they are victims; [...]

[...]

Like virtually all of the other commentary on the riot, however, Narváez's letter was silent on both the place and plight of Puerto Rican migrants in Harlem. Not
only did it fail to mention the large numbers of Puerto Ricans who would be identified—and might identify themselves—as "Negro workers." It also ignored the fact
that Puerto Ricans had been expressing for years the same grievances as African
Americans concerning housing, relief, and discrimination. This writer's silence on
these parallels reminds us of the pains taken not just by the elite but also by working
class, leftist Puerto Ricans to distinguish their countrymen from the black Americans
whose plight they so often decried. [...] The price of accepting the ascription imposed
by the racial binary in America—blackness as Negro, not just *negro*—was potentially
too steep even for Puerto Rican radicals.[22]

Challenging the Racial Binary, Part II

[...]

In the months following the Harlem riots, Puerto Ricans became the primary victims
of a new "anti-Hispanic campaign" in Washington Heights, where middle class Puerto Ricans had begun to settle earlier in the thirties. The Jewish and Irish landlords in
the neighborhood had begun raising rents sharply in an alleged effort to "drive out"
their Puerto Rican tenants. Spanish-speaking observers saw the landlords' coordi-
nated action as a reaction to two threats: first, that more and more of their Hispanic
tenants were recent arrivals of the "lower classes," and second, that these "brown-
skinned or darker" new tenants would bring with them the kinds of problems that
might turn Washington Heights into "a second Harlem." These observers saw a specifically racial prejudice against dark-skinned Puerto Ricans. "The situation in Washington Heights is not simply a situation of nationality, it is purely and unjustly a question of race," asserted one letter to *La Prensa*. Even the lighter-skinned among them
should not feel immune to this kind of discrimination, he warned, since no clear line
existed, here, between light and dark complexions; the only line was between *white*
and dark. "If it could happen to them, it could happen to you," he warned.[23] That is,

any Puerto Rican, no matter his or her complexion, could be discriminated against as a person occupying the non-white side of the binary—the black side.

In spite of the growing public concern about race-based discrimination against Puerto Ricans, there remained a firm impulse, from various sectors of the colonia, not to complain about the same injustices that African Americans objected to, and, still, not to talk about the Harlem riot as a Puerto Rican issue. When the New York State legislature voted to assemble a "Temporary Commission on Urban Colored Populations" two years after the riot, *La Prensa* editors applauded the move. "[It is] certain that there are many thousands of persons of the colored race living in Harlem under the saddest of social conditions," announced the editorial, skirting any mention of Spanish-speaking residents, especially Puerto Ricans, in the area.[24]

To "Buck the Color Line": Recognition Beyond the Binary

[...]

The more salient conflict for Puerto Ricans had to do with their persistent political invisibility not only as dark-skinned foreigners, but also as colonial citizens. In the realm of island politics, independentista migrants in the 1940s watched the disappearance of what they had seen as their wartime opportunity to hold politicians to account on the question of Puerto Rico's status. The famously radical-left Congressman Vito Marcantonio was the only elected official in America in that era who put issues affecting Puerto Ricans on the political agenda—and only rarely, when some other interest was at stake, did his Congressional colleagues even respond, much less vote in favor of Marcantonio's bills.[25] At the local level, Puerto Ricans' energetic activism had brought them no closer to securing the concrete privileges they hoped their American citizenship would give them, including access to decent housing, fair employment, and recognition as legitimate actors in local and national politics. Still fighting off a "Negro" identity, but failing to achieve an identity approaching "white," Puerto Ricans faced an invisibility that circumscribed their political power throughout the thirties, and then was compounded by the explosion of colonial tensions after 1937. [...]

[...]

[...] Puerto Ricans in New York in the thirties found that they were rarely regarded as white, and would not enjoy the privileges of whiteness unless they managed to "pass." These little-known details provide texture and depth to a very obvious point about the power of a rigid racist ideology to render disadvantage to those on the wrong side. They also illustrate a point only slightly less obvious, about the power of the racial binary to silence those historical actors who don't fit into its categories. [...]

SECTION III.

A *Nuyorican* Perspective

CHAPTER 9

Nuyorican Visionary: Jorge Soto and the Evolution of an Afro-Taíno Aesthetic at Taller Boricua

By Yasmin Ramírez

Founded in El Barrio, New York, in 1970 by Marcos Dimas, Adrian Garcia, Manuel "Neco" Otero, Martin Rubio, and Armando Soto, Taller Boricua/The Puerto Rican Workshop ranks as one of the oldest extant multi-disciplinary artist-run spaces in the United States. Taller Boricua's current directors, Marcos Dimas and Fernando Salicrup, take pride in noting that the workshop has adhered to its mission of using art as a tool for education and community building through sponsoring a wide-range of exhibitions, literary readings, dances, festivals, urban planning seminars and free art classes for over 35 years. The number of visual artists, writers, architects and musicians who have frequented Taller Boricua's workspaces in El Barrio is large and luminous. During the heyday of the Nuyorican art and poetry movement of the 1970s and early 1980s, for example, Taller Boricua's stable of collaborators included the following: Américo Casiano, Máximo Colón, Marcos Dimas, Sandra María Estevez, Gilberto Hernández, Adrian Garcia, Jesús "Papoleto" Meléndez, José Morales, Rafael Colón Morales, Néstor Otero, Manuel "Neco" Otero, Carlos Osorio, Martín "Tito" Pérez, Pedro Pietri, Armando Soto, Jorge Soto, Rafael Tufiño, Nítza Tufiño, Fernando Salicrup, Sammy Tanco and Manuel "Manny" Vega. Discussing the workshop's influence, Manny Vega once explained to New York Times art critic, Holland Cotter, that Taller Boricua comprised a "school" that he and other artists followed. "They're the East Harlem School," said Vega. "Eventually historians will get it."[1]

[...] [I]f Taller Boricua has served as a school of art, who among its many members can be regarded as the workshop's archetypical master—the artist whose images can illuminate the ideals and accomplishments of Taller Boricua on the whole?

Longstanding members of Taller Boricua such as Marcos Dimas, Fernando Salicrup, Nitza Tufiño, Jesús "Papoleto" Meléndez and Adrian Garcia were unani-

Originally published in CENTRO: Journal of the Center for Puerto Rican Studies 17(2): 23-41, 2005.

mous in nominating Jorge Soto Sánchez, the workshop's director in the mid–1970s, as an exemplary figure. [...] Soto's intellectual ambition coupled with a dedication to honing his craft made him the most critically acclaimed artist in the Taller Boricua circle in the late 1970s. [...]

[...] My discussion concentrates on analyzing the visual art [...] produced by Jorge Soto in the mid to late 1970s, a period when the poets and artists at Taller Boricua were first exploring Puerto Rico's African and Taíno heritages and determining how they could make work that linked their experience as New York- born Puerto Ricans to the legacy of art and literature in Puerto Rico. This essay begins a brief sketch of Jorge Soto's early life in order to place his work in context of the socioeconomic struggles that many New York-born Puerto Rican artists faced growing up in the 1950s and 1960s.

Soto's Early Years 1947–1971
Jorge Soto was born in El Barrio in 1947 and raised in a Spanish-speaking household. At the age of five, his family moved to the South Bronx, an area that was transition- ing from being a white ethnic enclave for working class Italians, Irish and Jews to a "ghetto" for African-Americans and Puerto Ricans. According to Patricia Wilson, who interviewed Soto in the early 1980s, Soto described himself as an introverted child who did not speak English well and took refuge in art.[2] Soto's elementary school teachers recognized his talent and he received a scholarship from Saks Fifth Avenue Department Stores to take drawing classes in composition and human anatomy. The anatomy classes that he took at age 10 had a lasting impact; a distinctive feature of Soto's mature work is the representation of figures inside out. But we cannot ignore the fact that Soto's many renderings of broken bodies and fascination with the gro- tesque relate back to scenes that he saw outside of art class. [...]

Soto's recollections reveal that art became a way for him to process the traumatic incidents that he witnessed during childhood. Perhaps to give Soto a respite from the escalating violence in the South Bronx, Soto's parents sent him to Puerto Rico for an extended stay in 1960. Returning to New York in 1961, Soto attended two years of high school while working part-time in a handbag factory. In 1963 he dropped out of high school and enlisted in the army.

[...]

Released from the Army in 1965, Soto returned to New York and determined to become an artist. Between 1965 and 1971 Soto established a pattern of working for six months to a year in menial jobs and then going on unemployment to devote himself full time to art. His first art history books were a pocket book primer entitled *Enjoying Modern Art* and John Berger's *The Success and Failure of Picasso*. He also began reading art magazines like *Art in America* and *Art News* and visiting museums and galleries on a regular basis. He credits the French Surrealists and the British Expressionist painter, Francis Bacon, as influences on his work at that time. In 1967, Soto had his first one-person exhibition at Studio 306, a storefront gallery/studio space in the West Bronx. [...]

Soto's Years at Taller Boricua 1971–1981

[...]

The visual artists who gathered at Taller Boricua in the early 1970s saw themselves as activists and were dedicated to creating "art for the people." Most of them had attended art schools in New York or on the island, were exposed to modern art, and read vanguard newspapers such as *Claridad* and *Palante*; therefore, they did not want to cater to the low-brow market for paintings of Puerto Rico's tropical landscapes. Instead, the artists at Taller Boricua heeded the directives of The Young Lords and Puerto Rican Students Union, which called for Puerto Ricans to educate themselves on the island's history, particularly the history of the enslaved African and Taíno peoples whose intermingling birthed Puerto Rico's resilient Creole culture.[3]

"We could all agree that there existed a cultural void in the Puerto Rican community," wrote Marcos Dimas in an essay detailing the early history of Taller Boricua. "As a gesture of solidarity and union, we adapted and personalized Taíno images, which became insignias that symbolically linked us with our ancestral root culture. That elusive aborigine—that mysterious being who had vanished from the face of Borinquen and had receded in our souls; the spirit of freedom that had disappeared into a number of myths, folk tales, and anthropological theories—has always been present in our ambience, lurking within our aura, and appearing in the language, mood, nuances, and gestures, as well as the physical appearance of the people. That mythical being, like the phoenix, was being resurrected at the corner of revolution and change."[4]

[...]

The aesthetic project that the artists initiated at Taller Boricua was freighted with limitations. In contrast to the Nuyorican poets, who primarily saw themselves as creating a "new language" and were not invested in finding precedents for their poetry among the island's writers, the artists at Taller Boricua aspired to work out of a pre-existing, if not "primordial," Puerto Rican visual arts tradition. However, there were relatively few examples of Afro-Puerto Rican and Taíno art in New York to examine for source material. In terms of establishing a direct artistic influence on the way that the Taller artists crafted their Afro-Taíno aesthetic, one must acknowledge the work of Rafael Tufiño. [...] Rafael Tufiño's images of *bomba* and *plena* musicians, masked *vejigante* revelers, and statuesque Afro-Puerto Rican women from Loíza Aldea became icons that supplied the younger generation with their primary pictures of Afro-Puerto Rican identity. Manuel "Neco" Otero's books and reproductions of Taíno art culled from publications issued by the Institute of Puerto Rican Culture were visual resources the artists consulted in the early years of the Taller. The artists also frequented the Museum of Natural History and the Museum of the American Indian. [...]

The exhibitions and visual arts workshops that Taller Boricua artists organized during the 1970s were acts of political/pedagogical intervention in a city that had little information or appreciation of Taíno and Afro-Puerto Rican artifacts. Jorge Soto's poster announcing an exhibit at Taller Boricua in 1974 demonstrates the multi-cultural direction that he [was] taking in his imagery. The poster depicts a vejigante carnival mask from Loíza Aldea besides a Taíno stone carving and is embellished by several examples of Taíno pictographs throughout the poster's upper zone. For viewers familiar with the Puerto Rican poster tradition, Soto's work may appear imitative of graphics rendered by the island's master printmakers: Rafael Tufiño, Lorenzo Homar and Carlos Raquel Rivera. But the script on the bottom half of the poster is uniquely New York Rican and articulates Soto's appreciation of the outlaw typography favored by subway graffitists who popularized "bubble style" letters in New York. Underscoring the graffiti allusion, Soto tagged the "I" in Boricua as though it were a subway column with the name of Taíno Cacique Urayoán, who led the first uprising against the Spanish in Puerto Rico. He also integrated symbols associated with other radical groups into his bubble letters. In addition to the Lares flag utilized by members of the Puerto Rican independence movement, Soto depicted a star and crescent moon in the left hand corner of the poster, a Muslim symbol often seen in newspapers circulated by followers of Black nationalist leaders like Malcom X. Far from being folkloric, or even purely "Puerto Rican," Soto's poster presents Taller Boricua as an artist's space whose members were aligned a multitude of vanguard political and aesthetic movements that operated above and below ground in the 1970s.

From Afro-Taíno to Shaman/*Santero*:
Santeria aesthetics in the works of Jorge Soto

The artists who worked at Taller Boricua were informed by knowledge gleaned from living alongside Afro-American and Afro-Caribbean peoples in New York. The totality of this experience generated an understanding of Puerto Rican identity that was cosmopolitan and transnational. One of the strategies that the Taller artists adopted to surpass the visual clichés of representing Afro-Puerto Rican heritage through well-worn tropes such as vejigante masks and bomba drums was to incorporate motifs in their work that quoted from iconography related to the Afro- Cuban practice of Santería.

[...]

Allusions to Santería are evident in works by Marcos Dimas, Adrian Garcia, Rafael Colón Morales, José Morales, Nitza Tufiño, Jorge Soto and Manuel Vega. In fact, when we examine Dimas' logo for Taller Boricua created in 1970 through an "afrocentric" perspective, we see that it is as much Yoruba as it is Taíno. The large curvilinear plant-like headdress that animates the figure, for example, is atypical in Taíno art. Instead, such headdresses are found in Yoruba and Afro-Cuban Shango figures, whose heads sprout double axes. Dimas's creature also has large almond-shaped eyes and a tight-lipped expression that is characteristic in Yoruba artifacts. Shango, the god of war, thunder and virility, is among the most popular orishas in the Afro-Cuban pantheon. Shango's many attributes includes being the guardian of drummers, an instrument that Dimas began playing when he was 12 years old.

The appearance of Santería motifs in Dimas' works and that of other artists in the Taller such as José Morales and Rafael Colón Morales is a consequence of the shared appreciation of Afro-Caribbean music and does not necessarily reflect the artists' religious affiliations. [...]

Jorge Soto's attitude towards Santería iconography went beyond formal appreciation for its music and regalia. He studied, if not practiced, the rituals and mythology of the Yoruba and other enslaved African and Native American peoples. Soto's scholarly engagement and Santería iconography enabled his work to attain an intellectual richness and a political charge that remains unmatched among his peers. The key to understanding Soto's images from 1974 onward is that they are poetic transcriptions of his ideas about Puerto Rican identity that make use of allegory, metaphors and myth. In Soto's drawing, *El matrimonio del Atabeya y Changó* (c. 1975), Taíno and Yoruba deities serve as allegorical figures that relate the history of co-mingling of African and Taíno peoples in Puerto Rico as a merger of two great civilizations whose combined experience of conquest and colonization birthed the Puerto Rican nation. The Yoruba/Santería deity Shango is depicted marrying the Taíno fertility goddess Atabeya. He reaches to remove a child from Atabeya's vagina while another child suckles at her breast. Their limbs stretch out and merge with each other's bodies, and motifs from each art heritage are fused. Taíno faces emerge from Shango's double axe and his body resembles a Taíno totem pole. Soto employs Picasso's cubist strategy of simultaneously depicting figures facing front and in profile to depict Atabeya's double identity. Facing front, Atabeya has a skeletal face with large round eyes and bared teeth, features that are typical in Taíno art. Her face in profile, however, is visibly black and resembles the female figures with almond-shaped eyes, tight-lipped smiles and full breasts that the Yoruba sculpt in dedication to Shango.

Soto's drawing can also be understood as an allegory of the Puerto Rican migration to New York and the birth of "Afro-Taíno" consciousness among his fellow artists at the Taller. In the artist's statement cited below, Soto describes the relationship between Puerto Rico and Africa as a "bondage of blood" that has enabled Puerto Ricans to claim kinship with African, Caribbean, Latin American and Native peoples across the globe [...].

In Soto's drawing, the mingling between Native and African peoples is celebrated as the union of two great civilizations, but there is a social subtext to this the image. In Puerto Rico, a popular response to someone who claims to be racially pure is to pose the following question: ¿y tu abuela donde está?[5] Soto's use of Santería aesthetics represents the artist's personal step of claiming buried ancestral legacies by bringing his grandmother's religious practices out of the closet. [...] As an adult, Soto came to understand that African and native peoples were not only physically but psychologically oppressed by a culture that stigmatized their healing rituals as evil. [...]

Soto's quest to uncover his ancestral roots took him back to Puerto Rico in 1972 during which time he made initial studies of Taíno artifacts and works of canonical Puerto Rican artists like José Campeche and Francisco Oller. In 1973 Soto had his first solo exhibition in Puerto Rico at Galería Tanamá in Arecibo, and his works continued to be displayed at several prestigious institutions on the island throughout the 1970s, including El Museo de la Universidad de Puerto Rico (1974); Museo de Ponce (1976); Instituto de Cultura Puertorriqueña (1976 and 1978); and Centro Nacional de la Artes (1979).[6] The institutional support that Soto's works received in Puerto Rico did not absolve him from being seen as a "Nuyorican" artist, and he experienced class and racial prejudice on his visits to the island. [...]

[...]

Soto's writings and art demonstrate a sincere, albeit ruthless, commitment to uncover the ideological myths about race, language and nationhood that kept Puerto Ricans on the island and the mainland apart. His employment of an Afro-Taíno visual language was a purposeful attack on the realist and social realist tradition that overshadowed the "nationalist" schools of Puerto Rican painting in the modern era, modes of representation that celebrated the distinctness of Puerto Rican heritage but also fetishized racial and regional differences among the Puerto Rican masses that modernization and circular migration were rapidly eroding.

In the mid-1970s, Soto created a series of prints and paintings that re-inscribed Puerto Rican national icons with Afro-Taíno imagery as a means to reflect continuity and change among Puerto Ricans on both sides of the Atlantic. Soto's Ricanstructions of Francisco Oller's *El velorio* (1893) and Homar's seal of the Institute of Puerto Rican Culture (1961) simultaneously expose the biases that underlie these images and assert that the racial, linguistic, and cultural hybridity that Puerto Ricans were experiencing as a result of transmigration was part of a historical continuum that stretched back to the Spanish conquest.

Francisco Oller's *El velorio* (1893) ranks among the great works of nineteenth-century realist art and touches on the subject of infant death and folk rituals in Puerto Rico. Puerto Rican folk belief once held that a child's death is cause for celebration because he or she is absolved of original sin and will therefore ascend to heaven. Oller's painting depicts a multiracial group of Puerto Rican peasants and clerics holding a riotous wake in a rural hut known as a *bohío*. *El velorio* contrasts an innocent child lying dead on a kitchen table with the depraved adults who drown their sorrows with food and drink. Despite its gruesome theme, *El velorio* is admired for its realistic portrayal of rural life and customs in Puerto Rico and is considered a national icon.

Jorge Soto's serigraph, *El velorio de Oller en Nueva York* (1975), reinterprets Oller's masterpiece to reflect continuity and change among Puerto Ricans living in New York at the last quarter of the twentieth century.[7] Like Oller, Soto portrays a group of mourners at a child's wake. The thatched roof interior where Soto's figures stand resembles the same hut that Oller carefully rendered. But the open door at the left hand corner of the room displays a cityscape, thus suggesting that the tenement apartment we see is an urban bohío. In contrast to Oller, whose realist aesthetic was couched in the anthropological interest of capturing the diversity of racial types in Puerto Rico, Soto employs his hybrid Afro-Taíno visual language to portray the mourners at the wake as a nation united by their mixed ancestry, proletarian social status, shared sufferings and syncretized spirituality. Accordingly, he represents the mixed ancestry of the Puerto Rican mourners by picturing

Taíno and African forms emerging from their bodies, sometimes distorting their physiques into fantastic shapes.

Soto's depiction of the dead child in the middle of the room offers an optimistic view of death and regeneration based on Native American and African beliefs. Rather than portray a lifeless child on a table, Soto represents it sitting up in a crossed-legged position as though its spirit had been reincarnated. Two additional alterations that Soto made to Oller's composition further convey that the child is undergoing a transformation. Firstly, Soto replaced the pious black man who is seen paying his respect to the child in Oller's painting with a representation of the Yoruba deity of the crossroads, Elegua, who is shown near the child in the middle of the room holding his traditional hooked staff. Secondly, whereas Oller hung a roast pig in the middle high ground of *El velorio* to symbolize the mourners' carnal desires, Soto placed a stylized bird, a symbol of peace and freedom, in the same spot to suggest that the ritual has uplifted the participants. Indeed the only scene of "depravity" that Soto retained from Oller's version of *El velorio* is the portrayal of a couple copulating in a corner, an act that can be seen within this context as life affirming.

El velorio de Oller en Nueva York was cover illustration for the Center for Puerto Rican Studies publication of papers delivered in the 1974 symposium: Critique and Debate: Culture and the Puerto Ricans (1976). The image gained wider attention when it was reproduced on the cover of the Association for Hispanic Arts (AHA) newsletter to commemorate Soto's solo exhibition at AHA in 1977. *El velorio de Oller en Nueva York* has since become Soto's most well-known work.

Soto's reinterpretation of Lorenzo Homar's seal of the Institute of Puerto Rican Culture (ICP) [c. 1961] was first reproduced in Critique and Debate: Culture and the Puerto Ricans and later graced the cover of Juan Flores' award-winning book *Insuralismo e idología burguesa* (1979).[8] Lesser-known today, Soto's ICP emblem merits equal recognition with *El velorio de Oller en Nueva York* because it summarizes his perspective on the origins and nature of Puerto Rican identity. The emblem that Homar designed for the Institute of Puerto Rican Culture represents Puerto Rico's tri-partite racial and cultural makeup through the figures of a Taíno Indian, a Spanish *caballero* and an African slave. The Indian holds a stone carving, the Spaniard holds a book and the African holds a drum to signify the cultural contribution that each race brought to the island. While the three races are presented on equal footing, the Spaniard's central position on the seal and the logo-centric framework of Puerto Rican national identity over-determines that Spanish language and heritage appear as the elements that unify Puerto Rican civil society. Although Homar designed the emblem in 1957 he excluded the United States as an agent of social change in Puerto Rico, an omission that rendered his image of Puerto Rican culture obsolete for its time.

Soto's reworking of Homar's emblem updates the historical forces that structured Puerto Rican culture in the 20th century. The Spanish caballero reappears in the center as a skeleton holding a skull wearing Uncle Sam's top hat. Here Spain and the United States are depicted not only as entities that brought death and destruction to the island, but also as representatives of the patriarchal culture of "dead white males" who pre-dominate in Euro-American retellings of history.

In contrast to Homar's patriarchal depiction of Puerto Rican heritage, Soto's rendering of the island's indigenous culture is figured by a voluptuous bird-headed female whose right breast is covered by a crescent moon shape and whose left breast and fertile womb are exposed. Soto heeded the feminist movement, and though he rendered many sexualized images of women, procreative female goddesses and the merging of male and female bodies to express universal harmony as a balance of male and female forces are persistent motifs in his works. Thus, here the female is joined at the hip to a male figure with huge round eyes that bears resemblance to representations of Yoka Hu, the Taíno god of life force. However, neither figure is purely Taíno. Bird-headed figures, for example, are prevalent in West African, Oceanic and Native North American artifacts, sources that Soto had been integrating into his visual language for several years.

Soto's twin-faced African male is a composite of Yoruba and Kongo iconography. Although his head is crowned by the double axe headdress that distinguishes Shango figures, instead of carrying Shango's sacred *bata* drum or the conga drum that Homar depicted in the original ICP seal, the African holds a skull in his right hand and carries a rapier in the left to reflect his Kongo ancestry. Like the Yoruba, the Kongo people were brought to the Caribbean during the slave trade. Kongo spiritual beliefs are grounded in ancestor worship and aspects of their ritual practices survive in Haitian Voodoo, Cuban *Palo* and Puerto Rican *Espiritismo*.[9] Indeed, the efficacy of Kongo rituals are so reknown in the Caribbean that Puerto Rican Espiritismo, which largely derives from the writings of the French spiritualist Allan Kardec, recognizes an African spiritual guide known as "El Congo" who is called upon to locate dead relatives.[10]

In Soto's image, the African male becomes the only figure capable of bridging the collective wisdom of Puerto Rico's past heritages with the present. In this context, the skull and rapier refer to instruments used in Voodoo, Palo and Espiritismo ceremonies, all which involve contacting ancestors and spirits for guidance and retribution. The rapier may be pounded against a drum or the ground to wake up ancestors and is also used to create symbols that empower the spirits or record what they say.

Soto's replacement of the conga drum with a skull is perhaps the most significant element in his reinterpretation of the ICP seal because it reveals the spiritual "truth" that Bomba and other forms of drumming and dancing circles impart to Nuyorican, Puerto Rican and other African-diasporic peoples. The skull is a metonymic symbol of the drum's capacity to connect individuals to minds of their ancestors, to sing, dance and worship as they once did. [...]

[...]

Conclusions

The Afro-Taíno motifs that appear in the works of Jorge Soto and other artists who comprised Taller Boricua's core membership are attributable to the confluence of several factors: (a) a desire among these artists to align their aesthetic ancestries back to great ancient civilizations in Africa and Latin America; (b) access to museums that house extensive collections of African, Afro-Diaspora and Native American art; (c) identification with the cultures and social struggles of an array of African, African-American and Afro-Latino and Native peoples across the Americas; (d) exposure to African-Diaspora religions such as Santería, Voodoo and *Cadomble* through popular music and/or direct engagement with these religious practices. As a consequence of all the above mentioned factors, the work of artists that were affiliated with Taller Boricua manifest a broader range of pan-African iconography and a greater tendency to fuse African and Taíno symbols than island-based Puerto Rican art dating from that era.

The work of Jorge Soto paralleled the hybrid structure of Nuyorican writing. His densely coded visual language was informed by several traditions: the carvings of the pre-Columbian Taíno natives of Puerto Rico; the artifacts of African and African-diasporic peoples; and the visual culture of New York's barrios. Whereas the Nuyorican poets invoked words that resonated in Spanish and English, Jorge Soto re-presented the island's pantheon of indigenous deities and nationalist icons in contemporary urban settings, thus allowing these mythic island figures new meanings for Nuyorican audiences. In this respect, Jorge Soto's approach towards image making is the mirror opposite of the documentary style that the Nuyorican poets adopted. The Nuyorican poets strove to make their poetic language reflect the concrete realities of daily life, while Jorge Soto strove to represent what he saw on the streets as the stuff of legends and myths. Nevertheless, like the Nuyorican poets whose Spanglish speech is punctuated by the staccato delivery of African-American and Afro-Caribbean poets and rappers, the work of Jorge Soto is a visual expression of the hybrid racial consciousness that distinguished Nuyorican cultural production in the 1970s and early 1980s.

The Nuyorican Movement was interdisciplinary. Visual artists, musicians, poets and dancers cohabited spaces and collaborated on staging cultural events and political actions. The re-vitalization of Afro-Puerto Rican folk art, music, song and dance traditions was understood as enabling contemporary artists to establish a trans-historical connection with the island's oppressed peoples of color, thus empowering Nuyoricans to dispute logocentric and Eurocentric constructions of Puerto Rican national identity.

CHAPTER 10

Central Park Rumba: Nuyorican Identity and the Return to African Roots

By Berta Jottar

[...]

Informed by the 1960s and 1970s Afro-Cuban jazz *descargas* and the ongoing salsa movement, the Nuyorican sound of rumba in Central Park was a montage of Cuban, Puerto Rican, and African American rhythms articulating this generation's hybrid cultural identity. However, unlike Cuban rumba, which was passed on from generation to generation through performance practice, since the 1940s, rumba in New York City and its Nuyorican manifestation was mostly the result of a knowledge transmitted through mechanical reproduction as percussionists learned Cuban rumba primarily from records and, later, audiotapes. Accordingly, from the late 1960s to the early 1970s, Central Park rumba became the intersection where the energy of the civil rights movement synchronized with the formation of an Afro-Boricua identity. Thus, rumba became a boricua articulation that constituted a performative nation, a post-national cultural space that functioned beyond the colonial geography and legacies of this Afro-Latin generation. Moreover, rumba became a third space: a sovereign performative nation exceeding the racial boundaries of the nation state through the performance of this Nuyorican hybrid identity.

   [...] Beyond Latin American nationalist discourses of hybridity as the result of *mestizaje* (cultural and racial mixing), this hybrid condition produces an artistic freedom that allows Latinos to experiment with African, Native American, and European aesthetic practices (Pacini Hernandez 2010). Rumba à la boricua is indeed a hybrid musical performance constituting the layered subjectivities of those Nuyoricans born in the mid and late 1950s.

Originally published in *CENTRO: Journal of the Center for Puerto Rican Studies* 23(1): 4–29, 2011.

[...]

By the early 1970s, Central Park rumba became a concentrated version of the ongoing corner rumbas/jam sessions taking place since the mid-1950s in the various neighborhoods shared by Latina/os and African Americans. In the following section, I analyze the multiple functions of Central Park rumba for this Nuyorican generation. Within the Central Park context, the performance of rumba articulated both a space of cultural pride and intra-racial negotiation.

Central Park Rumba at Bethesda Terrace (1960s–1970s)

It was in the late 1960s (the Boogaloo and Latin Soul era) and early 1970s (the beginning of the salsa revolution) that Bethesda Terrace in Central Park became the central location where Nuyoricans, African Americans, and other Afro-Latinos met at the rhythm of the drum. Paula Ballán[1] has remarked that the park's central fountain and open plaza resembled Puerto Rico's Spanish architecture, noting that "the summer weather allowed people to leave their closed, dark apartments to enjoy the park's openness; people wore their best clothes—newly ironed, just as Puerto Rican dress codes of the 1950s dictated" (personal communication, 1998). Ballán remembers first generation Nuyoricans and Puerto Rican immigrants attending jam sessions at Bethesda Terrace by the early 1970s.[2] For Ballán, however, "it was hard to call it a rumba; Central Park rumba was a social occasion more than a musical one" (personal communication, 1998).

Moreover, Félix Sanabria has remarked that, *"moreno americanos* [African Americans] had a major impact on Puerto Ricans by bringing their drums to the park. Jazz musicians like John Coltrane had arrived at the park with bongos and congas" (personal communication, 1998). Cecil Carter, an African-American drummer regular to the Terrace scene since 1968, recalls as many as four different drumming circles at a time playing their own variations of *Patato y Totíco* (1968) and Santería chants: "I wouldn't call it a rumba, but more of a drum circle with more Afrocentric influences without a main singer leading basic choruses like *agua que va caer"* (personal communication, 2010). By the mid-1970s, Mayor John Lindsay had legalized the live playing of musical instruments at Central Park.

[...]

Bethesda Terrace became the central area where Puerto Ricans, Nuyoricans, African Americans, and a few Dominicans congregated in small groups of friends, family, and lovers. Ballán remembers that Latinos also incorporated their transistor radios into the existing fountain scene, which was made up of *soneros*[3] with guitars, *bongoceros*,[4] and *pleneros*,[5] all practicing their musical knowledge.

[...]

For musicians like the González's brothers who frequented the Terrace, their musical content, form, and tastes were a reflection of their personal process of self-awareness, their identification with the "common struggles" ranging from "basic pride in Puerto Ricanness, 'New Ricanness' or Latinoness, to militant activism in the competition for resources and political access" (Singer 1982: 7). According to Lisa Knauer, "Cuba's support of anticolonial struggles and a cultural policy that foregrounded African Roots made Afro-Cuban culture a 'space' where many Puerto Ricans and African Americans could construct counter-hegemonic and nationalist imaginaries" (2009: 143). Roberta Singer contextualizes this era's musical production as identifying more generally with Third World liberation and pan-Latino movements (1988). [...]

[...]

Certainly, since the 1960s, music had become the vehicle of a "new consciousness, an Afro-Boricua pride and self-esteem" (West-Durán 2005). Indeed, this was an era of Puerto Rican ethnic pride typified by both the rise of the Young Lords and the Puerto Rican Independence Movement. Thus, the regular gathering at Bethesda Terrace was no exception; it supported the articulation of a Nuyorican sovereign identity. While the combination of live performance over recorded music recreated the soundscape of a larger pan-Caribbean world, the fountain scene was also aurally synchronized through the eloquent voice of Felipe Luciano's Sunday radio show on WRVR, *Latin Roots*.[6] Ballán argues that this radio show contributed greatly to the formation of Puerto Rican pride, particularly among those second- and third-generation boricuas who did not speak Spanish. Luciano's broadcast in English was an anti-colonial stand, a voice in favor of Puerto Rico's independence from the U.S. Thus, for a few hours on the weekends, Bethesda Terrace became an autonomous Puerto Rican space where politics and culture were synchronized via the musical performance of cultural pride and affirmation.

Probably for those outside Bethesda Terrace's rumba scene, the sound of these drum circles became the dissonant sounds of difference. Under mainland racial politics, boricuas of African descent were already categorized as African Americans (West-Durán 2005). Accordingly, these drum circles functioned as an acoustic declaration of this generation's cultural pride; they were aural articulations in which the repetition and reiteration of these particular sounds and rhythms produced a temporal space of cultural authority and presence:

> *"el boricua de New York City usa esta música para identificarse como Latino ... y es una forma de decir: el Americano tiene mi país, mi cultura, pero como quiera, yo me expreso como Latino." [The boricua in New York City uses this music to identify himself as a Latino...and it is a way to say: The American has taken my country, my culture, nevertheless, I express myself as a Latino].* (Yeyito, personal communication, 2009)

[...] For the dominant culture, Bethesda Terrace became an Afro-centric space of contestation.

The drum circles were also a performance of cultural defiance against a larger symbolic regime. The participants of Bethesda Terrace contested prevalent stereotypes of Puerto Rican "objectionable behavior" (Jiménez-Román 2008: 2). [...] Thus, as *salseros* fixed their experience in their music, salsa (infused of rumba rhythms) became an expressive form of liberation and decolonization, a movement of social change and national recognition (Berrios-Miranda 2004). For instance, album covers (e.g., Willie Colón's *El Malo, La Gran Fuga*, and *El Juicio*) signaled the stereotypical representations of Puerto Ricans as "delinquents" (Yglesias 2005; West-Durán 2005).

But the streets were another public arena were racialized groups fought nationwide these stereotypes. From the mid-1960s to the beginning of the 1970s, there was active resistance to the increase in claims of police brutality and the decrease of affordable housing, combined with deteriorating economic conditions in communities of color. This resulted in a series of nationwide riots not only in African American communities, but in Puerto Rican neighborhoods[7] in New Jersey and in Chicago (Santiago-Valles and Jiménez-Muñoz 2004: 96). [...] But in New York City's Central Park, the tumbadora and the bongo drums (central to the percussive African presence in Latin Jazz, Latin Soul and salsa) became the matrix between Nuyoricans and African Americans. As Gene Golden recalls, "our common concern was our love for Afro-descendant drumming traditions" (personal communication, 2010).

Within this larger socio-political context, the drum circles at Bethesda Terrace provided a multi-ethnic and multi-racial space in which the layered performance of Afro-Latino/a sound (rumba, salsa, bomba, plena), articulated a visible "black and proud" identity not only in opposition to prevalent U.S. racial politics, but also against prevalent Puerto Rican elitist discourse that privileged Puerto Rico's Span-ish roots. Indeed, Nuyoricans were caught between Puerto Rico's "myth of race-free color blindness and the reality of anti-Black racism" (Jiménez-Róman 2008: 3). Félix Sanabria remembers growing up with African Americans in the projects and how Nuyoricans were taught to discriminate against them in the name of "staying with your own people." However, located on the same socio-economic level as African Americans, Nuyoricans and Latino youth in general "developed a multiethnic con-sciousness" (Opie 2008) and began to identify with their neighbors:

> When you are living on the same floor, when you start liking the girls, when you start playing ball with the guys, you are in the same classrooms together, you real-ized that Afro-Latinos and Afro-Americans represented two branches of the same tree, after a while ... it is hard to tell the difference from one to the other ... and all these branches have grown out of the same living conditions. And when you are poor, you are not going to look at your neighbor and say 'because you are black, yo! If you are in the same boat, maybe we ain't the bad guys, maybe the guy that is charging us so much rent is the bad guy ... and you come together to fight for the same. (Félix Sanabria, personal communication, 2010)

[...]

Central Park Rumba Bench: Setting Down Roots

By the mid-1970s, the rumba was accorded a new location on the West Side near the Bow Bridge, by one of the park benches facing the idyllic, nineteenth-century landscape fram-ing the [El] Dorado and [The] Manhattan buildings. Two unrelated reasons were behind this development. First, people had started to organize their music *before* arriving at the park, forming ready-made groups that functioned differently than the spontaneous drum circles at the Terrace. Second, and most importantly, under pressure from local residents, the Parks Department began a series of "restorations" that fenced off Bethesda Terrace's area, effectively keeping people away from the fountain. Nevertheless, those committed to the music continued the rumba tradition on the Park's west side.

There are different origin narratives concerning this new rumba site. Some re-member the Jewish-American Morton Sanders,[8] with John Amira[9] and the African Americans John Mason,[10] Daffy Coleman, and others as choosing this particular bench to sit on while they played; however, some have argued that they mostly per-formed African music with a Latin flavor (see also Hiss 1976: 41). Others credit the Rumberos All Star, the first Nuyorican rumba ensemble in El Barrio for performing the first traditional rumba in this lake area.[11] By the late 1970s, Cuban rumba had become the official purpose for gathering. As in Cuba, music and socializing overlapped in the performance of traditional rumba in Central Park. Chatting, eating, and making new connections took place on the grassy area where drinks and food circulated, but the purpose of the gathering was also part of a larger project: the search for a shared African heritage.

In the 1970s, Puerto Ricans and Nuyoricans renewed their interest in the history of Puerto Rican, Cuban, and African traditional music forms (Singer 1982; Manuel 1994), which meant a return to their roots. However, the rumba was now no longer experienced over the collective listening to radio waves near the fountain; instead, participants were connected through a collective live performance with tumbadora drums. Ballán remembers that tumbadoras (or conga drums)[12] replaced portable radios and wind instruments, and that Puerto Ricans began to show off their Cuban rumba skills learned at home by listening and memorizing the available records of Cuban rumba in the U.S. But one may ask, why did performing rumba (rather than bomba) constitute a return to these young Nuyoricans of their African roots?[13] Yeyito and Félix Sanabria remember the experience of learning bomba and plena as almost impossible.[14] As will be discussed below, this generation was caught between Puerto Rican racial imaginaries (based on Spanish and then U.S. colonialism) and Puerto Rican nationalist discourses of authenticity.[15]

Puerto Rico's racial politics—a legacy of Spanish colonialism—continued to marginalize any form of Afro-Puerto Rican cultural expression: "[E]stamos hablando de música de negros, hay Puertorriqueños que no quieren asociarse con ese tipo de música de negros aunque sean negros" [We were talking about black music, and there are Puerto Ricans who don't want to be associated with this type of music even if they are black] (Félix Sanabria, personal communication, 2010). Furthermore, the U.S. erasure of Puerto Rican and Afro-Puerto Rican culture resulted in the lack of institutional support for traditional bomba and plena recordings. Although during the 1950s there was a plena revival in New York City, which helped Puerto Ricans to "overcome their regional divisions" and racial tensions (Lipsitz 2007: 215–6), the existing bomba records by Cortijo and Mon Rivera had been "Cubanized" and were "farther removed from the genre's roots." By the 1960s, the popularity of Cortijo was in decline (Manuel 1994: 260).

Ironically, while traditional bomba was disappearing from the cultural practices of working-class Puerto Ricans in New York, bomba was becoming a sign of Puerto Rican cultural nationalism and authenticity. If in Puerto Rico bomba never achieved the status of national music (Manuel 1994: 258), by the 1970s, many of the nationalists living in New York City did not want to teach bomba nor plena to Yeyito's friends because Nuyoricans were not considered "authentic" Puerto Ricans (Yeyito, personal communication, 2009).[16] Eddy Rodríguez also remembers the tensions between Puerto Ricans from the island and those from New York City, who were, and still are, cast as assimilated, inauthentic, and different from those from the island (personal communication, 1998). Moreover, those Nuyoricans not fluent in Spanish felt further alienated by language barriers (Flores 1993, 2000; Rivera 1996, 2001). [...]

On the other hand, López argues that the ongoing city rumbas (street drumming) channeled the community's creativity with "familiar antecedents in Puerto Rican and Caribbean cultures, objectively constitut[ing] an instrument for national survival and expression" (1976: 107). In Central Park rumba, the circle also became the space to acoustically negotiate this generation's linguistic, religious, and racial heterogeneity. The sound of the drum became the common language crossing internal boundaries: some musicians were Catholic and uninterested in the Afro-Cuban religions of Regla de Ocha or Palo Monte. Some individuals favored Puerto Rico's independence, others didn't. Furthermore, not all Nuyorican rumberos were Afro-descendant. However, being racially mixed, most of them identified primarily as belonging to the African diaspora, as "black," or as Afro-Latino. Indeed, rumba became an alternative third place that affirmed, as Maribel García Soto[17] has observed, the African presence within Puerto Rican culture (personal communication, 1999).

For this Nuyorican generation, traditional rumba functioned as the source to express their identification with Africa, whether they were black or not. For instance, Yeyito's relationship to rumba's Afro-descendant roots complicates an identification with "blackness" as purely racial. Yeyito, apparently not an Afro-descendant himself, argues that part of his identification with Afro-descendant drumming comes from his identification with Taíno[18] drumming culture (personal communication, 2009). Ironically, his identification asserts Puerto Rico's Taíno ancestry as one in solidarity with African Americans and functions contrary to Puerto Rican nationalist discourses and their "recreation of the indigenous past" as "the denigration of the 'third root'," or African culture (Duany 1999: 32). In this context, drumming becomes a political paradigm and praxis, a postcolonial claim against the erasure of Afro-descendants by way of Spanish and U.S. colonialism.[19] Traditional Cuban rumba provided a common musical paradigm that exceeded the territorial, national, and ideological features of this racially and linguistically diverse group. Rumba in Central Park became a post-national cultural performance that resisted Puerto Rico's Eurocentric racial politics as well as nationalist claims of authenticity while claiming a larger Afro-diasporic identification. Interestingly, the performance of rumba as "roots" conversely articulated the performance of a hybrid Nuyorian identity.

Rumba à la Boricua: Performing a Hybrid Identity

[...]

In their performance of rumba, this generation re-created their everyday inter-cultural experience. Their close contact with African American music (blues, bebop, and funk) and their bilingual/bicultural experience had created what I call "rumba with a difference," or rumba à la boricua. Rumba à la boricua was a hybrid cultural manifestation claiming both New York City and African roots within a larger African diaspora. Hybridity, "as an in-between site of enunciation" (Washburne 2008: x), produced their rumba sound, unique to their own "in-between" existence as Nuyoricans: "We are hybrids and we have the license to experiment; for instance, I might sing a columbia in a *jíbaro* singing form..." (Eddie Bobé, personal communication 1998).[20]

With this statement, Bobé also points to a Nuyorican form of making music that fits into a historical tradition of incorporating different musical forms in one song (Glasser 1995). Like salsa, (Quintero, as cited in Santos-Febres 1997: 178) rumba à la boricua was a hybrid form primarily based on the improvisation and the new combination of different musical forms; some Nuyorican rumberos would use traditional rumba guaguancó or columbia rhythms with different improvisational[21] styles, or they would use salsa *montunos* for rumba ones. [...]

By 1978, the older generation of Central Park drummers had stopped going to the rumba at the bench. According to Félix Sanabria, the innovations of his generation had changed the rumba scene because they "represented the merg[ing] between the Cubans and the Nuyoricans, the black New Yorkers and the New York City Dominicans" (personal communication, 2002). In fact, they were creating a hybrid style that juxtaposed the diverse rhythmic influences of a larger Afro-Latino diaspora while developing new musical skills.

Eddie Bobé identifies his generation with the ability to sing while playing multiple drums. [...] Re-inserting the singing voice into the rumba further contributed to the hybridity of rumba à la boricua; their voice was multilingual. For instance, Abraham Rodríguez sang rumba in Spanglish and English, in a doo-wop swing in Central Park. In other words, rumba à la boricua was a hybrid form, a way of improvising with their cultural and linguistic skills enriched by their knowledge of rhythms and musical accents reflecting their growing experience as part of the African diaspora.

The generation's search for its African roots resulted in hybrid experimentations of making both music and identity. But rumba à la boricua was also the result of the acquisition of rumba knowledge through mechanical reproduction. While Afro-Cuban tumbadora drums had replaced transistor radios, the performance of rumba à la boricua was primarily the result of a mediated memory, the memorization of traditional Cuban rumba from cassette tapes.

[...]

Conclusion

Historically, Cuban rumba itself is a hybrid form, a synthesis created during the late nineteenth century by Yoruba, Congo, and Carabalí slaves, freemen, and their descendants, coming together to play music and socialize on Sundays. Thus it could be argued that the hybridity nurtured in Bethesda Terrace, resulting in rumba à la boricua, mirrors its Cuban counterpart. As Fernando Ortiz (1963) argued in his theory of transculturation, new social constructions transform existing patterns of production, creating a new culture. In the Cuban context, the cultural manifestation was rumba; in New York City, rumba à la boricua. As Deborah Paccini has stated, there is nothing exceptional about hybridity within Latin/o American racial and cultural imaginary. Indeed, the hybridity of rumba à la boricua functioned as an in-between space of enunciation, not in favor of whitening, nor about racial blindness, but similar to what Jiménez and Flores have theorized as a "triple-consciousness," a multidimensional social experience and optic that evolved in the intersection of being "Latinos, Black and U.S. American" (2009: 321).

[...]

The 1960s and 1970s rumba à la boricua produced by Nuyoricans and Puerto Ricans, rather than being pure assimilation or appropriation of Cuban rumbas, reflects a number of historical and contemporary relationships within a diasporic Afro-Latino/a memory and imaginary. First, rumba à la boricua reflects a common Caribbean history of colonization through the continued use of Spanish language and references to *Tiempo de España* (the era of Spanish colonization). But, rumba in New York City reintroduced the African presence into Puerto Rican culture. In this sense, rumba à la boricua defies the late 1960s and 1970s hegemonic Puerto Rican discourses, the nationalist narratives of mestizaje that privilege whitening (*emblanquecimiento*). Second, rumba à la boricua forms a political connection to the African American diaspora within the U.S. After all, Nuyoricans are seen not only as Spanish or Taíno Indians, but also as black. As Eddy Rodríguez explains: "rumba in the U.S. is to the boricuas what blues is to African Americans. Rumba is the Nuyorican Soul" (personal communication, 1995).

Finally, rumba functioned as a post-national space—neither in Puerto Rico nor the U.S.—but rather as a sovereign *afro-boricua* experience in New York City, composed of working-class, racialized Nuyoricans: the children of Operation Bootstrap and the subsequent Civil Rights Movement. In the 1970s, rumba provided a space of negotiation and affinity, a space of possibility in the making of a hybrid Nuyorican subjectivity.

CHAPTER 11

Slipping and Sliding: The Many Meanings of Race in Life Histories of New York Puerto Rican Return Migrants in San Juan

By Eileen J. Findlay

In recent years, scholars have begun a rich conversation on the role of race in the experience of Puerto Ricans and their migration to the United States. They have de-lineated how Puerto Ricans in the U.S. not only struggle against poverty but have been persistently racialized, regardless of their phenotype, as inherently inferior to those ethnic groups deemed "fully white." Puerto Ricans' own racial diversity, which renders any claim to whiteness suspicious at best, their frequent resistance of the dominant U.S. white-black racial binary, their linguistic and other cultural differ-ences from mainstream U.S. society, and their homeland's longstanding colonial sub-jection by the U.S. have created enduring patterns of discrimination against them. Encountering this racism upon arrival in the U.S., scholars have noted, often pro-duces a new racialized identity among Puerto Ricans, somewhere in the nebulous ideological and political terrain between white and black—even Puerto Ricans who on the island were considered white are assigned to a position of "racial other" in the U.S. (Aranda 2007; Ayala and Bernabe 2007; Duany 2002; Cobas, Duany and Feagin 2009; Grosfoguel 2003; Grosfoguel and Georas 2000; Negrón-Muntaner 2007; Negrón-Muntaner and Grosfoguel 1997; Rodríguez 1994, 2009). This "inbetween," "non-white" identity, while imposed upon Puerto Ricans, has also often been actively claimed by migrants from the island and their descendants, as they have insisted on the integrity of Puerto Ricans as a whole, and as they have grappled with the rac-ism which they encountered in the U.S. (Aranda 2007; Duany 2002; Rodríguez 1994; Rumbaut 2009). Several authors have also noted that this new racial identity and consciousness have frequently fostered solidarity and creative collaboration with other marginalized, racialized groups, particularly migrants from Latin America and

Originally published in *CENTRO: Journal of the Center for Puerto Rican Studies* 24(1): 44–67, 2012.

other parts of the Caribbean, as well as African Americans (Flores 1993, 2009; Rivera 2007; Rodríguez 1994, 2009; Rumbaut 2009).

Scholars noting this hegemonic system of racialization in the U.S. differ, however, in the attention they give to the racial dynamics among Puerto Ricans themselves. Many assume or assert that Puerto Ricans by and large have been united by the discrimination they face in the U.S. A few, though, insist that racial difference is one of the primary internal fault lines of Puerto Rican collective identity. They point out that while blackness and black Puerto Ricans themselves have often been denied or excluded from hegemonic definitions of Puerto Ricanness, Puerto Ricans' own cultural production often have been rooted in Afro-diasporic forms and sensibilities. They also emphasize the importance of Afro-Puerto Ricans themselves as cultural and political workers in both the diaspora and the island. (Flores 1993, 2009; Jiménez Román and Flores 2010; Quintero Rivera 1988, 2009; Rivera 2003, 2007).

Scholars working on the island have begun to excavate the workings of race—especially understandings of blackness—among Puerto Ricans with great care. They have criticized Puerto Rico's own hegemonic racial ideology, which denies Puerto Rican racism and celebrates the island's alleged racial democracy, always in contradistinction to the U.S.' open racism. Puerto Rico's dominant racial regime is clearly more flexible than the U.S.' history of overt racial segregation, but it is still profoundly racist, these scholars argue; it accepts blackness only as a folkloric, romanticized identity buried in an allegedly victimized past of slavery or contained in particular geographic locations such as Loíza or Barrio San Antón of Ponce. According to the hegemonic nationalist discourse, Puerto Ricans may be deemed "racially mixed" or "mulato," but rarely *black*. These scholars have also analyzed how Puerto Ricans of African descent simultaneously participate in the dominant culture's silencing of blackness and keep black identities alive. Puerto Ricans' popular racial attitudes, identities, and practices then, can be profoundly contradictory, both eliding blackness and asserting its presence in daily life (Godreau 1999, 2002, 2006, 2008; Godreau, Reyes Cruz, Franco Ortiz, and Cuadrado 2008; Lloréns 2005; Martínez 2007; Quintero Rivera 1988, 1992). For many Puerto Ricans, even those who identify as being of African descent, blackness can be "fugitive"; "blackness suffers at once from 'erasure,' 'masking,' and 'denial' while simultaneously surfacing time and time again in public discourses about identity politics.... [I]t refuses to remain muted against attempts to minimize its relevance and existence. It surfaces and reappears..." (Lloréns 2005: 8, 16). These scholars, then, both denounce the silencing racism of an apparently racially inclusive society and suggest that even within large, overarching patterns, racial identities and meanings can take on multiple, even contradictory forms for Puerto Ricans.

In this essay I hope to contribute to this conversation about the effects of race on Puerto Ricans by analyzing the life history narratives of fifteen Puerto Ricans born and raised in New York City during the 1940s, 1950s, and 1960s. All of the narrators whose life stories I examine in this essay relocated to the San Juan, Puerto Rico, area as young adults during the late 1960s and early 1970s, where they have remained living until the present. I conducted the interviews in Puerto Rico during 2002.

The narratives provide a striking example of the discursive workings of "fugitive blackness" among New York-born Puerto Rican return migrants to the island. While at first glance race seemed to be a rather minor theme in the interviews, it soon became evident that commentaries on race actually marked crucial narrative turning points and delineated discussions of Puerto Rican authenticity. Race, then, despite its apparent marginalization as a theme, was both structurally and symbolically important to the oral histories. Also, these discussions of race on one level created consensual understandings of the past, especially in the New York-born narrators' interest in constructing a collective, empowered sense of themselves as legitimate Puerto Ricans vis-à-vis middle class islanders. At this consensus level, the narrators heartily confirmed the macro-level analyses of Puerto Rican racialization and internal solidarity within the U.S. On another level, however, the narrators asserted a surprisingly wide range of interpretations of Puerto Rican blackness. Thus, these narratives remind us that the meanings of race can be strikingly specific; sweeping observations about broad historical patterns of racialization, while important, only offer us a partial understanding of the complex workings of race for Puerto Ricans. Finally, the life stories remind us that racial meanings are emotional as well as political.

[...]

"A Different Kind of Puerto Rican"

Despite their long decades of residence, work, community building in Puerto Rico, and their deep love for the island, the vast majority of these narrators asserted that they were a "different kind of Puerto Rican" than those island-born and raised. These New York born-and-bred, long-term residents of San Juan consistently insisted on their dissimilarity from island Puerto Ricans—in language use, work habits, their claimed sophistication of world view, and particularly in their gendered expectations, values, and social practices. They deeply resented the discrimination they had experienced on the island as part of the New York diaspora, accused of bringing "foreign ways" to Puerto Rico.

The workings of race in these life histories, as is frequently the case in Puerto Rican contexts, was much more difficult to pin down than that of gender, which was a central theme in all the life histories. Questions of racial identity, instead, generally haunted the edges of the narratives, surfacing in quick references to historical experiences, or mythic familial struggles. However, comments about race were far from unimportant in these life histories. Through their discussions of racial prejudice and mixing among Puerto Ricans, and in their comments about racial and ethnic confrontation in the United States, the narrators simultaneously insisted on their legitimacy as Puerto Ricans, critiqued the U.S., and differentiated themselves from island Puerto Ricans. These New York Puerto Ricans residing in San Juan displayed unanimity in such commentaries.

All of them agreed that their generation of New York born-and-bred Puerto Ricans did not experience or practice racial prejudice among themselves. They also agreed that their parents and past generations, raised on the island, had been much more highly conscious of racial distinctions among Puerto Ricans than they themselves were. In addition, they insisted that racial prejudice haunted present islander Puerto Ricans in a way supposedly inconceivable for New York Puerto Ricans. Despite islanders' allegedly heightened racial prejudices and concern with racial differences among Puerto Ricans, which marked them in these narratives as more susceptible to intra-group racism than New York Puerto Ricans, the narrators implied that Puerto Rico offered more possibilities for racial social advancement and interracial love than did the U.S. They remembered the U.S., for the most part embodied in New York City, as defined by intense conflict among different racial or ethnic groups and a rigid binary racial system that imposed "black" or "white" identities on the more racially fluid Puerto Ricans.[1]

The experience and memories of such sharp aggression by racial and ethnic "others" in the U.S. produced a powerful solidarity among the Puerto Ricans who grew up in New York in the 1950s and 1960s and moved to Puerto Rico between 1968 and 1980. In their narratives, their experiences of ethnic/racial discrimination in New York City contrasted sharply with an alleged racial harmony among emigrant Puerto Ricans.

Upon arrival in Puerto Rico, however, they noted a subtle, yet persistent tendency on the island toward exclusion of Puerto Ricans of African descent; this racism echoed the hostility with which islanders met the narrators' New York-based cultural distinctiveness. The discourse of blindness to racial difference among Puerto Ricans raised in New York consequently became an important theme in their life narratives. Their understanding of race and its significance (or lack thereof) became a marker of their distinction from island Puerto Ricans, who had rejected them.

In these narratives, assertions of the invisibility of racial differences among Puerto Ricans in New York could morph into persistent hints of racism on the island. [...]

[...] Taken together, these life stories warn against the creation of a totalizing meta-narrative about the workings of race for these New York Puerto Ricans. As we will see, not only could racial meanings shift according to historical context; they could also vary from person to person, and even change in the process of a single person's storytelling. People's phenotypes could affect their historical experiences of race and the meanings they ascribed to them, but did not definitively determine them. Thus, we should not equate the particularities of racial experience and memory with the larger "racial regimes" which Puerto Ricans inhabited in New York City and on the island. The historical specificities of "the work race does" can operate on various levels—societal and individual, empirical and narrative—overlapping, contradicting, pushing each other in multiple directions.

Consensual Definitions

All the interviewees agreed that Puerto Ricans born and raised in New York during the great migration from the island in the 1940s and 1950s did not highlight racial differences among their Puerto Rican friends. [...] Aura Hernández told how as a child, "I don't think I saw Puerto Ricans with colors. I just saw them as Puerto Ricans. "Black" meant *moreno americano*. We looked at black Puerto Ricans and we saw them as Puerto Ricans.... I looked in the mirror and didn't see "white." I saw myself as Puerto Rican" (Aura Hernández [a] and [b]).

This allegedly race-blind social vision of the New York-born Puerto Ricans contrasted with the narrators' memories of their parents' and grandparents' generations in Puerto Rico as well as of other Puerto Ricans on the island. Gillie Rodríguez mentioned how islanders obsessively ferreted out traces of blackness in their neighbors and co-workers, making sly racist comments. "Those Puerto Ricans from the island—they smell it!" she cried (G. Rodríguez). Gladys Lugo agreed, commenting that her mother and extended island family were "very prejudiced against black people" (Lugo). Odette Pabón attributed her own more flexible racial understandings to the fact that she did not grow up around her grandfather and island cousins, who "constantly compared themselves to other people—'ay, yo soy un poquito más blanco,', like they do here [in Puerto Rico]" (O. Pabón). Indeed, several narrators claimed that their parents had originally emigrated to New York because their families of origin had refused to let them marry a person of African descent (Aura? Hernández; G. Rodríguez [a] and [b]; Lugo; O. Pabón).

On the other hand, Puerto Rico, however racist a place, still could countenance racial mixing; interviewees who considered themselves "white" affirmed this. [...] Marie Lebrón, whose light-skinned mother married her very dark father in New

York, remembered that her mother rarely spoke of racial hostilities on the island; rather, her mother told her that among poor people in Puerto Rico, racial differences had been immaterial. The most important thing was to marry and establish oneself in a home and job. Gillie Rodríguez excitedly noted that in Puerto Rico, blacks could become professionals—something she had never witnessed in New York. The boundaries of racial acceptance, although they existed, were markedly different in Puerto Rico than in New York—more subtle and individually flexible, if still persistent.

Once in New York, racial distinctions among Puerto Ricans seemed to diminish even further.[2] There, the primary ethno-racial boundaries remembered were those demarcating Puerto Ricans from other groups. The narrators agreed that the Bronx was more ethnically and racially diverse than El Barrio and some other areas of Manhattan, which were filled primarily by Puerto Ricans (Aida, Aura, and Victor Hernández; Matta; G. Pabón). This could have an effect on the New York-born generation's friendship options.

However, the narrators practically unanimously recalled an ethno-racial homogeneity in their intimate socializing, regardless of where they lived in the city. Marta Suárez told of African Americans, Cubans, Dominicans, and Puerto Ricans all living in the same buildings in the Bronx during the 1940s and 1950s. The Latin Americans often attended the same Catholic churches. But in her recollections these groups had very little interaction with one another. She remembered African Americans in particular as very distinct from the Spanish Caribbean groups; they spoke a different language, ate different foods, listened to different music, and were Protestant rather than Catholic.

[...] Not only did Puerto Ricans tend to be lighter-skinned than "the folks in Harlem," he alleged, but they dressed, danced, spoke, and even moved differently. Pabón insisted that African Americans' and Puerto Ricans' ethnic performances differed dramatically, with all Puerto Ricans, regardless of phenotype, sharing a common style.

Gladys Matta, who lived in the Bronx, talked of African American neighbors exchanging food and watching out for her, even sharing tales of personal travails with her as she worked at the neighborhood corner store. Friendly neighbors they might be, but never *amigas íntimas*—to invite into her home, have a party or attend a dance with, consider part of the close family-friend network. In these intimate spaces, she insisted, Puerto Ricans bonded solely with Puerto Ricans. [...]

[...]

Most of the narrators, however, recalled the streets of New York as a battleground, where different ethnic or racial groups frequently clashed over territorial boundaries. Gladys Lugo spoke sadly of her brothers having to defend themselves in fistfights with the Italians and Irish whose neighborhoods her family integrated. Marie Lebrón remembered her family being denied entrance to an apartment building in the Bronx, and later living under the opprobrium of Italians, Irish, Greeks, and Jews who resented their presence. She trembled with fear when recalling the blows her sister suffered from African American girls on the way home from school. [...].

The U.S.'s rigidly binary racial system that insisted on dividing people into the categories of "white" or "black" loomed over the ethno-racial complexity of New York neighborhoods, schools, and workplaces. Interactions with state institutions often forced Puerto Ricans to choose one side or the other of the dominant racial divide. Many elected to officially identify as "white" or were offended when categorically branded as "black," even when they acknowledged their own racially mixed ancestry. Luis Quiñones told of being taken for black by police in a Southern state—no laughing matter. George Pabón chuckled as he remembered the confusion of a military officer who could not definitively determine whether George was white or black. In the end, the officer turned to George's birth certificate, which listed him as "white." George's mother, María, chimed in to reminisce about the creation of such state documents. Although her Puerto Rican husband was black, she had applied for her children's birth certificates. As a result, both children were recorded as "white." Several of her husband's family members had done the same, ensuring that their very dark-skinned babies were officially defined as "white." "They didn't want to be the same as American blacks, you see," she asserted.[3] Such stories confirm many scholars' assertions that Puerto Ricans have been historically forced into the dominant racial binary by institutional structures and agents and that they frequently resisted being identified with African Americans, who unequivocally occupied the lowest rung of the racial hierarchy (Aranda 2007; Duany 2002; Thomas 2009, 2010; Rodríguez 1994, 2009).

Even those Puerto Ricans who tried publically to claim their blackness could be rebuffed. Marie Lebrón recalled a confounding incident in her sister's classroom: the teacher asked blacks and whites to stand up while "doing a survey." When Lebrón's sister stood with the black children, the teacher asked her where her parents were from. Upon hearing Puerto Rico, the teacher told her to sit down. "She came home con-fun-di-da. She'd always thought that she was black, and here they were telling her she couldn't be!"[4] Understanding herself as both Puerto Rican and black, but taunted by African-American schoolmates and denied her blackness by Anglo teachers, Lebrón's sister faced multiple levels of racialized exclusions in New York, enforced by both adults in state-run institutions and other children.

[...]

Despite their insistence on the racial undifferentiatedness of their own national group, Puerto Ricans struggled with how to define themselves and others in such a context. Carving out a working definition of blackness proved difficult for Marie Lebrón and her sisters, who braved street challenges from African American girls and teachers' rejection of their claims to blackness. Gillie Rodríguez, who did not identify as black, reported that none of the immigrants who surrounded her were "white." "Everyone in New York was where their parents were from. No one said they were 'American' except the American blacks. And the WASPS—like you—but I didn't know any of those then." Marie Lebrón, however, who articulated her blackness as a defining characteristic in her identity, disagreed. *"Sólo había blancos y de color. Los blancos eran de Europa—Italianos, Irlandeses, judíos. Y los de color eran los negros y puertorriqueños negros.* [pause] *y los otros puertorriqueños, de cualquier raza."* Dark-skinned Lebrón knew the pain and power of anti-black racism as the light-skinned Rodríguez never could. She also insisted—after reflection—on the unity of all Puerto Ricans, their solidarity in marginalization.

Making Further Racial Moves

[...]

Marie Lebrón identified as a black Puerto Rican [...]. [...], to Lebrón, racial and ethnic difference signified vulnerability, exclusion, and pain. [...] She recounted a memory from her early childhood of how her family was turned away from an apartment that her light-skinned mother had rented in the Bronx once the landlord and other tenants saw her dark-skinned father. Weeping, she told me how she and her family remained stranded in the street with all their personal belongings until a Puerto Rican friend of her mother's found them another apartment nearby. She then turned to another tale of her mother protesting the rude behavior of a Jewish woman at a New York hospital. The woman taunted Lebrón's mother, calling out " 'Why don't you go back to your country!' and my mother said—look, ma-am, better to have a country than to have none! They were Jewish—it was a Jewish hospital. That woman was furious! All red with fury, and all the other Jewish women around us, by the time we got to the window. And my mother, she was so peaceful. I couldn't believe she had said such a thing!"

Discrimination in the U.S. could be both racial and ethno-national—for Lebrón, these identities fused and reinforced each other in a narrative laced with physi-

cal threats and material vulnerability. She dwelt at length on her dark-skinned father's disabling accident, his tragic death while she was still a child, being left alone
in charge of the family as her mother worked double shifts, an assault which her
mother suffered walking home from a night shift job, the analogous attacks which
she and her sisters suffered by hostile neighborhood children—often African Americans—and her having to quit school early, despite her love of learning, to support her
mother and four younger siblings.

Lebrón closed the interview with a long description of a recent incident in the
suburban San Juan condominium where she presently lived. Several neighbors, all
white and economically comfortable, had gathered to meet the new "amigo" of a di-
vorcee friend, also white. "You could feel the coldness when they walked in. Everyone talking and everything still, but you could feel it. He's a *black* man. Puertorriqueño. You know, with his hair all up and everything. Maybe it was how he presented
himself, and maybe because this lady [with him] was so *white*, but you could feel it.
And these are people I *know*! And I thought—if you feel that way about *him*, how do
you feel about *me*? You've been accepting me for what I can do for you? Or for what I
am?" When a neighbor later informed Lebrón that her husband had forbidden her to
invite the new couple to their house because of the man's "appearance and attitude,"
Lebrón was angered, but did not openly challenge the woman, fearing the "loss of the
friendship." Instead, she had simply declined the woman's invitations to socialize.
Racism, then, lurked in the heart of moneyed, well-intentioned Puerto Ricans.

Despite such insidious betrayals, Lebrón remained very clear that Puerto Rican
race relations for her were preferable to those in the U.S. Overriding her acute awareness of social limits on the island (her physical self-presentation of contained female
respectability, with meticulously straightened hair and precise, controlled speech—
so different than the "*black* man...with his hair all up"—carefully acknowledged these
limits), Lebrón continued to articulate a deep identification with her Puerto Ricanness. "In Puerto Rico, I feel more [long pause] I feel like I can go anywhere. Like in
the States, there were times, when I was younger, when I'd say, God, I'd never be able
to go to Florida. I mean, this is as a *child*, ... I'd think, I'm here, I'm born here, and
there are so many places I can't go!" In the end, Puerto Rico's racism, which subtly
limited social intimacy between those identifying as white and those aggressively asserting a public black identity, was much safer than the brutal, often state-supported,
rigidly bifurcated racial hostility of the U.S., which affected even a careful, quiet, "respectable" black woman such as Lebrón.

[...]

In her closing words to me, Marie Lebrón returned to the proud black man who met such opprobrium at the Puerto Rican dinner party. Approvingly, she stated, "He knew who he was, he was proud. He had to be ready for the fact that other people aren't always going to accept you." Immediately afterwards, in response to my question regarding whether Puerto Ricans were one ethnic group, without distinctions of race, as historians often imply, she stated clearly, calmly, "yes, all my friends who were Puerto Rican were black, white. We all accepted one another." Lived racial exclusion in the Puerto Rican island present only fueled memories of a reconstructed, racism-free New York Puerto Rican community.

[...]

Conclusion

[...]

Race slips in and out of the interstices of island-dwelling New York Puerto Ricans' memory tales, winking, laughing, and moaning. In their life stories, these New York Puerto Ricans in San Juan spoke about race in many voices—sometimes in a homogenous, authoritative way, but also breaking out into ever more complex insights about community building, the birth of political consciousness, pain, and possibility. The transplanted New York Puerto Ricans who shared their stories with me created their understandings of race from their own life experiences and from broader discourses and political practices circulating in both post-war New York City and late twentieth-century suburban San Juan.

All the interviewees articulated a common narrative about a racially transcendent solidarity among oppressed Puerto Ricans in New York. Internal racial differences among Puerto Ricans, at least in the U.S. context, they insisted, were unimportant. In this, and in their insistence on the racialized discrimination that Puerto Ricans faced in New York, the narrators agreed with scholars who have emphasized the power of U.S. hegemonic racial regimes, most importantly a black-white hierarchical binary that Puerto Ricans uncomfortably negotiated and within which they rarely clearly fit. This racialization of Puerto Ricans within the U.S., the narrators noted, was imposed both by the state—through schools, the military, and the production of official documents, among other sites—and by the non-Puerto Rican individuals and groups who surrounded them—neighbors, classmates, bosses, landlords, even people standing in line at a hospital. Generally, these Puerto Ricans in New York, even when identifying as black or maintaining cordial relations with African American neighbors and workmates, resisted identification as African American, carving out instead an uneasy "non-white" identity. The narrators insisted that a hegemonic racism operated on the island also, albeit in a subtler, more individualized and more flexible form—none of the interviewees discussed the ways that institutions such as the state, mass media, or schools fostered the silencing or denigration of blackness.

A few of the narrators, however, also spoke passionately about the central importance of blackness in defining their own identity, both in New York and on the island. They articulated multiple meanings of race. New political consciousness and racial identities could emerge from lived, intimate relationships with other Afro-diasporic peoples. Blackness could function as a source of joy and empowerment in solidarity; for another narrator it could be a source of terrible pain and suffering. Puerto Ricans could both practice racism and transcend racial differences. Blackness could be biological or unrelated to phenotype, the product of a group's positioning in a colonial political economy. For some narrators, then, multiple interpretations of race could exist *simultaneously* and the emotions related to them could vary tremendously.

[...]

SECTION IV.

The Insidious and Ineffable Violence of Racial Discrimination

CHAPTER 12

The Social and Educational Inequalities of Black Students Studying English in Rural Puerto Rico

By Elena González Rivera

[...]

[...] It is common knowledge in Orocovis that Florencio is a very isolated black community. [...]

[...]

Living in a small, unindustrialized town like Orocovis for decades had its advantages and delights. Through the course of time, things stayed pretty much the same, making prevalent patterns of behavior visibly evident. The black members of our community were visible because they walked on the main road instead of riding in cars. They had poor roads leading to their homes, so they walked barefoot the distance from their homes to the main road with their shoes in their hands. Most of them lived in a sector of our community that I will call Florencio. The women were practicing Catholics and attended mass on Saturdays. They also worked doing domestic chores, while the men worked the farms of the white members of the community. At school, during recess and lunchtime, their children played mostly among themselves. They made up a large proportion of the Special Education clientele of our school, and many of them tended to have hygiene and health problems as well as a history of academic failures.

I wanted to better understand my students from Florencio because I believed it was the only way that I could teach them well. In order to formulate strategies for improving their classroom interaction patterns and suggest changes to school policy, it was necessary to delve into the social and cultural reality they experienced in the

Originally published in *CENTRO: Journal of the Center for Puerto Rican Studies* 20(1): 73–95, 2008.

black community of Florencio. This was achieved through an ethnographic study of Florencio (González 1997).

[...]

In rural Puerto Rico, students have practically no contact with native English speakers except for their English teachers, and even then many English teachers in rural Puerto Rico are non-native speakers of English. They are in a foreign language environment as opposed to a second-language environment. The bulk of students' interactions in English take place in the classroom with their classmates, all of who are also non-native speakers. In this particular sociocultural reality, a sense of identification with and acceptance by fellow classmates may work in favor of second-language learning. However, black students in predominantly white classrooms who are experiencing social distance and isolation due to race within their own first-language environment may demonstrate resistance to second-language learning. It may explain their tendency to want to remain silent during the English class and their general lack of motivation to learn English. [...]

[...]

[...] I found black first-graders from Florencio tended to play together with their cousins. If one of them fought, the rest of them followed, forming a protective shield against the aggressor. The older or larger children protected the younger or smaller ones. They spoke to each other in whispers or by shouting. When someone from another classroom approached them, it was usually a relative from another grade. They checked up on each other frequently. Very rarely did they interact with the white students or play with them.

In an interview, one of the black first-graders said: "I don't have any friends. The other kids don't want to play with me. They always tell me to go away and they hit me." On the occasions that I observed them, they generally acted in a protective manner towards each other and played in isolation from the rest of the student body. Their social interactions were exclusively among members of their primary group. [...]

Racial inequalities

In Puerto Rico, ambivalent attitudes toward race have been documented (González 1992; Lewis 1968; Rosario Carrión 1940; Seda Bonilla 1991; Victima 1996). Lewis is emphatic in stating that in Puerto Rico, social acceptance is determined by the whiteness of a person's skin. [...] This attitude is reflected in popular phrases (Rosario and Carrión

1940; Cancel 1995) and racial categories (Seda Bonilla 1991). One of the phrases that Rosario and Carrión mention is *"Nunca falta un mime en un vaso de leche"* (A glass of milk never fails to attract small, black insects). This saying has a connotative significance. It implies that a black person within a white environment is a cause of irritation.

On the other hand, others (Cancel 1995) insist that racial references in language are not a sign of ambivalence but instead denote racism and are neither accidental nor casual. [...] Even in our classroom practices and in textbook discourse, you can see the presence of the prevalent ideology of whitening (*blanqueamiento*), revealing an attempt to undermine, silence, trivialize, or simplify the contributions of blacks in Puerto Rico (Godreau et al. 2007). To negate the real contributions of blacks may be a sign of ignorance of the true nature of Puerto Rican culture (Zenón 1975). Today, these same basic problems of ambivalence towards race, social non-acceptance due to skin color, outright racism, preferred *mestizaje,* and the invisibility of the contributions of blacks still exist in Puerto Rico.

[...]

Methodology

During the academic year 1996-1997, I conducted a microethnographic case study of eight black ESL students from the community of Florencio. Four of the subjects were male, and four were female. Six of the subjects were in the seventh grade and two were in the ninth grade. Their ages ranged from 11 to 16 years. Only two students had the appropriate age for their grade levels, while the rest were older than their classmates.

[...]

Orocovis and Florencio

Orocovis is situated in the center of the island of Puerto Rico in the highest part of the central mountain range. [...] It is one of the largest towns on the island, with a territorial expansion of 42,313 acres of land divided into seventeen sectors or *barrios.* The climate of Orocovis is cool, unlike that of the coastal region. The economy of Orocovis depends on agriculture. It produces coffee, tobacco, bananas, plantains, minor fruits, a variety of vegetables, and cattle. In 1990, it had a population of 25,155 that decreased to 21,151 by 1999 (Population 2000). These statistics confirm a pattern of a diminishing population when compared to the 1960 figure of almost 30,000 inhabitants. [...]

[...] [I]n 1815 the Spanish crown passed a law called the *Real Cédula de Gracias* in order to promote agriculture and industry. With the passage of this law, black slave trade in Puerto Rico increased and, with it, the slave population. Prior to the passage of this law, it was difficult to find slaves in the interior of the island. By 1847, the total population in Orocovis was 2,731 inhabitants. Of these, 811 (30 percent) were of black descent including *mulattos*, freed slaves, or slaves. By 1872, the total population had increased to 6,001, and 2,380 (40 percent) were blacks. Of these, 103 (2 percent) were still slaves. Others may have been *cimarrones* or blacks hiding in the countryside in order to escape from slavery. [...]

[...]

Geographically, the community of Florencio is located in the sector of Orocovis known as Consejo (See Figure 1) isolated from the adjacent sectors of Dos Bocas and Cruz. Once you enter the community and drive a short distance, the first visible structure is a modest Catholic Church. Just as you approach the church, the road opens in two directions. If you go to the right, you enter the sector Hoyo Negro (Black Pit), but if you go up the hill and shortly after turn to the left, you will arrive at Pueblito, the poorest sector of Florencio. The name most commonly associated with Florencio was Hoyo Negro. There are different versions as to the origin of the name. Various theories were offered, including a reference to the skin color of the black members of Florencio, a reference to the type of primitive housing that predominated in the community (Caquías 2006b), or even a reference to the black blood sausages supposedly sold in the community. The most common theory, which I heard repeatedly from many people throughout the 25 years I lived in Orocovis, was the racial one. [...] [B]ut in Florencio there are whites as well as blacks. When the wife of an important farm product distributor built her second home there, she worked to bring about a change in the community's name. Through her efforts, the community's name was changed from Hoyo Negro to Florencio and officially publicized by means of an enormous sign marking its entrance.

[...]

Kinship ties

[...]

For purpose of analysis, I divided the seven families in the study into three groups based on their close kinship ties. The three family groups also tended to live close to each other. For example, the Flores family lived in the economically critical area called Pueblito, located to the left once you entered Florencio. The Díaz family lived in the area known as La Mina, located to the right once in Florencio. The Meléndez family lived in El Limón, located at the entrance of Florencio.

In the first traceable generation of the Flores family, the great grandmothers were sisters. [...] In the second generation of the Flores family, the grandmothers were also sisters. [...] They are the oldest living members of Pueblito. The parents of the third generation are all first cousins. The first marriage in the fourth generation of the Flores family was between second cousins. When the family trees of the other two families are examined, you see a similar pattern of intermarriage between *primos hermanos*.

[...]

Living Standards

[...] Oscar Flores had the lowest standard of living of the seven households that made up the three families in the study. [...]

Oscar's house did not have running water, a bathroom, or a telephone. The children had to be bathed in the front yard in a large tub with a hose connected to the plumbing of the house next door. Sandra, Oscar's mother, connected that same hose to the old-style washing machine she also kept there. Occasionally, and only during the day, they would ask permission to use the bathroom next door, yet most of the time they did their necessities in the neighboring woods or in the area around their home. She had just recently gotten electricity in her home, and they owned a run-down car. The eleven family members lived in a small wooden three-bedroom house. The mother cooked on an open fire. The hills leading to their house were unpaved and very eroded, requiring a four-wheel-drive vehicle. Due to the road condition, the municipal garbage truck could not enter Pueblito; therefore, the people created a makeshift dump about a 300 yards distance from its entrance. Walking on foot past it, you had to hold your breath and look away. Both of Oscar's parents, Sandra and Rafael, were illiterate. No one read the newspaper; there were no books, printed materials, or writing paper of any kind in the house.

The living standard of the student, Marta Marrero Díaz, who represented the Díaz family in Florencio, was not as critical as Oscar's. Her father, Julio Rivas, rebuilt their wooden home in cement. They now had a two-bedroom structure. They had a well-paved road, running water, electricity, an old-style washing machine, television, an old car, but no telephone. Marta's mother liked the old-style washing machine because she said it cleaned better than the automatic ones, so she didn't have to re-wash by hand to get things as white as she wanted.

Rose Casiano Meléndez lived in the sector El Limón close to the entrance of Florencio. She represented the Meléndez family and was the student who enjoyed the highest standard of living of all the other students in the study. Their house was off the main road leading to town and had a motorized gate at the entrance. The well-constructed cement road leading to their house was very wide and steep. Rosa lived in a four-bedroom cement house. They had a gas stove, running water, an automatic washing machine, television, radio, telephone, and two cars. Her father, Emilio Casiano Díaz, had a driver's license, and three of his children had driving permits. He worked full-time as a fumigator for the Department of Agriculture and worked in agriculture during his vacations. His oldest daughter was studying to be a nurse. It was the only household of the seven with a small library and an encyclopedia. Like all the mothers in the seven households, Wanda Díaz Meléndez was a full-time housewife.

Just as there were differences among the households, there were also similarities. For example, they were all affected by the location of the municipal dump in their neighborhood. None of the other communities wanted to have the dump placed within their boundaries but since the black community did not have any political power, the dump was placed in Florencio. Ironically the dump became a means of sustenance for the poorest black residents who would visit it daily in search of objects of value. This adverse practice may have contributed to their health problems. Furthermore, all of the houses had very poor illumination. The custom was to turn lights on only after the sun set as a way of conserving electricity. They all lived surrounded by blood relatives. Their social activities included family reunions, religious ceremonies, school activities, and cockfights. Most of the families had migrated to the United States. One grandfather had migrated 35 times, and one of the fathers had lived 6 months out of the year during 16 years in the United States until he had enough money to complete the construction of his home. All of the students in the case study valued their vernacular. They used Spanish all the time once outside the classroom, and when surveyed, they confirmed their preference for Spanish as a means of instruction. For example, one of the fathers expressed value for the Spanish language. He was very conscious of this when they were living in the States. He insisted that his daughter speak Spanish at home, although she was not using Spanish with her friends and classmates. He reminded her that when they returned to Puerto Rico, she was going to need her Spanish. At first she demonstrated a little resistance, but later complied with her father's request.

[...]

Social inequalities

The community had been labeled with the expression Black Pit that had negatively connoted the color of their skin. Although the name was officially changed, the effect of the change was minimal because the relationships between the black and white members of the community remained very much the same. The name change was purely cosmetic.

The custom of intermarriage limited their interactions with people outside of their immediate family group and resulted in a lot of inbreeding. Family members were neighbors as well as friends. All of their social activities entailed the celebration of important holidays exclusively with their family members. If they celebrated the holidays with people outside of the family circle, it was usually work related. They also went to school activities and religious services but, even there, they mostly kept to themselves. Once in a blue moon, they visited their relatives in Santa Isabel.

They did not have equal access to government services such as road repair and regular garbage collection because they had no political power. At school, faculty members wrote letters and had meetings with the mayor on their behalf and achieved resumption of minimal services. When Sila Maria Calderón won the governorship in 2000, she created the Project of Special Communities. Florencio became one of the special communities, and for the first time, they had a voice in deciding what type of government help was most important to them.

The low standard of living as well as the limited work opportunities are intimately related; nonetheless, unless the members of the community acquire new skills through training and education, it is very difficult to see an improvement in these areas. The social injustices, previously narrated and described through the history of the black community of Florencio, have a direct impact on the black children of Florencio and on their learning environment. It becomes more evident as they tell us their life histories.

Life histories

Despite all of the common factors among the three families, there were marked differences in their lifestyles. It was the range of subtle differences in their lifestyles, [...], that coincided with the children's degree of opportunities for academic success. The more detailed description of their personal lives will make the relationship of standard of living and school achievement clearer. It will also become evident how within the school environment they suffered inequalities for being members of the black community of Florencio.

a.) Oscar Díaz Flores, a Member of the Flores Family

The community of Pueblito was made up of seven households with 14 adults and 22 children, all of whom were members of the Flores family. Oscar's mother, Sandra Flores Díaz, was 33 years old and had completed the fifth grade. His father, Rafael Díaz Flores, was 39 years old and also studied as far as the fifth grade. They had nine children, and the oldest girl was handicapped. [...] When the child napped, [Sandra] washed the family clothes. Compared to all the other households in Pueblito, Oscar lived in the worst conditions. Their house was very overcrowded with only three bedrooms for eleven people. [...] The absence of a bathroom or running water made it difficult to eradicate problems of poor hygiene.

At the beginning of his academic life, Oscar confronted many difficulties. Perhaps the greatest drawback was that Oscar had not been enrolled in school until the age of nine. During that time, he lived in an even poorer and more isolated area than Pueblito and was accidentally discovered by the special education teacher, Nelly Fernández, in her routine community visits.

[...] At first, Oscar's parents did not want to enroll him in school, but the social worker told her that they could be sent to jail if Oscar was not enrolled. The threat convinced them, so, shortly afterwards, Rafael Díaz Flores accompanied his son to his first day of class. After initial psychological evaluations, Oscar was said to have moderate mental retardation. Learning to read was perhaps Oscar's greatest challenge. His second- and third-grade teacher recalled that Oscar first learned the mechanics of reading at the age of 12. Oscar admitted that having to learn English was the most difficult school task for him. Now in the seventh grade, he felt better in the English class because he had been handing in his assigned tasks and receiving help from his classmates.

All of these impediments were increased by the fact that Oscar stood out from the crowd because he was much taller and better developed than most students of his age. Yet members of the school community realized that, despite his advanced physical development, Oscar had remained academically behind the average student. He, along with several of his cousins with similar physical characteristics, soon became labeled by the school's policeman as *La Fuerza de Choque* (the Riot Squad), a term that soon caught on. *The Riot Squad* was made up of Tomás, Oscar, and Elmer, and everyone knew they couldn't mess with this trio, but later the term was used to refer to all of the kids from Florencio. Two teachers considered the term an affectionate one, yet others saw it as having negative undertones. The Spanish teacher, Emma Sandoval, saw the term as a label with negative connotations, a label that did not help her sixth grade homeroom rid itself of a bad self-image. She reported that her students would confidentially tell her: "They would point us out. They would point us out. We were the dummies. They would not give us any chances. They did not call on us like you do." [...]

Emma also recalled an incident at a faculty meeting where the director of the school referred to her homeroom using the term "The Riot Squad." She asked for a turn to speak and told everyone that she did not want anyone to use that term in relation to her group. She preferred that the group be called group 6-2. A large number of the faculty members laughed at her petition. She insisted that she was trying to improve the self-image of her group. She also said that she thought the group was not all that bad and that they were working. Her students had explicitly told her that the term "The Riot Squad" referred not to their discipline but to their learning. The implication was that they were big and strong, but they were not bright.

b.) Marta Marrero Díaz, a Member of the Díaz Family

Marta Marrero Díaz lived with her mother, father, and younger brother in Florencio, in the sector called La Mina. Hers was a small family compared to Oscar's. Her house was located on the main road a short distance from the church. She lived surrounded by her grandparents, aunts and uncles, and cousins, whose houses were lined up one next to the other. The conditions of the road were much better compared to Pueblito. Her grandmother, Aurora Díaz Martínez, was the sister of Orlando from Sector Pueblito. This was the blood link between the two groups of families.

Marta's mother, Marta Díaz Díaz, was 34 years old and a full-time housewife who worked four days a week picking coffee beans. She was the only working mother of all the households. During her spare time, she would collect aluminum cans and sell it to a middleman in order to help ends meet. She and her husband had completed the sixth grade and later studied plumbing at a vocational school in Barranquitas; nevertheless, neither of them ever actually worked as plumbers. Marta's mother thought she had learned everything she needed to know in order to raise her children, and now it was her children who needed to prepare themselves for their future.

Marta's father, Julio Ramos Rolón, was 35 years old. He had been my student many years ago. He completed the ninth grade, worked primarily as a farmer, and later on as an employee for an ornamental plant business. He injured his back while working and was pensioned due to hernia and blood pressure problems.

The first year that Marta started school she had acute absenteeism. She accumulated a total of thirty-five absences and eventually had to repeat the first grade. She did not like school and did not want to get on the school bus in the morning. Her mother would have to spank her in order to make her obey because she had no interest in school. The next year Marta repeated first grade and passed it, although she still did not know how to read. Her second-grade teacher helped her a bit with reading. Even so, her general achievement level was low, and her absences remained high (fourteen absences during the year). The third grade was a complete disaster for Marta. She failed three classes and continued to have a high level of absenteeism. By the fourth grade, she managed to turn things around. She started studying and working hard. Marta recalled, "I knew I could do it." She set out to prove to everyone that she could do the work, and in the process, the work got done and she grew intellectually. Marta was motivated because she had a reason, a purpose, and an aim. The fourth grade teacher motivated her students to read on their own with a project she entitled, A Bridge to Reading.

Marta insisted over and over again that there was no justification for having received Fs in the third grade. Marta truly believed that she knew the material and that the only reason she failed was because her third-grade teacher did not like her. Her seventh-grade homeroom teacher, Elba Sandoval, explained that she immediately sensed Marta's need to redeem herself. She wanted to prove that her failure in the third grade was not her fault. She was stigmatized for being one of the students labeled as "The Riot Squad" and had overcome it at a great price. That is why Elba wanted Marta to attend the honor roll activity and receive recognition in the company of her family members. In the seventh-grade English class, she handed in her work on schedule and completed it without anyone's help. She read independently and voluntarily in English.

c.) Rosa Casiano Meléndez, A Member of the Meléndez Family

The Meléndez family did not live within the perimeters of Florencio, although they did live very close by. There was a remote control gate and a small side gate at the entrance of their house. Their household was composed of the grandmother, the mother, the father, and her five brothers and sisters. In front of the gate across the main road, there was a makeshift basket where Rosa's brothers, cousins and uncles wore away the hours playing basketball. The basket was hung at a point on the main road that was curved and that had poor visibility of oncoming cars, making it a bit of a hazard. Rosa's two grandmothers were next-door neighbors. Her maternal grandmother, Doña Ana Díaz Díaz, lived with her. Her paternal grandmother, Doña Paula Díaz Díaz, lived down the hill in a separate house. Both women were sisters, making Marta's parents *primos hermanos*.

Rosa's mother, Wanda Meléndez Díaz, was 43 years old and worked as a full-time housewife. She was the only mother of the eight subjects in the study who had obtained a high school diploma. As a hobby, Wanda read from one of the encyclopedias they had purchased for their children. Wanda said that if it had not been for the high cost of university studies, she would have obtained a degree because she liked to study. Instead, she married right out of high school and started her family. In total, they had six children.

Wanda was convinced that the most important legacy she and her husband could leave their children was an education. She thought that with the scholarships available nowadays, a university degree was more accessible to those interested in studying.

Rosa's father, Samuel Meléndez Báez, was 45 years old and had a steady government job. It had not always been that way. The family had to endure many hardships in order to save up enough money to buy a piece of land and build their house. The father would migrate to the United States for six or seven months each year during the harvest season in Pennsylvania and Connecticut. The owner of the apple and fruit orchards would send him a plane ticket that he had to repay along with housing and food expenses. In addition to being employed as a migrant worker in the states, the father also worked for a local farmer. Later on, he applied for and got a job with the Agricultural Department in Naranjito. From there, he was transferred to Barranquitas. At the time of the study, he was still working for AFDA, but at the Orocovis branch. He had only a sixth-grade education.

[...]

Both parents worked hard to make it possible for their children to study and be employed. For example, Samuel took the oldest daughter to the university early each morning and picked her up at the end of the day. He also provided Emilio, his oldest son, with daily transportation to and from work. He did this very early in the morning so that he could arrive at work on time. On Christmas Eve, he customarily prepared a roasted pig for his son's boss and celebrated that holiday at his boss's home. He was not with his family on such an important event because he was paying a debt of gratitude to the person who had employed his son.

When we look at Rosa's academic work, we see that although she had some difficulties, she progressed from D's to C's in the first and second grades to C's and B's in the third to seventh grades. She recalls feeling very happy when she started to learn to read because learning to read was an important goal for her. Learning English was also important to her. Rosa was very responsible with her studies, she had impeccable personal hygiene, and her mother frequently visited the school.

Learning Inequalities

Through the life histories, we can see that the standard of living of these black children put them at a disadvantage, not only socially but also educationally. Oscar's parents had many children, were very poor and lived in extremely isolated conditions.

They neglected to send him to school until after he was nine years old. This late initiation in formal education took its toll on him. If he had been enrolled earlier, things might have been different. Marta, on the other hand, was the older of only two children, had a mother who took excellent care of her, an adequate vehicle, a fairly comfortable home, and plenty of running water in her home, making her standard of living much higher than Oscar's. Rosa had the highest standard of living of all the three with two cars, an automatic washing machine, a telephone, driver's licenses, paved roads, and a bathroom in the home. She also had a mother with the academic background to help her do her assignments and a personal library.

It is also evident that their initiation into the mechanics of reading was critical and constituted another disadvantage or inequality. For most of them, literacy acquisition did not occur until the third grade and after multiple failures. Once achieved, they assumed a positive attitude toward learning and demonstrated overall improvements.

The children also reported not being treated equally in relation to the other classmates and being rejected by teachers as well as by the general school population, including non-teaching personnel. They also perceived that they were purposely kept separated from the brighter students within their own grade level. But the greatest educational inequality was being labeled as "dumb" merely because they were part of the black community of Florencio.

The label, "The Riot Squad," negatively connoted their lack of intelligence or inability to compete intellectually with other students. It was like a ghost that followed them everywhere they went. It kept them marginalized and made them an out-group within their linguistic community. They were the focus of ridicule. The label may have been covering up latent feelings of racism never made explicit or public by the white members of the community. The label had the effect of curtailing and controlling the possibilities of academic opportunities and progress for the black children of Florencio. Yet, in response to this label, Marta progressed because she had a mission to redeem herself, to prove herself despite the racial, social, and educational inequalities.

The label coined by the school policeman was repeated by many of the non-teaching personnel, the students, and even the school director and teachers. Everyone knew it was not appropriate to reject others for their skin color, but labeling them (in this case, a covert form of racism) was socially and institutionally accepted. It took enormous resolve, as demonstrated by Marta, to overcome the effect of this covert racism and to overcome the educational inequalities that came with this label and other common labels such as "ese negrito(a)" y "San Martín" in reference to a black saint. Labels, as labeling theory predicts, may become self-fulfilling prophecies (Gouldner in Ballantine, 1989).

Conclusions

[...]

In Florencio, the parents at home and the children at school were labeled with subtle covert racial slurs like members of the Black Pit or "Riot Squad," San Martin or *negritos*, maintaining them separated from the white members of the community and making them outsiders in what should have been *their* community and school. Schools are supposed to strive to make students feel connected. Schools should be places of well-being where students should want to be, where they can feel that they belong, where their teachers are just, caring, and worry about them (Resnick et al, 1997). When the opposite occurs to any group within the school, then we have educational inequality, in this case rooted in social inequality. Furthermore, in their limited circle of social interaction (community and school), they were outsiders. It did not matter that everyone spoke Spanish. They lost their *de facto* membership in the Spanish linguistic community because of their skin color. They were considered outsiders and inferior. Within the classroom, there was an enormous social distance between them and their classmates.

How did being labeled as "The Riot Squad" affect the subjects' motivation to study? Marta became intrinsically motivated to learn English and all other subject areas because she wanted to prove everybody wrong. She was driven to excel, and with the support of her mother was able to overcome her early academic difficulties. Once she learned to read well in her vernacular, her academic work improved enormously. Contrary to Marta, Oscar was affected negatively by the labeling. He felt he was just too old (16 years old) and too big (5'10") to go on to the eighth grade and was thinking of giving up his studies at Dos Bocas and maybe enrolling in a vocational school.

On the other hand, the close kinship ties among the community members of Florencio may have been a way of overcoming the social, economic, and racial difficulties they encountered. Intermarriage as a customary behavioral pattern may have been a survival strategy.

In terms of education and language, it is evident that the households that best promoted learning were the households with the highest standard of living and vice versa. Parents' expectations and support were also fundamental factors in the children's academic success. Spanish functioned as an identity marker because the parents who migrated to the U.S. with their children did not want them to relegate Spanish to a secondary position. They considered Puerto Rico their home base and Spanish their primary language. They also supported and stimulated their children's interest in studying English as a second language, although they did not have the skills to help them with their English tasks.

[...]

CHAPTER 13

Slippery Semantics: Race Talk and Everyday Uses of Racial Terminology in Puerto Rico

By Isar P. Godreau

In July 1995, a fight almost broke out in Ponce, Puerto Rico, when a male friend of Doña Julia called her *"¡so negra!"* (yo' black woman!) as she walked by the streets of her barrio in San Antón.[1] Doña Julia knew her neighbor said this phrase jokingly to call attention to the fact that both of them were black. The verbal gesture established a sort of racial solidarity between them. However, another friend walking besides her interpreted the phrase as an insult and quickly jumped to her defense, declaring: *"¡Oye, Oye, que a esta señora hay que respetarla, ¿sabes?!"* (Hey, hey, you have to respect this lady, you know?!) Holding his rising arm with her hand, Doña Julia appeased him, stating *"Está bien, está bien, no te preocupes, es que él y yo bromeamos así"* (It's ok, it's ok, he and I joke that way).

It is a well-known fact among scholars of race relations in Latin America that racial terminology is highly situational and intimately linked to context of usage. *Negro*, for example, often caries pejorative connotations because of its association with slave status. Yet, in certain interpersonal exchanges such as the one described above, it can also be used to mark racial solidarity or "sameness" among those who openly identify themselves as black. Nonetheless, in other instances, the use of negro or its diminutive form *negrito* (or *negra, negrita*) may communicate affection and intimacy regardless of the skin color of the person to which it refers, but not regardless of the relationship between the speakers. Which meaning is to be ascribed depends on who says it, when, and how.

Likewise, the term *blanquito* is the diminutive for white, but the term is also utilized in Puerto Rico to refer to a person of the upper class, often times with pejorative connotations. Once again, this second sense, although bearing some relationship to skin color, does not depend on phenotypic variations. A wealthy black person may

Originally published in *CENTRO: Journal of the Center for Puerto Rican Studies* 20(2): 4–33, 2008.

be identified as blanquito, while the same may not necessarily be said of a white or light-skinned person who is poor. However, when the person called blanquito is a black person, the label can also be an accusation made for "acting like a white person." When a white person is called a blanquito, the charge has to do with an elitist, snobbish attitude or lifestyle. Other uses of the term blanquito may be deployed with a condescending attitude to describe a person who is too white and unattractive, as in *jincha* (ugly and pale) or *"pote de leche"* (milk container).

Determining the significance of racial categories becomes even more complicated with terms like *trigueño, de color*, and *indio*. The widely used term trigueño, for instance, is often used as a euphemism to classify people considered black because of the belief that negro is offensive. In this case, the meaning is similar to the more old-fashioned term de color (colored). Trigueño however, can also be used to indicate that a person's color is lighter than black or darker than white (Nazario 1961: 348–9; Godreau 2007). This second application responds to a three-tier classificatory system that distinguishes the mixed trigueño from other types that are understood as less phenotypicaly hybrid, such as negro or *blanco*. In such cases, applying trigueño is not necessarily informed by the belief that negro is offensive, but by the attempt to use and "accurate" description in a social context where "mixed" (i.e, trigueño) is interpreted as different from "black."[2]

[...]

The polysemic character of racial terms and its strong dependence on context and history has been an important focus of Latin American and Caribbean scholarship. [...]

In this [work], I argue that operating alongside this variance of factors that influence the use of racial terms, there is a particular linguistic pattern of "race talk" not previously identified in the literature, which I call "slippery semantics." By slippery semantics I mean a recurrent linguistic inconsistency in racial identification processes that takes place when people use different systems or logical grids of racial classification during a single conversation. Such grids can include the use of multiple racial terms to describe the same individual, the consistent use of binary black/white terminology, or the use of the same racial term to describe different "types of phenotypes" during a single narrative event. [...] [E]xamples in this [essay] will show how people can also suspend this multiplicity and adopt binary modes of racial classification that are consistent and clear-cut in the application of black/white identities.

I argue that this tendency towards polyvalency and inconsistency produces a destabilizing effect on the status of "race" as an identity-marker during the course of everyday conversations. This is not to say that Puerto Ricans do not classify each other racially, or that they do not act according to the racist implications of such classifications, but simply that such classificatory practices are not consistently or permanently verbalized as pertaining to fixed racial identities. Rather, what we see is a constant variance in the system of classification itself, combined with the recurrent switching of color and racial terms, and a general apprehension over the public ascription of racial labels to individuals. This slippery effect, I also argue, can reflect and construct different interpersonal relationships among those implicated or involved in the conversation indexing solidarity, intimacy, distance, or respect among speakers. In that process, social identities that go beyond race come into play, making racial meaning dependent and conflated with the social cleavages they summon during the conversation. Thus, more than determining the social weight of "race" vis-a-vis other identities, my aim in this article is to highlight their interdependence. In that sense, my concern is not "race-relations" per se or even "racial identity" as an autonomous category, but rather the everyday use of "racial identity labels" to mediate, represent, and reproduce social identities and hierarchies in the context of quotidian social encounters.

[...]

Examples of slippery ambiguity
The matriarch who took me into the community of San Antón in Ponce, Doña Julia, often made open reference to her black identity saying *"Yo soy una negra de San Antón"* (I am a black woman from San Antón). Her son and daughter were also equally vocal about their blackness. In fact, they objected to people using intermediate terms such as jabao (high yellow), mulato, and trigueño when referring to them. According to them, you are either blanco or negro, and on several occasions I heard them declare themselves very proud to be black.

Example 1
One day, concerned about her son's academic progress, Doña Julia went to visit the vocational public school to speak to her son's teacher. During their conversation, the teacher talked about the absence of black teachers and administrators in public schools and the negative impact this could have upon young black students, like her son. These were not his words exactly, though. He used at least five different terms to refer to the victims of racism during the course of the conversation with Doña Julia: trigueño, mulato, de color, *de barrio* (from the barrio), and *humilde* (of humble background).

The teacher often hesitated before using some of the more racially explicit terms. This is not unusual in exchanges where speakers do not know each other well, or are somewhat unsure about their interlocutor's racial identity politics. Exchanges like this one are often characterized by a certain nervousness and un-easiness, not just with the process of racial classification in general, but also with the term negro in particular. Thus, besides the use of euphemisms such as "de color" (colored) and the constant switching of terms, it is not unusual for people to stammer, hesitate, pause, repeat themselves, or look for comparisons, such as stating that "He's the same color as so-and-so" in order to avoid the stigma and the social hazards of using negro.

Pejorative connotations that equate the word negro with slave status can be traced to 19th century practices in Puerto Rico that distinguish between a non-white free population who called themselves *morenos,* or *pardos,* and the slave popula-tion who were "racialized" as "black" by both whites and non-whites (Nazario 1961: 346–7). In the Hispanic Caribbean, this negro-slave equivalency was facilitated by the rapid growth of a population of free blacks and mulattos who grew to become a majority and who sought to distinguish themselves from slaves (Mintz 1974; Torres-Saillant 2000: 1094; Guerra 1998: 222).

Much of the tentativeness and coyness that complements the use of euphe-misms has to do with this historical baggage and the challenges of coming to terms with the history of slavery. Yet slippery semantics is not just a cluster of euphe-mism. In fact, in some conversations people can use negro as part of the cluster of color terminologies and later substitute it by a term like *prieto* or *como yo* (like me) and so forth. And even in those instances when negro is avoided, people do not just use one, but various alternative euphemistic terms to describe the same individual during the course of the conversation.

Moreover, people often use these clusters of racial terms in combination with others that refer to social class, such as los *pobres, gente humilde, gente de barrio;* for the affluent, there are the terms blanquitos, *elitistas,* "those people from over there," the *come mierda* (stuck-up), o la *gente de buena familia* (of a wealthy family). The constant mixing of these terminologies and switching of racial terms in everyday in-teractions not only upsets the semantic stability of race as an as identity but also incorporates other, relevant dimensions of class, lifestyle, and education into the con-versation. In this case, when the teacher talked about racism and the lack of black role models in school, he defined those who are privileged and those who are less privileged in term of race but sometimes also in terms of class and class-informed attitudes such as de barrio (from the barrio) and humilde (humble).

[...]

In this sense, slippery semantics can help people construct alternative solidarities based on multiple positionalities such as social class, gender, religion, or political affiliation. Rather than level out and fix racial identities by using the binary terminology of blanco/negro, the constant oscillation, in some conversations, among terms allows for a multidimensional interpretation of power relationships in everyday encounters. Thus, using—or not using—multiple terms during the conversation may itself be an important factor in establishing sameness, difference, distance, or intimacy between speakers.

Example 2

In the next example, interlocutors did not build alternate solidarities based on class or other socially relevant criteria. Rather, the speaker's attempt was to distance himself from blackness and its assigned low social status through the popular aspiration of whitening or *"mejorar la raza,"* which literally means to "improve one's race" by having offspring with someone who is of a lighter complexion.[3]

The interview took place in 1996 in the central plaza of the city of Ponce. Sitting in one of the plaza's benches, a Puerto Rican man in his late 60s assured me that in Puerto Rico "there isn't any racism. Here blacks join with whites." He continued to explain:

"—I've got a son that lives in Texas, really white with blue eyes, and he married a *negrita* (diminutive form for black woman)."

"—Did anybody say anything? I asked."

"—Well, what can we say? She's a *triguueña elegante* (an elegant black woman). The only one who griped a little was me. I was improving the race (*adelantando la raza*), and he pushed it back"—he laughed. "Then my daughter—that one lives here, because, you see the way I am (referring to his looks), but my wife is white with green eyes, and I come from a white family too, you see? Then my daughter, who's a blond with blue eyes, also married a trigueño. His father is very negrito [black, diminutive form], but his mother is white with blue eyes. He was like me, trying to improve the race (mejorar la raza)."

"—And what's this thing about improving?" I asked.

"—Well, trying that they be white and not be prietos (black), so they won't have to pull their hair so much when they comb it."

"—And why do you think that people say "improve" toward the white side and "go backwards" toward the black side?"

"—That's what's always been said around here. Let's improve the race a little, so the kids can comb themselves better."

"—And don't you think that is racism?"

"—Well, it might be racism, but our way, the Puerto Rican way. Because, one likes to be a little lighter. Not me, because I'm "Puerto Rican colored,[4]" because I'm not prieto (black), I'm indio. Not this guy [pointing to a man who was sitting next to him], 'cause this guy's trigueño, but he has *pelo malo* (bad hair) right? [the man nodded]."

Besides the salience of *blanqueamiento* as a strategy that informs this man's unattained goal of *"adelantar la raza"* in his family, I want to call attention to his use of racial terminology. During the interview, he constantly shifted terms when alluding to people he considered "black," using one term in one sentence, another term in another sentence, and so forth. I am not talking about the mere use of euphemisms, because he did more than just substitute one term for another. Instead he used four different terms during our conversation to describe people he considered "black." These were "negro" (in his first assertion that in Puerto Rico blacks join with whites), prieto, trigueño, and negrito. During this conversation, the man interviewed also described himself as being of white ancestry, as being indio, and as being "Puerto Rican colored."

The lack of stability in racial terminology is furthered complicated in this interview by the fact that some of the racial terms I mentioned may not be used to mean the same thing. For example, the man interviewed used the word trigueña to describe his son's wife. In this sense trigueña served as a euphemistic label for someone he had previously characterized as black or as negrita. However, later on, he used trigueño to describe the person sitting next to him, commenting that he was trigueño but had "bad hair." When analyzed in the context of his previous assertion about being indio, one realizes that he is describing his trigueño friend as someone who could be mistaken for being indio if it wasn't for his pelo malo (bad hair). Hair here functions as a key racial marker for determining blackness (Candelario 2000; Godreau 2002b). Thus, he is saying that his friend's hair reveals his blackness, in spite of his trigueño or mixed looks. In this sense, trigueño and black are not synonyms.

One reason for this man's avoidance of the term negro to describe his friend, or any of his in-laws for that matter, might be because he considers the term negro and, more broadly, the condition of blackness undesirable. From this point of view, the correspondence we see in the interview between the content of the narrative (blanqueamiento) and the form (ambiguous semantics) is not purely coincidental. The same historically informed anxiety that tries to mitigate the stigma of blackness and whiten its mark of slave origin informs a language practice that leaves blackness without a stable mark of identity in the conversation. The only thing stable is the interlocutor's wish to distance himself from it.

Another factor to take into account when examining slippery semantics is that word choices are not only determined by the classifying system and values of the speaker, but also by the perception that the speaker has of his interlocutor's values and categories. [...]

[...]

[...]Each one of these terms must be analyzed within the context of the narrative in order to determine its significance as insult, as depiction, as euphemism, as status marker, or as a source of pride. This reliance on context is not a new finding. What I want to emphasize, however, is the recurrent linguistic slipperiness and multiplicity that complements the process. My analysis of the next set of examples maintains that such multiplicity of meanings can also include binary forms of racial classification that assume dichotomous black-white identities.

Examples of slippery binaries
Example 4
When I interviewed Felícita and her daughter Rosa in San Antón about the topic of racism, Rosa talked about an instance of racial discrimination that she had suffered in a store with a woman. Summarizing our conversation to her sister who had just come into the kitchen, she said:

"Those racist blancos!" "What about them?" her sister asked. "Well, if they see some-body who's prieto, someone de color ... whatever ... well, they reject him." Her sister agreed.

Rosa's use of "whatever" in this instance seems to suggest that, prieto and de color mean the same thing, as far as this conversation was concerned. At other points during our interview, however, Felícita and Rosa substituted their slippery semantics to introduce a more consistent binary system of classification. This occurred when the topic of the conversation changed to how racism was in the old days. Felícita said:

> "It used to be that a blanco couldn't walk in front of a *negro* and a *negro* couldn't walk by in front of a blanco.... Because, you know, you're walking by, and I come along, and you're giving me this dirty look because you don't want me walking by, you don't want me to even be there. But here you can't tell a negro, 'You can't walk there because that's for blancos, you can't walk there because that's for negros,' because these days everybody's all mixed together."

As she continued to talk about "nowadays" she used words like mulatos, prietos, de color, etc. However, when she referred to racism in the past—a kind of racism she understood to be more deep rooted—the social divisions between blancos and negros were explicit and consistent in her narrative. What changed in the mind of the informant to make this linguistic distinction? The answer could be inferred by what she said previously during the interview. Felícita believed that "nowadays" one could not find black people "because everybody is mixed." She associated the term "negro" with racial purity and, more important, with the past. Within this ideological framework, negro as a distinct identity from blanco might be better suited for describing past circumstances than present ones.

Felícita's construction of black as a "past identity" resonates with dominant national discourses in Puerto Rico that define all Puerto Ricans as heirs of The Spaniard (white), The Taíno (Indian), and The African (black) heritage. These "races" are understood as heritage symbols of a past that has been diluted and replaced by a new "mixed" present where the "pure," foundational "races" no longer exist. To the extent that being mixed and non-black is constructed as the representative identity of the modern Puerto Rican, blackness is not only relegated to the past but its applicability is essentialized to very narrow and stereotypical physical characteristics, such as having very dark skin color, kinky hair, and wide lips and nose shape (Zenón-Cruz 1975; Vargas-Ramos 2005: 4). Whiteness, on the other hand, is defined in Puerto Rico as an inclusive, flexible, wide-ranging category that can be impure and encompass people with different phenotypic features. [...]

In this discursive context, describing someone as "black" becomes problematic, not only because of its association with slave-status, but also because—to the extent that negro is construed as pure—it is considered unrepresentative of the Puerto Rican mixed present. [...]

Another context in which clear distinctions between blancos and negros are evident is when people want to establish ties of solidarity based on racial criteria [...]. Once equality in terms of racial identity has been recognized and valued between speakers, it is quite possible that the consistent use of fixed binary terms may prevail over multiple and ambiguous terminology in a conversation.

The dualism of blancos and negros is also common in jokes or in the heat of an argument, when unequivocal distinctions are made to humiliate the "other," or to show that he or she does not belong. Examples of such popular sayings are *"El negro, si no lo hace a la entrada, lo hace a la salida"* (The black man, if he does not do something as he enters, he will do it as he exists) or *"Ellos son blancos y se entienden"* (They are white and they understand each other).[5] Finally, binary forms or race talk are also commonly deployed to denounce racism.[6] [...]

Example 5

This interview was conducted in the interior town of Cayey at a public school. A teacher who described her sister as *prieta*, negrita, and "darker than me" changed her use of terminology during the interview when telling a story about racism among her kindergarten students. She narrated a story about a boy who called a girl in his class *negra sucia* (dirty black girl) [...]:

> Hearing that word, and hearing it used that way, like he told her, it really shocked me! And the kid was not white, which made me say, 'But how is it possible?' When the kids came in, I was forced to change what I had originally planned to do on that day ... because I was really angry. I stopped the boy in the middle of the room and decided to show... to let him see that he was black also... that the person he was rejecting was a black girl, but that he [himself] was black. And the boy ended up crying. But I didn't care that he cried, and his parents were called in for a meeting. At that moment, I was blinded, but how could I allow such a small girl to be called 'negra sucia'?

This example, in which intermediary and multiple color terms were suspended in the narrative in favor of a white/black binary, is not rare. Other teachers interviewed so far reported that when confronted with incidents of racial harassment in school, they try to make the perpetrators see themselves as black, telling them they are not white and that they have black features or black people in their family. In this way, assigning a black identity becomes a moral tool to undermine a bully's superior and arrogant stance towards black children. The problem with this strategy is that teachers did not challenge the racist logic that defines blackness as an inferior trait, but rather turned it into a "shared stain." Interestingly, teachers did not identify these bullies as "black" in other nonconfrontational contexts, but used more intermediate racial terminologies or alluded to specific phenotypic features to describe them (Godreau et al. 2008). In that sense, binary classifications mostly prevailed in their response to racial harassment.

[...]

Two models in conversation

Binary forms of racial classification might be distinct from those that rely on more ambiguous, intermediary terms. However, to the extent that people are familiar with and can move from one mode of race talk to another, I see them as forming part of the same linguistic culture of slippery semantics described above.[7] Both modes, I also argue, are equally affected by context, for people will use different linguistic grids to evade, conform, or confront racial hierarchies in everyday interactions.

These two different linguistic and conceptual patterns of race-talk (binary and ambiguous) have not been traditionally described as co-existing, but as representing two different racial models (see Hoetink 1967; Seda 1968; Tannembaum 1947; and Carrión 2005 among others). One variant, typically associated with the US, is described as operating according to the rules of "hypo-descent," which establish that "one drop of black blood" makes a person black. The other variant, associated with Afro-Latin America, is described as a more fluid model that recognizes a continuum and multiplicity of color categories.

The criteria scholars have used to establish and explain these two racial models have undergone a great deal of scrutiny since the 1950s. Previous analysts of Latin American race relations argued the difference resided in Latin American nations being less racist and more tolerant of interracial unions, a position advanced by scholars such as Caribbeanist Frank Tannenbaum (1947), Brazilian ideologue Gilberto Freyre (1975 [1933]), and Tomás Blanco (1942) and José Celso Barbosa (1937) in Puerto Rico. [...] Although comparative approaches continued to account for differences between Latin America and the US, scholars began to link the use of multiple racial terms in Latin America to ideological and discursive mechanisms that allow racist practices to prevail. [...] Hence some scholars in the US and Latin America have questioned the contrast between the US and the Latin American model of race relations, suggesting that there might be more similarities than previously acknowledged between them, particularly in terms of how racism and racial discrimination are naturalized and reproduced (Skidmore 1993; Winant 1992). [...]

[...], [A]ctivists and scholars have argued that the prevalence of intermediary racial categories such as mulato or trigueño, or pardo (Brazil) in everyday discourse hinders and dilutes political mobilization against racism in Latin America. The complex terminology is also said to mask racism and obscure fundamental differences in terms of the life chances and opportunities that exist between what are basically two segments: whites and non-whites (Telles 1999; Hasenbalg and do Valle Silva 1999). [...]

Taking a very different stance, there are those who argue that such binary divisions and essentialized constructions of race belong to the US and have little relevance for the Latin American context. These scholars interpret the theoretical deployment of racial binaries in places like Brazil or Puerto Rico as a manifestation of US imperialism or "ethnic ethnocentrism" (Bourdieu and Wacqant 1999; Carrión

1993) or the imposition of foreign racial norms and values (Rodríguez 1994; Duany 2002; Vargas-Ramos 2005).[8] [...]

My theorization of slippery semantics benefits and departs from the theoretical contributions posed by this scholarship. I argue, like others have done for Brazil, that multiple and ambiguous dynamics of racial identification do not preclude racist practices of exclusion based on binary forms of racial classification. Furthermore, as we saw, dichotomous constructions of racial identity can exist alongside more fluid models of racial identification and are deployed in a variety of Puerto Rican scenarios. Hence, defending the fluidity and cultural specificity of racial continuum as the only model operating in Puerto Rico does not account for those situations in which racism causes all other variables to collapse and black people are labeled, discriminated, and marginalized unequivocally because of their color in Puerto Rico and elsewhere in Afro-Latin America. It also ignores that people build solidarities and practice strategic essentialism based on racial criteria in response to their social reality. In that sense, I disagree with interpretations that represent essentialized white/black racial dichotomies as foreign or inadequate for the Afro-Latin American or Puerto Rican context.

On the other hand, interpreting the complex, slippery web of racial terminologies that co-exists with racist practices as a "cloak" mechanism that masks the true nature of racial hierarchies can also undermine what people are doing in other linguistic moments as a problem of "false consciousness." The use of intermediary terminology is thus reduced to a superficial/deceiving expression of a "more real" binary racial structure that lies underneath. Such dismissal of everyday race-talk can deter paying attention to how people create, through language, the construction of mixed-race identities, or selective solidarities as they mark, configure, and re-configure different social postures, etiquettes of behavior, identities, or essentialized expressions of group membership, depending on the context of usage. Thus, my take assumes that binary constructions of race are just as socially constructed and context driven as the multiple color categories people use in everyday discourse. For example, the use of euphemistic terms may have pragmatic implications on everyday encounters in terms of signaling respect, condescension, or blanqueamiento. At the same time, moments when people who consistently deploy racial binaries in race-talk can also create relationships of distance or solidarity between speakers, and have pragmatic effects upon everyday and formal encounters. As a concept that captures both, slippery semantics is an indicator of the fact that race is inherently informed by power dynamics and hierarchies that people will reproduce, challenge, or attempt to negotiate through language.

[...]

An incipient typology of contexts

Previously discussed examples of the use of binary and multiple racial categories in conversations imply that there are contexts that prompt black vs. white types of classifications and others that invite more ambiguous formulations. [...] Although more empirical evidence is needed to produce such a typology [of contexts], the examples discussed previously provide useful clues for deciphering some of the cultural norms that inform slippery semantics, which could be tested by further research. Binary forms of race-talk, for example, seem to prevail when racism is being denounced or practiced. Racial indictments can take place in formal or informal settings (in everyday conversations or in court, in a speech, an interview, or conference). Formal uses of binary race talk are also common when people refer to the past, as when Felícita talked about the old days. They are also common in historical narratives or when people talk about the founding ethnic groups of Puerto Rican culture (i.e, los negros, los blancos, y los indios) such as in school discourses about Puerto Rican history (see Godreau et al. 2008).

However, binary forms of race talk seem to be more prevalent in informal settings, when people make explicit racist remarks alluding to color or—on the other hand —for marking racial solidarity among speakers who consider themselves negros. Jokes, teasing, or mockery of others who appear to deny their "blackness" are common contexts in which stark contrasts between whites and blacks are drawn during informal conversations to offend or build alliances. On the other hand, the use of multiple and intermediary racial terms seems to prevail as the dominant "social etiquette" in Puerto Rico, especially in formal contexts when speakers do not know each other well.

[...]

Caribbean slipperiness: Some historical considerations

In documenting the co-existence of racial binaries with ambiguous forms of classification, it is important to ask what makes such shifts in slippery semantics socially apprehensible for Puerto Ricans? We have already mentioned the role of the state in constructing and erasing racial identities as well as the effects of broader, historical factors that date back to slavery and the plantation. Later, these factors informed the nationalist construction of Puerto Ricans as mixed and non-black. The stigma associated with "savages" coming from Africa, the various colonization processes, first by Spain then by the United States, also explain the "slipperiness" and discomfort people feel when discussing the subject of race, particularly when it is necessary to label anyone as "black."

The linguistic slipperiness of Puerto Ricans with race also makes sense when examined against the historical backdrop of survival strategies long associated with Creole cultures of the Caribbean that rely on syncretism, cooptation, camouflage, and the indirect confrontation of power structures. [...]

[...]

Scholars of the Caribbean have attributed this intangible cultural disposition of Caribbean people to the deeply stratified nature of slave societies and the determinative role played by the plantation system in framing contemporary Afro-American experiences (Burton 1997; Browne 2004; Benítez-Rojo 1989; Mintz 1974; Trouillot 1992; Safa 1987; Yelvington 2001). Their observations point us to colonized slave societies, in which slave participation in public institutions and other overt forms of cultural expression were prohibited. This resulted in a cultural system with a surreptitious quality that would challenge any attempts to neatly compartmentalize Caribbean life.

A number of Puerto Rican scholars have written about this surreptitious quality in Puerto Rican culture. Sociologist Ángel Quintero, for example, describes a multi-racial dispossessed, maroon-like peasantry in 16th century Puerto Rico, which sought to escape from the control of the Spanish crown by seeking refuge in the island's interior. Quintero argues that this sector avoided direct conflict with Spanish authorities by displaying certain Hispanic marks of identity as a way of appeasing any possible tensions between them and the Spanish crown. Thus, a cultural camouflage disguised those who could be perceived as foreign or black (Quintero 1992). In a similar vein, Arcadio Díaz Quiñones talks about *el arte de bregar* (the art of dealing with/working through something [my translation]) as a cultural code or non-written law, practiced among Puerto Ricans, that seeks to mitigate conflict without having to directly oppose the other, use violence, or "lose face" in the process of trying (Díaz Quiñones 2000: 22–3). [...]

The above descriptions of Creole dynamics as furtive, indirect, favoring the avoidance of conflict, and tolerant of contradictions resonate with certain aspects of slippery semantics and moments when speakers avoid the consistent use of racial labels during a conversation because they consider it offensive, because they want to refrain from constructing their interlocutor as a victim or perpetrator of racism, or because they can better construct solidarity based on other social variables such as gender, class, sexuality, geographic location, or political affiliation. At the same time, the possibility of shifting between binary modes of racial classification and more ambiguous modes also allows for the co-existence of different constructions of community and self, [...]. Rather than describing slippery semantics as a speech strategy that presupposes a shift of racial identities, it is best to consider it as a strategy that depends on the conceptualization of racial identities as mobile in the first place. Much like Creole dynamics that mirror structural power difference in their attempt to challenge, collapse, and mediate the social tensions of colonialism in post-slave societies, slippery semantics mirror tensions and contradictions informed by social asymmetry and racialization in the Caribbean and Puerto Rico (West-Durán 2005: 57–8).

Conclusion

In this [work], I define slippery semantics as a particular form of race talk, prevalent in Puerto Rico, that is consistently inconsistent in its use of racial terminology and in the system of racial classification itself. Grids of racial classification can include multiple racial terms to describe the same individual or the consistent use of binary white/black labels, or black vs. non-black identities. Such linguistic inconsistencies mirror the uncertain place of race in current public and private discourse, as well as the compromise that slavery and colonialism, first by Spain and then by the US, placed upon the humanity of the racialized subject in Puerto Rico.

In taking account of this historical trajectory, I argue that slippery semantics operates in the context of contradictory forces and tensions among blanqueamiento, ideologies of race mixture, racial democracy, and the institutional annulation of blackness in government discourses and bureaucracies of Puerto Rico. Caribbean dynamics of camouflage, syncretism, and ambiguity are also mentioned as providing historical foundation for this linguistic culture.

This [work] also addresses some of the social effects of using slippery semantics in everyday interactions. I argue that everyday exchanges, in which racial identity is inconsistently conferred, challenge the construction of stable marks of racial identity during the course of everyday encounters and conversations. For this reason, slippery semantics in race talk allows for various levels of typification and inclusion that might ease possible tensions, establish social distinctions, and/or build different kinds of solidarities (including racial solidarity) in everyday encounters. Thus, speakers might avoid the consistent use of racial labels during a conversation because they prefer cultivating social ties based on variables that are not racial; or use binary modes of race talk to clearly establish insider/outsider status based on race, among many other alternatives. In that sense, slippery semantics has important social effects, not only because of the complexity that it adds to the differentiation in question, but also because it reflects and constitutes relationships among speakers, creating or manifesting respect, distance, intimacy, or solidarity.

A final word of caution is in order regarding scholarship that links racial mixture and the multiplicity of racial terminologies to interpretations that minimize racial prejudice in Puerto Rico and Afro-Latin America. All the ethnographic examples presented in this [chapter] manifest that there is an evident racial hierarchy inform-ing the different stories told and the linguistic style people use to tell it. Emphasizing semantic fluidity and its strong dependence on context should not, therefore, render racial hierarchies less powerful in Puerto Rico or Latin America. On the contrary, the strong connection between racial identification processes and context of usage pre-cisely evidences the salience of "race" and people's efforts to maneuver its different social effects on their everyday relationships and conversations.

Thus, rather than interpreting slippery semantics as the cover of an otherwise straightforward racial reality, I consider it a malleable, historically informed speech strategy that people can employ to mediate the very complex effects that racial hierar-chies have upon social encounters. In the process, people might create and re-create classificatory grids of race as they engage in conversation to be strategically essen-tialist or ambiguous. Whether they succeed does not always depend on the speakers, but on how others perceive them and the somatic, socioeconomic restrictions that social and historical conditions place on their efforts. Hence, I am not arguing that people always have the power to define, negotiate, or determine the consequences of their racialization in everyday encounters. Racial semantics might be slippery, but racism is not. What I am arguing is that people will try to circumvent, get by, con-front, resignify, challenge, and, in some cases, reproduce those constraints through language. In this sense, I do not see slippery semantics as an escape from "race"—even if my previous use of the term "fugitive" in *semántica fugitiva* could indicate otherwise (Godreau 2000). Rather, I see it as a linguistic way of dealing with—though not necessarily resolving—the conflicts, contradictions, anxieties, and destabilizing effects of racism. Key questions that have guided this article are not, therefore, "What does slippery semantics hide?" or "How are US binary models of race misrepresent-ing Puerto Rico?" The key question is "What can these forms of race talk and their respective cosmologies tell us about people's efforts to deal with racial hierarchies in everyday encounters?" And, more important, "how can we incorporate the lessons learned into an antiracist agenda that empowers and doesn't alienate those who so skillfully try to maneuver their semantic effects."

CHAPTER 14

Domestic Work and Racial Divisions in Women's Employment in Puerto Rico, 1899–1930

By Elizabeth Crespo

The analysis of domestic work forces us to look at the inequalities of race and gender and leads to an examination of the multiplicity of experiences that have configured the history of women and work.

Scholarship on women and work in Puerto Rico during the early decades of [the twentieth] century has focused on the dramatic increase in women's labor force participation, in particular on women's work in the needle and garment industries (González García 1990; Baerga 1993). Little attention has been paid to domestic service,[1] which was the main source of employment for women during the first two decades of the century (Picó 1987; Díaz Caballero 1988; Tirado Avilés 1990). In fact, in 1899, 78 percent of employed women were domestic service workers, and in 1930, domestic service was still the source of employment for 30 percent of women who worked for wages or their equivalent.[2] Research on this topic and other realms of women's work may point to a much more diverse female labor force than is reflected by the literature on this period.

As we will see, the analysis of domestic work is also important because it was a much more significant source of employment for black women than for white women. White women moved out of domestic work and into manufacturing at a much faster pace than black women did, preserving marked distinctions between the proportions of white and black women in domestic and manufacturing employment. The focus on domestic work also points to differences in the timing of the incorporation of black and white women into the labor force. The most dramatic growth in women's labor force participation rates during the period discussed in this article occurred among white women and among women who lived outside the major cities. Data presented in this [work] will show that, in the three largest cities of the Island – particularly San Juan, black women had already been massively incorporated into

Originally published in *CENTRO: Journal of the Center for Puerto Rican Studies* 8(1&2): 30–41, 1996.

the labor force by 1899. Differences in the experiences of black and white women have been given very little attention in Puerto Rican women's labor history. This essay seeks to fill the gap.

An analysis of census data between 1899 and 1930 offers a rare opportunity to examine racial differences in the labor force. After the census of 1930, data on occupations are not presented by race. While some censuses present data for black, mulatto, and white, the only racial classifications that were carried consistently through all four censuses were white and black (or colored). Consequently white and black are the racial categories used in this [work].

Definitions of white and black used by the U.S. Census are consistent with the prevailing notions of racial purity and impurity in America at this time. In the census of 1920, for example, the instructions were to "report as "black" all full-blooded Negroes and as "mulatto" all Negroes having some proportion of white blood (U.S. Bureau of the Census 1920). Given these instructions, the distinctions between white, black, and mulatto made in the collection of data depended largely on the judgment of the enumerators. The category "mulatto" presented particular difficulties both in Puerto Rico and the United States. In the United States, it was found that black enumerators classified a greater proportion of blacks as mulattos than did white enumerators. The latter were more reluctant to classify black people as mulattos, preferring to classify them as black (U.S. Bureau of the Census 1920).

In Puerto Rico, the census questionnaire was administered in Spanish, and the enumerators were Puerto Rican. The numbers of individuals placed in each category were thus based on the perceptions of blackness and whiteness that predominated in Puerto Rico at that time. [...]

[...]

Domestic work and constructions of "other" under Spanish rule

To address the significance of patterns of employment, it is important to describe first the social stigmas historically associated with domestic work. A review of this history reveals ways in which domestic labor has been tied to sexual exploitation and constructions of deviance associated with race, sexuality, religion, the supernatural, and women's traditional roles as healers.

[...]

[...] Domestic slaves were a sign of material privilege. Since the early days of Spanish colonization, black and indigenous women, both free and enslaved, as well as poor white women, formed part of the pool of workers from which this labor was supplied. Nonetheless, enslaved women were the preferred source of labor. [...]

Indigenous and black women slaves were used widely as domestic servants by their owners and were also bought to hire out as domestic workers. In fact, the use of domestic workers was so extensive that the Spanish crown considered it excessive because it created an environment in which lack of work and discipline enabled slaves to become too intimate with their masters, and consequently lazy and prone to vice (Sued Badillo and López Canto 1986). [...]

[...] Domestic work performed by women involved cooking, cleaning, taking care of domestic animals, processing food, and manufacturing household items. Domestic duties also entailed wet nurse and nanny. Harsh working conditions were imposed on slaves, who were also often cruelly punished. Added to this mistreatment was the use of women slaves as sexual property. Rape was a form of establishing the power of the white, male slave owner over black women. Daughters of slaves were reserved for the first sexual relations of the sons of their owners. Nevertheless, rape was not a term used in relation to slave women. The term used was "prostitution" or "amancebamiento" – "concubinage"). In this way, black women were seen as the initiators of sexual relations with white men and treated as savage and nonhuman. [...]

[...]

[...] To this day, the images that associate black women with domestic work are used to establish differences between the status of black and white women.

Evidence of the continued presence of black women in domestic service is available in the 18th and 19th centuries. Although the data are not extensive, the presence of a growing number of women in San Juan, in particular black women, was noted in census data during the 18th century. Considering the limited economic opportunities for women it is assumed that many of them were domestic workers (Matos Rodríguez 1995).

More data are accessible for the 19th century. The census of 1846 indicates that four of five women who were listed as workers in San Juan were *parda*, mulatta or black. Many of them prepared food in establishments that catered to travelers, soldiers and sailors. Others were *mondongueras*, women who prepared mondongo, a tripe soup. These shops were considered suspicious by the authorities, who viewed them as potential meeting places for runaway slaves and other delinquents. While seamstresses tended to be of higher social status, many owning their own homes and earning higher wages, laundresses, servants, and cooks were most often of lower class and racial status. At least one third of laundresses were slaves. Some worked for the families that owned them while others also sold their services as a source of extra income. Some worked in military, state, or church institutions. Laundresses who gathered at wells or springs to do their work made colonial officials uneasy because as black women they were suspected of subversive activities. They were also considered promiscuous since their business required them to be outside their house, enter the homes of clients, or pass through city streets unaccompanied. Often they were objects of verbal and physical sexual abuse (Matos Rodríguez 1995).

Domestic Work in Early Twentieth Century Puerto Rico

The information presented above on mid-19th century San Juan confirms the U.S. census data of 1899, which indicates that a large proportion of women in San Juan and Ponce – in particular, black women – already formed part of the paid work force. Thus, one of the major changes in women's work during the first three decades of the 20th century in Puerto Rico was the rapid incorporation of women who lived outside the major cities, as well as white women and married women, into the paid work force. As a result of the restructuring of the Island's economy, male workers were displaced, while new sectors of women who had previously not worked for wages increasingly became an important source of cheap labor. Labor force participation rates of women 10 years old and over climbed from 14 to 22.9 percent, while those of men declined from 83 percent to 69.5 percent (U.S. Census Bureau 1930).

Notwithstanding the significance of this overall trend, we will focus our attention on the small but significant sector of women who at the turn of the century were already working for pay, primarily as domestic servants. Their importance goes beyond their numbers. The composition of this group is most revealing of its significance: 79 percent were single or widowed, and a large proportion worked in the cities and were black. The proportion of women who worked in the cities was two and a half times larger than the proportion who worked in the rest of the Island. Here, 26 percent of women worked for pay. In 1899, one-fifth of black women were already in the paid labor force, almost double the proportion of white women. The gap between the proportion of white and black women who worked outside the home increased steadily with age (U.S. War Department 1899). Although the proportion of black women in the labor force increased between 1899 and 1930, a more dramatic growth occurred among white women. While the percentage of black women ten years and older who worked in gainful occupations increased from 19 to 27 percent, the proportion of white women more than doubled rising from 10 to 21 percent (U.S. War Department 1899).

When we compare the growth in women's labor force participation in the cities with that of women in the rest of the Island, we find that the differences between the two localities gradually diminished during the period between 1899 and 1930. Nevertheless, in 1930, the proportion of women working in gainful occupations in the cities remained approximately one and a half times higher than that of women working in the rest of the island. In 1899, 33 percent of women ten years and older in San Juan and Ponce worked for wages or an equivalent, compared with 13 percent in the rest of the Island. In 1930, the percentage of women workers in San Juan, Ponce, and Mayagüez had only risen slightly, to 34 percent, while in the rest of the Island we observe a substantial increase to 21 percent (U.S. Census Bureau 1930).

In the largest cities there were marked differences in the proportion of black and white women in the labor force. For example, in San Juan in 1899, 42 percent of black women ten years of age and over were in the labor force, compared with only 15 percent of white women. In 1930, the labor force participation rate of black women in San Juan was 40 percent, compared with 26 percent for white women (U.S. Census Bureau 1930). The data for working women in Ponce and Mayagüez reveal a similar pattern, indicating that in the major cities black women's labor force participation rates did not increase during this period and were maintained at around 40 percent. In contrast, labor force participation rates for white women in the major cities almost doubled.

The data also show that labor force participation rates of white women in the cities were higher than those of their counterparts on the Island as a whole. In both 1899 and 1930, labor force participation rates for white women in the major cities were 5 percentage points higher than those of all white women in the Island (U.S. Census Bureau 1930).

Moving from rural areas to the cities, or from small Island towns to the capital, often meant that women had to work as domestics because it was the kind of work most often available. [...]

[...]

Some women moved to the cities because their husbands died or abandoned them. To provide for their children, they would leave them with a relative, move to the city, and live with the family they worked for. Work was arduous, and, as in the case narrated below, some girl children left behind also became domestic workers, although this is not reflected in statistics.

[...]

[...], [S]ome women went to live and work in *"casas de familia"* ("family households") leaving their children to be raised by relatives. For other women, the arrangement was to work in that household during the day and come home at night to continue cooking, cleaning, washing, and ironing for their own husband and children.

[...]

There were various types of domestic service workers, but in all four censuses between 1899 and 1930, the most common occupations listed under this category were servants and laundresses. In 1920, for example, 31,699 of a total of 32,482 female domestic and personal service workers were servants and laundresses (U.S. Census Bureau 1920). This work was done for wealthier individuals, for whom the personal service workers performed duties such as washing, ironing, cooking, cleaning, and care of infants and elderly people. Some lived with their employer, others worked in their employers' house only during the day, and some performed the work outside of the employers' home. The data indicate that only a small number of women performed these duties for institutions and commercial establishments. Some laundresses and ironers were hired in the embroidery and needlework industries (Report of the Governor 1930). Other occupations under the rubric of domestic and personal service included untrained midwives and nurses, hairdressers and manicurists.

The relations between the employer and the domestic worker were characteristic of systems of servitude in many ways. Some women did not work for a wage, but for an equivalent, for example in the form of room and board. Additionally, domestic work was situated in an intermediate position between the spheres of the public and the private and resulted in women submitting to an unending work day. Domestic work for the most part was not subject to the increasing governmental regulations related to work hours, piece work, employment of children, wages, and working conditions instituted during this period.[3] This was particularly true for those women who lived in their employer's home or worked on a day basis for individual families, but was also true for many who worked in institutions such as schools or hospitals[.]

[...]

Other women were paid by the dozen of clothes washed or ironed. In this case they had more control over the length of their paid work day, but their wages and working conditions also escaped supervision by the state.[4]

Table 1. Percent of Gainfully Employed Women Workers
10 Years and Older by Occupations and Race, Puerto Rico, 1899-1930

YEAR	BLACK			WHITE		
	Domestic Service	Manufacturing	All Other Occupations*	Domestic Service	Manufacturing	All Other Occupations*
1899	86.5	9.3	4.2	68.7	18.5	12.8
1910	70.0	18.5	11.5	48.1	27.9	24.0
1920	51.3	29.9	18.8	30.2	38.7	31.1
1930	44.7	44.5	10.8	23.2	55.8	21.0

*Includes clerical occupations, professional services, public service, trade, transportation, communication and agriculture. Source: U.S. Bureau of the Census, Thirteenth Census of the United States: 1910, Occupational Statistics, Table IX

Many employers considered that domestic workers were their sexual property[.]

[...]

Often, the boundaries between domestic servants and mistresses became quite blurred. In fact, various documents of the 16th through 19th centuries list "concubine" ("mistress") as an occupation along with washerwoman and cook (Sued Badillo and López Canto 1986). It was not unusual for wealthy men or clerics to have mistresses who were also their domestic servants. This situation continued into the early 20th century as well.

[...]

Between 1899 and 1930, employment in domestic work declined rapidly, from 78 percent of the female work force in 1899 to 30 percent in 1930. On the other hand, the proportion of women in manufacturing increased dramatically, from 14 to 52 percent (U.S. Census Bureau 1930). In spite of the overall decline in domestic work throughout these decades, such work continued to be a more important source of employment for black women than for white women.

As observed in Table 1, the percentage of black women employed in domestic work was approximately twenty points higher than that of white women in each census year. Although the importance of domestic work declined for both black and white women during this period, by 1920 it was no longer the most important source of employment for white women but continued to be for black women. In contrast, white women had more access to manufacturing jobs and to other occupations as well. In 1899, the percentage of white women who worked in manufacturing was twice as high as that of black women. Although this difference declined after 1899, in each census year the proportion of white women employed in this sector was approximately ten percentage points higher than that of black women.

On the highest end of the occupational queue, racial divisions can also be observed. While 5.5 percent of white women were professionals, only 2.2 percent of black women were professionals in 1930. The most common occupations for both white and black women in this category were teachers and trained nurses.

The racial divisions in the work force described above were coupled with differences in illiteracy and poor health conditions. Data on the city of Santurce in 1910 indicates that the proportion of domestic workers who could read and write was lower than the proportion of women in all other occupations except those who worked in trade, which was also a common occupation for black women. The percentage of surviving children, an important indicator of poverty and poor health, was smaller among domestic servants than in any other occupation (Díaz Caballero 1988; Picó 1987).

Conclusion

The first three decades of the twentieth century reveal a significant degree of racial division in women's work. Differences between white and black women are evident in the larger proportion of black women who worked for wages or their equivalent, and in the fact that high levels of participation in the paid work force occurred at an earlier date for black women. In addition, a significantly larger proportion of black women were relegated to domestic service, and were not able to move into manufacturing as rapidly as white women. Domestic work was the occupation most available to poor, immigrant, illiterate, and destitute women. The wages and working conditions of domestic workers were subjected to less regulation and supervision by the state, giving more opportunity for employers to exploit workers. Women who worked in the homes of their employers were particularly vulnerable to an unending work day. The low status of domestic work was also evidenced by the greater degree of poverty and the poorer health of these women. Physical proximity to their employers and the stereotypes associated with the sexuality of poor and black women made them very vulnerable to sexual abuse in the workplace. Racial divisions in the work force reinforced and confirmed the historical associations between domestic work, sexual exploitation, poverty, and blackness.

CHAPTER 15

Policing the Crisis in the Whitest of All the Antilles

By Kelvin Santiago-Valles

Puerto Ricans have a checkered history that crystallized in the nineteenth century, directly affecting racial taxonomies, attitudes, and identities among all of us to this very day. "Blackness" and anyone kindred to it is usually designated and experienced as "strange," "exotic" and/or "suspicious." More than any formal claim to explicit "ethnic" uniqueness, those uncommon Puerto Ricans self-defining themselves as "black" or "dark-mulatto" do so because they live an interiorizing social distance with respect to light-mulattoes and whites in/from the Island, toward U.S.-European Americans, and toward other lighter-skinned Latin Americans and Caribbean peoples (Barbosa 1937; Rosario and Carrión 1939; Picó 1972; Santos 1993).

It is largely an unwritten history and complex contemporary social analysis. Few Puerto Ricans of African descent explicitly identify themselves as such (Romano 1992), particularly among the poor masses, despite—or because of?—a long past of discrimination and a present of brutal (though furtively racialized) police persecution. Such is the reality summarized and explicated in this essay.

[...]

Current Socioeconomic Context

Like other peripherical areas under U.S.-capitalist hegemony, postwar Puerto Rico went from agro-monoculture to being a light-industry enclave for cheap factory labor. The appeal of low-waged but better-educated labor was enhanced by urban-based industrial programs and increased public services in Puerto Rico, which coincided with labor shortages in the U.S. Northeast. This resulted in large-scale migratory movements and demographic dislocations between 1940 and 1970: countryside to city within Puerto Rico, and from the Island to the United States. The entire process was compounded by an expanded official culture

Originally published in *CENTRO: Journal of the Center for Puerto Rican Studies* 8(1&2): 43–55, 1996.

(Creole and North American) of rapidly spreading schooling, radio, print media, and television.

Between the mid-1960s and the late 1970s, light-industry factories began being unevenly displaced by high-tech, capital-intensive plants, coinciding with massive waves of social unrest. The shift towards capital-intensive industry accelerated with the expansion of new social-control measures. Despite the fiscal constraints of the following decade, such regulatory measures have continued unevenly during the 1980s and early 1990s.

On one side of the social divide stood the heirs of the previous Creole elites—again, almost completely white and light mulatto. This aristocracy was composed of the junior partners of the new U.S. corporate investors and the upper strata of the rapidly expanding bureaucracy; and an overlapping ensemble of highly skilled professionals, technicians, and/ or managerial personnel spreading across all economic sectors. However restricted, the offspring of the old black/dark-mulatto intelligentsia also found a niche within this technocracy. The transition almost exclusively applied to non-white male professionals and/ or bureaucrats, their female counterparts being primarily limited to the petty professions (e.g., public school teachers, social workers, nurses, and so on) and academia. Such burgeoning—and gendered—social mobility was inclined to estrange the upper reaches of this non-white middle class from their racial kin among the new indigent majorities.

On the other side, a more socio-racially heterogeneous, much younger, no longer rural populace was growing. By the late 1960s, the group comprised two-thirds of Puerto Rico's population. The latter unevenly blurred (phenotypically and culturally) with the Island's *gente de color*. Though still below poverty level, this laboring mass was more literate and media-conscious and had higher social expectations than their predecessors. Most now lived in the public housing projects (called *caseríos* or *residenciales*), as well as in the shanty towns and laboring-poor suburbs, that—along with older, sometimes semirural, *pardo-libre* communities—were collectively, known as *barrios*. All were rapidly being absorbed by the urban sprawl.

This socio-racial amalgam is still composed of three groups: a nucleus of unskilled industrial workers whose initial growth ended by the mid-1970s, when capital-intensive industry expanded; a larger and unstable fusion of impoverished petty professionals, semiskilled clerical employees, unskilled wage-workers, and/or independent laborers in all service sectors; and a swelling, formally nonemployed sub-proletariat (the latter two groups tended to overlap). People of color, especially young males, appear to be overrepresented among many of these social sectors—the subproletariat, in particular.

Although between 1950 and 1990 men continued to comprise most of the employed population, their labor participation rates plummeted during this period as those of women laborers steadily rose. Official unemployment rates oscillated between 15 and 30 percent (both sexes) during this period, while all data indicate that it was mainly male laborers who increasingly were not even bothering to look for jobs in the legal labor market. The proportion of officially nonemployed people climbed from a little less than a third of the entire population in 1950 to almost half in 1985. As in the rest of the postwar Caribbean, these were the elements involved in most social strife since the late 1960s: wildcat strikes (1968-1973, 1978-1983), squatters movements (1966–1972, 1979-1983), riots, youth vagrancy, social violence, theft, and the uneven rejection of traditional-party loyalties (Ríos 1993; Silvestrini 1980; Anderson 1983; Silén 1978; Cotto 1993; Ferracuti et al. 1975).

[...]

New Settlement Patterns and Old Solidarities

In the Island, there is still a tendency to identify the multiracial population in the shanty towns, *caseríos* deteriorating laboring-poor suburbs, and the adjacent semirural localities as being of African descent. Despite existing governmental reforms, this demographic distribution was confirmed in the 1950s, among other things, by Caplow, Stryker, and Wallace's research of the colony's capital city. The study found that the beach-front, tourist, and high-class districts "had by far the lowest proportion of non-whites" of 1950, while "the New Suburbs, not yet urbanized"—i.e., where the poorest warrens were located—"had the highest." The authors concluded: "Segregation by color, although not unknown in San Juan, occurs by blocks or by neighborhoods." By the 1960s and early 1970s, anthropologist Helen Safa observed that even the poor themselves "tend to associate black and poor" (Caplow et al. 1964; Safa 1974).

Social services and public infrastructures deteriorated between the 1960s and the 1980s while sources of legal income (particularly factory lobs) shrank. This indigent urban mass thus reinstituted older forms of cooperation within new and more socioracially mixed (mulatto-ized) patterns of communal reciprocity. Safa says that, exchanges of "labor and skills in the repair and improvement of their homes" comprise "one of the main avenues of cooperation among men in the shantytown." The principal compensation assumes "the form of food and drink and, of course, the expectation that these favors will be reciprocated." According to this U.S. anthropologist, "The few possessions shantytown families own are usually shared with others." 'These are gendered patterns of solidarity: "Women borrow small articles like cups of sugar or electric irons, while men exchange tools and cooperate in the repair of their homes." Such patterns are also age-graded: "Even food is shared. Some old men living alone in the shantytown depend almost completely on neighboring families for their meals, for which they contribute nothing" (Safa 1974).

There is still an extreme dearth of even the most descriptive and cursory de-mographic, economic, and socio-cultural research specifically focusing on black and dark-mulatto Island "natives." One of the few recent studies suggests that it is mainly older poor women living in historically *pardo-libre*, semirural communities who fare the worst. These non-white women interviewees reported, however, that race rather than age was the greatest factor in determining the substandard quality of their lives (Quesada and Rivera Ramos 1985).

Roy Bryce-Laporte's 1968 investigation of former slum residents shows that reciprocal-aid practices accompanied this impoverished mass when they were reset-tled to *caseríos* and/ or to laboring-poor suburbs. Such networks of solidarity includ-ed "mutual economic and protective assistance, visiting and confidential exchanges, care in times of sickness and emergency," in addition to "disciplining of children, borrowing and sharing, and decision making on some subjects of common concern." Practices of this sort linked each family/community participant within a lattice of interdependent relationships so dense that, in order to "understand how individual members or individual units survived, it was necessary to know how they related to other units and operations of and within the network" (Bryce-Laporte 1968).

[...]

The Criminalization of Substance Activities

This period also witnessed an increase in the illegalization of survival practices (collective and individual) among the more non-white destitute majorities in ur-ban, suburban, and semirural settlements. Kurt Back's 1962 social-psychology study of *caserío* occupants in Puerto Rico indicates that "the residents frequently tapped power lines and hence did not have to pay for utilities" and that, in general, those interviewed "mentioned a great amount of extralegal activity" (Back 1962: 9-10, 32) In the early 1980s, British historian Raymond Carr commented: "The so-cial alienation of the lumpenproletariat, of which disadvantaged blacks constitute a significant section, is expressed...in deviance and delinquency" (Carr 1984: 248). Regulated or not by extralegal and informal social-control mechanisms, these are the social class, racial, and geographical spaces officially identified with illicit drug sales, squatting, resisting police evictions, participating in unreported incomes, shootouts, the underground lottery, etc. (Safa 1974; Picó 1988; Otero 1992; Osorio 1993; Centeno 1993; Cotto 1993).

To a great extent, the key issue is not whether crime statistics are quantitatively higher among the urban impoverished population in general and among its growing *gente de color* elements in particular. [The question is why?]

[...]

The local mass media and the Creole intelligentsia (of all political stripes, formally anticolonialist or not) have failed to see the structural logic, however disturbing, and much less the racial undertones, of this explosive social polarization. Instead, they have issued copious alarmist writings diagnosing such behavior as the "growing disease" of "a community against itself" (Rodríguez 1977; Silva de Bonilla 1981; Rivera Lugo and Gutiérrez 1993; Colón Martínez 1994). Few realize that the expansion of subaltern literacy levels and access to the mass media have flowed directly opposite the waning access to the growing social wealth created in the Island among the dispossessed "native" majorities.

The mentioned illegalities should be understood, among other things, as a response to the multiplication of gross and frequently, although tacitly, racialized social inequalities. One of the injustices that has provoked considerable resistance among the destitute masses is the land-use policy of the colonial government—local as well as federal—in turn, fueled by the activities of corporate speculators and ravenous real-estate developers. Increasingly, such schemes have placed residents in older, *pardo-libre* communities outside the law, while at the same time forcing a growing number of urban-poor families to unlawfully seize unused stretches of land because these laborers are unable to afford legal housing. In both cases, forced evictions are the ultimate official threat and/or actual practice. There have already been several notorious instances of this type of "cautionary tale," where the local police has brutally crushed the resistances of predominantly black/dark-mulatto, indigent residents. In 1980, the black, laboring-poor mother Adolfina Villanueva was gunned down by patrolmen while she defied an eviction in the Medianía Alta sector of the historically maroon municipality of Loíza. The "Villa Sin Miedo" squatters settlement—in whose organization poor women once again played a leading role—was razed by anti-riot platoons during a police assault and shootout two years later (O'Reilley 1984; Brentlinger 1989; Del Valle 1994; Archilla Rivera 1994).

Another outstanding example of criminalized responses to existing social inequalities stems from the local wage market's declining capacity to even attract—much less absorb—the spreading number of mostly destitute, more racially mixed (i.e., non-white), and disproportionately male youths. A case in point is the underground or illegal economy. In Puerto Rico, and contrary to its U.S. counterpart, illicit economic activities predominately involve laboring-poor, young men. They are the ones primarily absorbed by these burgeoning, now structurally fundamental, and volatile sources of income, whose most profitable endeavors are the distribution of controlled chemical substances, stolen goods in general, and firearms in particular.

Such activities, in turn, have been closely related to two factors negatively affecting postwar patterns of community solidarity, especially among increasingly mulatto-ized, urban, and indigent sectors. On the one hand, there is the increasingly perilous but lucrative nature of these leading, but by no means exclusive, sectors of the underground economy. On the other hand, there is the characteristically masculinist bravado of the male youth bands operating both within and outside of penal/juvenile institutions and fighting to control illicit operations at a neighborhood level. Although drawing on patterns of traditional *machismo* prevalent in Puerto Rico's society as a whole and in dispossessed urban localities in particular, such vicious competition to some extent has strained the community and family networks of reciprocity that the Island's illegal subsistence practices have historically depended on for protection, regulation, and support. This situation has undoubtedly informed the rising rates of local and domestic violence in general, especially of the battering of woman, within the *barrios* (López 1993; Picó 1988; Knudson 1987; Picó 1994). A few of the bands themselves–the "Ñetas" being the prime example–have attempted to counteract some of this social cannibalism by enforcing strict autonomous controls against indiscriminate violence.

From the late 1970s to the early 1980s the estimated volume of the underground economy oscillated between 3.5 to 4 billion dollars. The latter sum meant that more than a quarter of the Island's gross production went to the outlawed sectors of the economy at this time. Puerto Rico's illegal economic activities seem to be 50 percent to 100 percent greater than their U.S. equivalent and involving at least 500,000 Island laborers during the 1980s. This amounted to a little over half of Puerto Rico's active labor force: almost 25 percent of the entire population of employment age, both sexes (Russell 1982; Stewart 1984; Junta de Planificación 1987).

Government officials and advisors admit that unlawful practices such as the underground economy greatly weaken the hold of legal structures (local and federal) over the impoverished urban majorities in Puerto Rico (Stewart 1984). [...]

[...]

The Circuitous Racialization of Crime

Consequently and similar to what was happening in Great Britain during mid-1970s, in Puerto Rico at this time, as in the United States, there was a

> synchronization of the race and class aspects of the [economic] crisis. Policing *the blacks* threatened to mesh with the problem of policing *the poor* and policing *the unemployed*: all three were concentrated in precisely the same urban areas—a fact which of course provided that element of geographical homogeneity... The ongoing problem of policing the blacks had become, for all practical purposes, synonymous with the wider problem of *policing the crisis*. (Hall1978: 332)

In Puerto Rico, this racialization was being executed by the Creole institutions directly administering the colony and responsible for maintaining law and order.

But how can this be officially documented, given the absence of regular census statistics on Puerto Rico's racial subdivisions since 1950? One analytical alternative is to examine the Island police's continuing use of racial (or "color") taxonomies as part of its regular criminal/delinquent identification procedures. Nevertheless, practically all of the criminological studies during this period, whether informed by Puerto Ricans or not, have simply omitted any reference to (Vales et al. 1982; Silvestrini 1980; Peterson 1974; Vales 1987), or have explicitly disclaimed the pertinence of (Ferracuti et al. 1975), the police's race/color identification system.

The 1988 Nevárez-Muñiz and Wolfgang juvenile-delinquency study of a 1970 cohort in the San Juan Greater Metropolitan Area is one rare example to the contrary. Despite repeated disavowals and unlike similar work from the 1950s to the present, the authors cite and use the explicitly racial classifications employed by the police, the courts, and social services themselves: *"blanco," "trigueño,"* and *"negro."* Within their already defined delinquent cluster, these groupings were 54 percent *blanco*, 38 percent *trigueño*, and 8 percent *negro* (Nevárez-Muñiz and Wolfgang 1988).

The study reflects the received official Creole perception that those living in Island *barrios*—in particular, black males—were more inclined to be classified as criminals and delinquents. But although Nevárez-Muñiz and Wolfgang would present it otherwise, they give ample proof of how punitive agencies in the Island have singled out black and dark-mulatto poor-urban young males for a disproportionate amount of police identification and persecution.

According to this study, *negros* supposedly had almost twice the recidivism rates of *blancos*. More than twice as many male *negros* became delinquents by age 14 than their *trigueño* and *blanco* counterparts. Among male juveniles, *negros* were seen as more apt to commit severe crimes—particularly violent crimes (44 percent)—versus 36 percent of all *trigueños* and 32 percent of all *blancos*. *Negros* were reported also as having the highest rates of illicit drug use.

Hence, male-adolescent *negros* were more likely to be referred to the courts (72 percent) than *trigueños* (68 percent) or *blancos* (61 percent). Since the court system issued much harsher sentences to recidivists than to first-time juvenile offenders, *negros* were more prone to be locked up within juvenile detention centers or psychiatric units (14 percent), than *trigueños* (11 percent) and *blancos* (5 percent).

Although young women only made up 17 percent of all those classified as delinquents (both sexes), the non-white members of the female population were also criminally identified at disproportionately higher levels that were comparable to those of their male (*negro* and *trigueño*) counterparts (Nevárez-Muñiz and Wolfgang 1988).

In this sense, between the 1970s and early 1990s, Puerto Rico too, saw what Stuart Hall and co-workers have called a "synchronization" of race, poverty, and unemployment, "all three" being "concentrated in precisely the same urban areas." Meanwhile, policing has expanded on a much larger scale and with far more serious results. From early 1993 to the present the colony's PNP Governor has mobilized the militia-reserve units of the U.S. Army (or National Guard) to carry out joint police raids and to regularly patrol the public housing projects and laboring-impoverished suburbs. This troop deployment has transformed these areas into militarily occupied zones, formally and indefinitely under a state of siege (Archilla Rivera 1993; Picó 1993a; del Castillo 1993; Picó 1993b; Martínez 1994).

Such political and administrative practices suggest that, since the electoral base of Creole [-white] officialdom continues to be partly composed of the urban, non-white, destitute, and unemployed masses, then the local elites cannot maintain the openly racist discourses of the early twentieth century. But since the crisis requires policing and since the already mentioned race-slums-unemployment-crime "synchronization" still exists, being of African descent continues to be the absent referent in the way this "geographical homogeneity" is both imagined and regulated.

The Contradictory Mass Responses to the Racialization of Crime

As in the past, impoverished populations in the Island have reproduced racist inscriptions of social "threat." With the enormous influx of Dominican workers (legal and undocumented) into Puerto Rico since the mid-1970s, this mass-based racism has also meant envisioning Dominicans—who tend to be darker-skinned than most Puerto Ricans—as members of an "inferior race." Such practices have gone from mistaking black and dark-mulatto Puerto Ricans for Dominicans (and sometimes provoking the arrest of the former for failing to produce the "appropriate immigration papers") to graffiti calling for the murder of Dominicans residing in Puerto Rico (Vélez 1993; Guadalupe 1994).

Young, impoverished Puerto Rican *gente de color* unlike their Black-British counterparts, have not produced an Island equivalent of an openly "ethnically distinct class fraction" from the 1970s to the early 1990s. Instead of any explicit and frank "ethnic consciousness" in its principal forms of organization, the latter mainly adopted the form of bands or gangs outspokenly identified with the localities where certain individuals resided or are confined. The group leaders are "young black school-leavers... most exposed to the winds of unemployment." Such was the case of specific Río Piedras *caseríos* in the case of the "Manuel A. Pérez" clique; San Juan's former La Princesa jail where the legendary dark-mulatto convict, martyred social bandit, and prisoners-rights activist Carlos Torres Iriarte (a.k.a., Carlos La Sombra) organized the "Ñetas" or "Asociación de Confinados" (Convicts Association) and later the state penitentiary—one of the association's multiple current strongholds; public housing projects in Ponce where the "Avispas" operated; or entire urban centers such as the "Mayagüez" band whose name corresponds to that of the third largest city in the Island, and so on (Hall 1978, Picó 1994).

Yet there may be also a paradoxical undercurrent of self-identification locating these barrios and/or detention units themselves as distinct, Puerto Rican *negro/trigueño* spaces. The groundwork for such a consciousness is partially being laid by the media coverage and police interdiction practices described above. Perhaps more important, though, since the late 1960s and early 1970s to the present, such self-identification seems to be surfacing with the growing imbrication of two processes. On the one hand, there are the illegal survival practices of these impoverished youths in Island cities and U.S. ghettoes. On the other hand, there are the unevenly explicit Africanist-Antillean and Afro-U.S.-Latino, musico-cultural production of *salsa, merengue,* new *bomba-plena,* rap/hip-hop, as well as the partially candid Afro-Caribbean mix of semireligious initiations and habitual rituals, including *santería, espiritismo,* and *palo-mayombe.* Both the musical expressions and the rituals are extremely popular among the urban-poor in general and the gangs in particular; they even have pockets of adherents among the Island's middle-class (Muller 1983; Flores 1988; Fernández 1975; Nurse Allende 1982; Rivera 1992-1993; Alegría Pons 1992, 1991; Cámara 1991). This trend continues unabated up to the present, although it has not assumed openly self-conscious expressions.

Conclusion

In a 1988 study of one *pardo-libre barrio*, the Creole historian and Jesuit priest Fernando Picó remarked that today Island officialdom and the propertied, educated minorities "continue believing that their problem is drugs and crime and not the existing social conflicts resulting from racial discrimination and unequal opportunities" (Picó 1988: 14). As the bleak conditions of the Island's growing, mulatto-ized poor merges with the socioeconomic predicament of the destitute majorities, solving one situation cannot he separated from solving the other. This cannot be done without confronting the penury, racist policing, and socio-cultural under-evaluation being endured and resisted (however paradoxically) by these subaltern populations.

SECTION V.

The Racialization of Place and the Place for Racialization

CHAPTER 16

De la disco al caserío:
Urban Spatial Aesthetics and
Policy to the Beat of Reggaetón

By Zaire Zenit Dinzey-Flores

In April 2006, MTV Aired *My Block: Puerto Rico*, a newscast that turned popular *reggaetoneros* like Daddy Yankee, Tego Calderón, Don Omar, Calle 13, and Voltio into tour guides of their Puerto Rican neighborhoods. The show sought to understand the particular context from which *reggaetón* had emerged and provide "an inside view about where all those raps originate" (Illich nd). Among others, the Puerto Rican urban spaces visited on the show included public housing projects, the food kiosks of the Piñones coastal lands, the predominantly black town of Loíza, and the renowned urban slum neighborhood of La Perla, subject of anthropologist Oscar Lewis's book *La Vida*. The documentary began to formulate, particularly for the expansive audience that reggaetón has secured, a schematic rendering of the genre's urban Puerto Rican platform and context.

[...]

[...] [In this work] I seek to uncover the particular sets of urban elements and representations that reggaetón launches and that transmit specific knowledge and understandings of the Puerto Rican urban environment and experience. In particular, I ask what are the kinds of urbanity and urban community that the genre puts on exhibit and uses as a platform? [...]

[...] The [essay] presents the aesthetic elements and how they constitute the urban environment in profiling a particular image of the city. The concern here is content rather than frequency and examining the way that the urban articulations are made. In particular, I contextualize the images in the history of urban Puerto Rico and the everyday lives of people outside of the genre. The [essay] uncovers the particular notions

Originally published in *CENTRO: Journal of the Center for Puerto Rican Studies* 20(2): 34–69, 2008.

of the "city" managed in reggaetón and how they exist within popular and sociological conceptualizations of the city. It details how race, gender, poverty, and violence are engaged in representation of an "urban spatial aesthetic." The [essay] concludes with an examination of how the reggaetón-produced urban profile of Puerto Rico is legitimized and engaged in policy and sociopolitical discourses and practices.[...]

[...]

Reggaetón City, PR

Reggaetón is a musical genre that surfaced and existed in Puerto Rico through a journey that cannot be disconnected from the context of the city.[...]

Urbanism took hold in predominantly agricultural Puerto Rico in the early 1900s. This is not to say, however, that urban life was not already under way in Puerto Rico, with the establishment of urban Spanish colonial towns throughout the island. Due to a failing sugar economy and the advent of an urban industrialism rooted in the new political-economic relationship to the United States, many Puerto Rican agricultural laborers moved to the urban centers in search of better opportunities in the early 20th century. Dramatic population shifts took hold, as Puerto Rico became predominantly urban. Today, with a population of just under 4 million people, 94 percent of the entire Puerto Rican population lives in urban areas.[1]

Urban growth in Puerto Rico resulted in the creation of social "ghettos" where an urban underclass lived in substandard conditions. Urban slums became the major policy preoccupation for technocrats in addressing the growing urban population of the island in the mid-20th century.[2] A resulting and dominant policy to alleviate poverty and the "uncivilized" conditions of living was to create more adequate housing, which became the current *caseríos* (public housing projects) and *barrios* of the island. The eradication of slums, however, was not complete, and to this day, slums are characteristic in the island, the most legendary being La Perla [...]. The housing inequalities and urban locations that the policies of the early to mid-20th century Puerto Rico created are what structured the urban Puerto Rico of the late 20th, early 21st century and set the stage for the city that reggaetón will grow out of, and will perform, represent, idolize, criticize, debate, and sustain.[3]

Reggaetón's lyrics reflect Puerto Rico's urban landscape and reference the spatial geography and everyday city life of the island. The specific contextualization of reggaetón is an important indication of how the artists and the genre have constructed themselves and the Puerto Rican city. Furthermore, the spaces of reggaetón reveal a preoccupation with being authentically and genuinely urban. [...]

[...]

In centering public housing and barrios, reggaetoneros have attuned the image of public housing and barrios in Puerto Rico and moved away from negative caricature. Largely stigmatized, barrios and caseríos are represented in the media and in policy practices in ways that labels them unviable. The depiction of caseríos by reggaetoneros in some ways follows the line of how they are depicted in the media— hard places, full of struggle, poverty, and crime. However, reggaetoneros bring to the table the "have been there" possibility of redemption to their depictions of "el barrio." In this way, reggaetoneros' representations of their barrios are consistent with how other residents themselves perceive el caserío and el barrio. [...]

[...]

The urban aesthetics of reggaetón

Reggaetón as an urban symbol that locates itself in selective spaces can be examined from the perspective of urban sociologists, who theorized the conditions, culture, and social lifestyles that constitute city life. [...]

[...] The aesthetics of the city can be located in the very dynamics from which it emerged; dynamics that have resulted in a highly novel, ultramasculine, violently imagined, racially qualified, and typically antipodal space of redemption and contamination, utopia and dystopia, heaven and hell. The topics and locations of reggaetón illustrate urban Puerto Rico and the experiences of living in the cities of Puerto Rico for the many local and international audiences that have been captivated by the genre. But they also formulate and affirm ideas of what being urban and having urban culture is about. [...]

The violent poverty aesthetic

The most notable urban frame of reggaetón is poverty. The social and economic inequalities experienced by reggaetoneros are rearticulated in lyrics that highlight the plight of people who are poor, stigmatized, and vulnerable to violence. Specifically, the focus on urban barrios, caseríos, and the streets as a rhetorical constitutive element of the genre underscores the experience of urban poverty in Puerto Rico.

Poverty and inequality are intrinsic to the way the city has been formulated, imagined, and experienced. From the beginnings of urban research, the poverty apparent in centers to which migrants and immigrants had gravitated to was of major concern for policymakers. [...]

Puerto Rican cities today are characterized by rather obvious representations of urban inequality. Multi-million dollar shopping malls and gated communities of the wealthy often exist next to feared caseríos (public housing projects) and urban barrios.[4] The urban experience is characterized by high levels of poverty; in 1999, 48.2 percent of the island's population had an income below the poverty level (US Census 2000). The median household income in 1999 was a low $14,412, and 20 percent of households on the island received public assistance benefits (US Census 2000). The socioeconomic inequalities in the island are most visible in its distinct housing stratification. Puerto Rico holds the second largest public and assisted housing authority in the United States Federal Housing and Urban Development System, with over 55,000 units of public housing.

In their lyrics and public presentations, reggaetoneros show an intimate awareness of the marginality that characterizes their own lives and those who live the same brand of urbanity they lived. Most reggaetoneros come from humble backgrounds and experienced the realities of the barrios first hand. [...]

Attached to poverty, violence is another element of the urban aesthetic of reggaetón. As discussed above, about a tenth of the songs explicitly deal with violence. Violence and criminalization has long been a social dynamic of concern within urban environments. Given the high densities of the cities and suburban movements away from them, central districts have been characterized in the urban literature as prone to crime.

In Puerto Rico, crime is perhaps the biggest social preoccupation among islanders. During the 1960s and 1970s, crime rose dramatically in the island due to increased drug consumption, and by the late 1980s and early 1990s the island was experiencing what was deemed to be the worse crime wave ever (Rodríguez Beruff 1999). By 2004, with 790 murders, the mean homicide rate in Puerto Rico was three times that of the United States, greater than New York City, Los Angeles, and Chicago, and four times that of Europe (Rodríguez Beruff 1999).

Many reggaetoneros come from those specific places that are considered to be most violent in the island. And even if they don't, they typically don't come from privileged backgrounds. Public housing, caseríos, and barrios in particular have been recognized both in the media and by formal authorities as the sources of criminal activity. They are feared and avoided, and young males hailing from those places are labeled criminals. Violence is a part of the everyday life that reggaetoneros experienced and probably remain very close to. [...]

In addition to the violence they experienced growing up, being criminalized is a common experience among reggaetoneros. Many express being labeled and even arrested simply for coming from specific neighborhoods. Don Omar and Tego Calderón's song "Los bandoleros" exhibits this tendency of being labeled as outside of the law, resisting that label, and yet celebrating their origins in places that are feared. Don Omar, for example, expresses that his arrest was a result of persecution by the police, while Tego Calderón simultaneously engages and challenges the criminalizing label by stating that in doing music they are behaving better than before: "como quiera que lo pongas hago menos mal que antes" [however you see it, I'm doing less harm than before].

[...]

Masculine aesthetic

Reggaetón exemplifies the masculinization of the urban aesthetic. [...]

Masculinity is utilized to construct the dualistic, complex space that reggaetoneros experience and evince. Their representations of space are not only articulated through an attribution of maleness to urban space, but are also encapsulated in the deployment of the lyrics. The masculinization is perhaps most present in the introduction and conclusions of songs. All songs begin with the artists calling out their names and making claims for their current or future success. The songs similarly end with shout-outs by the artists and an affirmation of their lyrical, sexual, or gender prowess. Young men, as well as the handful of young women in the genre, subscribe to this format. In a genre that has been critiqued for sounding the same, the call-outs serve to identify the artists. Furthermore, they serve to contextualize the song in a masculine space. Often, the shout-outs identify the public, audience, or interlocutors for the songs. For example, some call out "*pal* caserío" or "de la calle." There is an interlaced construction of place, audience, ego, and prowess, which is encased in pseudo "calls of the wild." [...]

[...]

By asserting their masculine prowess, reggaetoneros have constructed the residential urban spaces they affirm as masculine with masculine traits (strong, hard, fearful), that tautologically confirms their invincibility and fearlessness. This portrait contradicts the demographic data of urban spaces in Puerto Rico. In the 2000 Census, 51 percent of Puerto Rico's population was female, and 21 percent of households were headed by single females.[5] But in areas of poverty, the proportion of women tends to be much higher, due to the particular conditions (violence and incarceration) that have reduced the number of males. For example, in two public housing sites in Ponce, the proportion of single female-headed households is higher than the national average.

Rather than the depiction of urban neighborhoods of reggaetón being an inaccurate representation of "real" urban life in Puerto Rico, the ultramasculine spaces they present are evidence of the masculinized urban aesthetics of the genre. Specifically, by claiming themselves, and the spaces that constitute their reality and their genre, as masculine spaces, reggaetoneros reposition themselves as strong, fearless products of tough, violent environments. Their prowess and potential for goodness are encased in their ability to struggle and rise above the tough street and violent caseríos. Thus, presenting the street as tough and masculine is exactly what positions reggaetoneros, and the spaces they exalt, as good, strong, and worthy of redemption. Masculinity thus is another vehicle by which urban spaces are consolidated as tough and hard, and at the same time are affirmed as good, worthy, courageous, and indicative of strength.[6] The masculine urban aesthetic that reggaetoneros formulate thus colors the important dualistic and complex rendering of reggaetón-produced conceptions of urban space.

The Black aesthetic

Race has been intrinsically tied to theoretical formulations of the city. Particularly in the United States, but also in the Caribbean, cities were formed under dynamics that solidified racial, ethnic, and class cleavages.[7] In Puerto Rico, reggaetoneros have brought to the fore an intrinsic connection between urban poverty and race. Many artists mention race and describe the profile of the people in their songs as being dark, using terms such as "negro," "moreno," "trigueña," etc. Of racial terms in songs, "negro" seems to be the most commonly used. "*Indio*" was used twice, once in Calle 13's "Atrevete te te" and once in Zion y Lennox's "Don't Stop." Thus, in their lyrics, reggaetoneros envision themselves as black or dark people whose disadvantaged position in Puerto Rican society has been linked to the intersection of class and race.[8]

The ultimate example of a reggaetonero who centralizes race in his lyrics, persona, and visual representations is the "happy to be nappy" Tego Calderón, who wears his hair styled in an afro and proudly emphasizes his African roots and black identity. In his collaboration with Yaga y Mackie "Yo quisiera," Tego was influenced by explicit racial rap acts such as NWA and his racial sensibilities carry through his image.[9] Generally, however, reggaetón has not been blind to race and in fact has attached blackness as an authentic identity of the genre. Eddie Dee claims that society stigmatizes him for being a rapper and looks at him as if it had never seen "un negro" in "Censurarme por ser rapero." Similarly, Don Omar repeatedly refers to himself as "el negro" o "*el negrito*" in a number of his songs (e.g., the introductory track of the *Sangre nueva* album).

Race is intimately linked to the genre through urban spaces. In the disco, morenas and negras get pursued by negros, and the pursuit is "*a lo niche.*"[10] Thus reggaetón gets contextualized in dark spaces with dark people. Daddy Yankee's Reebok ad displays this tendency to present dark people, as do Tego Calderón, his afro, and his videos. Tego, in fact, has in some ways helped to reconceptualize racist standards of beauty; suddenly, black women with afros have jobs on Puerto Rican television, in less politicized circumstances than they have experienced in the past.[11]

But race has also become a legitimizing agent for reggaetoneros, in large part because it is intimately tied with place and location. Being from the caseríos or barrios labels and stigmatizes reggaetoneros. The music itself becomes a path for seeking both inclusion and liberation from the stigma. Daddy Yankee, for example, can be seen in appearance as being a sanitized and more accepted version than other performers due to his lighter skin; this could be a potential contradiction to his caserío credentials, and may actually explain Daddy Yankee's vehement assertions of being from "el barrio," lest he be confused with some of the Latino pop idols of recent times. It might not be too outrageous to argue that Daddy Yankee's light-skinned phenotype has opened the doors to a mainstream audience. In fact, EMI Televisa affirmed that they signed their first reggaetón act, Tito "El Bambino" because "from the way he looks to the music he makes, he was the most (obvious) to make a cross over into pop music" (Cobo 2006). Looks, including race and phenotype, are intrinsic to the genre and negotiate the genre's image. Senior Vice President of marketing for Universal Music Latino also referred to Rakim & Ken-Y's looks as being ideal for a new, more pop-infused type of reggaetón marketing. As he stated: "Beyond the musical credibility they have as a reggaetón act, they have a certain look" (Cobo 2006).

Deciphering the "look" is not hard. Certainly, Tego or Don Omar's looks stick to the more traditional reggaetón street image than Tito "El Bambino" or Rakim & Ken-Y. Race and appearance, including hair and the use of "black" styles such as cornrows or dreadlocks thus lend some legitimacy and authenticity to reggaetón, which undoubtedly through their attachment, reference an urban poverty experience. Race thus is a managed urban quality that reggaetoneros seem to be largely aware of in establishing their legitimacy and urban truths.

[...]

Conclusion: Policy al ritmo de reggaetón

Toward the turn of the 2005–2006 year, the government of Puerto Rico enlisted Residente and Visitante of the newly popular reggaetón group Calle 13 in the fight against the practice of firing shots to celebrate the advent of a new year (Pérez 2005). An opinion poll suggested that the citizenry was encouraged by the participation of the artists in the social campaign (Pérez 2005). Calle 13 had not been the first group to be enlisted in political and social campaigns. Artists like Don Omar, Tego Calderón, Daddy Yankee, and others have been considered for different social campaigns. [...]

[...]

Many reggaetón artists have defended their music by emphasizing that their lyrics simply reflect real urban life.[12] This is no surprise given that the lyrical emphasis of the genre as a place for sharing the character of everyday life makes it ideal for spelling out the social and political realities of its actors. Furthermore, there is a premium in reggaetón on being "real" and accurate in the depiction of life.[13] This is true from the genre's beginnings. Reggaetón's origins are located within lyrics that address social realities and depict everyday urban life. Ruben DJ's first recording, made in 1989 and titled "La escuela," addressed school desertion, and Vico C's "La recta final" looked at the violent reality of the street that the youth of his generation faced. Other contemporaries like Liza M advocated safe sex by asking men to wear a hat ("pon ponte el sombrero"). Through these sociopolitical lyrics, and later through the sexualized songs of the 2000s, rappers and reggaetoneros in Puerto Rico have painted a picture of life as experienced in urban Puerto Rico.[14] [...]

[...]

Through aesthetic representations reggaetón has become a political force and engineer for alternative policy frames. The genre and its participants have realigned strategies to address poverty and have become active collaborators against poverty. Daddy Yankee, for example, funds a children's baseball team in the public housing project of Manuel A. Pérez, in Río Piedras (Vargas 2006). Tego Calderón recently participated in a national newscast regarding racism and unequal access of black people in the island (Rivera Esquilín 2003). They have also infused their people with energetic self-mobilization campaigns. Reggaetón has reminded the public that they too are participants in the polity and that they have something to say. In a recent case, the residents of Residencial Manuel A. Pérez put up a mural against repression, including that inflicted by police on residents due to "el largo y forma de su pelo o su color de piel" [the length and style of their hair and their skin color] and invited Calle 13 to perform in a concert against repression. [...]

[...]

CHAPTER 17

All This is Turning White Now: Latino Constructions of "White Culture" and Whiteness in Chicago

By Ana Y. Ramos-Zayas

Introduction

The three contiguous neighborhoods of Humboldt Park, Logan Square, and West Town are located to the Northwest Side of Chicago and together boast the largest concentration of Puerto Ricans in the so-called City of Neighborhoods. Until the early 1990s, Puerto Ricans in Chicago had the highest levels of residential segregation from both whites and blacks, with dissimilarity indexes of .89 and .81, respectively, than in any other U.S. city with significant Puerto Rican populations in the U.S. (Massey and Denton 1989:75). In the last decade or so, however, the area typically known as "Puerto Rican Chicago" has seen the increased presence of African American families; Mexican and Central American migrants and first-generation U.S.-born populations; and white artists and young professionals who commute to corporate downtown.[1] Despite the highly contested presence of various Latino nationalities and African Americans in a space traditionally marked as "Puerto Rican," it is the white residents whom Latinos[2] see as the embodiment of rapid urban change, particularly in West Town. A proliferation of trendy coffee shops, art supplies stores, and music clubs are tailored to the expanding white population. The complex landscape of meanings attached to this changing urban topography serves as metaphor for the production of racial and class difference.

[...] Region or locality—in this case, the particular urban context of Chicago's Northwest Side—has become a critical actor in the production and reproduction of a powerful language of social difference and racial formations or racialization.[3] Ricardo Gonzalez,[4] a worker at a Latino not-for-profit organization based in West Town, drew a map of "Puerto Rican Chicago" in a napkin to show me that there is "no Puerto Rican community here." Ricardo comments:

Originally published in *CENTRO: Journal of the Center for Puerto Rican Studies* 13(2): 73–95, 2001.

This area has value. This is a great area. Here's a train station. Here's another one. A few stops from downtown. Three hospitals. There's a nice park right here. Clemente, the third largest high school in Chicago, is also here.... You don't see Puerto Ricans around here [West Town] anymore. You know why? Because this community has been shrinking and shrinking. Because whites want this area now, so the rents are going up and we are being kicked out. Gentrification. That's what it's called. All this is turning white now.

Discussions of the creation, production, and protection of space in an increasingly Latinized "Puerto Rican Chicago" invariably implicate understandings of racial difference, not only in relation to blacks and among Latinos, but specially in reference to whites. Ricardo was not the only person to comment that the "better areas" of Puerto Rican Chicago are sold to "los blancos" or "los americanos" under less stigmatized names like "Wicker Park" as a section adjacent to West Town is called. Ricardo was specifically referring to the white professionals and a crowd of young "artists" moving into an "enclave" of renovated buildings rehabilitated in the otherwise deindustrialized surroundings of run-down factories. Nevertheless, Latinos living in the Northwest Side of Chicago have also shared physical—if not always social—space with ethnic whites and poor whites from the Appalachian region, as evidenced by the ethnographic data presented throughout this [chapter].[5]

This essay is an exploration into how Latinos in Chicago create "white culture" and generate ideas of whiteness in such a way that the identity of people racialized as "whites" are not guaranteed the privileged stand of securely being the racial norm. The intention here is to contribute to the literature on critical white studies[6] by changing the vintage glance that has characterized this relatively new academic field, and by expanding the field beyond concerns of how whites see racial Others or how whites see themselves also included is an understanding of how racial Others—namely, those racialized as "Latinos"—see whites, whiteness, and white culture. [...] [It] is an attempt to examine the success and limitations that Latinos face in uncovering the invisibility of privilege –particularly racial privilege or "whiteness". [...]

[...]

Los blancos: Racializing the "Invisible" Race

Latinos almost unanimously perceived the term "American" or "*americano*" as invariably conflated with those individuals racialized as white, the "white people."

While Mexicans and Puerto Rican migrants in Chicago were more likely to use the term *"los americanos,"* second-generation, U.S.-born Puerto Ricans used the literal translation of "whites"—*"los blancos."* Nevertheless, neither "white" nor *"blanco"* nor *"americano"* was ever used to designate someone who is Puerto Rican, Mexican, Cuban, or any other Latino nationality, regardless of individual phenotype. In fact, among U.S.-born and -raised Latinos, *"los blancos"* served to create a bond among Latino interlocutors—regardless of phenotype—to refer to non-Latino whites and draw distinctions between Latinos who may "look white" or even "act white," and people who are "real whites" (*los americanos*).

Some of the Latinos with whom I spoke in Chicago described "whites" in ways that are illustrative of the continuously produced and reproduced constructions of white culture and whiteness.[7] Occasionally, the racial term "whites" is a strategically essentialist term, deployed as a means to create a bond among Latino interlocutors— a *Latinidad*—even in instances when they share very little in terms of personal history and social location. Most frequently, however, "white culture" was constructed through discussions implicating various forms of dangerous, imperialist, corporeal, and stylistic locations in the neighborhood.

For instance, it was about *"los blancos"* that Antonio [...] referred to in a phone conversation about the Columbine High School tragedy. Antonio commented:

You know how they say we are violent and have guns and gangs and stuff? Well, look at Columbine, look at all the massive murders in all those schools. Who are they? They're white people! They live in the suburbs! So they complain about Clemente [High School] this, Clemente [High School] that, and they talk about us. But serial killers are white!

Antonio's comment is not only a challenge to the popular media depictions of the local public school, Clemente High School, as decidedly "Puerto Rican" (Ramos-Zayas 1997). Rather, Antonio's comment suggests a turning around of the logic of spaces racialized as white—in this case, the suburbs, suburban life, and suburban high schools. The underside of Antonio's statement is that "white people" possess the power to represent the "inner city" high school—an important cultural marker in the neighborhood—as a space of violence, which is of course racialized, while presenting the suburban high schools like Columbine as racially neutral. Antonio's comment speaks to this normalcy of whiteness. [...]

Whiteness as a "dangerous" location is a direct reference to the revision of the racial logic of space in terms of the "safe/law-abiding" suburbs versus "unsafe/criminal" so-called "inner city," as implicated in Antonio's purposefully counterintuitive views of the suburbs—and whiteness—as a site of ultimate violence. [...]

[...]

The greatest irony behind the characterization of whites as "dangerous," "bossy," and inclined to "take over" Puerto Rican agency, culture, and material resources is the general perception among Latinos that white people "lack a culture." The ambiguity of culture—and particularly "white culture"—is consistently deployed as explanation for the imperialist nature of whiteness. A commentary on white people's "lack of culture" by Elena Colon, a resident of Logan Square, illustrates Latino constructions of "white culture" as "cultureless." Born and raised in Chicago, Elena is a teacher at a popular education program for adults in West Town:

> Look, my husband is white. And I love my husband. He loves anything that's Puerto Rican. He is learning Spanish. He wants to eat rice and beans all the time. We go to Puerto Rico and my family loves him, because he pays atten-tion to the smallest little details of what they tell him or show him. They tell him, 'This is a pig or this is a cow' or whatever and there he is, paying attention...in awe [she laughs]. But, in a way, I resent his detached curiosity. It's detached, because he cannot be Puerto Rican as much as he may want to. Yet, I feel he uses my culture to satisfy his own curiosity. Through me he feels that he can sort of partake in this identity I'm starting to reclaim for myself. I resent that. I do, because it has taken me effort to be able to keep my culture. And now that I have a few potatoes, I'm not sure I'm ready to give one out to him. I think that now a lot of white people want to experience that...that sense of community...they're searching and searching. But they don't have a strong sense of identity based on community. I was invited to a Native Ameri-can sweat ceremony, but that doesn't mean that I belong or am a part of that. In fact, I felt I was intruding, even though I was invited. But there were a lot of white people there. And they were like...'ohhh'...all emotional [she mimics her point]. Because they don't have that, they don't.

The essentializing and totalizing aspects of Puerto Rican "culture" and white "culture" seem to dominate Elena's narrative. She resents her husband's exoticiza-tion of all things Puerto Rican, but not because she senses that he is misrepresenting her own view of Puerto Rican culture. Rather, she resents him for filling his own "cultural void" with the Puerto Rican culture that she, Elena, as a U.S.-born and raised Puerto Rican, has barely learned to claim.

The seeming dichotomy between Puerto Rican life as "culture" and white life as "cultureless" is ridden with slippage and contradictions in Elena's description. While, the lack of culture equals lack of community, white culture is nonetheless reified—reified as devoid of community and even of culture. Thus, white culturelessness, and hence whites' lack of a cultural community, only reinforces Elena's enhanced sense of being cultural—both by "learning" about Puerto Rican culture and by participating in the Native American ceremony. Elena does not feel part of the Native American sweat-lodge, and so she focuses on how the whites at the ceremony try to find community in ways that Elena would never or could never do. Whites' culturelessness actually allows white people easier identification with *all* cultures, something presumably not possible for people marked as Puerto Ricans or racialized as non-whites. Likewise, the fact that her white husband would want to be Puerto Rican is coupled with Elena's suggestion that, since being Puerto Rican is for her a "learned" process, this Puerto Ricanness is potentially available for appropriation by any white person who learns enough about the culture. Equally significant is Elena's view that Steve, her white husband, was drawn to her because of her culture, not in spite of it.

Despite the continuous assertions that whites are deficient because they do not have a culture and hence must appropriate other people's culture to experience a sense of community, a "white culture"—flawed, inadequate, and infantile—is produced and reproduced in social practice and discourse among Latinos. Narratives of whites' poor emotional balance and the location of whiteness in the body acquire particular prominence in my ethnographic data. Interracial relations are a primary medium through which Latinos construct white culture and talk about whiteness.

[...]

Latino constructions of white culture, as analyzed in this section, rely on ambiguous and ephemeral productions of *"los blancos,"* in which white identity is perceived as dangerous, imperialist, and capable of taking over Latinoness, both culturally and materially. In this sense, spaces marked as "Puerto Rican" or "Latino"—particularly the rapidly changing North West Side of Chicago—are always susceptible to appropriation by whites. Paradoxically, Latinos see white culture as the lack of a culture, a cultureless culture, which forces individuals racialized as "white" to develop complex identifications with non-white Others in order to gain a sense of community and collectivity. Racial formations in this sense depend on the context and on the significance people are interested in making out of racial difference, as well as the intermittent appraisals and reproductions of degrees of whiteness.

Shades of Whiteness

Whiteness in one of Chicago's largest Latino neighborhoods is the subject of frequent marking. As a cultural category, it is often chastised as being invasive or out of place in an area which many local activists and residents are trying to protect and culturally mark as Puerto Rican. The difference between whiteness and whites, in its continual repetition, assures an irregular terrain in which some whites always sit insecurely within the larger body of whiteness, while others have to struggle to create and enforce boundaries of exclusivity (cf. Hartigan 1997, 1999). When Latino residents invoke whiteness, they immediately mobilize class distinctions between themselves and the incoming whites, whom Latinos loosely categorize as "the yuppies," "the artists," ethnic whites and, in a few cases, the *"hillie-billies."* Rather than clearly bounded categories, these expressions of whiteness are malleable and contextual and are alternatively deployed to advance various grassroots agendas, including efforts to "reclaim," "protect," or "Puerto Ricanize" space. These categories of whiteness conflate race and class identities, and many Puerto Ricans tried to decipher the hierarchical orders and taxonomies that orchestrated the relationships among these "different" white groups, as well as between the multiple ladders of whiteness and Latino residents.

Los Yuppies: Corporate Whites and White Privilege

For many *barrio* residents, the yuppies were the most enigmatic contingency of whites. Older Puerto Rican residents like Maritza Colon did not understand why would "rich white people" want to pay what seems like inordinate amounts of money for a small-to-medium-size urban apartment instead of buying a "big house in the suburbs." [...] As Maritza assured me, "no Puerto Rican would pay $250,000 for a house in this area. For that amount of money they can move to the suburbs." The different readings of the same area contribute to the racialization of whites by Latinos, who stressed the irony that an area into which Puerto Ricans had tried to flee in the past would then become highly desired by a certain population of young and wealthy whites. This astonished Latino residents.

Latino *barrio* residents recognize whiteness and racial privilege as evidenced in the image of the "yuppie" as the quintessential gentrifier. However, this recognition of privilege, rather than leading to any form of class-based alliance among the poor, actually severed ties between the Latino poor and working poor and the Latino middle class. Latino middle-class community workers analyzed the shifting demographics of the neighborhood in ways that failed to recognize the systemic aspects of whiteness, by focusing on the role of the Latino *barrio* residents, most of whom are poor and working poor, in perpetuating the "disappearance of the Puerto Rican community." Latino professionals and community workers conflate the racial and class systemic privileges that allow continuous shifts in real estate values to favor a white corporate elite with a rhetoric that sees Latino area residents as responsible for "allowing" whites to take over. [...]

[...]

The yuppies [...] are the most recent neighbors in a line of various kinds of white residents that share urban space with Latinos in Chicago. A Mexican woman in her early 20s, Sylvia, [...] notices how the so-called yuppies did not move into Wicker Park when the area was racialized as "Puerto Rican." Rather, these white professionals moved into an area that had been "discovered" and inhabited by another type of whites: the white artists. [...]

In Sylvia's view, the process of gentrification occurs as a gradual whitening. Some whites become pioneers and venture into the exotic territory of a racially marked area in which they are initially the minority. When the area has turned "more white," then whites that are closer to whiteness start moving in as well. These white artist-pioneers have acquired a prominent symbolic and political role in everyday discussions about a changing space and the production of white privilege.

"The white artists": A Fashioned Whiteness

From the very beginning of my fieldwork in Chicago, I was confused by consistent referents to "the artists" to designate a population of white twenty-somethings living in the Wicker Park area. At times I felt that "the artists" and "the yuppies" were confused and represented ambiguous categories that did not designate anybody in particular. After all, while Latinos denounced the takeover of West Town by "yuppies," they also described the residents of Wicker Park in ways that seemed inconsistent with the popular views of young urban professionals circulating in the 1980s and early 1990s; a young Mexican woman in her mid 20s cleverly referred to them as having the "Harley Davidson Meets Morticia Adams" look.

Hilda Ayala emphasized the changing character of the West Town area where she lived before moving to a house in Humboldt Park. [...] Hilda insisted in showing me around Milwaukee Avenue and pointing out an aromatherapy shop, a cybercafé, various art supplies stores, and coffee houses that served as social spaces for the young white crowd. [...]

[...]

[...] Like the yuppies, the white artists are seen as imperialists, as able to manipulate at whim even "essential" traits like their gender identities and sexualities. Interestingly, of the people I met in Chicago, Brenda and her group of friends frequently socialized with these artists. While Brenda and her best friend, Elisa, often criticized the gentrification process and perceived whites as intruders in West Town, in their daily social practices the young women inhabited particular localities that admitted frequent interactions with the white artists. They even perceived these white artists to be somewhat "closer to" themselves, as race acquired a more passive presence and style, musical taste, age, and, in contradistinction to the yuppies, non-corporate inclinations took precedence.

Nevertheless, not unlike older Latino *barrio* residents, Elisa, Brenda, and their friend Tamika continue to perceive white youth not only as cultural imperialists, but also as "poor wannabees." In their view, these young white artists chose to be poor and even faked their poverty. "These white kids think that living in poverty is cool," commented Tamika, a young worker at a not-for-profit organization and part-time social work student. Elisa added: "They want to be friends with Latinos to pretend they are homeboys and homegirls themselves. You know, they go to the West Town clinic, eat at Ibis [local Puerto Rican-Cuban restaurant]. They're always asking for something...for a quarter, a cigarrette." Most significantly, this white artist "poverty" is perceived as chosen. The seeming inconsistency between being able to afford an expensive loft on coffee house wait-staff wages, while continuing to wear grungy clothes, evokes these white artists' privileged past and family background. [...]

[...]

Latino residents perceived these artists as superficial. They are thought of as blank-slated individuals clumsily trying on different identity costumes, rather than having a historical, emotionally grounded, community-committed consciousness. The artists' adventurous incursions into the City are perceived as evidence of an unencumbered, "individualistic" existence particularly condemned by Latino activists; these artists are able to "just pick up and go" on impulse. They can engineer—simply pick and choose—communities based on factors like style and musical taste, meanwhile maintaining their identity as "artists." By comparison, Latinos are almost inevitably committed, by themselves and others, to communities based on racial identity or nationality. Yet Latinos also construct these artistic communities as decidedly racial communities, and the racialness of these artists is always at the forefront of Latino understandings of white youth's lifestyles and interests, of their "white culture." Despite these generalizations around white culture, there are instances of momentarily racial passivity in which the racialness of whites is understood through more salient class identities. The rest of this [chapter] will consider Latino constructions of two such images of whiteness: the "ethnic whites" and the *"hillie-billies."*

The Ethnic Whites: Whites Who Do Have a Culture

While the yuppies and the artists are perceived as "new" to the neighborhood, Puerto Rican *barrio* residents oftentimes distinguished these "gentrifiers" from oldtime white residents—the "ethnic whites." Whereas the artists and the yuppies represent a cultural void or culturelessness, the ethnic whites—particularly, the Polish and Italians—are perceived to "have a culture" in ways similar to the ways in which Puerto Rican or Mexican residents "have a culture." Latinos' racialization of these ethnic whites involve an emphasis on symbolic rituals and cultural markers, such as festivals, foods, music, migration tales, etc., as evidence of the existence of an "Italianness" or "Polishness" in the North West Side. What determines whether a white person is identified as "ethnic white" rather than as "just plain white" is the intensity of the social contact between the Latino interlocutor and the white individual in question. Hence in individual situations in which whites had a direct, frequent, and ongoing relationship with Latinos—as landlords in their buildings or as owners of local restaurants and stores, for instance—they cease being "just whites" and become characterized by their ethnicity. If these white people had a relationship with Humboldt Park and vicinity that required their social or commercial engagement with Latino *barrio* residents, they are somewhat "darkened" or distinguished from the cultureless whites.

While Latinos still perceived these ethnic whites to be financially better off than themselves, they also recognized the class mobility that marks the difference between the ethnic whites who stayed in Humboldt Park, West Town, and Logan Square and those who left for the suburbs along the Milwaukee Avenue corridor. Latinos are aware that those ethnic whites who stayed may have done so for economic reasons, rather than for a sense of urban adventure as the artists did, or for geographical convenience as the yuppies did. For instance, multiple narratives of older ethnic whites who are never visited by their suburban children abound in my interviews with Latino *barrio* residents. Latino interviewees recognized that their white ethnic neighbors are somewhat disconnected from those whites who left the North West Side for reasons involving the racial composition of the area and who moved to the suburbs in search of a more homogenous zone.

Carmen Santiago, a 43-year old Puerto Rican woman who moved to Chicago from Puerto Rico when she was four years old, recalled that the Polish store owners in the Logan Square area where she grew up always tried to prevent her mother from buying at their stores. [...]

Carmen's description of Latino relations with ethnic whites is emblematic of the many memories of incidents of discrimination many interviewees described. As newcomers racialized as being similar to blacks, Puerto Ricans in the largely Polish and Italian areas of Logan Square had very limited positive memories of these interracial encounters. A critical aspect of Carmen's narrative is that "Polish" and "Italians" are decidedly different from "whites," despite preserving some of the local commercial power oftentimes associated with whiteness. Like other Latinos, Carmen views the incoming "yuppies" as responsible for shifting whiteness away from the old-time ethnic whites, in ways that unsettle these Italian and Polish residents' whiteness. The ethnic whites become more similar to the Mexican, Cuban, and Puerto Rican residents precisely by the incorporation of the upwardly mobile white yuppies into the racial order of the area.

It is important to emphasize that the consistent distinction between unmarked whites and ethnic whites does not suggest that ethnic whites do not share in the privileges of whiteness. Rather, it shows how, for ethnic whites, an unmarked whiteness is something to be earned. Most significantly, ethnic whites seem to earn this unmarked whiteness precisely by distancing themselves from those people racialized as non-white, particularly Latinos. Moving out of the neighborhood or emphasizing dominant class identities are means by which "Italians" and "Polish" move closer to being white. Yet Latinos do recognize that the ethnic whites in the neighborhoods of Humboldt Park, Logan Square, and West Town share some of the privileges of whiteness at the most immediate, localized level. [...]

[...] [C]lass identities shape the sites in which Latino *barrio* residents ethnicize whites as whites whose whiteness is incomplete and characterized by elements similarly present in the racialization of Latinos and blacks. While class is always the already present thread in narratives involving Latino ethnicization of whiteness, class identities as cultural identities become even more salient in Latino descriptions of the white poor or *"hillie-billies."*

Los "hillie-bilies": Whites with nothing but whiteness[8]

There are some kinds of whiteness that lack power in the eyes of Puerto Ricans and Latinos—the whiteness of the poor whites. Yet despite the common economic deprivation that Latinos may share with poor whites in Chicago, the two groups are kept apart by the meanings of whiteness. Latino *barrio* residents hold on to their cultural and urban savviness as assets, while poor whites hold on to their whiteness as a valuable possession and oftentimes their sole property.

The people my interviewees called the *"hillie-billies"* or *"hilbilos"* (as a Mexican woman Pérez (2000) interviewed in Chicago called the urban Appalachians)[9] are perceived by Latinos as the lowest echelon in the ladder of whiteness. These are whites who are rejected by "their own people"—that is, the more affluent whites who avidly attempt to draw the boundaries of whiteness by using terms like "white trash" or "trailer trash."[10]

The first time that I heard the term *"hillie-billie,"* a derivative of "hillbilly," was from Cristina Rodriguez, a Puerto Rican parent-volunteer at the local high school. When I arrived at Cristina's house to interview her and help her son with a Social Studies project, I saw that Cristina had just said good-bye to a young woman who had been visiting with her. Cristina mentioned how the woman's uncle had just returned to Cincinnati, leaving the young woman with the responsibility of paying the rent of their apartment all by herself. Cristina mentioned that she had met this woman, whose name was Besty, because Betsy's uncle, Gary, used to work with Cristina's brother as an automechanic in a neighborhood garage. Cristina commented: "Betsy's uncle...he couldn't get used to the city. He was here for a few months. He lived in Cincinnati before Chicago, but he couldn't get used to that either. They are originally from Kentucky, I think. They are *hillie-billies*, you know. That's what people call them here. It's hard for them to get used to the city, so they come to try, but then they end up going back." At the time, I found the term *"hillie-billie"*— or for that matter "hillbilly"—odd, and just disregarded it as an offhanded characterization of someone who was perhaps from a rural area of the Midwest. Cristina suggested that the *"hillie-billies"* had a hard time adjusting to city life because of their rural origins. While this may be similar to the predicament of other migrants in the city who come from rural areas, the distinction is that these Appalachian-descent migrants never get to adjust; thus, they remained permanently "out-of-place" and unencumbered.

[...]

Like Cristina, Roberto recognized that the poor whites Latinos called the *"hillie-billies"* did not participate in the same order of power and racial privilege typically associated with whiteness. In fact, while Roberto still considered the white Appalachian poor as a "type" of white, it was evident from his narrative that these whites were subjected to forms of prejudice and stereotyping which rendered their racial identity a matter of shifting, everyday contexts.

Latinos did not reject these poor whites necessarily for their rural background, since many Puerto Ricans and Latinos in general harbored very positive, even idyllic, views of the rural landscapes and lifestyles of their respective countries of origin. In fact, Puerto Rican quintessential image of national character and authenticity is the *jíbaro*, a member of good-natured countryfolk residing in the mountainous areas of Puerto Rico. Nevertheless, whenever Latinos referred to "hillbillies" or "Appalachians," the terms carried social contempt and inscribed particular class inflections that divided these poor whites from the yuppies, the artists, and the ethnic whites in the neighborhood. Oftentimes, passing comments, jokes, and forms of ironic humor, as well as an implicit emphasis on the lack of social skills or cultural capital were used in conversations among Latinos to express views of the hillbillies largely influenced by Hollywood's characterization of Appalachian populations.

A critical aspect of Latino constructions of whiteness is that distinctions among whites are made in sites characterized by poverty and marginality, such as the high-poverty North West Side neighborhoods that constitute "Puerto Rican Chicago." Likewise, the whites are essentialized in sites associated with racial privilege or whiteness, such as Chicago magnet high schools or the "better" areas of the neighborhood. The concept of "poor white" implies both race and class, while the concept of "working class" could imply an approach across racial and ethnic lines. These poor whites are noted for their marked difference from the older generation of "working class" ethnic whites, "corporate" yuppies, and "bohemian" artists.

Conclusion: Whiteness, Privilege, *Latinidad*

The vocabulary around "racism" creates a discourse of discrimination and oppression, but generally hides the systemic and ideological everyday mechanisms that makes racial oppression possible and efficient. "White supremacy" is associated with a "lunatic fringe," not with the everyday life of well-meaning white citizens. Most significantly, discussions about "racism" that center exclusively on how oppression operates oftentimes conceal the existence of specific, identifiable beneficiaries of oppression, who are not always the actual perpetrators of discriminatory acts. This essay has attempted to broaden discursive engagements of "racism" that undermine or altogether overlook the aggressive new nativism in the United States, and the particular interests at play in maintaining the nation as predominantly white.

This is especially the case at a time when the media and popular speculation about "the browning of America" has acquired paranoid proportion. Evidenced in fiscal measures directly implicating Latinos, such as the explicit battles over migration and citizenship rights and the dismantling of social welfare programs, this new nativism relies on the consistent concealment of the operations of racial privilege, even in the post–Civil Rights era, when racial bigotry is publicly condemned.

An examination of Latino constructions of white culture and whiteness facilitates the process of making systems of privilege visible by exposing how Latinos navigate the ideological, systemic, and material conditions that, along with subordination, sustain racial discrimination in the United States. As evidenced in Latinos' production and reproduction of white culture through everyday social practices and local narratives in the context of rapidly changing demographic and cultural spaces, Latino *barrio* residents recognized the multiple elements of the power structures responsible for reconfiguring resources and benefits. Among the Latinos with whom I spoke, the complex links between domination, subordination, and the resulting privilege were articulated through the seemingly counterdirectional tendencies of formulating essentialist notions of "white culture" and simultaneously recognizing the gap between a white identity and whiteness as a system of privilege. Hence, while Latinos claim that whites have "no culture," they simultaneously engage in the production of a bounded "white culture," which is strategically deployed to denounce instances of racial privilege in the particular geographical, cultural, and ideological locality that is "Puerto Rican Chicago." Likewise, this denunciation of privilege, while initially associated with a generic "white culture," becomes more nuanced as various cultural taxonomies are deployed to racialize particular social interactions with whites.

The "yuppies," the "artists," the "ethnic whites," and the *"hillie-billies"* are not simple bounded categories, but rather cultural taxonomies that straddle the slippery surfaces of class and racial identities, and condition everyday relationships between Latinos and whites. As Latinos in this Chicago neighborhood recognized the heterogeneity among individuals racialized as "white," the more hegemonic perception of the United States as a "classless society" interrupts the process of class-based alliances between individuals who share the similar consequences of being poor. These poor white's are not "real" whites because despite the nuances in everyday practices, whiteness and white culture are too conflated with notions of upward mobility, middle-classness, and ultimately, Americanness. Their authenticity is questioned based on their closeness or distance from dominant social decorum, as well as the nature of these whites' relation to the cultural and geographical spaces marked as "Puerto Rican" or "Latino."

Nevertheless, while "white culture" is constructed and brought out of its privileged invisibility, the system of privilege and whiteness is quickly elided and its own hegemony is reasserted. Fears of "losing the neighborhood" are more related to prejudice against African American *barrio* residents and struggles over U.S. citizenship among Latino groups of various nationalities than about a Latino recognition of systemic discrimination and white privilege. In this sense, racial formations among Latinos in Chicago's North West Side result from shifts in economic structures and the historical and ideological movements of people through a constantly changing urban space. These fluid spaces provide the basis for refashioning political and residential orders and orchestrating the continuous production and reproduction of models of representation.

SECTION VI.

Institutional Racialization and the Racialization of Self

CHAPTER 18

Changed Identities: A Racial Portrait of Two Extended Families, 1909-present

By Gabriel Haslip-Viera

Haslip-Peña and Viera-Santiago are the names of my parental extended families, whose shifting ethno-racial identities demonstrate the arbitrariness, confusion, and inconsistency of racial classification in the United States and Puerto Rico. They also illustrate how Puerto Ricans can ignore, obfuscate, or repress an African or Afro-Latin@ background or origin, and how different cultural and social environments can influence the adoption or construction of an ethno-racial identity by individuals or entire families in a forced or self-serving manner. In addition to the role of social privilege and prejudices, much of this confusion also reflects how census enumerators and other bureaucrats on the island or mainland made frequent mistakes, cut corners, and often failed to apply the expected "one drop rule" of hypodescent for persons of African or part African background when classifying people by race prior to 1960, when changes in policy began to permit a degree of self identification in official and unofficial documents (Gibson and Jung 2002; Davis 1991; Rodriguez 2000; Duany 2002). It is true that there has been some predictability in the direction and/or motivation for change in racial classification in both Puerto Rico and the United States over the years (Loveman 2007; Loveman and Muniz 2007; Rodriguez 2000; Duany 2002). However, there have also been on-going problems with biased judgments, poorly articulated questions, inconsistency, and sheer laziness and/or incompetence on the part of census enumerators and bureaucrats that have not, and may not be accounted for. These problems and others (Candelario 2007; Godreau 2008; Duany 2002; Thomas 2009), along with the changes in policy themselves, have also contributed to the unreliability of racial statistics in official documents—especially when it comes to Puerto Ricans and other persons of mixed background.

Originally published in *CENTRO: Journal of the Center for Puerto Rican Studies* 21(1): 37–51, 2009.

The Haslip-Peña Family in the U.S. Census and Other Official Documents, 1909–1955[1]

Nicholas (Nicolás) Gabriel Haslip, my paternal grandfather, was born on the island of Curaçao in the Netherlands West Indies in 1883, the offspring of a European Dutch father, and Regina, who was possibly of Jamaican or part Jamaican origin. Raised solely by his mother and apparently educated in the elementary and secondary schools of Curaçao, he joined the merchant marine as a young man and traveled throughout the Caribbean before establishing residence and a small dry goods store in Puerta de Tierra, the port of San Juan, Puerto Rico. He also married Mérida Peña Torres, my paternal grandmother, a native of Guayama, in 1909.

Nicholas Gabriel was a man who would be described as a *"jabao"* or *"grifo"* in the Spanish-speaking Caribbean, or even as a white person, which was certainly the case when he lost most of his hair in the middle years of his life (cf. Stephens 1999, Duany 2002). By contrast, his wife Mérida was clearly someone who would be categorized as a mixed race *"mulata"* in the Spanish-speaking Caribbean and as "Negro" or "Colored" in the United States, which were the terms in use when she lived in New York between 1915 and 1945. At the time of his marriage in 1909, my paternal grandfather was classified as *"pardo"* or brown, a term traditionally used in Puerto Rico and Latin America to define persons of mixed African and European background, along with mulato (Álvarez Nazario 1974; Stephens 1999). However, in the 1910 U.S. census for Puerto Rico, he and his wife Mérida, along with his brother-in-law, José Peña Centeno, were listed as "N" for *negro* or Black in Spanish (cf. Loveman 2007; Loveman and Muniz 2007).

In the years that followed, Nicholas Gabriel's racial classification and that of his family, as recorded by bureaucrats and census enumerators, changed unpredictably and erratically. For example, after coming to New York and establishing residence in Brooklyn in 1915, he was listed as "black" in skin color ("BL") on his February 1918 "Alien Seaman's Identification Card." However, seven months later, his "race" was listed as "white" on his draft card for the U.S. military during World War I. Afterwards, Nicholas Gabriel was recorded as being "white" in the 1920 census, "white" with "dark" complexion on his 1921 "Certificate of Naturalization" (U.S. citizenship), "yellow" in complexion on his 1923 passport application, Negro ("NEG") in the 1930 census, and again as "white" with "dark" complexion on his military draft card for World War II.

Members of Nicolás Gabriel's immediate family and other relatives who lived in his household also experienced shifts in their racial categorization during these years, with changes usually reflecting how he was classified. Despite the expected application of the "one drop rule," and as a result of inconsistent record keeping, Mérida, my mulata-looking paternal grandmother, was listed as "white" in the 1920 census, "NEG" or Negro in the 1930 census, and "Spanish" on her 1945 death certificate. All of my grandfather's children, including my father James (Jaime), and my uncle Julius (Julio), who had tightly curled hair and light to medium brown skin color, were listed as "white" in the 1920 census, and Negro ("NEG") in the 1930 census.[2] This erratic pattern is also seen in my father's official records around the time of his marriage in 1937. In January of that year, he was listed as having a "brown" complexion on his Merchant Marine "Protection Certificate." However, six months later, he was recorded as having a "dark" complexion on his Merchant Marine "Certificate of Identification." In World War II he was also listed as having a "dark" complexion on his military draft card, but in this case, the term "dark" was part of a hierarchical list of categories that ranged from "Sallow" to "Light, "Ruddy," "Dark," "Freckled," "Light Brown," "Dark Brown," and finally "Black." Later, my father was also listed as "Negro" on my own 1941 birth certificate, and again as a "Negro" when he was profiled with several African-American and Afro-West Indian employees of the United States Customs Service in an article that appeared in *Ebony* magazine in October 1950.

My father's classification as "Negro" or as a person of color probably continued in the years that followed, but other labels were also used with increased frequency, especially after 1960, when a change in government policy allowed people to self identify on census forms and other documents to some degree. More often than not, my father came to be classified as a racially undifferentiated Puerto Rican, or Puerto Rican/Hispanic,[3] but he was also listed as "white" on my younger brother's birth certificate as early as December 1951—only about a year after the publication of the article in *Ebony* magazine. This change in classification may also have resulted from an arbitrary decision made by a hospital bureaucrat, but there was also the possibility of pressure from my father, who at this stage in his life was able to exhibit an assertive, authoritarian demeanor as a relatively tall, stocky, well-dressed official of the U.S. Customs Service. Ten years earlier, in 1941, he had also tried to change the listings for race on my own birth certificate, but with only partial success. According to the story, there was an argument with a hospital bureaucrat that resulted from a typed birth certificate which listed my mother as "White," my father as "Negro" and yours truly as "Negro," but with the word "Negro" crossed-out and replaced in handwritten ink with "Puerto Rican." Thus, I may have become one of the earliest members of the "Puerto Rican" race on the U.S. mainland—a label that became commonplace for Puerto Ricans in official documents by the 1950s, along with "White," "Negro," and "Other."[4]

The Viera-Santiago Family in the U.S. Census
and Other Official Documents, 1910–1950

Changing racial classifications are also seen on the matrilineal side of my family. However, in this case, there is a decided overall shift from "mixed race" categories to whiteness in the period from 1910 to 1930, providing some support for recent research and speculation on how race was classified in Puerto Rico by locally recruited agents of the U.S. Census in defiance of Bureau policies (Loveman 2007; Loveman and Muniz 2007; Rodríguez Domínguez 2005; López 2006; Guerra 1998; Duany 2002). Isidra Mercado de Santiago, my maternal great grandmother, was classified as "MU" or "mulata" in the 1910 census for Caimito, Río Piedras, as were her mother, Demetria Jorge de Mercado, her son Ángel Santiago, and her daughter, María Santiago, my maternal grandmother. Isidra's son, Ángel, was also classified as "mulato" in the 1920 census, soon after he married and established his own household, but two years earlier, he had been classified as "negro" on his 1918 military draft card—reflecting in this case, the apparent application of the "one drop rule" for persons of African or part African background.

It was during the 1920 census that the move towards whiteness clearly manifested itself in the Viera-Santiago family as a result of subtle changes in the instructions for enumerators and other factors that may have influenced the classification of persons by race (Loveman 2007; Loveman and Muniz 2007). In these records, and in contrast to the 1910 census, my great-grandmother, Isidra, now living in Santurce, was categorized as "B" for *blanca* or "white," along with my grandparents, María and Juan Viera, and their children. All of these individuals varied in appearance to some degree. Juan Viera, my maternal grandfather, was described as "looking like a typical Spaniard." My grandmother María was apparently darker, but no picture of her has survived. Their children, including my mother Virginia, ranged in color from white to medium brown, but all had very straight hair which was considered, and continues to be considered, an important factor when it comes to racial classification and the determination of status in the Spanish-speaking Caribbean. Juancho, the oldest, my mother Virginia, and two other siblings born in the 1920s, Irma and Roberto, came out looking "Spanish." In contrast, my uncles Luis, Raúl, and Ramón came out looking somewhat *trigueño* or Indian, with two other siblings, Ernesto and Francisco, falling somewhere in between. Other family members were also recorded as living in this large household in the period from 1920 to 1930. These included two younger sisters of my grandmother: Nemencia, who died soon after, and Simona Santiago Cruz, who as I remember, could surely have been classified as mulata, along with her two daughters and her darker, African-looking son, Carlos. However, in the 1930 census, they too were listed as "white."

Racial Trajectories: 1950-Present

How my maternal and paternal grandparents viewed race, and how they identified racially is unknown to me. Both my maternal grandparents died in Puerto Rico in the early 1930s. Mérida, my paternal grandmother, also died suddenly and unexpectedly in her Brooklyn home in 1945, but Nicholas Gabriel died several years later in 1951 when I was ten years old. Based on what I remember and what I have learned since then, it appears that he might have tried to minimize or ignore the race issue as much as possible. He married a woman who was much darker in complexion than he was, and had children whose color ranged from "almost white" to medium brown—all with very wavy or tightly curled hair. His friends, and his work and business associates varied by race and nationality. [...] [H]e may have tried to emphasize the ideals of a color-blind North American, Puerto Rican, and/or internationalist identity,[5] which in part was the view asserted in the late 1960s by my uncle Robert (or Norberto) Haslip, his oldest son and a jabao, who interrupted a conversation that I was having with several cousins on the race issue by declaring that "all of this talk about race is silly" because "we are all Americans and that's the way it should be." However, my father's view toward race and ethno-racial identity evolved differently from that of his older brother and other siblings.[6]

The ethno-racial environment that I first witnessed as a child growing up in New York's East Harlem in the late 1940s was quite complex, yet seemingly harmonious. By the time I was seven or eight years old, I became aware that there were all sorts of people living and working in the neighborhood. Italian-Americans were concentrated in the eastern part of East Harlem. Puerto Ricans and other Latinos were largely situated in the western part of the neighborhood. We lived in the Italian section, but in the East River Houses, an ethnically mixed "municipal housing project" that included families of mostly Italian and Irish background, other European ethnics, some African Americans, and only four Puerto Rican families, including ours. I attended an elementary school with students who mostly represented the groups resident in the Italian part of the neighborhood, I played in the streets with the Italian-American and Irish kids, I bought my soda, candy and chewing gum in the Italian-American grocery and candy stores, and I walked with my parents to visit relatives and friends in the Puerto Rican section of the neighborhood to the west of Lexington Avenue. No significance that I can remember was ever placed on differences in physical appearance during this period, and there was never any mention of Africa or an African background in the family conversations. I was told that we lived in "America," that we were Puerto Ricans, and that we had relatives—including my paternal grandfather—who came from the Dutch West Indies. But I was also told that none of these differences really mattered. The family discourse, especially that of my father, focused on individuals and nationality groups, except for the "colored people" (i.e. African Americans), but we were not "colored people," and it didn't matter anyway as long as they were [...] "good people." As far as my father and other family members were concerned, the important issues were "proper" individual behavior, a degree of intelligence, good manners, personal cleanliness and good grooming, proper dress, and whether or not people's homes were fastidiously clean and orderly.

[...] As I reached my teenage years, I began to hear subtle and not so subtle references to family members who had entered into marriages or relationships that were considered correct or incorrect based on the idea of *mejorar la raza*—a concept historically prevalent in Latin America and the Spanish-speaking Caribbean that encourages non-white persons to make every effort to improve the family racial stock by marrying "white" or as "white" as possible. What resulted in the Haslip-Peña family were racial trajectories that went in different directions, depending in large part on the relationships or the marriage decisions that were made and the neighborhoods where family members lived.

According to the tidbits of conversation that slipped-out over the years, my medium dark complexioned uncle Julius and my lighter complexioned father supposedly made the correct decisions when they married women who were defined as white (Italian-American), or passed for white (my Puerto Rican mother). By contrast, my light complexioned uncle Robert, Nicholas Gabriel's oldest son, made the wrong decision when he married a dark complexioned Puerto Rican woman and continued to live in the Bedford Stuyvesant section of Brooklyn as it became increasingly Black in the years between 1930 and 1960.[7] Over time, my uncle Julius became somewhat de-racialized[8] because he lived in multi-family dwellings in the Italian-American sections of South Brooklyn and Kensington with his large extended family of Italian-American in-laws. His two daughters, who originally looked jabao and even somewhat mulato in appearance, also became Italian American or "white" because they grew up in these environments and married Irish and Italian-American husbands. By contrast, my Uncle Robert's three children went in two different directions. The oldest child, a daughter, and the second son became Black in cultural orientation because of their appearance, their surname (Haslip only), and because they grew up in Bedford Stuyvesant, married Black or Black West Indian spouses, and continued to live in Black neighborhoods.[9] The oldest son, by contrast, eventually developed a mixed race identity because of a perceived African/Indian appearance, his surname (Haslip only), and because he married a Puerto Rican woman who could pass for white. He also fathered three daughters—two of whom could easily pass for Latinas, and one of whom became Black in social and cultural orientation.

In contrast to the Haslip-Peñas, the racial trajectory of the Viera-Santiago family followed a different but consistent path during this period because of their surnames, their time of arrival in New York, and despite variations in their appearances. My light complexioned mother and her light complexioned older brother, Juancho, were immediately defined as "white" when they came to New York in the early 1930s. They also soon became "Puerto Rican" when Puerto Ricans were recognized as an ethnic group and subsequently defined as an undifferentiated racial group in the years between the early 1930s and the early 1950s. The other siblings who came to New York also had similar experiences. My aunt Irma and my uncle Roberto, who looked "white," and my uncle Ernesto, who was a bit trigueño, were also quickly categorized as undifferentiated Puerto Ricans when they came to New York in the late 1940s.[10] Their experience also replicated the path followed by my maternal grandmother's mulato-looking younger sister, Simona Santiago Cruz, who came to New York with her children in the mid-1930s. Despite their hair texture and skin color, which ranged from light to medium dark brown, they too became undifferentiated Puerto Ricans by the late 1940s. Overall, the African background of the Viera-Santiago family vanished during this period. They became or accepted classification as Puerto Rican in the 1940s and 1950s, Puerto Rican and Hispanic by the late 1960s, and for the most part, they have also continued to self identify in this way up until the present time.

The establishment of a Puerto Rican/Hispanic category in official documents during these years also allowed my father to continue to emphasize and privilege the Puerto Rican as a racially undifferentiated identity and further diminish the importance of his African background in notable contrast to those members of his extended family who became increasingly Black or Afro-West Indian in their social and cultural orientation. The shift toward a Puerto Rican identity was also reinforced by the move that my parents made in November 1955 from the northeast Bronx to the town of Huntington in suburban Long Island, where I first experienced real racial polarization and crude, blatant bigotry as a fourteen- year-old. At the time, the town was rigidly segregated into Black and white sections. The residents were primarily assimilated, upper and lower middle class persons of Irish and German-American background, but there were also a considerable number of Italian-Americans, some White Anglo-Saxon Protestants, and other European descended ethnics. The African Americans were largely poor, marginalized and politically passive. Most of them lived in a restricted, rigidly segregated enclave north and south of the railroad tracks, which cut through the middle of the township. A few Puerto Ricans also lived near the tracks, but these were mostly poor, male, and largely invisible migrant farm workers employed in the declining potato, vegetable, and duck farms of Long Island. My father bought his house in one of the white, lower middle class sections of town, but near the frontier with the Black section. Some of our white neighbors were not too pleased by our presence when we moved in, but they were soon neutralized by my father's tactful, yet authoritarian demeanor, and by his now mid-level bureaucratic position in customs enforcement. He also made it clear in a subtle, diplomatic manner that he was superior to his neighbors in various ways, and that we were Puerto Ricans of Hispanic culture and language and not like those "colored persons" who lived in the Black section of town.

[...] During these years he became somewhat de-racialized, but I was nevertheless quite surprised to find out that he was declared "white" on his death certificate when he passed away in 1999. I had concluded, wrongly as it turned out, that defining persons by race on these types of documents was passé by this time.

As it turns out, increasingly complex racial trajectories have been the rule for individuals of my generation and those that have emerged since the 1970s and 1980s. Most of the individuals on the Haslip-Peña side of the family have solidified their connections to the African American or Afro-West Indian communities—self-identifying or accepting classification as Black, although even here, there are many times when reference to a Latin@ connection is made. Others have contributed through intermarriage, professional attainment, and in other ways, to an evolving racial mix that has allowed their offspring to adopt white, Latin@, or other identities with the mixing destined to continue in unpredictable ways in the years to come. On the Viera-Santiago side of the family, identity and classification as Latin@ continues to be the norm with some exceptions. There is a trend toward whiteness among those individuals, primarily females, who have married white husbands and have become middle class. At the same time, the grandchildren and great-grandchildren of Simona Santiago Cruz have continued to identify as Puerto Ricans, or they have become Black or undifferentiated Latin@s because of their surnames and because of the neighborhoods where they live—again demonstrating the ultimate futility of trying to accurately classify Latin@s (and other groups) by race in an era that permits racial self-identification in official documents, and in many official and unofficial settings.

My own racial trajectory has also followed a somewhat circuitous route. As a teenager, I internalized my father's identity as a racially undifferentiated Puerto Rican; but this aspect of my identity was very secondary to my sense of self as an individual. In the years that followed, I continued to see myself primarily as an individual who happened to be Puerto Rican despite the varied and sometimes negative experiences I had with regard to race in art school, the U.S. army, and the commercial art business. I adopted the prevailing liberal position toward race and race relations as I lived through the final years of the integrationist phase of the civil rights movement; however, a major change took place in my mid-twenties, when I moved from my parent's house to the East Elmhurst section of Queens and started spending time in central Harlem as a result of a relationship I had with an Afro-West Indian woman, whose family had connections with leaders in the Harlem community. Among other notables, I "hung out" with Harold Cruse, the author of *The Crisis of the Negro Intellectual*— a book that opened up a whole new world for me—along with other books on African and African-American history and politics that I read for the first time. As an un-hyphenated Mr. Haslip, I was also assumed to be Black by many of the people I met during this period, which was no problem because I had already begun to internalize the reality of my partly African background. However, another change took place in the fall of 1969 when I started taking evening classes at New York's City College

At this point, I met new friends who were mostly Puerto Rican, cautiously joined the student protests at the College, hyphenated my name, and developed an identity and sense of self as a mixed race Puerto Rican with part African and possibly Amerindian ancestry.[11] [...] Since that time, I have continued to articulate a mixed race identity, although like most of my immediate friends and professional colleagues, I have also adopted the position that race has no scientific validity, that race is socially constructed, and that claims for a significant Amerindian background for Caribbean Latinos has little or no basis in the scientific and historical evidence. I even had my genetic background tested in an effort to determine what my alleged racial mix might be, and whether there was any Amerindian background. As it turns out, these tests are crude, simplistic, and unreliable, and their accuracy has been challenged by scientists in academic journals and other publications (Duster n.d.; Brown 2002; Elliott and Brodwin 2002; Weiss and Fullerton 2005; Cabrera Salcedo 2006; Brusil-Gil de Lamadrid and Godreau 2007; Bolnick et al. 2007; Yang 2007; Nixon 2007). However, the results in my case confirmed what I already knew or suspected. My mother's distant ancestry through her maternal line (mitochondrial DNA) came out to be sub-Saharan African despite her white appearance, and my father's distant ancestry through his paternal line (y-chromosome) came out to be European despite his medium to light brown skin color and tightly curled hair.[12] The results of my recently concluded "admixture" test also confirmed what I already knew or suspected. Despite an alleged South Asian, Amerindian, Gypsy, or Arab appearance, I was told that my genetic background was in fact 71 percent European and 29 percent sub-Saharan African, with absolutely no evidence of an Asian or Amerindian background.[13] This means that I can identify in various ways depending on the context or situation.

Based on how race is currently constructed in U.S. society, I can identify and be identified as an undifferentiated Puerto Rican, Latino, or Black person, but, in addition, I can also be identified (and have identified) as a mixed race Puerto Rican, a mixed race Latino, a mixed race Black person, an Afro-Puerto Rican, an Afro-Boricua, and an Afro-Latino.[14] Having listed all of these somewhat different and even problematic identities, the reader might ask which one is preferable, or which one I would choose. In a society that to some degree permits self-identification, "ideological code switching," silence and denial, and "strategic ambiguity," (Candelario 2007; Godreau 2008; Thomas 2009; Duany 2002) and rejecting all concepts of race as biologically and socially bogus, I would privilege none of these identities. However, we in fact live in a race conscious environment and not in an ideal world. Therefore, in a society where one has to play the game of race with some frequency, and given the presumptions and misinformation that permeate this issue, I can still articulate all of these identities, some of them, or none of them, with complete confidence and comfort, depending on the context or situation; however, I also firmly believe that every effort should be made to correct all misconceptions and misinformation with regard to this issue. [...]

CONFLICTING CLASSIFICATIONS: NICOLÁS GABRIEL HASLIP AND MÉRIDA PEÑA TORRES (AUTHOR'S PATERNAL GRAND-PARENTS) AND OF JAMES HASLIP PEÑA (AUTHOR'S FATHER).

Nicolás Gabriel Haslip

1909: marriage certificate (Puerto Rico): *"pardo"* (colored)

1910: US Census (PR): Negro

1918: Alien Seaman ID Card (New York): black

1918: Military draft card (NY): white

1920: US Census (NY): white

1921: US Certificate of Naturalization (NY): white with dark complexion

1923: US Passport application (NY): yellow in complexion

1930: US Census (NY): Negro

1940s: Military draft card (NY): white with dark complexion

Mérida Peña Torres

1909: marriage certificate (Puerto Rico): *"parda"* (colored)

1910: US Census (PR): Negro

1920: US Census (NY): white

1930: US Census (NY): Negro

1945: Death certificate (NY): Spanish

James (Jaime) Haslip Peña

1920: US Census (NY): white

1930: US Census (NY): Negro

1937: Merchant Marine Protection Certificate (NY): brown complexion

1937: Merchant Marine Certificate of Identification (NY): dark complexion

1940s: Military draft card (NY): dark complexion

1941: On author's birth certificate (NY): Negro

1950: In *Ebony* magazine profile (NY): Negro

1951: On author's brother's birth certificate (NY): white

1960s: On different occasions (NY): Puerto Rican

1999: On death certificate (NY): white

CHAPTER 19

Acculturation under Duress: The Puerto Rican Experience at the Carlisle Indian Industrial School, 1898–1918

By Pablo Navarro-Rivera

Juan José Osuna arrived at the Carlisle Indian Industrial School (CIIS) in Carlisle, Pennsylvania at six o'clock on the morning of May 2, 1901. He was fifteen years old, stood four feet six inches in height, and weighed just 80 pounds. Osuna, who would become a noted Puerto Rican educator, wrote of his arrival at Carlisle:

> We looked at the windows of the buildings, and very peculiar-looking faces peered out at us. We had never seen such people before. The buildings seemed full of them. Behold, we had arrived at the Carlisle Indian School! The United States of America, our new rulers, thought that the people of Puerto Rico were Indians; hence they should be sent to an Indian school, and Carlisle happened to be the nearest (Osuna 1932).[1]

Carlisle was a massive *molino de piedra*, a set of millstones through which some 10,700 human beings would be sent from the time that it opened its doors in 1879 until the last student left in 1918. The mission of this institution operated by the United States (U.S.) federal government on a former military base in Carlisle, Pennsylvania, was formulated by its founder Richard H. Pratt, who directed the school until 1904. Pratt stated:

> A great general has said that the only good Indian is a dead one, and that high sanction of his destruction has been an enormous factor in promoting Indian massacres. In a sense, I agree with the sentiment, but only in this: that all the Indian there is in the race should be dead. Kill the Indian in him, and save the man (Pratt 1892).

Originally published in *CENTRO: Journal of the Center for Puerto Rican Studies* 18(1): 223–257, 2006.

By the time the school was closed in 1918, almost 11,000 human beings had been subjected to one of the most ambitious experiments in the destruction of cultural identity and forced acculturation in United States history.[2] Research is very limited on the human tragedy represented by the Carlisle Indian Industrial School. What is even less well known is that about sixty young Puerto Ricans were subjected to the experiment at Carlisle, almost all of them sent there by the United States colonial government on the island.[3]

In her research on the CIIS, Bell (1998) found that the school's history had received very little attention. The studies that had been conducted, she said, had not sufficiently examined the school "within a broader socio-cultural system of federal/Indian relations, nor do they document the range of individual responses to institutionalization at Carlisle" (Bell 1998: 6). Carlisle has barely been examined in Puerto Rican historiography, despite its importance for understanding the first efforts of the United States government to adapt Puerto Rican society to its colonial status. The presence of Puerto Rican youth at the CIIS is mentioned in passing in the works of Bell (1998) and Landis (2001). Osuna (1949), and Negrón de Montilla (1971) also mention the sending of Puerto Ricans to study in the United States, but specify neither the schools to which they were sent nor their missions or objectives. In his doctoral dissertation, José Manuel Navarro (1995) alludes to the sending of Puerto Ricans to Carlisle, and includes a summary of the school's origin and goals.[4]

In 2003, the online journal *Kacike: Journal of Amerindian Caribbean History and Anthropology* published an article by Sonia M. Rosa about the Puerto Ricans who studied at Carlisle. In this article, which suffers from weaknesses of content and methodology, the author brings up the possible Taíno Indian origin of the Puerto Rican students at Carlisle: "An important question remains: Were those kids who were sent to the Carlisle Indian Industrial School Taíno Indians? I believe that there is no right answer to that question" (Rosa 2003).

To support her suggestion, Rosa refers to the work of Juan Martínez Cruzado (2002), also published in the journal *Kacike*. Martínez Cruzado maintains that he has found a Taíno genetic heritage in the populations of Puerto Rico and the Dominican Republic. However, Martínez Cruzado's article makes no reference to the CIIS or to the Puerto Rican students sent there. With regard to Carlisle, the subject of this essay, there is no evidence that the United States specifically sent Taíno Indians who had presumably survived the Spanish conquest.

To the leadership of the United States, both Puerto Ricans and Cubans were "colored" and should be educated in the same way as the Blacks and Indians in the United States. They set up public school systems in Cuba and Puerto Rico and established scholarships to send students to schools in the United States such as the Hampton Institute in Virginia, the Tuskegee Normal School in Tuskegee, Alabama, and the Carlisle Indian Industrial School in Carlisle, Pennsylvania. The selection of Puerto Rican students was based not on any possible Taíno origin, but on other factors such as the connections between their families and the regime in power in Puerto Rico.

[...]

Background

The wave of U.S. expansionism in the nineteenth century very closely followed the pattern set previously by the British Empire. Economic interests that drove the expansion were interwoven with theories of natural superiority and divine mandates or manifest destiny. However, the United States government did not adopt the British practice of governing its colonies indirectly. In fact, the United States did not formally recognize that it had "colonies," preferring to establish "territories." U.S. soldiers arrived in Puerto Rico in 1898 in order to impose United States doctrine and economic interests. According to principal leadership elements in the United States, Puerto Rico was an economically and militarily important country, but was inhabited by inferior beings who would need to be "civilized" in order to maximize the potential benefits of the conquest. This was the same evaluation that they made of Indians and Blacks in the United States, as well as Cubans and Filipinos (Zimmerman 2002). In the words of Charles Eliot, president of Harvard University at the time of the 1898 colonial war, and one of the most influential educators in the United States, "I am inclined to the belief that we shall be able to do Cuba and Porto Rico some good; though to do so we shall have to better very much our previous and existing practices in dealing with inferior peoples."[5]

Notwithstanding the above, to some Puerto Rican sectors at the end of the nineteenth and the beginning of the twentieth century, the advent of United States rule represented possibilities for social justice and a democratic political system that had been unimaginable under Spain. These people regarded the 1898 invasion with optimism. However, their idealization of the United States was not borne out. After an initial period of military rule, the occupation forces established a civilian government under their own absolute control.

In the wake of its military victory in 1898, the United States government initiated in the Caribbean what the dominant discourse called the "civilizing," "Americanizing," or "assimilationist" mission to be applied to Cubans and Puerto Ricans, the same process that had previously been applied to North American Indians, Africans, and African-Americans, and that would subsequently be extended to the Pacific in Hawaii and the Philippines. However, rather than any "civilizing," "Americanizing," or "assimilationist" mission, the process of domination in fact was to grind down or "pulverize" the constituent elements of conquered people's cultural identities.

A process of reacculturation went hand in hand with the grinding down of the young among conquered peoples, a process achieved by the integration and forced adaptation of students within the educational environment. To this end the United States established a public school system in Puerto Rico in 1898 and a Normal School for teacher education in 1900, following the model already in use in the United States for the education of Indians and African-Americans (Torres González 2003). In 1899, the U.S. government established a series of scholarships for vocational and university study in the United States, and in 1903 it founded the University of Puerto Rico.

With the use of the new scholarship funds, the colonial legislature in Puerto Rico began to send Puerto Rican students to institutions such as Carlisle, Hampton, and Tuskegee. Among the stated goals of these schools was the adaptation of students to the expectations of the dominant society and their instruction in vocational arts. In order to set up an initial teaching corps appropriate to the new colonial order, the United States government sent 1,600 Cuban teachers to Harvard University in the summer of 1900 and more than 400 Puerto Rican teachers to Harvard and Cornell Universities in 1904.

The leaders of the U.S. government, sponsor of the scholarships, knew the director of Tuskegee very well and considered that the work he had been doing with African-Americans should be extended to Cubans and Puerto Ricans. Booker T. Washington[6] was by this time a leading educational and political figure in the country and a supporter of the 1898 war. On March 15, 1898, Washington wrote a letter to John Davis Long, United States Navy Secretary from March 1897 to May 1902, stating the following:

The climate of Cuba is peculiar and dangerus (sic) to the unaclimated (sic) white man. The Negro race in the South is accustomed to this climate. In the event of war I would be responsible for placing at the service of the government at least ten thousand loyal, brave, strong black men in the South who crave an opportunity to show their loyalty to our land ....[7]

In reference to Cubans, Washington, the first director of Tuskegee, wrote:

I believe all will agree that it is our duty to follow the work of destruction in Cuba with that of construction. One-half of the population of Cuba is composed of mulattoes or Negroes. All who have visited Cuba agree that they need to put them on their feet the strength that they can get by thorough intellectual, religious and industrial training, such as given at Hampton and Tuskegee. In the present depleted condition of the island, industrial education for the young men and women is a matter of the first importance. It will do for them what it is doing for our people in the South.

If the funds can be secured, it is the plan of the Tuskegee Normal and Industrial Institute at Tuskegee, Ala., to bring a number of the most promising Negro young men and women to this institution to receive training, that they may return to Cuba, and start in the interest of the people industrial training on the island. Tuskegee is so near Cuba that it is conveniently located for this work.[8]

Washington added, "What I have said about Cuba applies as well to Porto Rico, where over half the population are Negroes."[9] The first Cubans arrived at Tuskegee in 1899.

The first to be put in charge of Puerto Rican education after 1898 was General John Eaton, who was a great friend and sympathizer of the Carlisle Indian Industrial School. In January 1899, the same month in which General Eaton was appointed to his post on the island, the Carlisle Indian Industrial School's periodical, *The Indian Helper*, published the following:

It is eminently fitting that the school teacher should follow the soldier into Porto Rico. If there is anyone who can successfully light the lamp of learning in the island it should be General Eaton, who started so successfully the same work among the freedmen of the south at the close of the civil war.

General Eaton is one of Carlisle's staunchest friends, and we are glad that he has been selected for such an honored position as Commissioner of Education in Porto Rico, which he so eminently fortified by experience and influence to fill.[10]

Soon thereafter, Eaton initiated the process by which young Puerto Ricans would be sent to Carlisle. Serious health problems forced Eaton to resign his post about a year after arriving in Puerto Rico to organize the public school system.

Martin G. Brumbaugh, Commissioner of Education for the colonial government in Puerto Rico in 1900 and 1901, indicated in his 1900 annual report that the island had neither good schools nor institutions of higher education, and that it lacked the resources to establish them. On this basis he recommended that the colonial legislature establish scholarships to send 45 students to study in the United States each year. Twenty-five males would be sent to preparatory schools and universities and a second group of twenty males and females would receive scholarships of $250 each year to study in institutes such as Carlisle, Tuskegee, and Hampton (Commissioner of Education 1904: 25). Brumbaugh, who characterized his educational policy for Puerto Rico as part of a program for "the Americanization of the island," mandated that English be imposed as the language of instruction.[11] By winning scholarships for Puerto Rican students to study in the United States, he extended the scope and range of the education policy that the colonial government had been developing on the island itself since 1898.

Samuel McCune Lindsay came from the University of Pennsylvania to serve as Commissioner of Education in Puerto Rico from 1902 to 1904. In his annual report for 1904, Lindsay specified that:

> Under sections 68 to 77 of the "compiled school law" a number of students are maintained in various schools in the United States at the expense of the government of Porto Rico. These sections comprise two separate acts, which are known as "house bill 35" and "council bill 12." Under house bill 35, 25 young men are sent to the United States for literary and professional training in such institutions as may be determined by a commission consisting of the president of the executive council, the speaker of the house of representatives, and the commissioner of education (1904: 25).

In another section of the same report, Lindsay further stated:

> Under council bill 12, for the technical education of Porto Rican young men and women, 20 young men and women are awarded scholarships with the understanding that they are to be sent to a technical or industrial school.

In the same 1904 report (Lindsey 1904: 26–7), Lindsay listed the following recipients of scholarships for vocational studies, and specified the place where each one would be sent to study:

JASPER, N. Y.:
Antonio Pérez

TONGALOO UNIVERSITY, TONGALOO, ALA.
[The correct name was Tougaloo University, Tougaloo, Mississippi]:
Carlos Schmidt

Jesús Negrón
Felipe Orta
TUSKEGEE NORMAL AND INDUSTRIAL INSTITUTE,
TUSKEGEE, ALA.:
Lola Tizol
Josefina Trilla
Berenice Rodríguez
Félix Reina
María Rodríguez Avilés
María Moreno
Virginia Aponte
Eugenio Lecompte
Luis Méndez
Francisco Barrios
Antonio Arroyo
Luisa González Nieves
Felipe Sagardía

In this report, however, the Commissioner of Education made no mention of the students at Carlisle, and did not explain the omission. He also failed to mention the Cuban students who had been sent to Tuskegee.

In 1901, as part of his effort to see that Puerto Rican students would study in the United States, Brumbaugh communicated with educators such as Booker T. Washington, who was president of the Tuskegee Normal and Industrial Institute in Tuskegee, Alabama. In his letter to Washington, Brumbaugh said that

> *The Legislature of Porto Rico has recently made provision to send from this Island to your school and to Hampton, Va., and to other similar institutions, twenty boys and girls, who will be able to leave this Island as soon after July 1st as you advise in view of the conditions at your school. How many of these twenty can you receive, and at what cost per capita, and under what conditions would you be willing to accept them? It is my desire to send as many to you as you can conveniently accommodate, as I believe you are doing the best work for the colored race that is now being done anywhere in the United States.[12]*

In the same letter, Brumbaugh added:

It has occurred to me that in order to break up their Spanish language we might scatter some of them into similar institutions; upon this subject, however, I am not clear and I write to you in perfect frankness for your advise (sic). Would you recommend any other schools besides your own and Hampton for these colored children? If so, will you be kind enough to give me the name and address of such institutions in order that I can take up the question with them? I write this frankly to you because I know that you have the interests of the race at heart and my whole purpose is to do the largest good for these twenty children.

In his book *A History of Education in Puerto Rico*, Osuna (1949: 158) states that a total of 219 Puerto Ricans were studying in the United States in 1901, though he identifies neither the students nor the institutions involved. Osuna says the following:

Besides the teachers, picked youths from the public schools were sent to preparatory schools in the United States. By the summer of 1901, 219 pupils had been sent North and were under the personal oversight of the Commissioner of Education. Some of these pupils were sent to very good schools, while others were not so fortunate, mistakes having been made in selecting some of the schools. Nevertheless the majority of them succeeded, and many of them returned later and made and are making their contribution to the educational as well as to the general progress of the Island.

Osuna was himself one of those students who traveled to the CIIS in May 1901. In his book, he does not specify the errors that were made in selecting United States schools, nor does he explain his view on the implications of such errors.

For her part, Negrón de Montilla (1971: 38) limits herself to stating, in reference to Education Commissioner Martin. G. Brumbaugh, that

...through his personal effort young men and women were sent to the States for advanced study. The legislative assembly under Dr. Brumbaugh's pressure enacted two laws, "H. B. 35" and "S. B. 12" providing for the education in the United States of 25 young men, each of whom was given $400 for each year of maintenance and education.

Negrón de Montilla does not mention the schools or the aims of their programs. She limits herself to stating that 25 males were given scholarships to study at preparatory schools and universities.

In her study of Carlisle, Bell (1998) offers a perspective on the school that was absent from previous studies, particularly that of Ryan (1962). In the preface to her doctoral dissertation, Bell states that "This dissertation revisits the Carlisle Indian Industrial School—the flagship of the American Assimilation era's education program" (1998: vi). Bell adds:

> To understand the Carlisle Indian School is to interrogate its popularized representations, and arguably the most powerful images of the Carlisle Indian School consist of a series of photographs taken before and after students' admission. At the time, these photographs were seen and sold as irrefutable proof that it was possible to raise Indians out of savagery and transform them into model pupils and citizens. A century later, those same photographs seem shocking, serving as an enduring reminder of the power and brutality of the American State (1998: 5).

[...]

Bell's thesis is that:

> In the late nineteenth and twentieth centuries, the American nation-state, operating through the Bureau of Indian Affairs and various other federal agencies, engaged in a policy of assimilation: indigenous peoples were to be detribalized and incorporated as individual citizens into the American nation... (1998: 6).

My findings in researching the Puerto Rican experience at Carlisle are consistent with those of Bell for North American Indian students there; [...].

The philosophical principles at work at Carlisle and the corresponding practices instituted at the school did not fundamentally differ with regard to Indians and Puerto Ricans. The information available in the existing studies of the CIIS, particularly those of Bell and Ryan, provides a context for understanding the experiences of students from other nations such as Puerto Rico and the Philippines.

Carlisle

Carlisle operated along the lines of a military institute. Upon arriving there, students would pose for a "before" photograph which would later be used to contrast their savage appearance with the civilized persons that they were to become. The student would then get a bath, a haircut, "civilized" clothing, and a Christian name. The use of vernacular languages was forbidden; English was the only language permitted both day and night (Ryan 1962; Lesiak 1991; Navarro 1995; Bell 1998). By the time that the first Puerto Rican student arrived at Carlisle in 1898, the practice of taking "before" and "after" photographs had been discontinued.

Students at Carlisle were constantly observed, and measures were taken to ensure that they did not socialize with others from the same nation or language community. According to Bell:

> Students were subject to constant surveillance, both explicit and implicit. Most activities occurred under the watchful eye of teachers, wardens and peers who were prefects. They socialized in restricted areas, and associations between students from the same tribal/National group were actively discouraged. Dormitories, overseen by wardens, were arranged in such a way that students never roomed with someone from their home community or language group (1998: 249).

Just as the "Negro Problem" in the United States had led to the founding of the Hampton and Tuskegee Institutes, the "Indian problem" led to the founding of the Carlisle Indian Industrial School in 1879. The conquest of additional new peoples in 1898 added yet another such "problem," and the Hampton, Tuskegee, and Carlisle models were useful in devising methods for their adaptation. In the case of the Indians, the perceived "problem" was their resistance to the United States appropriation of their national territories and the Federal campaign to destroy them as peoples. In addition to military force, the government used the educational system to suppress indigenous resistance. Between 1873 and 1880, the number of government and religious schools for Indians[13] increased from 286 to 393, with an increase in student population from 6,061 to 13,338 (Ryan 1962: 64). According to Ryan, the proportion of school age Indians who were attending school was still only one in twelve, despite these increases.

Pratt, who proposed the creation of Carlisle, had dedicated his military career to fighting Indians, and then to their "civilization," when he was administrator of 72 Indian prisoners of war at Fort Marion, in St. Augustine, Florida. The "success" of Pratt, at that point a lieutenant, in Indian education, first at Fort Marion and then at the Hampton Institute in Virginia, led to the establishment of the CIIS and the naming of Pratt as its first director. Carlisle was established on the grounds of an inactive military base in the town of Carlisle in central Pennsylvania, 19 miles from Harrisburg. Modeled after Hampton Institute, the vocational school for African-Americans, Carlisle was the first Indian school to be founded by the Federal government off of a reservation. When the school was formally inaugurated on November 1, 1879, it had 147 students from various Indian reservations and agencies, including 11 of the former prisoners from Fort Marion.[14]

The guiding policy of Pratt's "civilizing mission" was called "acculturation under duress" (Ryan 1962: 23). The rationale for this policy was the supposition that
once "thoroughly subjugated" (Ryan 1962), Indians would have no means by which
to resist their forced acculturation in institutions such as Carlisle. Three important
components of the acculturation program were vocational education, the exposure
of students to the dominant model of social and economic organization, and the
strenuous imposition of Protestant principles.

On March 3, 1819, the Federal government had established a "Civilization Fund"
for the purpose of "civilizing" Indians, and made an initial appropriation of $10,000
for this purpose.[15] The operation of the CIIS was financed through this fund from
1879 to 1882, when it began to receive a dedicated appropriation from Congress.

This was Pratt's description of the Carlisle academic mission:

> ... to teach English and give a primary education and a knowledge of some com-
> mon and practical industry and means of self-support among civilized people. To
> this end regular shops and farms were provided, where the principal mechanical
> arts and farming are taught the boys, and the girls taught cooking, sewing, laun-
> dry, and housework (1973).

In 1901, the Federal government approved a curriculum for Indian schools, stip-
ulating that "this course is designed to give teachers a definite idea of the work that
should be done in the schools to advance the pupils as speedily as possible to useful-
ness and citizenship" (Reel 1901: 5). In Reel's view, the stated curriculum would make
it possible for students to develop a higher level of morality, as well as become more
patriotic and Christian citizens.

[...]

The power that Carlisle had over its students, and the manner in which that
power was wielded as an instrument of control, had a great impact on the students, including the Puerto Ricans. Bell mentions that Carlisle, as an agency of
the Federal government, utilized its enormous power to facilitate or hinder the
employment of its Native American students. Federal power over Indian individuals was enhanced by the fact that Indians were not granted United States
citizenship until 1924, six years after Carlisle closed.[16] The reality of this legal
inferiority and political disenfranchisement also affected the Puerto Rican students, as Puerto Rico was a colony at the time that they attended the CIIS. The

United States would not grant citizenship to Puerto Ricans until 1917, just one year before the school closed.

A document describing the history of Carlisle states that "in pursuance of this policy every inducement was offered to retain pupils, to prevent their return to reservation life, and to aid them to make for themselves a place among the people of the east." Concerning the task of Carlisle, Pratt said that "We are doing what we can to make the Indians like other people, capable of meeting the obligations of life in this country," and in the same letter, Pratt added that "until that is accomplished, there is an Indian problem."[17]

In an 1888 statement by Pratt to Frances E. Willard, he said the following:

There are about two hundred sixty thousand Indians in the United States, and there are twenty-seven hundred counties. I would divide them up, in the proportion of about nine Indians to a county, and find them homes and work among our people; that would solve the knotty problem in three years' time, and there would be no more an "Indian Question."[18]

[...]

In the view of Pratt and that of the United States government, the fundamental objectives of Indian education were the obliteration of native identities and the definitive displacement of indigenous people from their traditional lands.

As stated in a 1905 document (see note 18) issued by the Bureau of Indian Affairs:

In his first annual report on the conduct of the school, Lieut. Pratt announced that two boys and one girl had been placed in the families of prosperous citizens of Massachusetts, and subsequently that five girls and sixteen boys had found homes with white families in the vicinity of Carlisle during the summer months, thus enabling them by direct example and association to learn the ways of civilization. This was the commencement of the "outing system" that has come to be a distinctive civilizing feature not only of the Carlisle school but of the Indian school service generally (Ibid).

[...]

As I have pointed out, many Carlisle graduates returned to their indigenous communities. However, only 600 of Carlisle's 10,700 students actually graduated. In the documents consulted for this study, no information has been found with regard to the proportion of

Carlisle students, including Puerto Ricans, who later returned to their communities of origin. This lack of information makes it difficult to analyze the phenomenon of return. We do know, however, that a significant number of Puerto Ricans who left the island to go to Carlisle either stayed in the United States or migrated frequently between the two countries.

The fact that many students fled Carlisle, including five Puerto Ricans, is not given much attention in official reports. However, between 1879 and 1918, at least 1,850 students escaped from the school (Bell 1998: 210).[19] Considering that a student's return to his or her community would typically require a rail journey of several days duration, we can understand Bell's assertion that a student's decision to flee must have been in response to quite serious problems. This would have been even truer for Puerto Rican students, who would have had to return home by sea.

Carlisle as an Educational Model

Carlisle generated a great deal of interest both in the United States and in other countries. People from many parts of the world visited the school. [...]

Carlisle was also visited by representatives of educational institutions interested in Pratt's "civilizing" and "assimilationist" experiment. Among the institutions that sent representatives were Bucknell, Millersville State Normal School, Wyoming Seminary, Keystone Academy, Gettysburg, Ursinus, Dickinson, and Lafayette Colleges.

The nature of visits by Cubans to Carlisle is a matter of some interest. We know that Cubans, like Puerto Ricans, were viewed as inferior people by U.S. government officials, and that institutions such as Carlisle, Hampton, and Tuskegee could serve as models for the work that the United States would undertake in the newly acquired colonies such as Cuba. The Register, unfortunately, does not include the reasons for the visits, and school records do not list any of its students as Cuban.

Visits to Carlisle by distinguished persons were promoted by Pratt in his campaign to portray the school as a successful experiment in "civilization" that could play a role in solving the "Indian problem." To this end, Pratt invited visits from prominent state and federal legislators and other important government officials. Pratt stated that these visits were important factors in winning public and private funding for the school. He stressed that it was of great importance that visitors leave with a good impression of the institution.

[...]

[...] It was imperative to the school's first superintendent that there be clear criteria for the admission of students. To this end, the school's application forms and student records included the student's Indian name and his or her proportion of Indian blood, indigenous nation of origin, and the federal agency for indigenous affairs that had referred him or her to the school. The same application forms and transcripts were used for all students, including the Puerto Ricans. Although some school documents do describe the races of Puerto Rican students Vicente Figueroa and Dolores Nieves, their applications and student records do not; thus they were not officially categorized as to race. This was very probably due to the fact that Pratt founded Carlisle as a school for Indians, and he did not in fact favor educating Native Americans and African-Americans in the same institution (Ryan 1998). This very problem was among the reasons that Pratt, in 1879, had left the Hampton Institute, which was a vocational school for African-Americans in Virginia, where he had directed a special program for Indians. Pratt believed that the white population was more tolerant of Indians than of African-Americans and that mixing the two populations would hinder the acceptance of the former (Ryan 1998).

One important factor that merits further examination is the racial and ethnic discourse common in the United States in the late nineteenth and early twentieth centuries, the manner in which the residents of new United States colonies were characterized within that discourse, and how this was reflected at institutions like Tuskegee, Hampton, and Carlisle (Duany 2002; Guridy 2002).

On the list of tribes represented at Carlisle, for example, there is one by the name of "Porto Rico." Osuna had no doubt that Puerto Ricans were considered Indians at Carlisle: thus the name of his 1932 article on his experiences at the school: "An Indian In Spite of Myself." The staff at Carlisle wrote "Porto Rico" on the records of Puerto Rican students in the space indicated for tribe of origin. Duany (2002) likewise found that the Smithsonian Institution referred to Puerto Ricans as Indians during this period.

However, others, such as Martin G. Brumbaugh, put Puerto Ricans and Cubans in the category "colored." In a letter to Brumbaugh, Booker T. Washington referred to the populations of Puerto Rico and Cuba as predominantly Black. As Duany has suggested, this suggests an ambivalence in the use of ethnic and racial categories. It is interesting to note that Puerto Rican students invariably crossed off the terms "Indian" and "Tribe," replacing them with "Puerto Rico" or "Puerto Rican."

Notwithstanding any possible ambivalence in U.S. racial and ethnic discourse, however, the perceived inferiority of Blacks, Indians, Puerto Ricans, and Cubans in the United States and its new colonies was a constant. It was therefore critical, as Pratt proposed in *The Indian Helper* in 1899, to "light the lamp of learning" for these peoples.

[...]

Conclusion

[...]

Between 1879 and 1918, Carlisle functioned as a molino de piedra, intended to mentally crush its students. Nearly 11,000 North American Indians, Blacks, Filipinos, Alaskans and 60 Puerto Ricans passed between these millstones. Almost all of those who came from Puerto Rico expected that they would receive a professional education and their families on the island had been given the same impression. Although the existing correspondence between the students and their families is not abundant, other studies of Carlisle and the available documents of the school itself indicate that its objective was to adapt students to the roles and identities prescribed by Pratt and his concept of "civilization." This adaptation necessarily began with the destruction of incoming students' cultural identities, most particularly the substitution of English for their vernacular languages.

According to Pratt, the substitution of "civilization" for the students' native cultural identities would make it impossible for them to return to their societies of origin. In fact, this itself was one of Pratt's principal goals: to ensure that the Indian students of Carlisle did not return to the communities from which they had come. Pratt failed in his attempt to keep the Indian students in the East. However, while many students opted to return home, the Indians who left Carlisle had lost much of the identity that defined them when they began the eastern journey years before. They returned as strangers in their own communities, as foreign in those environments now as they had been to those in the East who perceived them as savages.[20]

It is not clear to what extent the Puerto Rican experience in Pennsylvania coincided with that described above. The dearth of information available makes it difficult to reconstruct the Puerto Rican experience at Carlisle with a degree of historical accuracy. For example, we do not know how many of the Puerto Ricans returned to their country or how they experienced that return. Other than what can be gleaned from a small number of letters, we know little about these young people, participants in the initial stage of what would later be known as the Puerto Rican diaspora.

No evidence at all has been found that the United States had a policy of sending Taíno survivors of the Spanish conquest to Carlisle. When the new Puerto Rican government distributed circulars announcing scholarships for study in the United States, they made no mention of Taíno identity as a criterion for selection. The student records of Puerto Ricans at Carlisle, which include their initial applications, contain no references to Taíno heritage, and no such reference has been found in any documentary source that was consulted for this study.

Language is one of the evident preoccupations encountered in the relevant documentary sources. More than 100 years after the founding of Carlisle, words like "Americanization" and "assimilation" continue to have currency. We still hear the word "American" used to mean "from or having to do with the United States." These words and definitions, which were used by Brumbaugh, Pratt, and many others, were repeated by Ryan in 1962 and Bell in 1998, among other scholars, without any reflection or criticism of their meaning, contextual effect, or descriptive imprecision. These words and concepts used in historical reflection and discussion remain those brought to prominence by the architects of colonial wars like that of 1898 and of identity-crushing grindstones like Carlisle.

The impact that the CIIS had on its Puerto Rican students is one of the areas that warrant further study. The adaptive, identity-molding influence of the institution and its ideology extended beyond the school's grounds in Carlisle. According to Pratt, the "outing" program was Carlisle's "supreme Americanizer." Based on an examination of the letters and other communications between officials at Carlisle and its former students, this program must certainly be taken into account. Though the great majority of the Puerto Ricans did not stay in touch with the school, some did write letters and/or complete the questionnaire that was sent to former students.

In this correspondence we find positive evaluations of the experience that some students had at the school. For example, in 1911 Enrique Urrutia thanked Carlisle for the education that made possible his career in the United States Army. In Urrutia's opinion, there is no greater honor for a human being than to serve in the United States Army. Urrutia must have been one of the first Puerto Ricans ever to serve in the United States armed forces, just 13 years after they had invaded his country. A very small minority, Urrutia among them, stayed in touch with the school, and even fewer commented favorably on their experiences there. Even after his retirement, Pratt continued to receive letters from about 300 former students, in which they addressed him as "Dear Father," and described how thankful they were to him, as Carlisle's first director, for the education they had received there (Ryan 1998).

Other former students reproached the officials of Carlisle for the way they had been treated. Dolores Nieves rebuked Carlisle for its role in the difficult times she had to endure under its auspices, particularly in the "outing" program. Osuna, who apparently did not stay in touch with Carlisle, wrote in "An Indian in Spite of Myself" that his overall experience there was negative. To a great extent, Osuna's evaluation of Carlisle coincided with that expressed by the Puerto Rican students to Muñoz Rivera in 1901, when they said that the authorities in Puerto Rico who were administering the legislatively established scholarships for study in the United States had not been truthful about the nature of Carlisle. As a result, five Puerto Ricans ran away from the school, and at least 11 students returned to Puerto Rico on the orders of their parents.

Although Osuna left the CIIS campus in Carlisle, he spent years in Orangeville, Pennsylvania under the "outing" program. According to Pratt, the "outing" program was the most effective "civilizing" initiative that Carlisle had. Orangeville was a puritanical town, the ideal environment that Pratt and the federal government of those years sought for the reacculturation of Carlisle students. In this sense, as has been stated above, Osuna did not leave Carlisle as long as he was part of the "outing" program. Orangeville was an extension of Carlisle, or to an even greater extent, Carlisle was an extension of Orangeville.

SECTION VII.

Is Race in the Genes?

CHAPTER 20

The Politics of Taíno Revivalism: The Insignificance of Amerindian mtDNA in the Population History of Puerto Ricans. A Comment on Recent Research

By Gabriel Haslip-Viera

At various times during the past few years, a number of newsgroup and newspaper articles have appeared with headlines such as "UPR study finds high Taíno DNA rate: Tests contradict theory of extinction in P.R.," "DNA research upsets Puerto Rico history," and "Study suggests large number of Puerto Ricans descended from Taíno Indians."[1] These articles have reported on genetic research conducted on Puerto Rican islanders by Dr. Juan Carlos Martínez-Cruzado and a team of investigators from the University of Puerto Rico at Mayagüez. Focusing on human mitochondrial DNA (which is passed exclusively through the female line), Martínez-Cruzado and his team have determined that the maternal Native American contribution to the Puerto Rican gene pool is 61.3 percent.[2] They claim that this figure is "significant," but up until the present time, they have failed to adequately clarify or explain why this is the case. They also have failed to adequately explain or demonstrate that "the Taíno contribution to the current population" of Puerto Ricans "is considerable," that the "DNA analysis reveals substantial Native American ancestry," and that "some of the Taíno physiognomic traits are still present" in the Puerto Rican population (Martínez Cruzado et al. 2001; Martínez Cruzado et al. 2005).

Mitochondrial DNA has been used in recent years to trace the genetic ancestry of human populations. For example, a recent comparison of samples of mitochondrial DNA suggests that all humans have descended from a single female who lived in East Africa. Australian, European, New Guinean, and Native American ethnic groups have also revealed a specific number of mitochondrial

Originally published in *CENTRO: Journal of the Center for Puerto Rican Studies* 18(1): 261–275, 2006.

types. The comparison of these types of mitochondrial DNA over time have enabled scientists to construct a family tree that shows when these groups began to evolve away from each other.[3] However, broad ethnic or racialist conclusions based on this kind of research have limited utility when Puerto Ricans and other populations of mixed ancestry are analyzed.

Based on a study of a "random sample" of the island population, Martínez-Cruzado and his team have concluded "that the mtDNA pool of Puerto Ricans is predominantly Amerindian" or "indigenous Taíno." However, they have minimized or have failed to report that in many instances, this genetic material may have been passed on to a living Puerto Rican by a single, or very few, sixteenth-century Taíno or Amerindian females, who contributed DNA to this individual through their female descendants, despite the birth of mixed offspring that resulted from a consistent pattern of unions between these females and males of African, European, Asian, and mixed background. In other words, the contribution of Taíno or Amerindian females to a contemporary Puerto Rican may be quite trifling when the actual biological history of that individual's family is traced back over the generations to the early sixteenth century (Martínez Cruzado 2002; Hanis et al. 1991; Bonilla et al. 2004; Fernández Cobo et al. 2001). There also is the distinct possibility that Puerto Ricans, with dark brown skin, tightly coiled hair, and facial features assumed to be "Black African," may also have Taíno mitochondrial DNA (Parra et al. 2003; Martínez-Cruzado et al. 2005; Martínez-Cruzado et al. 2001; Rando et al. 1998; Pereira, Prata and Amorin 2000; Richards et al. 2002; González et al. 2003; Plaza et al. 2003; Díaz Soler 1970.)

As most Puerto Ricans know, the island was originally populated by waves of Native Americans in the millennia leading up to the European discovery in 1493 (Rouse 1992). After the European settlement process began, the Native or "Taíno" population (currently estimated at no more than 50,000) began to decline rapidly as a result of warfare, abuse by the Spaniards, and the introduction of Eurasian and African diseases, among other factors. In 1530, the Spaniards reported that the Amerindian population had been reduced to a mere 1,537 (or 1,162) individuals (Brau 1966; Anderson-Córdova 1990; Silvestrini and Luque de Sánchez 1988; Martínez-Cruzado et al. 2005). By the end of the sixteenth century and continuing until the 1770s, persons defined as "Indians" were no longer recorded in population estimates or official documents. Nevertheless, historians and other social scientists have discussed the probability that a number of Taínos may have survived near the coast or in the interior regions of the island, away from the main centers of European settlement (Brau 1966; Fernández Méndez 1970; Figueroa 1974; Silvestrini and Luque de Sánchez 1988; Anderson-Córdova 1990; Sued Badillo 1995b; cf. Martínez-Cruzado et al. 2001). Martínez-Cruzado and his team (2001: 503) claim "that the 1530 census ignored what could have been thousands of Taínos living in the inhospitable mountains of the central region of Puerto Rico," and that "many survived and adapted to the conditions imposed by the colonial order" (Martínez-Cruzado et al. 2005: 133, 148). However, convincing evidence is not provided for this claim, and the assertion is ultimately meaningless given the on-going and well-documented ethnic mixing that took place between surviving Taínos and other groups in the decades and centuries that followed.

What is clear is that a significant number of Taínos were able to leave or escape from Puerto Rico to join other indigenous groups in the Eastern Caribbean (Anderson-Córdova 1990; Sued Badillo 1995a). The Spaniards also soon began to import other Native men and women into Puerto Rico from neighboring regions, along with enslaved persons from West Africa, and persons of African and mixed African and European ancestry already resident in Spain and other parts of Europe. Historical documents demonstrate that starting in 1510, Native Americans from the Bahamas, Florida, the Eastern Caribbean, Brazil, the Gulf coast of Mexico, and the Caribbean coast of the Yucatan, Belize, Honduras, and Venezuela were brought to Puerto Rico in significant numbers to replace the native Taíno population, which was declining rapidly and was near extinction by 1550 (Sued Badillo 1995b). According to Karen Anderson-Córdova, an estimated total of about 34,000 enslaved Native Americans were brought to both Hispaniola and Puerto Rico between 1509 and 1544 (Anderson-Córdova 1990; Martínez-Cruzado et al. 2005). A breakdown of this estimate for each island is not provided, but Anderson-Córdova suggests that the majority of "Indians" enumerated in the 1530 census were already of foreign origin (Anderson-Córdova 1990; Figueroa 1974). Although there is some evidence that the Amerindian population might have been larger than reported because only enslaved Indians or Indians in "encomienda" were counted, there is no reason to believe that "pure blooded" Indians, whether Taíno or foreign, had survived in significant numbers by the end of the sixteenth century (Brau 1966; Figueroa 1974; Fernández Méndez 1970; Anderson-Córdova 1990).

[...]

Advocates of Amerindian/Taíno identity and survival in the United States and Puerto Rico are inclined to exaggerate the importance of the "pure Indians" that suddenly appear or reappear in the historical record after an absence of 195 years (Haslip-Viera 2001). As reported most recently by Martínez-Cruzado and others, there were 1,756 "Indians" in the partido of San German in 1777 and 2,302 "Indians" in the same partido in 1787. For advocates of Amerindian survival, these figures are extremely significant because they demonstrate an alleged Taíno continuity (Martínez-Cruzado et al. 2001; Silvestrini and Luque de Sánchez 1988; Anderson-Córdova 1990; Brau 1966, 1969; Figueroa 1974; Jiménez de Wagenheim 1988). However, from a demographic, ethnic, and genetic standpoint, this population is of no importance when compared to the substantial numbers of mostly Africans and Europeans that began to arrive in Puerto Rico after the 1760s (Sued Badillo 1995b; Pike 1983; Picó 1986; Haslip-Viera 1999).

The historical record demonstrates that Africans of free and enslaved status were brought to Puerto Rico very soon after the colonization process began. In the years of economic stagnation and depopulation that followed the virtual extinction of Native Americans, the total official population of the island hovered between 3,500 and 8,000 persons (Vila Vilar 1974; Silverstrini and Luque de Sánchez 1988; Fernández Méndez 1970). By 1530, the African population may have already equaled or exceeded the combined Amerindian and European population. As noted earlier, an identifiable mixed African, Indian, and European population had also emerged at the beginning of the seventeenth century. With the continued arrival of mostly Africans and Europeans in the years between 1600 and 1750, the mixed population became increasingly "mulato," or of mixed European and African ancestry. The details for this period are skimpy, but the trend is clear.

[...]

In an attempt to exaggerate the Amerindian element in the biological history of Puerto Ricans, Martínez-Cruzado and his team have defined the term "pardo" as referring to persons of mixed European and Amerindian ancestry (Martínez-Cruzado et al. 2001). They cite no source for this truly extraordinary claim, which is not supported in the historical record, or by contemporary historians, anthropologists, and linguists. As would be expected, the term pardo is best translated into English as "brown," and was used in medieval Spain to define a person who had "brownish skin." The term was also used as the equivalent of "loro" when applied to humans, and was connected to the word "mulato" which defined persons of African with European or Amerindian ancestry in both Spain and the Americas during the sixteenth century (Álvarez Nazario 1974, 1982).

By the late seventeenth century, the term "pardo" had become a somewhat more respectable alternative to the more derogatory "mulato." In the Caribbean and in Puerto Rico, the term "pardo" was increasingly used to define the "free colored" population in contrast to "mulato," which was applied to persons of the lowest status and slaves of mixed African and European ancestry. Government officials, visitors to the island, and the census records of the eighteenth and nineteenth centuries are clear on this (Álvarez Nazario 1974, 1982; Kinsbruner 1996). The census of 1775 shows that the largest identified casta in Puerto Rico (46.7 percent) was of mixed ethnic background (defined as pardos libres) when compared to "Whites" (40.4 percent), "Free Blacks" (negros libres) and "slaves" (12.9 percent). [...]

The census of 1775 and those that followed from the late eighteenth to the end of the nineteenth century are also important because they demonstrate that the biological or population history of Puerto Ricans has been determined primarily by persons of European and African background, and not Taínos or Native Americans. Starting with a high birth rate (Picó 1986; Scarano 1993; Silvestrini and Luque de Sánchez 1988), the continued arrival of immigrants from the Canary Islands, the granting of freedom to runaway slaves from the non-Hispanic Caribbean, and new policies that fostered economic growth in commercial agriculture, the population of Puerto Rico began a dramatic period of growth that started in the early eighteenth century and continued until the 1790s, when other factors reinforced the pattern of growth. These included the arrival of French planters from Haiti, Spanish Creoles from Santo Domingo, their slaves, and other refugees from the slave uprisings and wars that engulfed the island of Hispaniola after 1791. They also included increased numbers of enslaved Africans for the expanding sugar and coffee sectors, and a dramatic increase in the number of impoverished immigrants from Spanish Galicia, Asturias, the Canary Islands, the Basque Country, Mallorca, and also from France, Corsica, Lebanon, Syria, and other parts of Western Europe, the Levantine Mediterranean, and the Americas (Álvarez Nazario 1974; Cifre de Loubriel 1962; Díaz Soler 1970, 1994; Fernández Méndez 1970; Figueroa 1974; Kinsbruner 1996; Marazzi 1974; Ortiz 1983; Picó 1986; Rivera 1992; Scarano 1993; Silvestrini and Luque de Sánchez 1988; Jiménez de Wagenheim 1988; Martínez-Cruzado et al. 2005).

[...]. Nevertheless, it is apparent that the high birth rate and the arrival of substantial numbers of Africans and "whites" had a dramatic impact on the overall make-up of the island population. [...]. Although a number of Amerindian and indo-mestizo convict and "contract" laborers were brought to Puerto Rico from Mexico and other areas to work on San Juan's fortifications and other projects from the late seventeenth to the early nineteenth centuries (Picó 1986; Sued Badillo 1995b; Pike 1983; Haslip-Viera 1999; Aguirre Beltrán 1972), it is clear that the most significant contribution to the biological makeup of contemporary Puerto Ricans came from Europeans and persons of mixed background. In terms of raw numbers and percentages, "whites" and persons of mixed, and mostly African and European background, clearly outranked persons defined as "Black" or "Indian." From the important base date of 1775 and up until 1897, persons defined as "white" constituted between 38.4 percent and 63.9 percent of the total population (51.5 percent to 63.9 percent from 1860 and 1897). At the same time, the population of mixed background varied from 32.2 percent to 46.7 percent of the total during the same period. Thus, given the complex ethnic history of the island's population, it is no wonder that individual Puerto Ricans can be said to look like "whites," "Arabs," "Hindus," "Amerindians," "Black Africans," "Chinese," and every other possible combination in between, with the continued use of terms such as "blanco," "colorao," "rubio," "trigueño," "Indio," "grifo," "jabao," "moreno," "mulato," "negro," and "prieto," as part of everyday parlance in the popular culture.

Martínez-Cruzado and his team have also sent decidedly mixed messages on the conclusions they have drawn from their research. On the one hand, they admit that after "1542," the Taínos "were slowly assimilated through the following decades or centuries by the settler population," that "an immigration wave with strong European and African components helped increase the population of Puerto Rico over thirteenfold during the 19th century," and that this immigration wave has resulted in a Puerto Rican population that is "highly mixed" or "the product of centuries of admixture."[4] On the other hand, they have also insisted that the population of western Puerto Rico "had a very high Amerindian ancestry in 1776," and that "the Taíno contribution to the current population is considerable," which are assertions not supported by the substance of their research (Martínez-Cruzado et al. 2001).

Martínez-Cruzado, himself, has also articulated these claims much more forcefully in a series of interviews with reporters from the popular media. [...] Again, these are claims that are not substantiated by the research.

Advocates of Taíno survival have used what they call "the myth of extinction" to unfairly discredit or attack those scholars who have been critical of their claims. Martínez-Cruzado, himself, has been quoted as saying that his research "challenges the traditional view that Indians in Puerto Rico became extinct in the early 16th century.[5] But in reality, academics have been very cautious about this issue. As previously noted, modern historians and anthropologists have discussed the possibility of Taíno or Amerindian survival in Puerto Rico for several decades. Salvador Brau first raised the issue in his *Historia de Puerto Rico* way back at the beginning of the twentieth century. However, any conclusion on whether the Taínos survived or became extinct depends on how the term extinction is defined. Ironically, Martínez-Cruzado and his team have made a very strong scientific case for extinction.

Using various criteria, anthropologists and historians have discussed how the Taínos may have survived physically, culturally, or through an assimilation process with other groups after contact was established with European and African populations, but from the standpoint of genetics, there seems to be little doubt that the Taínos became extinct. In their writings and pronouncements, Martínez-Cruzado and his team repeatedly admit that the Taínos inevitably mixed with Spaniards and Africans (Martínez-Cruzado et al. 2001; Martínez-Cruzado 2002). This means that they produced offspring of mixed background called mestizos, mulatos, pardos, and morenos during the colonial period, and not Taínos. In order to make the case against extinction, Martinez Cruzado and his team would have to locate individual Puerto Ricans who are "Amerindian" and demonstrably pure from a biological standpoint. However, it appears that locating such individuals would be highly unlikely if not impossible.[6]

CHAPTER 21

Amerindian mtDNA in Puerto Rico: When Does DNA matter?

By Jorge Estevez

This is a response to Haslip-Viera's (2006) essay published in CENTRO Journal and titled "The Politics of Taíno revivalism: The insignificance of Amerindian mtDNA in the population history of Puerto Ricans." In it Haslip-Viera critically comments on the recent mtDNA research, analysis, and conclusions of Dr. Juan Martínez Cruzado, who demonstrated that up to 61 percent of Puerto Ricans have Amerindian ancestors. Although eloquently written, as is always the case with the author, the article seems to miss the point of current research entirely. Further, the author's claims are based on the assumption that history is not biased and therefore cannot lend itself to scrutiny or re-interpretation due to new evidence that may arise to the contrary. The aim of this [essay] is to offer a different perspective. It explains why 61 percent of the current population of Puerto Rico is indeed a significant number and how this revelation can only re-enforce Puerto Rican identity.

It is clear that Puerto Ricans can and do identify with either European or African ancestry without fear of ridicule or otherwise. On the other hand when Puerto Ricans identify with their native heritage, they are often labeled racists, or at best fanatics. In fact, identifying with the Indian component of this tripartite population is somehow seen as a denial of Negritude and misguided romanticism. The obvious implication of Taíno DNA in modern Puerto Ricans suggests that perhaps the history of the island must be re-evaluated. If this is the case, then people claiming Taíno descent are not delusional, as some have stated, but rather part of a growing trend among Caribbean peoples to learn the truth about their past. The extinction of the Taíno is a myth, and like all myths, eventually this one will die out as well.

As most people who are familiar with the Caribbean know, there are no Amerindians in the region, at least this is what has been traditionally said, written, and accepted. For this very reason, news of Native American mtDNA in the modern population of Puerto Rico is causing quite a national and international stir. In March 1999, Dr. Juan

Originally published in *CENTRO: Journal of the Center for Puerto Rican Studies* 20(2): 219–228, 2008.

C. Martínez Cruzado, a biology professor at the University of Puerto Rico in Mayagüez, conducted a mitochondrial DNA restriction study on 800 people selected based on the 1990 Census of Population and Housing by a random and systematic method designed to choose a sample set representative of the Puerto Rican population. The study found that a staggering 61 percent had mtDNA deriving from a female Indian ancestor. Mitochondrial DNA is passed down through the mother's line to her children; however, only her female children can pass along the mtDNA. For some this was not particularly surprising. Indeed, it certainly was not surprising to those involved in what is commonly called the Taíno Restoration Movement. Also not surprised were many indigenistas who in the past had to publicly adhere to the conservative view of the island's supposed "extinct" Taíno population, while privately agreeing that there are indeed varying degrees of cultural, linguistic, and biological survival. Clearly, science is proving that even things that appear to be set in stone can be refuted with modern investigative techniques and tools.

[...] Dr. Martínez Cruzado has made it clear that of the 61 percent showing mtDNA in Puerto Rico, 16 percent show that they are descendants of Indians who were probably brought to the island as slaves or in migrations from other Latin American countries. It is the remaining 84 percent that either pose a problem for some or offer a solution to others as to the true fate of the islands native population.

When many scholars first became aware of these mtDNA studies, they suggested that the results must be wrong. This argument later changed into a vague admission of native descent on the island. Some proposed that these native genetic traits must come from migrations from abroad or possibly from Indian slaves brought to the island during colonial times. If this were true, surely there must be some record, somewhere, clearly stating that the number of Indian slaves being brought to Puerto Rico was higher than the importation of African slaves. But there isn't any. In addition, this DNA study was based on females. The majority of slaves, African, Indian, or otherwise, who were brought into Puerto Rico and the other Caribbean Islands were mostly male.

Mitochondrial DNA is located in the mitochondria, and 100 percent of this DNA is inherited from the mother. In contrast to most DNA of eukaryotic organisms, this is found in the nucleus. Branches of mtDNA (female) or Y-DNA (male) are known as "Haplogroups." Native American mtDNA haplogroups are as follows; A, B, C, and D. These are found throughout the Americas. Within the Haplogroups there are different sequence types called "Haplotypes," and these run into the thousands. [...]

Dr. Martínez Cruzado's analysis found that 88 percent of Puerto Rican Native American mtDNAs are composed of Haplogroups A and C, with A being the most dominant. Within these two Haplogroups, which are also found throughout the Americas, there are Haplotypes that are not found in North, Central, or South America. In other words, they are geographically specific, localized Haplotypes. In a smaller, but certainly not conclusive study conducted in the Dominican Republic, Dr. Martínez Cruzado found that 80 percent of the Native American mtDNAs belonged to Haplogroups A and C. The fact that Haplogroups A and C dominate on both islands suggests a common origin. In comparing the Haplogroups between the two islands, there was no clear match with Haplogroup A. The best explanation is that the Native American populations of both islands had a common origin but separate evolutionary processes within their respective domains. Separate evolutionary processes could happen only if they have been on those islands for thousands of years, which the classic Taíno were.

Many archeologists maintain that anywhere between 6000 to 7000 years ago native groups from Central America, possibly from the Yucatan, arrived in the Caribbean. About 4000 years later, migrations from the Orinoco river basin in South America began arriving. It was a mixture of all these different peoples that eventually gave rise to the classic Taíno. It stands to reason, then, that the classic Taíno did not and could not belong to a single Haplogroup. In Puerto Rico, Haplogroup A samples indicate the last wave of Arawakan speakers to enter the region.

In April 2005 the *National Geographic* selected FamilyTreeDNA to head the Geographic project, a massive undertaking focusing on tracing human migrations. People from around the world submitted inner-mouth swab samples for the project (this is how DNA samples are extracted). Of the Puerto Ricans that independently submitted samples (mostly people doing genealogical investigations), 70 percent are showing Haplogroups A and C with minor B and D. A smaller number of Dominicans and Cubans have also submitted samples. Roughly 50 percent of each of these populations is showing Haplogroups A and C as well. In short, this independent study is confirming, without setting out to do so, Dr. Juan Martínez Cruzado's original findings.

So what does this all mean? For starters, one cannot simply dismiss DNA as some people would have us believe. DNA analysis and conclusions are complicated and not easily understood by non-geneticists. When it is shown that 61 percent of a population is of Amerindian origin, and there isn't supposed to be any persons with such a background, the results are very impressive. Dr. Gabriel Haslip-Viera's assertion that mtDNA is insignificant in Puerto Rican demographics inspires the following question: if 61 percent is not significant, then what percentage is? Haslip-Viera's paper claims that the 61 percent showing mtDNA may have derived from a population of as little as 125 native females (this kind of analysis is usually done by molecular anthropologists), but it could also have come from as many as 800 or even 8000 females.

There is no way to know for sure. The fact remains that 61 percent of the population does indeed have native mtDNA.

Is there Taíno ancestry on the island? It is a question that has been asked many times before. The answer has come swiftly, with a scientifically definitive yes. So why the continued denial and staunch opposition? [...]

Of course to many historians it seems that if the current scientific evidence does not support the historical "facts" model, then the data must be faulty. But if we take a closer holistic approach to the question of Taíno survival along with the DNA evidence, a clearer picture emerges. Native linguistic influence on Caribbean Spanish, material culture, and other dimensions of Taíno culture are rarely studied, and when they are, it is usually superficially. The fact is that the amount of linear succession is remarkably uniform and vast throughout Puerto Rico and the other major islands of the Caribbean. Let us take a look at some of these.

Linguistics

Two hundred everyday words and expressions in addition to several thousand attested toponyms of Taíno lexicon are used in the Spanish spoken in the Caribbean. This is no casual linguistic influence. In most books the classic Taíno are credited with leaving only a few words, such as barbecue, hurricane, savannah, hammock, or canoe. One would assume that if this is all that is left of the Taíno language, then surely the classic Taíno's influence on the modern Spanish of the region is minimal and further proof of the virtual demise of the population. But upon closer inspection it becomes clear that the classic Taíno left a substantially deeper impact on the Spanish language. Two hundred words are neither minimal nor coincidental, but are in fact direct evidence of this people's continuity and survival.

Many historians in the past have tried to reconcile this obvious linguistic legacy with the "fact" of Taíno extinction. How can people that supposedly died out thirty years after contact, as many historians claim, leave so many of their words? The most immediate assumption is that the Spaniards, not having names for the new things they encountered, borrowed the existing Taíno names. While this is certainly plausible in some cases, it certainly cannot be applied to the multitude of Taíno words used today. [...]

In this case we see that the Spanish had not one but two names for the single-piece wooden tray (*dornajo* and *gamello*) that the classic Taíno called *batea*. In Puerto Rico and the other Caribbean islands both the word batea and the instrument are still used today. But why do we still call it batea? Unless the Spanish collectively decided to exchange either name they had for these trays for the Taíno name *batea*, it makes no sense why we would still call these instruments by their ancient native name.

[...]

Some modern linguists have stated that not enough research has been done on the remnants/influence of classic Taíno language on the Spanish of the region (Granberry 2004). In contrast, the English-speaking countries of the Caribbean have very few words stemming from the Taíno language. In places like Jamaica (which does in fact have Taíno/maroon continuity) we find few Taíno words. The names of flora and fauna have been replaced with English names. Fruit such as *guanábana*, a Taíno name that is commonly used in Puerto Rico, is now called soursop. Could it be that the English (who also had contact with the Taíno) were able to "make up" or exchange their own names for certain things they were not familiar with and the Spanish could not?

Material Culture
It is inexplicable if not irresponsible to keep Taíno in the realm of the past. This trend, however, is certainly not unique to Puerto Rico, for it seems to be the ideology in most Latin American countries. My opinion on this is that social Darwinism is a rule that is followed to the letter regarding any connection to the indigenous past, making us then descendants of *"savages"* rather than the Spanish conquerors.

On 15 September 2006 I attended the opening of "The New Old World Photographic Exhibit" at the Museo de las Américas in Puerto Rico. This exhibit was on loan from the Smithsonian National Museum of the American Indian, featuring photographer Marisol Villanueva's work on Taíno/Carib material culture.

The exhibit was Caribbean wide in scope and focused on the surviving material culture of both the Taíno and Carib. It was very clear from the exhibit that both of these two peoples share very similar cultural traits. The rural cultures of Puerto Rico and the other Caribbean islands have retained a significant degree of customs and practices from our Taíno ancestors. I felt that at last the Taíno legacy was receiving some recognition.

There was another exhibit, titled "Our African Heritage," which displayed many strikingly beautiful objects from across Africa. Ironically, none of the objects were made in Puerto Rico or by Puerto Ricans. The objects came from a private collection donated by Dr. Ricardo Alegría. While there certainly are many cultural icons that do reflect the African cultural legacy in Puerto Rico, I felt that this was a poor example of it.

One thing that disturbed me about this exhibit was a case displaying an object that is clearly Taíno: the *güiro*, a rasping instrument that is used in merengue, salsa, and bachata music. This instrument, traditionally attributed to the Taíno, has now become African!

According to Ricardo Alegría, who is the father of Puerto Rican archeology, the güiro must be African simply because there is no mention of it by the Spanish chroniclers. I pointed out that the chroniclers also never mentioned the Taíno stone collars used during the course of *batu/batey* games our ancestors played. In other words one can only guess at the number of cultural objects and customs the Spanish did not record simply because it did not hold their attention, and of course today's scholars assume it must be African if said objects are not Spanish. As my friend and colleague Dr. Max Forte, head editor of the Caribbean Amerindian Centrelink webpage, says, "African seems to be the default identity in the Spanish Caribbean." If it is not clearly Spanish, then it must be vaguely African.

The word güiro itself is of Taíno origin. It stems from Native words such as *higuera* (Caribbean gourd), *güichara, güira,* etc. Unless the Africans brought the güiro over from Africa and then decided to give it a Taíno name, there is absolutely no reason why the güiro should be considered African. Besides, anyone familiar with African cultures knows that the güiro is not used in Africa, neither in tribal music nor in the contemporary African music scene. It simply is not an African instrument.

It would be wonderful to see an exhibit in Puerto Rico focusing on Taíno material culture and customs, beyond the archeological findings. Such an exhibit would shed light on *casabe* making, *mabi* preparation, the nets used for catching *jueyes* (crabs), basket weaving (*jabas*), and fishing nets (*nasa*), *pasteles*, endemic medicinal plant use, and the multitude of Taíno customs that have continued to be a part of Puerto Rican culture. But these are rarely mentioned and often overlooked; hence many people on the island are not even aware of just how much Taíno cultural continuity there is.

Census

I will not offer much in the way of census records simply because I do not believe in them. As a native from the Dominican Republic, I find that today, in the age of computers, we cannot get an accurate census count. In the Dominican Republic there is no accurate number of illegal Haitians living in the country. Why? The Haitians for obvious reasons do not want to be counted. The same can be said of illegal Dominicans living in Puerto Rico. How many are there? There are only estimates, but no one knows for sure. Some people believe census takers have hidden agendas and refuse to be counted. It seems highly unlikely that, 450 to 500 years ago, when our ancestors were fleeing and hiding for their lives, few of them would have wanted to be counted. For the Spanish it would have been nearly impossible to count people who were living in the most remote areas of the island. Although Puerto Rico has a small landmass, it is also extremely mountainous. In the past it was easier to have material goods delivered from outside the island than from its interior!

To support his argument Haslip-Viera (2006) used many quotes from Karen F. Anderson-Córdova's dissertation (1990). It is clear that we cannot discount the fact that natives were imported from other parts of the Americas into the Caribbean— as Anderson-Córdova states in her dissertation. But were these slaves female or male? Most of the slave trade focused on males for obvious reasons; after all, men were thought to be better suited for working the gold mines and the sugarcane fields. That said, the mounting evidence of Taíno mtDNA survival only adds to the hypothesis that there is indeed a native element in the Caribbean. The problem I find with Anderson-Córdova's otherwise brilliant work is that at the time she wrote it, mtDNA studies were a few years in the future. Mitochondrial DNA could have either substantiated her hypothesis or lent it a wider scope. At the time the only evidence to support her theories were based on historical records. These records reveal that the Spanish historians manipulated records or reported from a very biased viewpoint for selected audiences.

American historian Dr. Lynne Guitar, who has done extensive historical and ethnographic work in the Dominican Republic, writes that "colonists and Spanish administrators in the sixteenth century manipulated their reports, letters, censuses and histories for their own social, economic and political gain." Closer inspection of the historical record reveals that in one form or another Indians are mentioned in Puerto Rico's history as well as in Cuba and the Dominican Republic. It is evident that the supposed extinction of the people is a point of view created by past historians and perpetuated by their modern counterparts. Dr. Guitar also demonstrates that the islands were never governed in their entirety. The Spanish had outposts, towns, and a few cities, but most of the inaccessible regions of the islands remained isolated. Below are a few examples of Taíno's mentioned in Puerto Rican history:

In 1543 it was reported to the King of Spain by the bishop of San Juan, that there were but 60 Native Indians remaining in the entire island of Puerto Rico. Yet when the Earl of Cumberland, who had captured San Juan, fled the island, the King of Spain sent an armada, commanded by General Don Francisco Coloma, to re-conquer the colony in 1599, and was surprised to find the city of San Juan inhibited almost entirely of Indians. (quoted in Steiner 1974:17)

The one of most interest is the indio, or that of the descendants of inhabitants found on the island at its discovery and settlement. They form a great mass of the country laborers over the island, especially in the centre and northeastern section. They have much of the serious appearance of the North American Indian, with his high cheek bones, but their color is less red and more swarthy. (Harrington 1899:174)

As a result of their battles with the Spanish, of disease and emigration to other islands, of hard labor in the mines, and other unaccustomed drudgery, the Native population of Puerto Rico rapidly disappeared, so that there were but 60 Native Indians remaining in the island. At this time there are a few traces of them remaining, at least this census has not discovered any. Still in such matters no census can vie with the trained observer, and therefore attention must be called to the following statements of Captain W.S. Shuyler in a report on August 30, 1899: while work was being done on the roads, I had the occasion to watch crowds of 700 or 800 men gathered around the pay tables at Las Marias, La Vega, and Anasco. The frequency of the Indian type was very noticeable. While it is almost certain that there is today no single Indian of pure stock in PR it is equally sure that the type can be seen everywhere in the mountain settlements. At San German I noticed a woman whose color, hair, and features were true Indian as seen in the Southwest of the US. (Davis 1900)

El Yunque, where marked Indian features were casually observed everywhere, especially in the isolated mountainous regions, where the inhabitants still preserve Indian features to a marked degree. (Fewkes 1970:24-5)

Today there are no pure Taínos...Mestizos are found in the rural towns of Oriente plateau in Cuba, also in the woods of El Yunque massif on Puerto Rico. (Lovén 1979:499)

...the Taínos were a people that long ago became extinct. Such relics in the form of objects still used, or ancient superstitions occurring in folklore, as may still be found among the mestizo "descendants" in the Yunque Rainforest, of Oriente in Cuba, or among the Negro interbred population of the Dominican Republic. (Lovén 1979: 657)

Puerto Rican Identity

As a native from the Dominican Republic it feels awkward for me to speak on Puerto Rican identity. Identity for the most part is a personal issue. That said, it could be assumed that all identities are created. For example, there were no Dominicans or people identifying with being Dominican 164 years ago, when the Republic was formed and the island renamed. How long did it take before people began calling themselves Dominican? The same can be said for Puerto Rican identity.

People who identify with their Taíno ancestry are in fact reidentifying with a sense of self, a consciousness that was long ago suppressed due to historical inaccuracies and local politics. That sense of "I am from here" is an indigenous sentiment that should be extended to anyone identifying with the Spanish or African components of this tripartite nation of people. From an early age people associate with the cultural icons around them, and before it is "revealed" to them that they are Puerto Ricans, they already know. In the past, however, native customs, linguistics, and material culture were never clearly defined as native, certainly not in schools or popular literature. When they are, people begin to take a deeper look into their past and identities. Some realize that perhaps their connection to the classic Taíno is stronger than what they have been led to believe by academics.

It is indeed perplexing for many Puerto Ricans who relate to certain Taíno cultural practices, such as casabe bread making for example, only to be ridiculed for identifying with the very people who contributed this custom to us. But people today are asking concrete questions about our historical past and making connections not just culturally but now also genetically with our Taíno ancestors. This phenomenon may appear new, but it is not. It has been brewing for quite some time.

The persistence of a Taíno genetic component in contemporary Dominican life, along with the survival of certain undeniably indigenous beliefs and traditions, requires the recognition of a native substratum in our midst today (García Arévalo 1990: 275). This observation not only applies to the Dominican Republic and Cuba, but to Puerto Rico as well. Fortunately, many young scholars, some of whom are of Caribbean/Puerto Rican descent, are taking a closer look at our histories and are asking new questions and questioning old answers.

Conclusion

If we, as if by magic, were to extract all things Taíno, including the names of flora and fauna, place names, culture, and customs from the Spanish Caribbean, would we still be the same unique people we are today? Indeed, it would be interesting to find another "extinct" culture that has influenced the language and material culture of another as much as the classic Taíno have. We can conclude that if we could extract all things native from the island, we would be unrecognizable as Puerto Ricans, Cubans, or Dominicans. Of course, it can also be argued that if we extracted the Spanish and the African influence we would not be the same people either. But guess what? We would still be indigenous, which is the point that those involved with Taíno reclamation and reidentification have been trying to express all along. Embracing the Taíno does not imply a hatred for the Spanish or racism toward the African, far from it. After all, if the classic Taíno were a mixture of many different ethnicities—and they were—then nothing has really changed. We continue to be a people of mixed blood.

It is a fact that at least 61 percent of the Puerto Rican population has mtDNA that is native, and mostly of Taíno extraction. Does this mean that all Puerto Ricans are Indians? No, but it does suggest that people who identify with their native roots should be taken as seriously and with as much respect as anyone claiming African or Spanish descent. Imagine how many folktales, home remedies, oral traditions, etc. have disappeared simply because when the word "Indio" is attached to them, they somehow lose their validity and thus are rendered unauthentic. This is shameful, considering how many Puerto Ricans claim to have a grandmother or grandfather who identified strongly with their Taíno roots.

Taíno ancestry, culture, and customs have always been with us. It is time to elevate the Taíno to their proper place in history. Our ancestors contributed many things that are central to us still to this day. It should not come as a surprise that we also have a genetic connection. Taíno self-identification is on the rise. It is not going to go away. It is time to take a serious look into this phenomenon. Perhaps it is also time to look into the phenomena of staunch denial and opposition of all things native on the island. [...]

CHAPTER 22

Amerindian mtDNA Does Not Matter: A Reply to Jorge Estevez and the Privileging of Taíno Identity in the Spanish-speaking Caribbean

By Gabriel Haslip-Viera

In his article "Amerindian mtDNA in Puerto Rico: When does DNA matter?" Jorge Estevez makes a spirited defense of indigenous identity and the mtDNA research completed on Puerto Rican islanders and other Caribbean Latin@s by the geneticist, Juan Carlos Martínez Cruzado and his colleagues. However, this defense of genetic research connected to indigenous identity is deficient in a number of ways. For the most part, Mr. Estevez merely reiterates the assertions made by Martínez Cruzado and his colleagues, without really engaging my assessment of this research. He also raises a number of issues with regard to culture and linguistics that were not discussed in my article, and he suggests that I hold certain assumptions and made certain statements that I did not make in my critique.

mtDNA Research and genetic ancestry testing in general
For starters, I never claimed that the percentages provided by Martínez Cruzado and his team on mtDNA in Puerto Ricans were inaccurate, even though I also have serious reservations about the scientific validity of this research. It was clearly stated in my article and its subtitle that the indigenous mtDNA found in 61 percent of Puerto Rican islanders is insignificant because almost all the persons in an individual's family tree dating back to the 16th century are not analyzed. All persons living today have two parents, four grandparents, eight grandparents, sixteen great grandparents, and thirty-two great, great grandparents (see Figure 1). Projecting further back in time, each of us had 128 parental ancestors in 1790, 1,024

Originally published in *CENTRO: Journal of the Center for Puerto Rican Studies* 20(2): 228–237, 2008.

in 1700, and 16,384 in the 1580s, when *pure blooded* Taínos (my emphasis) probably became extinct.[1] In actuality mtDNA, which is traced through a single female line (see black boxes in diagram), only constitutes a tiny element or residue of the total genetic composition of each Caribbean Latin@ if the family tree is projected back to the end of the sixteenth century. This means that Martínez Cruzado and his team have traced the indigenous mtDNA of only fifteen females in a family tree of 16,384 individuals over the course of fifteen generations.

Martínez Cruzado and his team have also completed preliminary but unpublished research on the Y-chromosome of Puerto Rican islanders; however, this research has not received the kind of attention and hyped-up publicity that the mtDNA research has received. Unlike mtDNA, the Y-chromosome is passed exclusively through the paternal line (father, grandfather, great-grandfather, etc.), and like mtDNA, it represents a very small part of each individual's genetic history. As reported to journalist Juan González, 70 percent of 800 Puerto Ricans sampled by Martínez Cruzado had the Y-chromosome of Europeans, 20 percent had the Y-chromosome of Africans, and only 10 percent had the Y-chromosome of Amerindians (not necessarily Taíno).[2] This constitutes almost the reverse of the ethnic background for percentages of female mtDNA in the same population and provides strong evidence for demonstrating that the Puerto Rican population is thoroughly mixed. The limitations of this research for mixed populations was also demonstrated in my own case about a year ago when I was informed that my mtDNA was of African origin despite the appearance of my white-complexioned mother, and my Y-Chromosome was of European origin despite my father's "mulatto" appearance.[3]

At one point in his essay, Mr. Estevez challenges me to answer the following question: "If 61 percent is not significant, then what percentage is?" The answer to this challenge is not to be found in mtDNA or Y-chromosome research, but potentially in what is referred to as "genetic ancestry testing" or "admixture mapping," which attempts to determine the relative contribution of selected ancestral populations to an individual's genome. This kind of test analyzes an individual's "autosomal DNA," or the majority portion of a person's genetic material in an effort to determine the ethnic breakdown in percentages of an individual's genetic make-up. Unfortunately, there are currently major problems with this kind of testing because of incomplete databases, contradictory results, disagreements on how to define ethnic groups, and the curious anomalies that sometimes emerge, such as the finding that a South Asian Punjabi had 8 percent Amerindian ancestry (Koerner 2005; Yang 2007). In any case, a number of persons claiming a Taíno pedigree have been shocked to learn that their Amerindian ancestry is quite minor or practically nonexistent as a result of these tests.

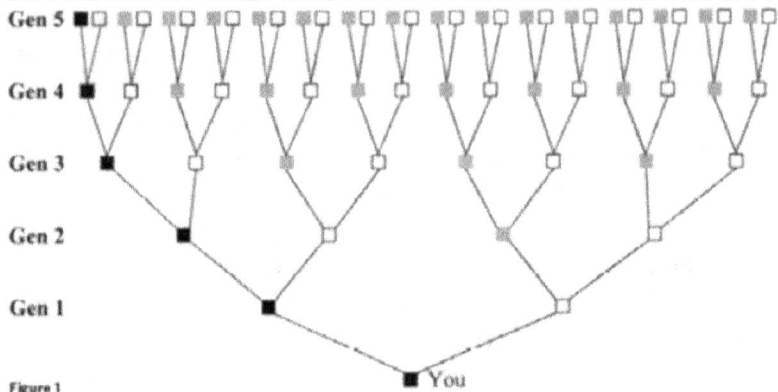

Figure 1

In an internet posting, "Marisol" is shocked to learn that her ancestry is 80 percent European, 16 percent Asian, and only 3 percent Native American. "Marisol" is subsequently consoled by a number of respondents who equate Asian ancestry with the Native American, but who nevertheless ignore the importance of the 80 percent figure for European ancestry.[4] In another internet posting, "Elder" Jim Runningfox (aka: James López) of the "Aymaco Taíno Tribe," is surprised to learn that his ancestry is 80 percent European, 13 percent Sub-Saharan African, and only 7 percent Native American, with 0 percent East Asian. In a statement to tribal members, Mr. Runningfox describes how he is particularly puzzled by the European and the "South Sahara African results," which he feels are "too high." He also considers quitting the Aymaco tribe because of the test results, but is dissuaded by respondents, including Mr. Estevez, who claim that 7 percent Amerindian ancestry (Mr. Estevez), or even "1 drop of Taíno blood" (Cacike Coqui) is sufficient for continued membership in the tribe.[5]

Mr. Estevez also fails to mention the results of his own admixture test, which appears in a book chapter that he co-authored with anthropologists Lynne Guitar and Pedro Ferbel-Azcarate (aka: Peter Ferbel) (Guitar, Ferbel-Azcarate and Estevez 2006). Mr. Estevez reports that he has "a significantly high quantity of indigenous markers" but fails to provide the percentages "within five generations" that he states are provided by the company, DNA Print Genomics.[6] He also states that he was told that "just four generations ago" his ancestors "were what used to be called 'full-blooded' natives." However, companies of this type have been criticized for telling clients what they would like to hear (Bolnick et al. 2007; Nixon 2007). Curiously, Mr. Estevez also minimizes the importance of genetic testing in his section of the co-authored chapter while emphasizing its importance in the response to my article. He states that "we Taíno as a people, validate the DNA evidence, not the other way around," and that "the journey of self discovery...is about culture, not genes, for genes say little about us as a people" (Guitar, Ferbel-Azcarate and Estevez 2006:61)

History

Despite suggestions or claims to the contrary, I do not assume that "history is without bias" and "cannot lend itself to scrutiny or re-interpretation." On the contrary, professional historians are trained to continuously search for new evidence that may result in historical reinterpretation. The discovery of important new evidence and the reinterpretation of that evidence is what often elevates the reputation and status of historians in the discipline. [...]

Mr. Estevez is very selective when it comes to his acceptance of historical evidence. He is dismissive of the census enumerations that were done by the Spanish authorities during the course of the colonial period in Puerto Rico (cf. Haslip-Viera 2006). However, he is quick to accept without question the racialist judgments of Anglo-American officials and anthropologists who reported on the populations of Cuba, Puerto Rico, and the Dominican Republic in the aftermath of the 1898 Spanish American War. It is not clear, for example, why Jesse Walter Fewkes and Sven Lovén are quoted. They refer to "mestizos," or persons of mixed background who "still preserve Indian features to a marked degree." They are not referring to surviving Indians or Taínos.[7] The quotes from Michael Harrington, and U.S. Army General George W. Davis, who briefly served as governor of Puerto Rico, are equally problematic (cf. Schmidt-Nowara 2006). We need to be reminded that in the aftermath of the Spanish American War, Anglo-American officials, anthropologists, and others were generally mystified by the diversity in physical appearances that they encountered in the Spanish-speaking Caribbean— especially within families. As would be expected, Harrington and Davis applied and articulated their own racialist ideas and stereotypes on the people they described in their reports and publications. In their travels, they encountered people in Cuba and Puerto Rico whom they thought conformed to the Amerindian physical stereotype as conceptualized in Europe and the United States, but in actuality, we do not know what the pre-Columbian Taínos looked like with any kind of precision.

Mr. Estevez and other advocates of Taíno survival also suggest or claim that hundreds or perhaps thousands of Taínos were able to establish independent communities in the mountainous interior regions of the islands during the course of the sixteenth century, and that these populations are the basis for indigenous survival into the twenty-first century (cf. Barreiro 2006). Mr. Estevez quotes or paraphrases the work of anthropologist Lynne Guitar, who states that "colonists and Spanish administrators in the sixteenth century manipulated their reports, letters, censuses and histories for their own social, economic and political gain," and that the Spaniards had only a few outposts, towns, and cities and never governed the islands in their entirety (Steiner 1974). These comments are nothing new and have been articulated elsewhere by others (Sued Badillo 1995a); however, there is no evidence that large numbers of Amerindians were able to establish independent communities in isolation of the Spaniards. The Spaniards were fully capable of scouring the islands in search of Indians to enslave or employ in the gold mining enterprises and plantations, as was the case in Hispaniola in 1493–1495, or in Brazil with the *Bandeirantes* and other slave traders in the seventeenth and eighteenth centuries (Wilson 1990; Hemming 1995a, 1995b). The historical evidence shows that impoverished Spaniards and Africans also fled or migrated into the interior regions of the islands, and as a result, what emerged over the centuries is what is seen at the present time— mixed populations of mostly African and European background with minor vestiges of the indigenous (Haslip-Viera 2006; Candelario 2007; Duany 1985; Moya Pons 1985; Pérez 2006).

Culture

The apparent suggestion that I may have claimed that Taíno culture is extinct is also not true. I did not discuss culture or cultural influences in my article, but a number of assertions made by Mr. Estevez with regard to indigenous cultural influences are also problematic. For starters, it is not true that Taíno culture has been minimized in the Spanish-speaking Caribbean. On the contrary, the influence of Taíno culture has been exaggerated out of all proportion to its actual importance. A tripartite cultural heritage that combines European, indigenous, and African elements has been promoted in Cuba, Puerto Rico, and to a lesser degree, in the Dominican Republic since at least the late nineteenth century; the indigenous (or "second root" after the Spanish) is seen as more important than the African (Duany 2002; Candelario 2007; Roberts 2001; Sagás 2000; Schmidt-Nowara 2006). In Puerto Rico, there are many more museums devoted to the Taíno and their legacy than there are museums devoted to African culture and its influence.[8] In the Dominican Republic, the Museo del Hombre Dominicano (Museum of the Dominican Man) continues to devote a much larger space to the indigenous than it does to the African despite the greater importance of African culture in that country. In a recent book, sociologist Ginetta Candelario has shown how the cultural establishment in the Dominican Republic continues to resist the inclusion of displays that highlight the African legacy (Candelario 2007). There also is no truth to the claim that the influence of the Taíno language on the vernacular of the Spanish-speaking Caribbean has been minimized. Mr. Estevez fails to make reference to the important work that has been done on this topic by Manuel Álvarez Nazario (1977, 1995), David Cruz de Jesús (2003), Edwin Miner Solá (2002), Rodolfo Cambiaso (1974), and Emilio Tejera (1977), among others (Fonfrías 1969, Perea and Perea 1941). At one point, Mr. Estevez also states that "it would be interesting to find another 'extinct' culture that has influenced the language and material culture of another to the extent the Classic Taíno have." This thoroughly overblown statement seems to ignore the many "extinct cultures" that have had a much more profound influence on the peoples and cultures of the modern world—the most obvious being the influence of ancient Greece, Rome, and the Mediterranean world in the areas of art, architecture, language, law, philosophy, politics, and religion. The issue here is not the extinction of Taíno culture, which has had some influence on the contemporary cultures of the Spanish-speaking Caribbean, but the near annihilation of the Taíno population by the beginning of the seventeenth century and the subsequent mixing of the remnants with Europeans, Africans, and others. The cultural mixtures that have resulted do not justify the privileging of a Taíno identity or pedigree in the contemporary period.

Identities

Mr. Estevez laments the fact that persons who claim a Taíno identity or pedigree may be ridiculed for doing so. But it should be understood that such ridicule may result from a valid understanding that ethnic and cultural purity does not exist in the Spanish-speaking Caribbean or anywhere else. Most Caribbean Latin@s know that they are of mixed background, that Europeans, Africans, Asians, Middle Easterners, and the Indigenous have all contributed to the biological diversity and cultural history of the Spanish-speaking Caribbean in some way, and that ideally, no single group, whether European, African, Indigenous, or whatever, should be privileged with regards to their identity or pedigree. Mr. Estevez also states that "our ancestors have contributed many things that are central to us still to this day," and that the time has come "to elevate the Taíno to their proper place in history," but as noted earlier, the influence of the Taíno has been exaggerated out of all proportion to its actual importance. Historically, the Taíno and the indigenous have been used in the Spanish-speaking Caribbean to marginalize or denigrate Africans and their cultural contributions. As Mr. Estevez knows, all non-white persons in the Dominican Republic by definition are referred to and are asked to identify as some type of *Indio* or Indian regardless of their skin color and appearance, under the assumption that Dominicans cannot possibly be Black. Yet in the Dominican Republic, there also is the concept articulated in the phrase "Black behind the ears," which means that regardless of a claimed European, Asian, Middle Eastern, or Indigenous ancestry or pedigree, there is the likelihood of an African ancestry that should not be ignored—a concept that also exists in Puerto Rico in the phrase "¿Y tu abuela, donde está? (And your grandmother, where is she?) (Candelario 2007; Sagás 2000; Roberts 2001).[9]

At this point, it appears that the effort by Caribbean Latin@s to claim an exclusive European, African or indigenous identity based on biology is floundering badly with predictions that such ethnic exclusivity will not be supported by scientific research in the future. In particular, those persons who claim a privileged Taíno ancestry or pedigree and have taken the admixture test are finding out that the Indigenous component in their genome is quite minor when compared to the European or the African component. These tests, which have been commercialized to an extraordinary degree on the internet and other media, also need to be monitored and their results subjected to a rigorous, scientific peer review process in order to avoid what is already beginning to happen—the deliberate and public distortion of test results.[10] We also need to be reminded of the realities of race and ethnicity in the United States and the Spanish-speaking Caribbean and its social construction in the contemporary period. For example, all those who claim an exclusive Taíno identity or pedigree should remember that a Caribbean Latin@ with stereotypical Black African features and tightly coiled hair may indeed have indigenous mtDNA or the Y-chromosome (etc.), but this individual will still be considered Black in the Spanish-speaking Caribbean and the United States[11] and will be treated or mistreated accordingly.

REFERENCES

Abbad y Lasierra, Fray Iñigo. 2002 (1866, 1776). *Historia geográfica, civil y natural de la Isla de Puerto Rico.* 3ra. ed. Madrid and San Juan: Editorial Dos Calles and Centro de Investigaciones Históricas.

_____. 1788. *Noticias de la historia geográfica, civil, y politica de Puerto Rico.* Madrid.

About the Schomburg Center for Research in Black Culture. n.d. Gale. Accessed 1 March 2006. <http://www.gale.com/free_resources/bhm/literature/schomburg.htm>.

Acosta-Belén, Edna, ed. 1980. *La mujer en la sociedad puertorriqueña.* Río Piedras: Ediciones Huracán.

Acosta-Belen, Edna. And Korrol, Virginia Sánchez. 1991. The World of Jesús Colón. In *The Jesús Colón Papers.* ed. Centro de Estudios Puertorriqueños New York: Centro de Estudios Puertorriqueños, Hunter College, City University of New York.

_____. 1993. 'The World of Jesús Colón,' to Jesús Colón. In *The Way it Was and Other Writings.* Houston: Arte Público.

Aguirre Beltrán, Gonzalo. 1972 (1946). *La población negra de México.* Mexico City: Fondo de Cultura Económica.

Albizu Campos, Pedro. 1972. *La conciencia nacional puertorriqueña.* México, D.F.: Siglo XXI.

Alegría Pons, J.F. 1992. Aspectos de la religiosidad popular en Puerto Rico. *Claridad* 27 December - 2 January: 16-17.

_____. 1991. Latin Empire: Puerto Rap. *CENTRO: Journal of the Center for Puerto Rican Studies* 3(2): 77-85.

Álvarez Nazario, Manuel. 1974 [1961]. *El elemento afronegroide en el español de Puerto Rico: Contribución al estudio del negro en América.* San Juan de Puerto Rico: Instituto de Cultura Puertorriqueña.

_____. 1977. *El influjo indígena en el español de Puerto Rico.* Río Piedras: Editorial Universitaria, Universidad de Puerto Rico.

_____. 1982. *Orígenes y desarrollo del español en Puerto Rico* (siglos XVI y XVII). Río Piedras: Editorial de la Universidad de Puerto Rico.

_____. 1995. *Arqueología linguística: estudios modernos dirigidos al rescate y reconstrucción del arahuaco taíno.* San Juan: Editorial de la Universidad de Puerto Rico.

Ancheta, Angelo. 2006. Filipino Americans, Foreigner Discrimination, and the Lines of Racial Sovereignty. In *Positively No Filipinos Allowed: Building Communities and Discourse*, eds. Antonio Tiongson, Jr., Edgardo Gutiérrez, and Ricardo Gutiérrez. Philadelphia: Temple University Press.

Anderson-Córdova, Karen. 1990. Hispaniola and Puerto Rico: Indian Acculturation and Heterogeneity, 1492–1550. Unpublished Ph. D. dissertation, Yale University.

Anderson, Robert. 1983. The Party System: Change or Stagnation. In, pp. 3-26, *Time for Decision: The United States and Puerto Rico*. Jorge Heine, ed. Lanham, MD: North-South Publishing Co.

Andreu Iglesias, César. 1984. *Memoirs of Bernardo Vega: A Contribution to the History of the Puerto Rican Community in New York*. New York: Monthly Review Press.

Aparicio, Frances. 1998. *Listening to Salsa*. Hanover, NH: University Press of New England/Wesleyan University Press.

Aponte, Lola. 1995. Para inventarse el Caribe: la construcción fenotípica en las Antillas hispanófonas. *Bordes* 2: 5-14.

Appadurai, Arjun. 1991. Global Ethnoscapes: Notes and Queries for a Trans-national Anthropology. In *Recapturing Anthropology: Working in the Present*, ed. Richard Fox. Santa Fe, New Mexico: School of American Research Press.

Aranda, Elizabeth. 2007. *Emotional Bridges to Puerto Rico: Migration, Return Migration, and the Struggles of Incorporation*. Lanham, MD: Rowman and Littlefield.

Archilla Rivera, Milvia.Y. 1993. Guerra contra los pobres y militarización del país. *Claridad* 5-11 February: 4.

_____. 1994. Expropiación de Las Picúas: legislatura defiende a los ricos. *Claridad* 29 April 29-5 May: 3.

Ayala, César, and Rafael Bernabe. 2007. *Puerto Rico in the American Century: A History Since 1898*. Chapel Hill: University of North Carolina Press.

Babín, María Teresa. 1958. *Panorama de la cultura puertorriqueña*. New York: Las Americas Publishing Co.

_____. 1978. The *Jíbaro*: Symbol and Synthesis. In Proceedings of the Comparative Literature Symposium, Texas Tech University. Volume IX. *Ethnic Literatures since 1776: The Many Voices of America*. Part 2, eds. Wolody-myr T. Zyla and Wendell M. Aycock. Lubbock: Texas Tech Press.

Back, Kurt. 1962. *Slums, Projects, and People*. Durham: Duke University Press.

Baerga, María del Carmen, ed. 1993. *Género y trabajo: la industria de la aguja en Puerto Rico y el Caribe hispánico*. San Juan: Editorial de la Universidad de Puerto Rico.

Bairros, Luiza. 1996. Orfeu e Poder: Uma perspectiva afro-americana sobre a política racial no Brasil. *Afro-A'sia* (Centro de Estudos Afro-Orientais, UFBA) 17: 173-186.

Balce, Nerissa. 2006. Filipino Bodies, Lynching, and the Language of Empire. In *Positively No Filipinos Allowed: Building Communities and Discourse*, eds. Antonio Tiongson, Jr., Edgardo Gutiérrez, and Ricardo Gutiérrez. Philadelphia: Temple University Press.

Ballantine, Jeanne. H. 1989. *The Sociology of Education: A Systematic Analysis.* 2nd ed. Englewood Cliffs, NJ: Prentice Hall.

Barak, Julie. 1998. Navigating the Swamp: Fact and Fiction in Rosario Ferré's *The House on the Lagoon. Midwest Modern Language Association* 31(2): 31-38.

Baralt, Guillermo, A. 1982. *Esclavos rebeldes: conspiraciones y sublevaciones de esclavos, 1795- 1873.* Río Piedras: Ediciones Huracán.

Barbosa de Rosario, Pilar. 1937. *Problema de Razas: Documentos para la historia.* San Juan de Puerto Rico: Imprenta Venezuela.

Barbosa, José Celso. 1896. No esta en la cierto. *El País.*

———. 1909. El problema del color. *El Tiempo.*

———. 1920. Negrofobia. *El Tiempo.*

———. 1937. *El problema de razas.* San Juan: Imprenta Venezuela.

Barreiro, José. 2006. Taino Survivals: Cacique Panchito, Caridad de los Indios, Cuba. In, pp. 21-39, *Indigenous Resurgence in the Contemporary Caribbean: Amerindian Survival and Renewal.* Maximiliam C. Forte, ed. New York: Peter Lang.

Bell, Genevieve. 1998. *Telling Stories Out of School: Remembering The Carlisle Indian Industrial School, 1879–1918.* Ph.D. dissertation, Stanford University.

Belpré, Pura. n.d.[c]. February 2, 1899. Unpublished essay. Box 1, Folder 4. The Pura Belpré Papers, Archives of the Puerto Rican Diaspora. Centro de Estudios Puertorriqueños, Hunter College, CUNY.

———. n.d.[e]. Agreement. Unpublished book contract. The Pura Belpré Papers, Archives of the Puerto Rican Diaspora. Centro de Estudios Puertorriqueños, Hunter College, CUNY.

———. n.d.[f]. I Wished to Be Like Johnny Appleseed. Unpublished Essay. The Pura Belpré Papers, Archives of the Puerto Rican Diaspora. Centro de Estudios Puertorriqueños, Hunter College, CUNY.

Benítez Rojo, Antonio. 1989. *La isla que se repite: El Caribe y la perspectiva posmoderna.* Hanover, NH: Ediciones del Norte.

———. 1996. *The Repeating Island: The Caribbean and the Postmodern Perspective.* 2nd ed. Trans. James E. Maraniss. Durham: Duke University Press.

Berger, Maurice. 1998. Introduction: The Crisis of Criticism. In *The Crisis of Criticism,* ed. Maurice Berger. New York: The New York Press.

Bernotas, Bob. 1997. Profile: Ray Vega steps out as a band leader and remembers the glory days on New York radio. *New York Latino.*

Berríos-Miranda, Marisol. 2004. Salsa Music as Expressive Liberation. *Centro: The Journal of the Center for Puerto Rican Studies* 16(2): 158-173.

Betances, Samuel. 1972. The Prejudice of Having No Prejudice in Puerto Rico, Part I. *The Rican: A Journal of Contemporary Puerto Rican Thought* 2: 41-54.

_____. 1973. The Prejudice of Having No Prejudice in Puerto Rico, Part II. *The Rican: A Journal of Contemporary Puerto Rican Thought* 3: 22-37.

Bethell, Leslie. Ed.1987. A Note on the Church and the Independence of Latin America. In *The Independence of Latin America*. Cambridge: Cambridge University Press.

Blanco, Tomás. 1975 [1935]. Elogio de la plena. In *Antología del pensamiento puertorriqueño 1900 1970, Vol. II*, ed. Eugenio Fernández Méndez. Río Piedras: Editorial de la Universidad de Puerto Rico.

_____. 1985 [1942]. *El prejuicio racial en Puerto Rico*. Río Piedras, Puerto Rico: Ediciones Huracán.

Bliss, Peggy Ann. 1991. The island deals with race bias during WWI. *The San Juan Star: Sunday Magazine*.

_____. 1995. Black, White, Puerto Rican All Over. *The San Juan Star*. March 22

Bodenheimer, Rebecca. 2010. Cross-genre Hybridizations in Rumba and Cuban Popular Music and Racialized Discourses of Musical Influence. In *Sound Ecologies, 55th. Annual Meeting Society for Ethnomusicology*. Los Angeles, California.

Bolnick, Deborah A., Duana Fullwiley, Troy Duster, Richard S. Cooper, Joan H. Fujimura, Jonathan Kahn, et al. 2007. The Science and Business of Genetic Ancestry Testing. *Science* 318 (19 October): 399-400.

Bonilla, Carolina, Mark D. Shriver, Esteban J. Parra, Alfredo Jones, and José R. Fernández. 2004. Ancestral Proportions and Their Association with Skin Pigmentation and Bone Mineral Density in Puerto Rican Women from New York City. *Human Genetics* 115(1): 57-68.

Bontemps, Arna. 1944. The Schomburg Collection of Negro Literature. *The Library Quarterly* July.

Bourdieu, Pierre and Loic, Wacqant. 1999. On the Cunning of Imperialist Reason. *Theory, Culture & Society* 16(1): 41-58.

Brau, Salvador. 1996 (1904). *Historia de Puerto Rico*. San Juan: Editorial Borinquen.

_____. 1969 (1907). *La colonización de Puerto Rico: desde el descubrimiento de la Isla hasta la reversión a la corona española de los privilegios de Colón*. San Juan: Instituto de Cultura Puertorriqueña.

Brentlinger, John. 1989. *Villa Sin Miedo ¡Presenté!*, Claves Latinoamericanas, México.

Brown, Kathryn. 2002. Tangled Roots? Genetics Meets Genealogy. *Science* 295 (1 March): 1634-1635.

Browne, Katherine E. 2004. *Creole Economics: Caribbean Cunning under the French Flag*. Austin: University of Texas Press.

Brusi-Gil de Lamadrid, Rima and Isar P. Godreau. 2007. ¿Somos indígenas? *Diálogo* (March–April): 10-11.

Bryan, William S. 1899. *Our Islands and Their People, as seen with Camera and Pencil.* New York: n.d., Thompson Publishing Co.

Bryc, Katarzyna, C. Velez, T. Karafet, A. Moreno-Estrada, A. Raynolds, A. Auton, M. Hammer, C. D. Bustamante, and H. Ostrer. 2010. Genome-wide Patterns of Population Structure and Admixture among Hispanic/Latino Populations. *Proceedings of the National Academy of Sciences* 107: 8954-8961, suppl. 2.

Bryce-Laporte, Roy S. 1968. Family Adaptation of Relocated Slum Dwellers in Puerto Rico: Implications for Urban Research and Development. *The Journal of Developing Areas* 2 (4): 533-540.

Bunche, Ralph. 1973. The *Political Status of the Negro in the Age of FDR.* Chicago: University of Chicago Press.

Burdick, John. 1992. The Myth of Racial Democracy. *Report on the Americas* 25(4): 40-44.

Burton, Richard D.E. 1997. *Afro-Creole: Power, Opposition and Play in the Caribbean.* Ithaca: Cornell University Press.

Butler, Paul. 2004. Much Respect: Toward a Hip-Hop Theory of Punishment. *Stanford Law Review* 56 April: 983-1016.

Cabranes, José. 1978. Citizenship and the American Empire: Notes on the Legislative History of the United States Citizenship of Puerto Ricans. *University of Pennsylvania Law Review* 127: 391-492.

Cabrera Salcedo, Lizette. 2006. Búsqueda de explicaciones históricas en el AND. *Diálogo* (October – November): 4-9.

Calderón, Tego. 2002. Loíza. In *El Abayarde.* White Lion Music, WL004.

Caldwell, Kia Lilly. 2004. Look at Her Hair: The Body Politics of Black Womanhood in Brazil. *Transforming Anthropology* 11(2): 18-29.

Calvin, Floyd J. 1927. Race Colleges Need Chair in Negro History—A. A. Schomburg. *Pittsburgh Courier.*

Cámara, D. 1991. Las iniciaciones rituales de Palo Monte o Mayombé como fuentes de conocimiento y evolución humana. *Africanías* 7: 3-4.

Cambiaso, Rodolfo Domingo. 1974. *Pequeño diccionario de palabras indo-antillanas.* Santo Domingo: Secretaría de Educación.

Candelario, Ginetta. 2000. Hair Race-ing: Dominican Beauty Cultural and Identity Production. *Meridians* 1(1): 128-156.

————. 2007. *Black Behind the Ears: Dominican Racial Identity from Museums to Beauty Shops.* Durham: Duke University Press.

Caplow, Theodor, Sheldon Stryker, and Samuel E. Wallace. 1964. *The Urban Ambience: A Study of San Juan, Puerto Rico.* Totowa: The Bedminster Press.

Caquías Cruz, Sandra. 2006b. Un pueblo que entiende de señas. *El Nuevo Día* October 22.

Carr, Raymond C. 1984. *Puerto Rico: A Colonial Experiment.* New York: Vintage Books.

Carrión, Juan Manuel. 1993. Etnia, raza y la nacionalidad puertorriqueña. In, pp. 3-18, *La nación puertorriqueña: ensayos en torno a Pedro Albizu-Campos,* eds. Juan Manuel Carrión, Teresa C. García Ruíz and Carlos Rodríguez Fraticelli. Río Piedras: Editorial de la Universidad de Puerto Rico.

_____. 1996. *Voluntad de nación: ensayos sobre el nacionalismo en Puerto Rico.* San Juan, PR: Ediciones Nueva Aurora.

_____. 2005. Two Variants of Caribbean Nationalism: Marcus Garvey and Pedro Albizu Campos. *CENTRO: Journal of the Center for Puerto Rican Studies* 17(1): 27-45.

Carroll, Henry K. 1899. *Report on the Island of Porto Rico.* Washington, D.C.: Government Printing Office.

Castro, Fidel. 1975. *La revolución cubana.* Mexico: Ediciones Era.

Cancel Miranda, Rafael. 1995. *Pólvora y palomas.* Mayagüez: Imprenta Hostos.

Centeno, D. 1993. Un llamado a valorar la opinión de los residentes. *Diálogo.* (September): 14.

Centro de Estudios Puertorriqueños. 1991. *The Jesús Colón Papers: Finding Aid.* New York: Centro de Estudios Puertorriqueños, Hunter College, City University of New York.

_____. n.d. Guide to the Pura Belpré Papers. Accessed 1 March 2006. < http://centropr.org/lib-arc/faids/belpref.html>.

Cifre de Loubriel, Estela. 1962. *Catálago de extranjeros residentes en Puerto Rico en el Siglo XIX.* Río Piedras: Editorial de la Universidad de Puerto Rico.

_____. 1964. *La inmigración a Puerto Rico durante el Siglo XIX.* San Juan: Instituto de Cultura Puertorriqueña.

_____. 1975. *La formación del pueblo puertorriqueño: la contribución de los catalanes, balearicos y valencianos.* San Juan: Institutio de Cultura Puertorriqueña.

_____. 1988. *La formación del pueblo puertorriqueño: la contribución de los gallegos, asturianos, y santanderinos.* Río Piedras: Editorial de la Universidad de Puerto Rico.

_____. 1995. *La formación del pueblo puertorriqueño: la contribución de los los isleños-canarios.* San Juan: Centro de Estudios Avanzados de Puerto Rico y el Caribe.

Cobas, José A., Jorge Duany, and Joe F. Feagin, eds. 2009. *How the United States Racializes Latinos: White Hegemony and Its Consequences.* Boulder: Paradigm Publishers.

_____. 2009. Racializing Latinos: Historical Background and Current Forms. In, pp. 1-15, *How the United States Racializes Latinos: White Hegemony and Its Consequences,* eds. José A. Cobas, Jorge Duany, and Joe F. Feagin. Boulder: Paradigm Publishers.

Cobo, Leila. 2006. New Artists Sustain Reggaetón's Appeal. May 16. http://news. yahoo.com.

Code, Lorraine. 1993. Taking Subjectivity into Account. *In*, pp. 15-48, *Feminist Epistemologies*, eds. Linda Alcoff and Elizabeth Potter. New York: Routledge.

Cohen, David and Jack Greene, eds. 1974. *Neither Slaves Nor Free: The Freedmen of African Descent in the Slave Societies of the New World*. Baltimor: Johns Hopkins University Press.

Coll y Toste, Cayetano. 1924. Origen etnológico del campesino de Puerto Rico y mestizaje de las razas blanca, india y negra. *Boletín histórico de Puerto Rico* 11: 127-159.

Colón, Jesús. 1946. El Prejuicio y la Independencia. *Liberación* 19 June.

———· 1956a. A Judge in New Jersey. *Daily Worker*. 16 January.

———· 1956b. Is Language a Barrier? *Daily Worker*. 30 January.

———· 1956c. The Library Looks at the Puerto Rican. *Daily Worker* 5 March.

———· 1956d. Little Things are Big, *Daily Worker* 27 June.

———· 1956e. Hiawatha Into Spanish, *Daily Worker* 13 November.

———· 1957a. Because He Spoke in Spanish, *Daily Worker* 9 April.

———· 1957b. Pilgrimage of Prayer, *Daily Worker* 14 May.

———· 1957c. I Went to School on Friday in Washington, D. C. *Daily Worker* 21 May.

———· 1957d. Phrase Heard in a Bus. *Daily Worker* 2 July.

———· 1957e. Little Rock," *Daily Worker* 8 October.

———· 1958a. Pilgrimage of Prayer; Marching in the Snow. *Daily Worker* 2 March.

———· 1958b. As I See it From Here. *The Worker* 7September.

———· 1958c. The Powell Campaign. *The Worker* 14 September.

———· 1958d. The Question of Voting for Your Own Kind. *The Worker* 5 &12 October.

———· 1958e. Ten to 30 Years—For 2 Cigarettes. *The Worker* 16 November.

———· 1959a. Racism in Glendale and Ridgewood. *The Worker* 5 July.

———· 1959b. I Appear Before the Un-Americans. *The Worker* 29 November.

———· 1959c. The Un-Americans and the Americans. *The Worker* 6 December.

———· 1960a. The Negro in Puerto Rican History. *The Worker*. 7 February.

———· 1960b. The Negro in Puerto Rico Today. *The Worker* 13 March.

———· 1961. How to Rent an Apartment Without Money; The Day My Father Got Lost. In *A Puerto Rican in New York and Other Sketches*. New York: Masses and Mainstream.

———· 1993. Angels in My Hometown Church; Statement by Jesús Colón to the Walter Committee on Un-American Activities. In *Colón, The Way it Was and Other Writings*. Houston: Arte Publico Press.

———· 2002 [1961]. *A Puerto Rican in New York and Other Sketches*. New York: International Publishers.

Colón López, Joaquín. 2002. *Pioneros puertorriqueños en Nueva York, 1917-1947*. Houston: Arte Público.

Colón Martínez, Noel. 1994. Consenso frente a la criminalidad. *Claridad* 28 January 28, 3 February.

Cotter, Holland. 1998. A Neighborhood Nurtures Its Vibrant Cultural History. *The New York Times* 16 March, section E, p.3.

Cotto, Liliana. 1993. The Rescate Movement: An Alternative Way of Doing Politics. In, pp. 119-130. *Colonial Dilemma: Critical Perspectives on Contemporary Puerto Rico*. Edwin Meléndez and Edgardo Meléndez, eds. Boston: South End Press.

Covas Quevedo, Waldo D. 2002. Prevención al ritmo del 'reggaetón.' *El Nuevo Día* 17 June.

Cruz de Jesús, David. 2003. *Los indigenismos en el español de Puerto Rico: apreciaciones sobre su historia y vigencia*. San Juan: Editorial Plaza Mayor.

Daniel, Yvonne. 1991. Changing Values in Cuban Rumba, A Lower-class Black Dance Appropriated by the Cuban Revolution. *Dance Research Journal* 2(23): 1-10.

Dávila, Arlene. 1997. *Sponsored Identities: Cultural Politics in Puerto Rico*. Philadelphia: Temple University Press.

———· 1999. Local/diasporic Taínos: Towards a cultural politics of memory, reality, and imagery. In *Taíno Revival: Critical Perspectives on Puerto Rican Identity and Cultural Politics*, ed. Gabriel Haslip-Viera. New York: Centro de Estudios Puertorriqueños, Hunter College, City University of New York.

Davis, David Brion. 1966. *Problems of Slavery in Western Culture*. Ithaca: Cornell University Press.

Davis, George W. 1900. Report of General George W. Davis. War Department Census of Puerto Rico 1899. Washington, DC: Government Printing Office.

Davis, Paul A. 1979. The Black Man and the Caribbean as Seen by Nicolás Guillén and Luis Palés Matos. *Caribbean Quarterly* 25(1/2): 72-79.

Davis, James F. 1991. *Who is Black? One Nation's Definition*. University Park: Pennsylvania State University.

De Genova, Nicholas, and Ana Y. Ramos-Zayas. 2000. Racialization and the Politics of Citizenship among Mexicans and Puerto Ricans in Chicago. Paper presented at the American Anthropological Association, November.

de la Fuente, Alejandro. 2001. *A Nation for All: Race, Inequality, and Politics in Twentieth-Century Cuba*. Chapel Hill: University of North Carolina Press.

del Castillo, N. 1993 Militarización de los caseríos. *El Diario* 24 June 18.

Del Moral, Solsiree. 2013. *Negotiating Empire: The Cultural Politics of Schools in Puerto Rico, 1898-1952*. Madison: University of Wisconsin Press.

del Río, Zaida, et. al. 1990. *Herencia clásica: oraciones populares ilustradas por Zaida del Río*. Ciudad de la Habana: Centro de Desarollo de las Artes Visuales.

Del Valle, S. 1994. Vecinos de Loiza enfrentan desahucio. *Claridad* 31 December-6 January: 4.

Delgado, Richard, and Jean Stefancic, eds. 1997. *Critical White Studies: Looking Behind the Mirror*. Philadelphia: Temple University Press.

Demarest, Arthur. 2005. *Ancient Maya: The Rise and Fall of a Rainforest Civilization*. New York: Cambridge University Press.

Demarest, Arthur, Prudence M. Rice and Don S. Rice, eds. 2005. *The Terminal Classic in the Maya Lowlands: Collapse, Transition, and Transformation*. Boulder: University Press of Colorado.

Den Tandt, Catherine. 1999. All That Is Black Melts into Air: Negritud and Nation in Puerto Rico. In *Caribbean Romances: The Politics of Regional Representation*, ed. Belinda J. Edmonson. Charlottesville: University Press of Virginia.

Denton, Nancy A. and Jacqueline Villarrubia. 2007. Residential Segregation on the Island: The Role of Race and Class in Puerto Rican Neighborhoods. *Sociological Forum* 22(1): 51-76.

Díaz Caballero, Arlene. 1988. Las trabajadoras asalariadas en Santurce. *Anales de Investigación Histórica* 1: 1-119.

Díaz Quiñones, Arcadio. 1982. *El almuerzo sobre la hierba*. Río Piedras, Ediciones Huracán.

———· 1985. Introducción. In *El prejuicio racial en Puerto Rico*, Tomás Blanco. Río Piedras: Ediciones Huracán.

———· 1993. *La memoria rota*. Río Piedras: Ediciones Huracán.

———· 2000. *El arte de bregar: Ensayos*. San Juan: Ediciones Callejón.

Díaz Soler, Luis M. 1970. *Historia de esclavitud negra en Puerto Rico*. Río Piedras: *Editorial* Universitaria.

———· 1994. *Puerto Rico desde su origenes*. Río Piedras: Editorial de la Universidad de Puerto Rico.

Dietz, James. 1986. *The Economic History of Puerto Rico: Institutional Change and Capitalist Development*. Princeton: Princeton University Press.

Dimas, Marcos. 1990. Artist Statement. In *Taller Alma Boricua: Reflecting on Twenty Years of the Puerto Rican Workshop: 1969–1989*. New York: El Museo del Barrio.

Dinzey-Flores, Zaire Z. 2005. Fighting Crime, Constructing Segregation: Crime, Housing Policy, and the Social Brands of Puerto Rican Neighborhoods. Unpublished Ph. D. dissertation, University of Michigan.

———· 2013. *Locked In, Locked Out: Gated Communities in a Puerto Rican City*. Philadelphia: University of Pennsylvania Press.

Dodson, Howard. 1986. Introduction. In *The Legacy of Arthur Alfonso Schomburg: A Celebration of the Past, A Vision for the Future*, ed. Schomburg Center for Research in Black Culture. New York: Schomburg Center.

———. 1989. Introduction. In *Ernestine Rose and the Origins of the Schomburg Center*, ed. Celeste Tibbets. Schomburg Center Occasional Papers Series, Number Two. New York: Schomburg Center for Research in Black Culture, The New York Public Library.

Dolan, Jay P. Vidal, Jaime R. 1994. *Puerto Rican and Cuban Catholics in the U. S., 1900-1965*. Indiana: University of Notre Dame Press, Quintero Rivera.

Domingo, W. A. 1925. Gift of the Black Tropics. In *The New Negro: An Interpretation*, ed. Alain Locke. New York: Albert and Charles Boni Inc.

Dominguez, Bernardo Garcia. 1988. Garvey and Cuba. In *Garvey: His Work and Impact*, eds. , Rupert Lewis and Patrick Bryan. Kingston: Institute of Social and Economic Research, University of the West Indies.

Domínguez, Virginia. 1994. A Taste of 'the Other': Intellectual Complicity in Racialization Practices. *Current Anthropology* 35(4): 333-348.

Duany, Jorge. 1985. Ethnicity in the Spanish Caribbean: Notes on the Consolidation of Creole Identity in Cuba and Puerto Rico, 1762–1868. *Ethnic Groups* 6(2): 99-123.

———. 1997. From the Bohío to the Caserío: Urban Housing Conditions in Puerto Rico. In, pp. 188-216, *Self-Help Housing, the Poor, and the State in the Caribbean*, eds. Robert Potter and Dennis Conway. Knoxville: University of Tennessee Press.

———. 1998. Reconstructing Racial Identity: Ethnicity, Color, and Class among Dominicans in the United States and Puerto Rico. *Latin American Perspectives* 25:147-172.

———. 1999. Making Indians out of Blacks: The revitalization of Taíno identity in contemporary Puerto Rico. In, pp. 31-56, *Taíno Revival: Critical Perspectives on Puerto Rican Identity and Cultural Politics*, ed. Gabriel Haslip-Viera. New York: Centro de Estudios Puertorriqueños, Hunter College, City University of New York.

———. 2000. El censo, la raza y los puertorriqueños. *El Nuevo Día*. 18 February.

———. 2002. *The Puerto Rican Nation on the Move: Identities on the Island and in the United States*. Chapel Hill, NC: University of North Carolina Press.

DuBois, W.E.B. 1898. *Philadelphia Negro*. Philadelphia: University of Philadelphia Press.

———. 1999 [1903]. *The Souls of Black Folks*. Critical edition by H.L. Gates and Terri Hume Oliver. New York: W.W. Norton.

Duster, Troy. nd. Deep Roots and Tangled Branches. *The Longview Institute* <http://www. longviewinstitute.org/research/duster/deeproots>.

Elizabeth, Léo 1974. St. Domingue. In *Neither Slave Nor Free: The Freedmen of African Descent in the Slave Societies of the New World*, eds. David Cohen, Jack Greene. Baltimore: Johns Hopkins University Press.

Elliott, Carl and Paul Brodwin. 2002. Identity and Genetic Ancestry Tracing. *British Medical Journal* 325, (28 December): 1469-1471.

Estevez, Jorge. 2008. Amerindian mtDNA in Puerto Rico: When Does DNA Matter? *CENTRO: Journal of the Center for Puerto Rican Studies* 20(2): 219-228.

Fagen, Patricia Weiss. 1976. Antonio Maceo: Heroes, History, and Historiography. *Latin American Research Review* 11(3): 69-93.

Falcón, Angelo. 1984. A History of Puerto Rican Politics in New York City: 1860s to 1945. In *Puerto Rican Politics in Urban America*, eds. James Jennings and Monte Rivera. Westport: Greenwood Press.

Fernández Cobo, Mariana, David V. Jones, Richard Yanagihara, Vivek R. Nerurkar, Yasuhir Yamamura, Carolina F. Ryschkewitsch, and Gerald L. Stoner. 2001. Reconstructing Population History Using JC Virus: Amerinds, Spanish, and Africans in the Ancestry of Modern Puerto Ricans. *Human Biology* 73(3): 385-402.

Fernández Méndez, Eugenio. 1970. *Historia cultural de Puerto Rico, 1493–1968.* San Juan: Ediciones El Cemí.

Fernández, Raúl. 2003. Si no tiene swing no vaya' a la rumba. In *Jazz Planet*, ed. Taylor Atkins. Mississippi: University Press of Mississippi.

Fernández-Soberón, Miriam. 2004. Daddy Yankee se inspira en el barrio. *El Nuevo Día* 19 August.

Fernández, W. 1975. Sepia del Bajo Mundo: música al compás de La Perla. *Avance* 2(75): 24-31.

Ferracuti, Franco et al. 1975. *Delinquents and Nondelinquents in the Puerto Rican Slum Culture.* Columbus: Ohio State University Press.

Ferré, Rosario. 1998 [1986]. *Maldito amor y otros cuentos.* New York: Vintage Español.

————· 1995. *The House on the Lagoon.* New York: Farrar Strauss Girouox.

————· 1996. *La casa de la laguna.* New York: Vintage.

Ferrer, Ada. 1991. Social Aspects of Cuban Nationalism: Race, Slavery, and the Guerra Chiquita, 1879-1880. *Cuban Studies* 21: 37-56.

Fewkes, Walter J. 1970 [1917]. *The Aborigines of Porto Rico and Neighboring Islands.* New York: Johnson Reprint Co.

Figueroa, Loida. 1974. *History of Puerto Rico: From the Beginning to 1892.* New York: Anaya Books.

Findlay, Eileen J. 2009. Portable Roots: Latin New Yorker Community Building and the Meanings of Women's Return Migration in San Juan, Puerto Rico, 1960–2000. *Caribbean Studies* 37(2): 3-43.

Fitzpatrick, Joseph. 1959. Delinquency and Puerto Ricans. New York: Migration Division, Department of Labor.

Flores, Juan. 1982. Foreword. In *The Jesús Colón Papers*, ed. Centro de Estudios Puertorriqueños New York: Centro de Estudios Puertorriqueños, Hunter College, City University of New York.

———· 1984. The Puerto Rico that José Luis González Built: Comments on Cultural History. *Latin American Perspectives* 11(3): 173-184.

———· 1988. Rappin', Writin', & Breakin'. *CENTRO: Journal of the Center for Puerto Rican Studies* 2(3): 34-41.

———· 1993. *Divided Borders: Essays on Puerto Rican Identity*. Houston: Arte Público Press.

———· 2000. *From Bomba to Hip-Hop: Puerto Rican Culture and Latino Identity*. New York: Columbia University Press.

———· 2009. *The Diaspora Strikes Back:* Caribeño *Tales of Learning and Turning*. New York: Routledge.

Fogelson, Robert and Richard Rubenstein, eds. 1969. The Complete Report of Mayor LaGuardia's Commission on the Harlem Riot of March 19, 1935. New York: *Arno Press and the New York Times*.

Foner, Philip. 1977. *Antonio Maceo: The "Bronze Titan" of Cuba's Struggle for Independence*. New York: Monthly Review Press.

Fonfriás, Ernesto Juan. 1969. *De la lengua de Isabel la Católica a la taína del cacique Agüeybana (origen y desarrollo del habla hispano-antillana)*. San Juan: Editorial Club de la Prensa.

Forte, Maximillian C. 2006. Searching for a Center in the Digital Ether: Notes on the Indigenous Caribbean Resurgence on the Internet. In, pp. 253-270, *Indigenous Resurgence in the Contemporary Caribbean: Amerindian Survival and Revival*, ed. M.C. Forte. New York: Peter Lang.

Franco Ortiz, Mariluz. 2003. Manejo de experiencias de racismo cotidiano con niñas y jóvenes: Un estudio transversal en escuelas de Loíza, Puerto Rico. Río Piedras, PR: Universidad de Puerto Rico, unpublished Ph.D. dissertation.

Frankenberg, Ruth, ed. 1997. *Displacing whiteness: Essays in social and cultural criticism*. Durham: Duke University Press.

Frazier, E. Franklin. 1939. *The Negro Family in the United States*. Chicago: University of Chicago Press.

———· 1951. A Study of the Negro Family. In *The Integration of the Negro into American Society*. Moorland Spingarn Research Center, Howard University.

French, John D. 2000. The Missteps of Anti-Imperialist Reason: Bourdieu, Wacquant and Hanchard's Orpheus and Power. *Theory, Culture, and Society* 17(1): 107-128.

Freyre, Gilberto. 1975 [1933]. *Casa Grande e Senzala. Formaçao da familia brasileira sob o regime da economia patriarcal*. Rio de Janeiro: Livraria J. Olympio Editora.

———— 1986. *The Master and the Slaves: A Study in the Development of Brazilian Civilization*. Berkeley: University of California Press.

Fry, Peter. 2000. Politics, Nationality, and the Meanings of "Race" in Brazil. *Daedalus* 129(2): 83-118.

Fuson, Robert H. 1987. *The Log of Christopher Columbus*. Camden Maine: International Marine Publishing Company.

García Arévalo, Manuel. 1990. Transculturation in the Contact Period and Contemporary Hispaniola. In, pp. 169-180, *Columbian Consequences. Volume 2: Archeological and Historical Perspectives on the Spanish Borderlands East*, ed. D.H. Thomas. Washington, DC: Smithsonian Institution Press.

Garvey, Amy Jacques. 1970. *Garvey and Garveyism*. New York: Macmillan.

Garvey, Marcus. 1983 *The Marcus Garvey and Universal Negro Improvement Association Papers* Vol. 2, 3. University of California Press.

Géliga-Vargas, Jocelyn A. 2015. On Racial Silence and Salience: Narrating "African Things" in Puerto Rico Oral History. *a|b: Auto/Biography Studies* 30 (1): 31-52.

Géliga-Vargas, Jocelyn A., Irmaris Rosa Nazario and Tania Delgado. 2009. Testimonios Afropuertorriqueños: Using Oral Testimonies to (Re) Write Race in Contemporary Puerto Rico. *Sargasso* 2007-2008 (1): 115-130.

Gelpí, Juan G. 1993. *Paternalismo y literatura en Puerto Rico*. Río Piedras: Editorial de la Universidad de Puerto Rico.

Gibson, Campbell and Kay Jung. 2002. Historical Census Statistics on Population Totals by Race, 1790-1990, and by Hispanic Origin, 1970-1990 for The United States, Regions, Divisions, and States, Working Papers Series, No. 56. Washington, DC: United States Census Bureau.

Gilbert, Peter. 1971. *The Selected Writings of John Edward Bruce: Militant Black Journalist*. New York: Arno Press.

Gilroy, Paul. 1993. *The Black Atlantic, Modernity, and Double Consciousness*. Cambridge: Harvard University Press.

Glasgow, Ivette. 1997. Whites With Nothing But Whiteness. In *Critical White Studies: Looking Behind the Mirror*, eds. Richard Delgado and Jean Stefancic. Philadelphia: Temple University Press.

Glasser, Ruth. 1995. *My Music Is My Flag: Puerto Rican Musicians and Their New York Communities, 1917–1940*. Berkeley: University of California Press.

Godreau, Isar Pilar. 1995. "Where is Race in this Gumbo? The Slippery Semantics or Semantics Fugitiva in Puerto Rican Race and Color Talk." Paper delivered at the Annual Meeting of the American Anthropological Association. Washington, D.C.

———— 1999. Missing the Mix: San Antón and the Racial Dynamics of "Nationalism" in Puerto Rico. Santa Cruz, CA: University of California, unpublished Ph.D. dissertation.

————· 2000. La semántica fugitiva: raza, color y vida cotidiana en Puerto Rico. *Revista de Ciencias Sociales (Nueva época)* 9: 52-71.

————· 2002. Changing Space, Making Race: Distance, Nostalgia, and the Folklorization of Blackness in Puerto Rico. *Identities* 9(3): 281-304.

————· 2002b. Peinando diferencias, bregas de pertenencia: el alisado y el llamado 'pelo malo' (Combing Differences, Searching for Belonging: Hair Straightening and So-called Bad Hair). *Caribbean Studies* 30(1): 82-134.

————· 2006. Folkloric 'Others': *Blanqueamiento* and the Celebration of Blackness as an Exception in Puerto Rico. In, pp. 171-187, *Globalization and Race*, eds. Kamari Maxine Clarke and Deborah A. Thomas. Durham: Duke University Press.

————· 2007. Trigueño. In *International Encyclopedia of the Social Sciences.* 2nd edition, ed. William A. Darity, Jr. Farminton Hills, MI: Macmillan Reference USA.

————· 2008. Slippery Semantics: Race Talk and Everyday Uses of Racial Terminology in Puerto Rico. *CENTRO: Journal of the Center for Puerto Rican Studies* 20(2): 5-33.

————· 2015. *Scripts of Blackness: Race, Cultural Nationalism, and U.S. Colonialism in Puerto Rico.* Urbana: University of Illinois Press.

Godreau, Isar, Mariolga Reyes Cruz, Mariluz Franco Ortiz, and Sherry Cuadrado. 2007. The "Third Root" in the Third Grade: Racism, Mestizaje, and Representations of African Heritage in an Elementary School. Unpublished manuscript. Cayey: Institute of Interdisciplinary Research, University of Puerto Rico.

————· 2008. The Lessons of Slavery: Discourses of Slavery, Mestizaje, and Blanqueamiento in an Elementary School in Puerto Rico. *American Ethnologist* 35(1): 115-135.

Godreau, Isar and Vargas-Ramos, Carlos. 2009. "Which box am I?": Towards a Culturally Grounded, Contextually Meaningful Method of Racial and Ethnic Categorization in Puerto Rico. Cayey, PR: Institute of Interdisciplinary Research: University of Puerto Rico,

González, Ana M., Antonio Brehm, José A. Pérez, Nicole Maca-Meyer, Carlos Flores, and Vicente M. Cabrera. 2003. Mitochondrial DNA Affinities at the Atlantic Fringe of Europe. *American Journal of Physical Anthropology* 120(4): 391-404.

González García, Lydia Milagros. 1990. *Una Puntada en el Tiempo, La industria de la aguja en Puerto Rico 1900-1929.* San Juan, Santo Domingo: CEREP— CIPAF.

González, José Luis. 1980. *El país de cuatro pisos y otros ensayos.* Río Piedras: Ediciones Huracán.

————· 1990. The Four-Storeyed Country. In *Puerto Rico: The Four-Storeyed Country and Other Essays.* Trans. Gerald Guinness. Mapplewood, NJ: Waterfront Press.

González Rivera, Elena. 1992. Factors Associated with Achievement in a Poor Rural School. Paper presented at El Tercer Congreso Puertorriqueño de Investigación. Río Piedras, Puerto Rico: Universidad de Puerto Rico.

———· 1997. A Microethnographic Case Study of Intermediate Level of English as Second Language Students from a Culturally Different Community. Unpublished Ed.D. Thesis, University of Puerto Rico.

Gordon, Maxine W. 1949. Race Patterns and Prejudice in Puerto Rico. *American Sociological Review* 14(2): 294-301.

Granbery, Julian and Gary Vescelius. 2004. *The Languages of the Pre-Columbian Antilles*. Tuscaloosa: The University of the Alabama Press.

Gravleee, Clarence C., William W. Dressler and H. Russell Bernard. 2005. Skin Color, Social Classification, and Blood Pressure in Southeastern Puerto Rico. *American Journal of Public Health* 95(12): 2191-2197.

Green, Jack and David Cohen. 1974. *Neither Slave Nor Free: The Freedman of African Descent in the Slave Soceities of the New World*. Baltimore: Johns Hopkins University Press.

Greenberg, Cheryl. 1991. *Or Does it Explode? Black Harlem in the Great Depression*. New York: Oxford University Press.

Griffiths, Frederick T. 2001. Ralph Ellison, Richard Wright, and the Case of Angelo Herndon. *African American Review* 35(4): 615-636.

Grosfoguel, Ramón. 2003. *Colonial Subjects: Puerto Ricans in a Global Perspective*. Berkeley: University of California Press.

Grosfoguel, Ramón, and Chloé Georas. 2000. Coloniality of Power and Racial Dynamics: Notes Toward a Reinterpretation of Latino Caribbeans in New York City. *Identities* 7(1): 85-125.

Grube, Nikolai, ed. 2008. *Maya: Divine Kings of the Rainforest*. Duncan, SC: H.F. Ullman/ Langenscheidt Publishing Group.

Guadalupe, R. 1994. Del graffiti como medio de expresión racista. *Claridad* 22-28 July: 24.

Guerra, Lillian. 1998. *Popular Expression and National Identity in Puerto Rico: The Struggle for Self, Community, and Nation*. Gainesville: University Press of Florida.

Gugliota, Guy. 2007. The Maya: Glory and Ruin. *National Geographic* (August) <http://ngm.nationalgeographic.com/2007/08/maya-rise-fall/gugliotta-text>.

Guinness, Gerald. 1993. Here and Elsewhere, I. Luis Palés Matos. *In*, pp. 1-41, *Here and Elsewhere. Essays on Caribbean Literature*. Río Piedras: Editorial de la Universidad de Puerto Rico.

Guitar, Lynne. 1998. Cultural Genesis: Relationships among Indians, Africans and Spaniards in Rural Hispaniola, First Half of the Sixteenth Century. Unpublished Ph.D. dissertation, Vanderbilt University.

Guitar, Lynne, Pedro Ferbel-Azcarate, and Jorge Estevez. 2006. Ocama-Daca Taíno (Hear Me, I Am Taíno): Taíno Survival on Hispaniola, Focusing on the Dominican Republic. In, pp. 41-67, *Indigenous Resurgence in the Contemporary Caribbean: Amerindian Survival and Renewal*, ed. Maximilian C. Forte. New York: Peter Lang.

Guridy, Frank Andre. 2002. Racial Knowledge in Cuba: The Production of a Social Fact, 1912–1944. Ph.D. dissertation, University of Michigan.

Guterl, Matthew Pratt. 2001. *The Color of Race in America 1900–1940*. Cambridge: Harvard University Press.

Gutiérrez, David. 1995. *Walls and Mirrors: Mexican Americans, Mexican Immigrants, and the Politics of Ethnicity*. Berkeley: University of California Press.

Hall, Douglas. 1974. Jamaica. In *Neither Slave Nor Free: The Freedmen of African Descent in the Slave Societies of the New World*, eds. David Cohen, Jack Greene. Baltimore: Johns Hopkins University Press.

Hall, Neville. 1987. Education for Slaves in the Danish Virgin Islands, 1732-1846. In *Education in the Caribbean: Historical Perspectives*, ed. Ruby Hope King. Kingston: Faculty of Education, University of the West Indies.

————· 1992. *Slave Society in the Danish West Indies: St. Thomas*. St. John and St. Croix. Kingston: University of the West Indies Press.

Hall, Stuart. 1978. *Policing the Crisis: Mugging, the State, and Law and Order.* London: Macmillan.

Hanchard, Michael. 1992. *Taking Exception: Race and the Limits of Liberal Nationalism in Cuba, Mexico and Brazil*. Paper presented at Latin American Studies Association Conference.

Handler, Jerome. 1974. *The Unappropriated People: Freedmen in the Slave Society of Barbados*. Baltimore: Johns Hopkins University Press.

Handlin, Oscar. 1959. *The Newcomers: Negroes and Puerto Ricans in a Changing Metropolis*. Cambridge, Mass.: Harvard University Press.

Haney López, Ian F. 1996. *White By Law: The Legal Construction of Race*. New York: NYU Press.

————· 1998. Race and Erasure: The Salience of Race to Latinos/as. In *The Latino/a Condition: A Critical Reader*, eds. Richard Delgado and Jean Stefancic. New York: NYU Press.

Hanis, Craig L., David Hewett-Emmett, Terry K. Bertin, and William J. Schull. 1991. Origins of U.S. Hispanics. Implications for diabetes. *Diabetes Care* 14(7): 618-627.

Harlan, Louis, ed. 1975. *The Booker T. Washington Papers*. Vol. 4, 1895–98. Urbana: University of Illinois Press.

————· and Smock, Raymond W., eds. 1977. *The Booker T. Washington Papers*. Vol. 6. Urbana: University of Illinois Press.

Harrington, Michael R. 1921. *Cuba Before Columbus*. New York: Museum of the American Indian.

Harrington, Michael W. 1899. Porto Rico and the Porto Ricans. *Catholic World* 70(416): 161-177.

Harris, Robert, Nyota Harris and Grandassa Harris. 1992. *Carlos Cooks and Black Nationalism: From Garvey to Malcolm*. Dover, Mass: The Majority Press.

Harrison, Hubert. 1917. *The Negro and the Nation*. New York: Cosmo-Advocate Publishing Co.

Hartigan, John. 1997. Locating White Detroit. In, pp. 180-213, *Displacing Whiteness: Essays in Social and Cultural Criticism*, ed. Ruth Frankenberg. Durham: Duke University Press.

——— 1999. *Racial Situations*. Princeton: Princeton University Press.

Hasenbalg, Carlos and Nelson do Valle Silva. 1999. Notes on Racial and Political Inequality in Brazil. In *Racial Politics in Contemporary Brazil*, ed. Michael Hanchard. Durham: Duke University Press.

Haslip-Viera, Gabriel. 1999. Crime and Punishment in Late Colonial Mexico City, 1692–1810. Albuquerque: University of New Mexico Press.

———. ed. 1999. *Taíno Revival: Critical Perspectives on Puerto Rican Identity and Cultural Politics*. New York: Centro de Estudios Puertorriqueños, Hunter College, City University of New York.

———. ed. 2001. *Taíno Revival: Critical Perspectives on Puerto Rican Identity and Cultural Politics*. Princeton: Markus Wiener.

———. 2006. The Politics of Taíno Revivalism: The Insignificance of Amerindian mtDNA in the Population History of Puerto Ricans. *CENTRO: Journal of the Center for Puerto Rican Studies* 18(1): 260-275.

———. 2007. The Taíno Movement Among Caribbean Latinas/os in the United States. In, pp. 417-426, *A Companion to Latina/o Studies*, eds. Juan Flores and Renato Rosaldo. Malden, MA: Blackwell Publishing.

———. 2008. Amerindian mtDNA Does No Matter: A Reply to Jorge Estevez and the Privileging of a Taíno Identity in the Spanish-speaking Caribbean. *CENTRO: Journal of the Center for Puerto Rican Studies* 20(2): 228-237.

———. 2009. Changed Identities: A Racial Portrait of Two Extended Families, 1909-Present. *CENTRO: Journal of the Center for Puerto Rican Studies* 21(1): 37-51.

Hayden, Dolores. 2002. *Redesigning the American Dream: Gender, Housing, and Family Life*. New York: W. W. Norton & Company.

Helg, Aline. 1995. *Our Rightful Share: The Afro-Cuban Struggle for Equality, 1886-1912*. Chapel Hill: University of North Carolina Press.

Hemming, John. 1995a (1978). *Red Gold: The Conquest of the Brazilian Indians*. London: Papermac/Harvard University Press.

_____. 1995b (1987). *Amazon frontier: The Defeat of the Brazilian Indians*. London: Papermac/Harvard University Press.

Hernández, Carmen Dolores. 1997. *Puerto Rican Voices in English: Interviews With Writers*. Westport, CT: Prager Publishers.

Hernández-Delgado, J. L. 1992. Pura Teresa Belpré, Storyteller and Pioneer Puerto Rican Librarian. *The Library Quarterly* 62: 425-440.

Herskovits, Melville. 1960. The ahistorical approach to Afroamerican studies: a critique. *American Anthropologist*, 62(4): 559-568.

Hernández, Tanya K. 2002. Multi-Racial Matrix: The Role of Race Ideology in the Enforecement of Anti-Discrimination Laws, a United States-Latin America Comparison. *Cornell Law Review*, 87: 1093-1169.

Higrnan, Barry. W. 1976. *Slave Population and Economy in Jamaica, 1807-1834*. Cambridge: Cambridge University Press.

_____. 1984. *Slave Populations of the British Caribbean, 1807-1834*. Baltimore: The Johns Hopkins University Press.

Hiss, Tony. 1976. Drums. In *New Yorker* 29 September.

History Task Force, Centro de Estudios Puertorriqueños. 1979. *Labor Migration Under Capitalism, The Puerto Rican Experience*. New York: Monthly Review Press.

Hoernel, Robert B. 1976. Sugar and Social Change in Oriente, Cuba, 1898-1946. *Journal of Latin American Studies* 8(2): 215-249.

Hoetink, Harry. 1967. *The Two Variants in Caribbean Race Relations: A Contribution to the Sociology of Segmented Societies*. London: Oxford University Press.

_____. 1970 The Dominican Republic in the Nineteenth Century: Some Notes on Stratification, Immigration, and Race. In *Race and Class in Latin America*, ed. Magnus Mörner. New York: Columbia University Press.

_____. 1974. Surinam and Curaçao. In *Neither Slave Nor Free: The Freedmen of African Descent in the Slave Societies of the New World*, eds. David Cohen, Jack Greene. Baltimore: Johns Hopkins University Press.

_____. 1982. *The Dominican People, 1850-1900: Notes for a Historical Sociology*, Baltimore: Johns Hopkins University Press.

_____. 1985. "Race" and Color in the Caribbean. In, PP. 55-84, Sidney Mintz and Sally Price, eds. *Caribbean Contours*. Baltimore: Johns Hopkins University Press.

Hoffnung-Garskof, Jesse. 2001. The Migrations of Arturo Schomburg: On Being Antillano, Negro, and Puerto Rican in New York, 1891–1938. *Journal of American Ethnic History* 21.

Howes, Kelly King. 2001. *Harlem Renaissance*. Detroit: UXL Press.

Hutson, Jean Blackwell. 1969. The Schomburg Collection. In *Harlem: A Community in Transition*, ed. John Henrik Clarke. New York: Citadel Press.

Ilich, Tania. n.d. My Block: Puerto Rico on MTV. http://latinmusic.about.com/

James, Winston. 1998. *Holding Aloft the Banner of Ethiopia: Caribbean Radicalism in America, 1900–1932.* New York: Verso.

Jiménez de Wagenheim, Olga. 1988. *Puerto Rico: An Interpretive History from Pre-Columbian Times to 1900.* Princeton: Markus Wiener Publishing.

————. 1985. *Puerto Rico's Revolt for Independence: El Grito de Lares.* Princeton and New York: *Markus Wiener Publishing.*

Jiménez, Félix. 2004. *Las prácticas de la carne: Construcción y representación de las masculinidades puertorriqueñas.* San Juan: Ediciones Vertigo.

————. 1985. Playa, fritura y sol en Piñones: Fin de semana de antojos criollos. *El Nuevo Día,* April 10.

Jiménez-Muñoz, Gladys. 1993. *A Storm Dressed in Skirts: Ambivalence in the Debate on Woman's Suffrage in Puerto Rico, 1927-1929.* Ph.D. dissertation. SUNY, Binghamton.

Jiménez Román, Miriam. 1996. Un hombre (negro) del pueblo: José Celso Barbosa and the Puerto Rican "Race" Toward Whiteness. *CENTRO: Journal of the Center for Puerto Rican Studies* 8:9-29.

————. 2008. Boricuas vs. Nuyoricans—indeed!: A Look at Afro-Latinos. *ReVista: Harvard Review of Latin America* Spring.

Jiménez-Román, Miriam and Juan Flores. 2009. Triple-consciousness? Approaches to Afro-Latino Culture in the United States. *Latin American and Caribbean Ethnic Studies* 4(3): 319-328.

————. eds. 2010. *The Afro-Latin@ Reader: History and Culture in the United States.* Durham: Duke University Press.

Jorge, Angela. 1979. The Black Puerto Rican Woman in Contemporary American Society. *In* Edna Acosta-Belén, ed. *The Puerto Rican Woman.* New York: Praeger Publishers.

Junta de Planificación,. 1987. *Informe económico al Gobernador.* San Juan: Oficina del Gobernador.

Justiniano, Carmen Luisa. 1994. *Con valor y a como dé lugar: memorias de una jíbara puertorriqueña.* San Juan: Editorial de la Universidad de Puerto Rico.

Kaiser, Ernest. 1982. "Schomburg, Arthur Alfonso." *Dictionary of American Negro Biography.* Ed. Logan, Rayford. Winston, Michael. New York: W. W. Norton and Co.

Keeran, Roger. 1989. "The International Workers Order and the Origins of the CIO." *Labor History,* 30(3): 385-408.

Kelley, Robin. 1998. *Yo' Mama's Disfunktional!: Fighting the Culture Wars in Urban America.* New York: Beacon Press.

Kim, Claire Jean. 1999. The Racial Triangulation of Asian Americans. *Politics and Society* 27: 105-138.

Kinsbruner, Jay. 1996. *Not of Pure Blood: The Free People of Color and Racial Preju-dice in Nineteenth-Century Puerto Rico*. Durham: Duke University Press.

Kiple, Kenneth. 1976. *Blacks in Colonial Cuba, 1774-1899*. Gainesville: University Presses of Florida.

Kisseloff, Jeff. 1989. *You Must Remember This: An Oral History of Manhattan from the 1890s to World War II.* New York: Schocken Books.

Knauer, Lisa Maya. 2009. Racialized Culture and Translocal Counter-publics Rum-ba and Social Disorder in New York and Havana. In, pp. 131-168, *Caribbean Migration to Western Europe and the United States Essays on Incorporation, Identity, and Citizenship*, eds. Ramón Grosfoguel, Margarita Cervantes-Rodriguez, and Eric Mielants. Philadelphia: Temple University Press.

Knight, Franklin. 1970. *Slave Society in Cuba During the Nineteenth Century*. Madi-son: University of Wisconsin Press.

_____. 1985. Jamaican Migrants and the Cuban Sugar Industry, 1900-1934. In *Between Slavery and Free Labor*, ed. Manuel Moreno Fraginals. Baltimore: Johns Hopkins University Press.

_____. 1990. *The Caribbean: The Genesis of a Fragmented Nationalism, 2nd ed*. New York: Oxford University Press.

Knudson, D.G. 1987. "Que nadie se entere": la esposa maltratada en Puerto Rico. In, pp. 139-154, *La mujer en Puerto Rico*. Ed. Azize Vargas, Yamile. Río Piedras: Ediciones Huracán.

Koerner, Brendan I. 2005. Blood Feud. *Wired* 13.09 (September) <http://www.wired.com/ wired/archive/13.09/seminoles.html>.

Korrol, Virginia E. Sánchez. 1983. *From Colonia to Community: The History of Puerto Ricans in New York City*. University of California Press.

Kutzinski, Vera. 1993. *Sugar's Secrets: The Erotics of Cuban Nationalism*. Charlottes-ville, VA: University Press of Virginia.

Labrador-Rodríguez, Sonia. 1999. Mulatos entre blancos: José Celso Barbosa y Anto-nio S. Pedreira. Lo fronterizo en Puerto Rico al cambio de siglo (1896-1937). *Revista Iberoamericana* 65(188-189): 713-731.

Laguna-Díaz, Elpidio. 1987. Flying Bus. In *Images and Identities: The Puerto Rican in Two World Contexts*. Asela Rodríguez de Laguna, ed. New Brunswick: Transaction Books.

LaGumina, Salvatore John. 1969. *Vito Marcantonio: The People's Politician*. Dubuque, Iowa: Kendall/Hunt Publishing Co.

Landale, Nancy S. and Oropesa, R.S. 2002. White, Black, or Puerto Rican? Racial Self- Iden-tification among Mainland and Island Puerto Ricans. *Social Forces* 81(1): 231-254.

_____. 2004. What Does Skin Color Have to Do with Infant Health? An Analysis of Low-Birth Weight among Mainland and Island Puerto Ricans. *Social Science and Medicine* 61: 379-391.

Landis, Barbara. 2001. Carlisle Indian Industrial School History.http://home.epix. net/~landis/ histry.html.

Laviera, Tato. 1985. *AmeRícan. Houston: Arte Público Press.*

Ledru, André Pierre. 1935. *Viaje a la isla de Puerto Rico.* San Juan: University of Puerto Rico. (Translated by Julio L. De Vizcarrondo)

Lee, Sharon M. 1993. Racial Classification in the U.S. Census, 1890–1990. *Ethnic and Racial Studies* 16(1): 75-94.

Lesiak, Christine. 1991. *In the White Man's Image.* Video. Public Broadcasting System.

Lewis, David Levering. 1982 [1979]. *When Harlem Was In Vogue.* New York: Vintage Books.

Lewis, Gordon K. 1963. *Puerto Rico: Freedom and Power in the Caribbean.* New York: Monthly Review Press.

——. 1968. *Puerto Rico: Freedom and Power in the Caribbean.* 2nd ed. New York: Harper Torchbooks.

——. 1969. Race Relations in Britain: A View From the Caribbean. *Race Today* 1(3): 79-81.

——. 1983. *Main Currents in Caribbean Thought: The Historical Evolution of the Caribbean in its Ideological Aspects, 1492-1900.* Baltimore: Johns Hopkins University Press.

Lewis, Oscar. 1965. *La Vida: A Puerto Rican Family in the Culture of Poverty—San Juan and New York.* New York: Random House.

Lewis, Rupert. 1987. *Marcus Garvey: Anti-Colonial Champion.* London: Karia Press.

Lindsay, Samuel McCune. 1904. Annual Report. Commissioner of Education for Porto Rico.

Lipsitz, George. 2007. *Footsteps in the Dark: The Hidden Histories of Popular Music.* Minneapolis: University of Minnesota Press.

Llanos, Victoria. 1981. Como pintan a los negros. In *Poesía afroantillana y negrista,* ed. Jorge Morales. Rio Pedras: Universidad de Puerto Rico.

Lloréns, Hilda. 2005. Fugitive Blackness: Representations of Race, Power, and Memory in Arroyo, Puerto Rico. Ph. D. dissertation, University of Connecticut.

——. 2014. *Imaging the Great Puerto Rican Family: Framing Nation, Race and Gender during the American Century.* Lanham, MD: Lexington Books.

López, Irene. 2006. Puerto Rican Phenotype: Understanding Its Historical Underpinnings and Psychological Associations. *Hispanic Journal of Behavioral Sciences* 30(2): 161-180.

López, Lillian. n.d. Oral History with Pura Belpré. Lillian López Papers, Archives of the Puerto Rican Diaspora. Centro de Estudios Puertorriqueños, Huter College, CUNY.

López, René. 1976. Drumming in the New York Puerto Rican Community: A Personal Account. In *Black People and Their Culture: Selected Writings from the African Diaspora*, eds. Bernice Reagon, Rosie L. Hooks, and Linn Shapiro. Washington, DC: Festival of American Folklife.

Lopez, R. 1993. Una vuelta al punto: el negocio y la cultura de Ia drogas al detal. *Diálogo* February: 14-15.

Loveman, Mara. 2007. The U.S. Census and the Contested Rules of Racial Classification in Early Twentieth-Century Puerto Rico. *Caribbean Studies* 35(2): 79-114.

Loveman, Mara and Jeronimo O. Muniz. 2007. How Puerto Rico Became White: Boundary Dynamics and Inter-Census Racial Reclassification. *American Sociological Review* 72: 915-393.

Lovén, Sven. 1979 [1935]. *Origins of Tainan Culture, West Indies*. New York: AMS Press.

Lowe, Lisa. 1996. *Immigrant Acts: On Asian American Cultural Politics*. Durham: Duke University Press.

Lynch, John. 1989. *Bourbon Spain, 1700–1808*. Cambridge: Basil Blackwell.

Maldonado-Dennis, Manuel. 1980. *The Emigration Dialectic: Puerto Rico and the USA*. New York: International Publishers.

Malone, Cheryl Knott. 2000. Toward a Multicultural American Public Library History. *Libraries & Culture* 35(1): 77-87.

Manuel, Peter. 1994. Puerto Rican Music and Cultural Identity: Creative Appropriation of Cuban Sources from Danza to Salsa. *Society for Ethnomusicology* 38(2): 249-280.

Marazzi, Rosa. 1974. El impacto de la inmigración a Puerto Rico, 1800 a 1830: análisis estadístico. *Revista de Ciencias Sociales* 18(1–2): 1-41.

Martin, Simon and Nicolai Grube. 2008. *Chronicle of the Maya Kings and Queens*, 2nd Edition. New York: Thames & Hudson.

Martin, Tony. 1976. *Race First: The Ideological and Organizational Struggles of Marcus Garvey and the Universal Negro Improvement Association*. Westport, Conn.: Greenwood Press.

Martínez, A. 1994. Una división especial para vigilar los residenciales. *El Nuevo Día* 1 June: 15.

Martínez-Cruzado, Juan Carlos. 1999. Ethnic Contributions to the Puerto Rican Mitochondrial Gene Pool. *Human Biology* 73(4): 491-511.

———. 2001. G. Toro-Labrador, V. Ho-Fung, M. Estévez-Montero, A. Lobaina-Manzanet, D. Padovani-Claudio, H. Sánchez-Cruz, P. Ortiz-Bermudez, and A. Sánchez-Crespo. 2001. Mitochondrial DNA Analysis Reveals Substantial Native American Ancestry in Puerto Rico. *Human Biology* 73(4): 491-511.

_____. 2002. The Use of Mitrochondrial DNA to Discover Pre-Columbian Migrations to the Caribbean: Results from Puerto Rico and Expectations for the Dominican Republic. *Kacike: Journal of Caribbean Amerindian History and Anthropology* <www.kacike.org/MartinezEnglish.html>.

_____. G. Toro-Labrador, J. Viera-Viera, M. Rivera-Vega, J. Startek, M. Latorre-Esteves, A. Román-Colón, R. Rivera-Torres, I. Navarro-Millán, E. Gómez-Sánchez, H. Caro-González, H. Caro-González, and P. Valencia-Rivera. 2005. Reconstructing the Population of History of Puerto Rico by Means of mtDNAPhylogeographic Analisis. *American Journal of Physical Anthropology* 128: 131-155.

Martínez-Echazábal, Lourdes. 1998. *Mestizaje* and the Discourse of National/Cultural Identity in Latina America, 1845-1959. *Latin American Perspectives* 25(3): 21-42.

Martínez, Samuel. 2007. *Decency and Excess: Global Aspirations and Material Deprivation on a Caribbean Sugar Plantation*. Boulder: Paradigm Publishers.

Martínez-Vergne, Teresita. 1999. *Shaping the Discourse on Space: Charity and Its Wards in 19th-Century San Juan, Puerto Rico*. Austin: University of Texas Press.

Marx, Anthony W. 1998. *Making Race and Nation: A Comparison of South Africa, the United States and Brazil*. New York: Cambridge University Press.

Massey, Douglas, and Nancy Denton. 1989. Residential segregation of Mexicans, Puerto Ricans and Cubans in selected U.S. Metropolitan Areas. *Sociology and Social Research* 73(2) (January): 73-83.

Mathews, Thomas G. 1974. The Question of Color in Puerto Rico. *In*, pp. 299-323, *Slavery and Race Relations in Latin America*, ed. Robert Brent Toplin. Westport, CT: Greenwood.

Matos, Félix V., and Linda C. Delgado, eds. 1998. *Puerto Rican Women's History: New Perspectives*. Armonk, NY: Sharpe.

Matos Rodríguez, Felix V. 1995. Street Vendors, Pedlars, Shop-Owners and Domestics: Some Aspects of Women's Economic Roles in Nineteenth-Century San Juan, Puerto Rico (1820-1870). In *Engendering History- Caribbean Women in Historical Perspective*, eds. Verene Shepherd, Bridget Brereton and Barbara Bailey. New York: St. Martin's Press.

McKay, Claude. 1935. Harlem Runs Wild. *The Nation* 3 April.

_____. 1940. *Harlem: Negro Metropolis*. New York: E. P. Dutton & Co.

McKillop, Heather. 2006. *The Ancient Maya: New Perspectives*. New York: W.W. Norton.

Meyer, Gerald. 1989. *Vito Marcantonio: Radical Politician, 1902-1954*. Albany, New York: State University Press of New York.

_____. 1992. Marcantonio and El Barrio. *Centro de Estudios Puertorriqueños Bulletin* 4(2): 66-87.

Miner Solá, Edwin. 2002. *Diccionario taíno ilustrado*. San Juan: Ediciones Servilibros.

Middleton, DeWight R. 1981. The Organization of Ethnicity in Tampa. *Ethnic Groups, 3: 281-306*.

Mills-Bocachica, Wanda. 2003. Identity, Power and Place at the Margins: Negotiating Difference in "El Barrio San Antón" Ponce, Puerto Rico. New Brunswick, NJ: Rutgers University, unpublished Ph.D. dissertation.

Miner Solá, Edwin. 2002. *Diccionario taíno ilustrado*. San Juan, PR: Ediciones Servilibros.

Mintz, Sidney. 1966. Puerto Rico: An Essay in the Definition of a National Culture. In *U.S.-Puerto Rico Status Commission, Status of Puerto Rico*. Selected background studies prepared for the *U.S.-Puerto Rico Status Commission on the Status of Puerto Rico*, Washington, D.C., U.S. Government Printing Office.

_____. 1974a. *Caribbean Transformation*. Chicago: Aldine Publishing Co.

_____. 1974b. *Worker in the Cane: A Puerto Rican Life History*. New York: W. W. Norton.

_____. 1978. The Role of Puerto Rico in Modern Social Science. *Revista/Review Interamericana* 8(1): 7-16.

Mintz, Sidney and Sally Price. 1985. *Caribbean Contours*. Baltimore: Johns Hopkins University Press.

Moore, Carlos. 1989. *Castro, the Blacks and Africa*. Los Angeles: Center for Afro-American Studies, University of California, Los Angeles.

Moore, Robin D. 1995. The Commercial Rumba: Afro-Cuban Arts as International Popular Culture. *Latin American Music Review* 16(2): 165-198.

_____. 1997. *Nationalizing Blackness*. Pittsburgh: University of Pittsburgh Press.

Morales Carrión, Arturo. 1983. *Puerto Rico: A Political and Cultural History*. New York: W. W. Norton.

Moreno Fraginals, Manuel, Frank Moya Pons and Stanley Engerman, eds. 1985. *Between Slavery and Free Labor: The Spanish-speaking Caribbean in the Nineteenth Century*. Baltimore: Johns Hopkins University Press.

Moreno Fraginals, Manuel. 1964. *El ingenio: El complejo económico social cubano del azúcar*. Tomo 1, 1760-1860. Habana: UNESCO.

Moreno Vega, Marta. 1998. The Purposeful Underdevelopment of Latino and other Communities of Color. In, Marta Moreno Vega and Cheryll Y. Greene, eds. *Voices from the Battlefront: Achieving Cultural Equity*. Trenton: Africa World Press.

Mormino, Gary R. and Pozzetta, George E. 1987. *The Immigrant World of Ybor City: Italians and Their Latin Neighbors in Tampa, 1885-1985*. Urbana: University of Illinois Press.

Morón, María Teresa. 1986. Un paseo por Piñones. El Reportero, January 29, p. 18.

Morrison, Toni. 1992. *Playing in the Dark: Whiteness and the Literary Imagination*. Cambridge: Harvard University Press.

Moscoso, Francisco. 1986. *Tribu y clases en el Caribe antiguo*. San Pedro de Macorís, República Dominicana: Ediciones de la Universidad Central del Este.

Moya Pons, Frank. 1998. *The Dominican Republic: A National History*. Princeton: Markus Wiener.

———. 2007. *History of the Caribbean: Plantations, Trade and War in the Atlantic World*. Princeton: Markus Wiener.

———. 1985. The Land Question in Haiti and Santo Domingo: The Sociopolitical Context of the Transition from Slavery to Free Labor, 1801-1843. In Moreno Fraginals et al, eds., *Between Slavery and Free Labor: The Spanish-speaking Caribbean in the Nineteenth Century*. Baltimore: Johns Hopkins University Press.

Muller, K.C. 1983. "Santería," *Sunday San Juan Star Magazine* 22 May: 2-3.

Muñoz Rivera, Luis. 1901. Una visita al Indian School. *The Puerto Rico Herald* 1 September 14. [From *Revista de Genealogía Puertorriqueña* October, 2000.]

Nagel, Joane. 1995. American Indian Ethnic Renewal: Politics and the Resurgence of Identity. *American Sociological Review* 60(6): 947-965.

Naison, Mark. 1985. *Communists in Harlem During the Great Depression*. New York: Grove Press.

Nash, Gary B. 1995. The Hidden History of Mestizo America. *Journal of American History* 82(3): 941-962.

Navarro, José Manuel. 1995. Creating Tropical Yankees: The "Spiritual Conquest" of Puerto Rico 1898–1908. Ph.D dissertation, University of Chicago.

Navarro Rivera, Pablo. 2000. *Universidad de Puerto Rico: de control político a crisis permanente 1903–1952*. Río Piedras: Ediciones Huracán.

Nazario, Manuel Álvarez. 1961. *El elemento afronegroide en el español de Puerto Rico: contribución al estudio del negro en América*. San Juan: Instituto de Cultura Puertorriqueña.

Negrón de Montilla, Aida. 1971. *Americanization in Puerto Rico and the Public-School System 1900–1930*. Río Piedras: Editorial Edil.

Negrón-Muntaner, Frances, ed. 2007. *None of the Above: Puerto Ricans in the Global Era*. New York: Palgrave Macmillan.

Negrón-Muntaner, Frances, and Grosfoguel, Ramón, eds. 1997. *Puerto Rican Jam: Essays on Culture and Politics*. Minneapolis: University of Minneapolis Press.

———. 1997. Beyond Nationalist and Colonialist Discourses: The *Jaiba* Politics of the Puerto Rican Ethno-Nation. In, pp. 1-38, *Puerto Rican Jam: Essays on Culture and Politics*, eds. Frances Negrón-Muntaner and Ramón Grosfoguel. Minneapolis: University of Minneapolis Press.

Negrón Muñoz, Angela. 1973. "Hablando con Don Luis Palés Matos," a 1932 interview reproduced in José I. De Diego Padró, *Luis Palés Matos y su trasmundo poético*. Río Piedras: Ediciones Puerto.

Negrón Portillo, Mariano. 1990. *Las turbas republicanas, 1900-1904*. Río Piedras: Ediciones Huracán.

Nevárez-Muñiz, D. and Wolfgang, M. 1988. Delincuencia juvenil en Puerto Rico: cohorte de personas nacidas en 1970. San Juan: Senado de Puerto Rico. (November).

Newton, Velma. 1984. *The Silver Men: West Indian Labor Migration to Panama, 1850-1914*. Kingston: Institute of Social and Economic Studies, UWI.

The New York Public Library. n.d. Countee Cullen Branch Information. Accessed 21 April 2006. <http://www.nypl.org/branch/local/man/htrinfo.html>.

_____. n.d. Schomburg Center for Research in Black Culture. Accessed 8 July 2006. <http://www.nypl.org/research/sc/sc.html>.

Ngai, Mae. 1999. The Architecture of Race in American Immigration Law: A Reexamination of the Immigration Act of 1924. *The Journal of American History* 86: 67-92.

_____. 2004. *Impossible Subjects: Illegal Aliens and the Making of Modern America*. Princeton: Princeton University Press.

Nieves Falcón, Luis. 1993, La ruta del legado colonial. In Comisión Puertorriqueña para la Celebración del Quinto Centenario del Descubrimiento de América y Puerto Rico (ed.) *La tercera raíz: Presencia africana en Puerto Rico*.

Nistal-Moret, Benjamin. 1985 Problems in the Social Structure of Slavery in Puerto Rico During the Process of Abolition, 1872. In *Between Slavery and Free Labor*. Fraginals, Manuel Moreno et al. eds. Baltimore: Johns Hopkins University Press.

Nixon, Ron. 2007. DNA Tests Find Branches But Few Roots. *New York Times* (Sunday Business, 25 November): 1, 7.

Nobles, Melissa. 2000. *Shades of Citizenship: Race and the Census in Modern Politics*. Palo Alto: Stanford University Press.

Nolla, Olga. 1998. *El manuscrito de Miramar*. México, D. F.: Alfaguara.

Nurse Allende, L. 1982. Los Pleneros de la 23 Abajo: creando un nuevo concepto de la plena y la bomba. *Hómines* 6(1): 251-255, (January-June).

Oboler, Suzanne. 1995 *Ethnic Labels, Latino Lives*. Minneapolis: University of Minnesota Press.

Ojeda Reyes, Félix. 1978. *Vito Marcantonio y Puerto Rico: Por los trabajadores y por la nación*. Rio Piedras: Ediciones Huracán.

_____. 1992. Vito Marcantonio and Puerto Rican Independence. *Centro de Estudios Puertorriqueños Bulletin*. New York: Hunter College

Opie, Frederick D. 2008. Eating, Dancing, and Courting in New York: Black and Latino Relations, 1930-1970. *Journal of Social History* 42(1): 79-109.

O'Reilley, P. 1984. Town Without Fear: Making the Land Their Own. *No Middle Ground*, 3-4: 72-76, Fall.

Ortega, Julio. 1991. *Reapropiaciones: Cultura y nueva escritura en Puerto Rico*. Río Piedras: Editorial de la Universidad de Puerto Rico.

Ortiz, Alragracia. 1983. Eighteenth-Century *Reforms in the Caribbean: Miguel de Muesas, Governor of Puerto Rico, 1769–1776*. Rutherford NJ: Fairleigh Dickenson Press.

————. ed. 1996. *Puerto Rican Women and Work: Bridges in Transnational Labor*. Philadelphia: Temple University Press.

Ortiz, Fernando. 1963. *Contrapunteo cubano del tabaco y del azúcar*. La Habana: Consejo Nacional de Cultura.

Ortiz, Victoria. 1986. Arthur A. Schomburg: A Biographical Essay. In *The Legacy of Arthur Alfonso Schomburg: A Celebration of the Past, A Vision for the Future*. Ed. The Schomburg Center for Research in Black Culture. New York: Schomburg Center for Research in Black Culture.

Osorio, I. 1993. Hablan los jóvenes del caserío. *Diálogo* (August): 16, 18.

Otero, R. 1992. Yo soy de Canales: entrevista a Cruz Rivera. *Piso 13*, 1(1): 2-3.

Osuna, Juan José. 1932. An Indian in Spite of Myself. *Summer School Review* 10(5).

————. 1949. *A History of Education in Puerto Rico*. Río Piedras: Editorial de la Universidad de Puerto Rico.

Pacini Hernandez, Deborah. 2010. *Oye Como Va! Hybridity and Identity in Latino Popular Music*. Philadelphia: Temple University Press.

Padilla, Elena. 1947. *Puerto Rican immigrants in New York and Chicago: A study in comparative assimilation*. Unpublished M.A. thesis, Department of Anthropology, University of Chicago.

Padilla, Felix. 1987. *Puerto Rican Chicago*. Indiana: University of Notre Dame Press.

————. 1992. The quest for community: Puerto Ricans in Chicago. In *In the barrios: Latinos and the underclass debate*, eds. Joan Moore and Raquel Pinderhughes. New York: Russell Sage Foundation.

Palés Matos, Luis. 1978. *Poesía completa y prosa selecta*. Caracas: Biblioteca Ayacucho.

————. 1993. *Tuntún de pasa y grifería*. Edición de Mercedes López-Baralt. Río Piedras, Editorial Universitaria.

Pantonja, Antonia. 2002. *Memoir of a Visionary, The Autobiography of Antonia Pantoja*. Houston: Arte Público Press.

Parés Arroyo, Marga. 2006. Campaña infantil contra el humo y el cigarillo. *El Nuevo Día*, 6 April.

Parra, E. J., R. A. Kittles, and M.D. Shriver. 2004. Implications of correlations between skin color and genetic ancestry for biomedical research. *Nature Genetics* 36 (11): S54-60.

Parra, Flavia C., Roberto C. Amado, José R. Lambertucci, Jorge Rocha, Carlos M. Antunes, and Sérgio D. J. Peña. 2003. Color and Genomic Ancestry of Brazilians. *Proceedings of the National Academy of Sciences* 100(1): 177-182.

Pedreira, Antonio S. 1937. *Un hombre del pueblo: José Celso Barbosa*. San Juan de Puerto Rico: Imprenta Venezuela.

———. 1934 (1992). *Insularismo: Ensayos de interpretación puertorriqueña*. Río Piedras, PR: Editorial Edil.

Perea, Augusto and Salvador Perea. 1941. *Glosario etimológico taíno-español, histórico y etnográfico*. Mayagüez, P.R.: Tip. Mayagüez Printing.

Perea, Juan. 2001. Fulfilling Manifest Destiny: Conquest, Race, and the Insular Cases. In *Foreign in a Domestic Sense: Puerto Rico, American Expansion, and the Constitution*, eds. Christina Duffy Burnett and Burke Marshall. Durham: Duke University Press.

Pereira, L., M.J. Prata, and A. Amorin. 2000. Diversity of mtDNA Lineages in Portugal: Not a Genetic Edge of European Variation. *Annals of Human Genetics* 64(6): 491-506.

Pérez, Gina. 2000. Mejicanas sufridas y puertorriqueñas rencorosas. Paper presented at the American Anthropological Association, November.

Pérez, Lisandro. 1982. Iron Mining and Socio-Demographic Change in Eastern Cuba, 1884-1940. *Journal of Latin American Studies* 14(2): 381-405.

Pérez, Louis A. 1986. Politics, Peasants, and People of Color: The 1912 "Race War" in Cuba Reconsidered. *Hispanic American Historical Review* 66(3): 509-539.

———. 1995. *Cuba: Between Reform and Revolution, 2nd ed*. New York: Oxford University Press.

Pérez, Louis A, Jr. 2006. *Cuba: Between Reform and Revolution, 3rd ed*. New York: Oxford University Press.

Pérez, René. 2005. Figura del momento. *El Nuevo Día*, 28 December.

Pérez y Mena, Andrés Isidoro. 1991. *Speaking with the Dead: Development of Afro-Latin Religion Among Puerto Ricans in the United States*. New York: AMS Press.

Peterson, J. 1974. *Evaluación de la estadística criminal de la Policía de Puerto Rico: años 1969-70 a 1973-74*. San Juan: Departamento de Justicia.

Picó, Fernando. 1981, *Amargo café*. Río Piedras: Ediciones Huracán.

———. 1987. Las trabajadoras del tabaco en Utuado, Puerto Rico, según el censo de 1910. *Homines* 10(2): 173-186.

———. 1988, *Historia general de Puerto Rico*. Río Piedras: Ediciones Huracán.

———. 1988. *Vivir en Caimito*. Río Piedras: Ediciones Huracán.

———. 1990. *Historia General de Puerto Rico, 5th Ed*. Rio Piedras: Edición Huracán.

———. 1993a. Criminalidad y violencia: mano dura contra la mano dura. *Diálogo*. (February): 12-13.

———. 1993b. Crisis de autoridad y la autoridad por la fuerza. *Diálogo*. (August).

_____. 1994. *El día menos pensado: historia de los presidiarios en Puerto Rico (1793-1993)*. Rio Piedras: Ediciones Huracán.

_____. 1986. *Historia general de Puerto Rico*. Río Piedras: Huracán-Academia.

Picó, I. 1972. "Entrevista de LA HORA: El racismo en Puerto Rico," *La Hora*, 8 September.

Piñeiro de Rivera, Flor. 1989. ed., *Arthur Alfonso Schomburg: A Puerto Rican Quest for His Black Heritage*. San Juan: Centro de Estudios Avanzados de Puerto Rico y el Caribe.

Pike, Ruth. 1983. *Penal Servitude in Early Modern Spain*. Madison: University of Wisconsin Press.

Plaza, S., F. Calafell, A. Helal, N. Bouzerna, G. Lefranc, J. Bertranpetit and D. Comas. 2003. Joining the Pillars of Hercules: mtDNA Sequences Shows Multi-directional Gene Flow in the Western Mediterranean. *Annals of Human Genetics* 67(4): 312-328.

Population Studies Branch. 2000. *PR-99-1 Estimates of the Population of Puerto Rico Municipalities, 1 July 1999, and Demographic Components of Population Change: 1 April 1990 to 1 July 1999*. http://www.census.gov/population/estimates/puerto-rico/ prmunnet.txt. (accessed on 11 February 2007)

Poyo, Gerald. 1989. *With All, and for the Good of All: The Emergence of Popular Nationalism in the Cuban Communities of the United States, 1848-1898*. Durham, NC: Duke University Press.

Pratt, Richard H. 1973. The Advantages of Mingling Indians with Whites, 1892. In, pp. 260-271, *Americanizing the American Indians*, ed. Francis P. Prucha. Cambridge: Harvard University Press.

Puerto Rico. Department of Education. 1904. Annual Report of the Commissioner of Education, 1904. Washington, D.C.: Government Printing Office.

Quesada, Pura and Rivera Ramos, Alba Nydia. 1985. La satisfacción de vida de la mujer envejeciente puertorriqueña blanca y negra en dos áreas geográficas de Puerto Rico. In *La mujer puertorriqueña: investigaciones psico-sociales*, ed. Alba Nydia Rivera Ramos. San Juan, Puerto Rico: Centro para el Estudio y Desarrollo de la Personalidad Puertorriqueña.

Quintero Rivera, Ángel G. 1988. *Patricios y plebeyos: burgueses, hacendados, artesanos y obreros. Las relaciones de clase en el Puerto Rico de cambio de siglo*. Río Piedras: Ediciones Huracán.

_____. 2009. *Cuerpo y cultura: las músicas mulatas y la subversión del baile*. Madrid: Editorial Iberamericana.

_____. 1992. El tambor en el cuatro: la melodización de ritmos y la etnicidad cimarroneada. In, pp. 43-55, *La tercera raíz: precencia africana en Puerto Rico*. San Juan: CEREP & ICP.

_____. 1994. The Camouflaged Drum: Melodization of Rhythms and Maroonage Ethnicity in Caribbean Peasant Music. In *Music and Black Ethnicity: The Caribbean and South America*, ed. Gérard H. Béhague. Coral Gables: North-South Center University of Miami.

Ramírez, Yasmin. 2002. Jorge Soto Sánchez. In *Voces y Visones: Highlights from the Permanent Collection of El Museo del Barrio*. New York: El Museo del Barrio.

Ramos Mattei, A. Andrés. 1981. La importación de trabajadores contratados para la industria azucarera puertorriqueña: 1860– 1880. In, pp. 125-141, *Inmigración y clases sociales en el Puerto Rico del siglo X I X*, ed. Francisco Scarano. Río Piedras: Ediciones Huracán.

Ramos Rosado, Marie. 1999. *La mujer negra en la literatura puertorriqueña*. 2nd ed. San Juan: Editorial de la Universidad de Puerto Rico.

Ramos, Toni-Ann. 1995. Maintenance of Taino Traditions within Puerto Rican Culture. Unpublished M.A. thesis, The University of Arizona.

Ramos-Zayas, Ana Yolanda. 1997. 'La patria es valor y sacrificio': Nationalist ideologies, cultural authenticity, and community building among Puerto Ricans in Chicago. Unpublished Ph.D. dissertation, Columbia University.

_____. 2003. *Performing the Nation: Class, Race and Space in Puerto Rican Chicago*. Chicago: University of Chicago Press.

Ramos-Zayas, Ana Yolanda, and Nicholas De Genova. 2000. Racialization and the Politics of Citizenship among Mexicans and Puerto Ricans in Chicago. Paper presented at the American Anthropological Association, November.

Rando, J.C., F. Pinto, A.M. González, M. Hernández, J.M. Larruga, V.M. Cabrera, and H-J. Bandelt. 1998. Mitochondrial DNA Analysis of Northwest African Populations Reveals Genetic Exchanges with European, Near-Eastern, and sub-Saharan populations. *Annals of Human Genetics* 62(6): 531-550.

Reel, Estelle. 1901. *Course of Study for The Indian Schools of the United States*. Superintendent of Indian Schools. Washington: Government Printing Office.

Reid, Ira. 1939. *The Negro Immigrant: His Background, Characteristics and Social Adjustment, 1899-1937*. New York: Columbia University Press.

Report of the Governor of Porto Rico, 1929. 1930. Washington: Government Printing Office.

Resnick, Michael D., et al. 1997. Protecting Adolescents from Harm: Findings from the National Longitudinal Study on Adolescent Health. *Journal of the American Medical Association* 278(10): 823-832.

Richardson, Bonham. 1985. *Panama Money in Barbados, 1900-1920*. Knoxville: University of Tennessee Press.

_____. 1989 Caribbean Migrations, 1838-1985. In *The Modern Caribbean*, eds. Franklin Knight, Colin Palmer. Chapel Hill: University of North Carolina.

Richards, Martin, V. Macaulay, A.o Torroni, and H.-J. Bandelt. 2002. In Search of Geographical Patterns in European Mitochondrial DNA. *American Journal of Human Genetics* 71(5): 1168-1174.

Riis, Jacob A. 1890. *How the Other Half Lives*. New York: Penguin.

Ríos, Palmira N. 1993. Export-Oriented Industrialization and the Demand for Female Labor: Puerto Rican Women in the Manufacturing Sector, 1952-1980. In, pp. 89-102, *Colonial Dilemma: Critical Perspectives on Contemporary Puerto Rico*. Edwin Meléndez and Edgardo Meléndez, eds. Boston: South End Press.

Risch, Neil, S. Choudhry, M. Via, A. Basu, R. Sebro, C. Eng, K. Beckman, S. Thyne, R. Chapela, J.R. Rodriguez-Santana, W. Rodriguez-Cintron, P.C. Avila, E. Ziv, and E. Gonzalez-Burchard. 2009. Ancestry-related Assortative Mating in Latino Populations. *Genome Biology* 10 (11): R132.

Rivera Esquilín, Eileen. 2003. Tego y la raza negra. *El Nuevo Día* 22 May.

Rivera Lugo, C. and Gutiérrez, P. 1993. Puerto Rico, Puerto Pobre: los senderos de la desintegración social o el camino de Ia esperanza. *Diálogo* Febuary: 16-17.

Rivera-Ortiz, Marcos. 2001. *Justicia negra: Casos y cosas*. Hato Rey, PR: Ediciones Situm

Rivera, Raquel Z. 1992-1993. "Rap Music in Puerto Rico: Mass Consumption or Social Resistance?,"*CENTRO: Journal of the Center for Puerto Rican Studies* 5(1): 52-65.

_____. 1996. Boricuas from the Hip Hop Zone. *CENTRO: Journal of the Center for Puerto Rican Studies* 5(1/2): 202-215.

_____. 2001. Hip Hop, Puerto Ricans, and Ethno-racial Identities in New York. In pp. 235-261, *Mambo Montage*, eds. Agustín Lao-Montes and Arlene Dávila. New York: Columbia University Press.

_____. 2003. *New York Ricans From the Hip-Hop Zone*. New York: Palgrave Macmillan.

_____. 2007. Will the "Real" Puerto Rican Culture Please Stand Up? Thoughts on Cultural Nationalism. In, pp. 217-232, *None of the Above*, ed. Frances Negrón-Muntaner. Boulder: Paradigm Press.

_____. 2010a. New York Bomba: Puerto Ricans, Dominicans, and a Bridge Called Haiti. In, pp.178-199, *Rhythms of the Afro-Atlantic World: Rituals and Remembrances*, eds. Kiddoe Nwankwo Ifeoma and Mamadou Diouf. Ann Arbor: University of Michigan Press.

Rivera Tudó, Ángela. 1931. The Puerto Rican Indians. Translated by Vilma Santiago-Irizarry. *La Correspondencia de Puerto Rico*, 3 January.

Rivera Vargas, Daniel. 2005. Protesta a son de música. *El Nuevo Día* 3 December.

Rivero, Yeidy M. 2005. *Tuning Out Blackness: Race and Nation in the History of Puerto Rican Television*. Durham: Duke University Press.

Robbins, Corrine. 1979. *The Drawings of Jorge Soto Sánchez*. New York: El Museo del Barrio.

Robert, Karen. 1992. Slavery and Freedom in the Ten Years' War, Cuba, 1868-1878. In *Slavery and Abolition* 13(3): 181-200.

Roberts, Peter. 2001. The (Re)Construction of the Concept of 'Indio' in the National Identities of Cuba, the Dominican Republic and Puerto Rico. In, pp. 99-120, *Caribbean 2000: regional and or national definitions, identities and cultures*, eds. Lowell Fiet and Janette Becerra. San Juan: University of Puerto Rico.

Rodríguez Beruff, Jorge. 1999. *Fronteras en conflicto: Guerra contra las drogas militarizacion y democracia en el Caribe, Puerto Rico y Vieques*. San Juan: Red Caribena de Geopolitica, Seguridad Regional y Relaciones Internacionales.

Rodríguez, Clara. 1980. Puerto Ricans: Between Black and White. In *The Puerto Rican Struggle: Essays on Survival in the U.S.*, eds. Clara Rodríguez, Virginia Sánchez Korrol, and José Oscar Alers. Maplewood, NJ: Waterfront Press.

————. 1994. *Puerto Ricans: Born in the U.S.A.* Boulder: Westview Press.

————. 1994. Challenging Racial Hegemony: Puerto Ricans in the United States. In, pp.131-145, *Race*, eds. Steven Gregory and Roger Sanjek. New Brunswick: Rutgers University Press.

————. 2000. *Changing Race: Latinos, the Census, and the History of Ethnicity in the United States*. New York: NYU Press.

————. 2009. Counting Latinos in the U.S. Census. In, pp. 37-72, *How the United States Racializes Latinos: White Hegemony and Its Consequences*, eds. José Cobas, Jorge Duany, and Joe F. Feagin. Boulder: Paradigm Publishers.

Rodríguez Cruz, Juan. 1965. Las relaciones raciales en Puerto Rico. *Revista de Ciencias Sociales 9(4): 373-386*.

Rodríguez Domínguez, Víctor. 2005. The Racialization of Mexican Americans and Puerto Ricans, 1890s-1930s. *CENTRO: Journal of the Center for Puerto Rican Studies* 17(1):71-105.

Rodríguez, Joselin. 2006. Baby Ranks dice que el reggaetón es un espejo de la sociedad que lo rodea. *HOY 2*, 2June.

Rodríguez Juliá, Edgardo. 1983. *El entierro de Cortijo*, Río Piedras: Ediciones Huracán.

————. 1991. Piñones: Una crónica. *El Nuevo Día, Revista Domingo*. Setpember 22, pp. 4-9.

Rodríguez-Morazzani, Roberto P. 1994–95. Linking a Fractured Past: The World of the Puerto Rican Old Left. *CENTRO: Journal of the Center for Puerto Rican Studies* 7(1): 20-30.

Rodríguez-Silva, Ileana. 2012. *Disentangling Blackness, Colonialism, and National Identities in Puerto Rico*. New York: Palgrave Macmillan.

Rodríguez Vázquez, José J. 2004. *El sueño que no cesa: la nación deseada en el debate intelectual y político puertorriqueño 1920–1940*. San Juan: Ediciones Callejón.

Rodríguez, W. 1977. "Puerto Rico: sociedad enferma salad mental, gran serie no. 1," *El Nuevo Día* 27 October.

Rogers, J. A. 1972. "Arthur A. Schomburg: 'The Sherlock Holmes of Negro History' (1874-1938)," "Schomburg is the Detective of History." *World's Great Men of Color, Vol. 2*. New York: Macmillan Publishing Company.

Rogler, Charles 1948. Some Situational Aspects of Race Relations in Puerto Rico. *Social Forces*, 27: 72-77.

_____. 1944. The Role of Semantics in the Study of Race Distance in Puerto Rico. *Social Forces* 22(4): 448-453.

Romano, C.M. 1992. Yo no soy negra. *Piso 13* 1(4): 3.

Romberg, Raquel. 2003. *Witchcraft and Welfare: Spiritual Capital and the Business of Magic in Modern Puerto Rico.* Austin: University of Texas Press.

Rosa del Romeral, Ramón Romero. 1976. The Social Question and Puerto Rico: A Friendly Call to Intellectuals. *Workers' Struggle in Puerto Rico: A Documentary History,* ed. Angel Quintero Rivera. New York: Monthly Review Press.

Rosa, Sonia M. 2003. The Puerto Ricans at the Carlisle School. *Kacike: Journal of Caribbean Amerindian History and Anthropology* <www.kacike.org/SoniaRosa.html>.

Rosa-Vélez, Sonia Migdalia. 2002. Acercamiento a los mitos y leyendas taínos en la literatura puertorriqueña y caribeña. Unpublished M.A. thesis, Universidad de Puerto Rico, Mayagüez.

Rosario, José Colombán and Justina Carrión. 1939. Problemas Sociales: El negro: Haití-Estados Unidos-Puerto Rico. *Boletín de la UPR* 10(2): 127-134.

_____. 1940. *El Negro: Haiti, Estados Unidos y Puerto Rico.* San Juan: Universidad de Puerto Rico.

Rosario Rivera, Raquel. 1992. *Los emigrantes llegados a Puerto Rico procedentes de Venezuela entre 1810–1848.* Hato Rey: Esmaco Printers.

Rosario, Rubén del, Esther Melón de Díaz, and Edgar Martínez Masdeu, eds. 1976. *Breve enciclopedia de la cultura puertorriqueña.* San Juan: Editorial Cordillera.

Rose, Ernestine. 1937b. Letter to Franklin Hopper. 18 October.

Rosenwaike, Ira. 1972. *Population History of New York City.* Syracuse: Syracuse University Press.

Rouse, Irving. 1992. *The Taínos: The Rise and Decline of the People Who Greeted Columbus.* New Haven: Yale University Press.

Roy-Fequiere, Magali 2004. *Women, Creole Identity, and Intellectual Life in Early Twentieth-century Puerto Rico.* Philadelphia, PA: Temple University Press.

Rumbaut, Rubén. 2009. Pigments of Our Imagination: On the Racialization and Racial Identities of "Hispanics" and "Latinos." In, pp. 15-36, *How the United States Racializes Latinos: White Hegemony and Its Consequences,* eds. José Cobas, Jorge Duany, and Joe F. Feagin. Boulder: Paradigm Publishers.

Russell, T. 1982. "Underground Economy" Here is a Huge Activity, *Caribbean Business.* 21April: 1-2.

Ryan, Carmelita S. 1962. The Carlisle Indian Industrial School. Ph.D. dissertation, Georgetown University, Washington, D. C.

Safa, Helen I. 1974. *The Urban Poor of Puerto Rico: A Study in Development and Inequality*. New York: Holt, Rinehart and Winston, Inc.

_____. 1987. Popular Culture, National Identity and Race in the Caribbean. *New West Indian Guide* 61(3–4): 115-126.

_____. 2001. Talk: Discourses on Color and Race. In *Dreaming Equality: Color, Race and Racism in Urban Brazil*. New Jersey: Rutgers University Press.

Sagás, Ernesto. 2000. *Race and Politics in the Dominican Republic*. Gainesville: University Press of Florida.

Sagrera, Martin. 1973. *Racismo y política en Puerto Rico: La desintegración interna y externa de un pueblo*. Río Piedras, Puerto Rico: Editorial Edil, Inc.

Said, Edward W. 1978. *Orientalism*. New York: Pantheon Books.

Sánchez González, Lisa. 2001. *Boricua Literature, A Literary History of the Puerto Rican Diaspora*. New York: NYU Press.

_____. 2005. Pura Belpré Legacy. In *Latina Legacies: Identity, Biography, and Community*, eds. Vicki L. Ruiz and Virginia Sánchez-Korrol. New York: Oxford University Press.

Sánchez Korrol, Virginia E. 1983. *From Colonia to Community: The History of Puerto Ricans in New York City*. Westport: Greenwood Press.

_____. 1994. *From Colonia to Community: the History of Puerto Ricans in New York City*. Berkeley: University of California Press.

Santaliz, Coqui. 1988. Divina herencia en Vacía Talega. *Puerto Rico Ilustrado, El Mundo*. May 1, pp. 12-13.

Santiago, Roberto, ed. 1995. *Boricuas: Influential Puerto Rican Writings—An Anthology*. New York: Ballantine Books.

Santiago-Valles, Kelvin A. 1994, *Subject People and Colonial Discourses: Economic Transformation and Social Disorder in Puerto Rico, 1898-1947*. Albany: State University of New York Press.

_____. 1995. Puerto Rico. *In*, pp.139-161, *No Longer Invisible: Afro-Latins Today*, ed. Minority Rights Group. London: Minority Rights Publications.

_____. 1996. Policing the Crisis in the Whitest of All the Antilles. *CENTRO: Journal of the Center for Puerto Rican Studies*, 8(1&2): 43-55.

Santiago-Valles, Kelvin and Gladys M. Jiménez-Muñoz. 2004. Social Polarization and Colonized Labor: Puerto Ricans in the United States, 1945-2000. In, pp. 62-149, *The Columbia History of Latinos in the United States, 1960 to the Present*, ed. David Gutierrez. New York: Columbia University Press.

Santos Febres, Mayra. 1996. *Pez de vidrio, Río Piedras: Ediciones Huracán*.

_____. *1997. Geografía en decibeles: Utopías pan-caribeñas y el territorio del rap. In Primer Simposio de Caribe 2000: Re-Definiciones: Espacio global/nacional/cultural/personal caribeño, eds. Lowell Fiet and Janette Becerra. Río Piedras:*

Facultad de Humanidades, Universidad de Puerto Rico.

———. 1997. Salsa as Translocation. In, pp. 175-188, *Everynight Life, Culture, and Dance in Latin/o America*, eds. José Muñoz and Celeste Fraser. Durham: Duke University Press.

———. 2000. *Sirena Selena vestida de pena*. Barcelona: Mondadori.

———. 2006. *Nuestra Señora de la Noche*. España: Espasa Autor.

Santos, Mayra. 1993. A veces miro mi vida. *Diálogo*. October.

Scarano, Francisco A. 1984. *Sugar and Slavery in Puerto Rico: The Plantation Economy of Ponce, 1800-1850*. Madison: University of Wisconsin Press.

———. 1993. *Puerto Rico: cinco siglos de historia*. NewYork: McGraw-Hill.

Schmidt-Nowara, Christopher. 2006. *The Conquest of History: Spanish Colonialism and National Histories in the Nineteenth Century*. Pittsburgh: University of Pittburgh Press.

Scott, Rebecca. 1985. *Slave Emancipation in Cuba: The Transition to Free Labor, 1860-1899*. Princeton: Princeton University Press.

Seda Bonilla, Eduardo. 1961. Social Structure and Race Relations. *Social Forces*, 40(2): 141-148.

———. 1973. *Los derechos civiles en la cultura puertorriqueña*. Río Piedras, PR: Ediciones Bayoán.

———. 1968. Dos modelos de relaciones raciales: Estados Unidos y América Latina. *Revista de Ciencias Sociales* 12(4): 569-598.

———. 1991. *Los derechos civiles en la cultura puertorriqueña*. Río Piedras, PR: Edictorial Universitaria, Universidad de Puerto Rico.

Sereno, Renzo. 1945. Cryptomelanism: A Study of Color Relations and Personal Insecurity in Puerto Rico. *Psychiatry* 10(3): 261-269.

Sharer, Robert and Loa Traxler. 2005. *The Ancient Maya*, 6th edition. Stanford: Stanford University Press.

Sheriff, Robin E. 2000. Exposing Silence as Cultural Censorship: A Brazilian Case. *American Anthropologist* 102(1): 114-132.

Shoemaker, Nancy. 1997. How Indians Got to Be Red. *The American Historical Review* 102: 625-644.

Shriver, Mark D. and Rick A. Kittles. 2004. Genetic ancestry and the search for personalized genetic histories. *Nature Reviews: Genetics* 5: 611-618.

Silén, Juan Ángel. 1977. *La generación de escritores de 1970 en Puerto Rico (1950-1976)*. Río Piedras: Editorial Cultural.

———. 1978. *Apuntes para una historia del movimiento obrero puertorriqueño*. Río Piedras, PR: Editorial Cultural.

Silva de Bonilla, R. 1981. Un análisis de la violencia, el crimen y los criminales: anatomía de un quehacer ideológico de los científicos sociales en Puerto Rico. *Revista del Colegio de Abogados* 42(2): 127-138.

Silvestrini, Blanca G. 1980. *Violencia y criminalidad en Puerto Rico, 1898-1973*. Río Piedras: Editorial Universitaria.

Silvestrini, G. Blanca, and María Dolores Luque de Sánchez. 1988. *Historia de Puerto Rico: trayectoria de un pueblo*. San Juan: Editorial La Biblioteca.

Singer, Roberta L. 1982. My Music Is Who I Am and What I Do: Latin Popular Music and Identity in New York City. Ph.D. dissertation, Indiana University.

Sinnette, Elinor Des Verney. 1962 Arthur Schomburg and Negro History. *The Worker*.

———. 1989. *Arthur Alfonso Schomburg: Black Bibliophile and Collector, A Biography*. New York: New York Public Library and Wayne State University Press.

Sitkoff, Harvard. 1978. *A New Deal for Blacks: the Emergence of Civil Rights as a National Issue*. New York: Oxford University Press.

Skidmore, Thomas E. 1993. Bi-racial USA vs. Multi-racial Brazil: Is the Contrast Still Valid? *Journal of Latin American Studies* 25(2): 373-386.

Smith, Rogers. 2001. The Bitter Roots of Puerto Rican Citizenship. In *Foreign in a Domestic Sense: Puerto Rico, American Expansion, and the Constitution*, eds. Christina Duffy Burnett and Burke Marshall. Durham: Duke University Press.

Steiner, Stan. 1974. *The Islands: The World of the Puerto Ricans*. New York: Harper Row.

Stephan, Nancy Leys. 1991. *The Hour of Eugenics: Race, Gender and Nation in Latin America*. Ithaca: Cornell University Press.

Stephens, Thomas M. 1999. *Dictionary of Latin American Racial and Ethnic Terminology*, 2nd ed. Gainsville: University of Florida Press.

Steward, Julian H. 1956. *The People of Puerto Rico*, Champaign-Urbana, University of Illinois Press.

Stewart, J.R. 1984. Notes on the Underground Economy in Puerto Rico. *Puerto Rico Business Review* 9(4): 23-30. 1 July.

Storm, John Roberts. 1999. *Latin Jazz: The First of the Fusions, 1880s to Today*. New York: Schirmer Books.

Strassler, Robert B. ed. 2008. *The Landmark Thucydides. A Comprehensive Guide to the Peloponesian War*. New York: The Free Press.

Suárez-Findlay, Eileen J. 2000. *Imposing Decency: The Politics of Sexuality and Race in Puerto Rico, 1870–1920*. Durham: Duke University Press.

Sued Badillo, Jalil. 1995a. The Island Caribs: New Approaches to the question of ethnicity in the early colonial Caribbean. In, pp. 61-89, *Wolves from the Sea: Readings in the Anthropology of the Native Caribbean*, ed. Neil L. Whitehead. Leiden: KITLV Press.

_____. 1995b. The Theme of the Indigenous in the National Projects of the Hispanic Caribbean. In *Making Alternative Histories: The Practice of Archaeology and History in Non-Western Settings*, eds. Peter R. Schmidt and Thomas C. Patterson. Santa Fe: School of American Research Press.

_____. 2001. *El dorado borincano: la economía de la conquista*, 1510–1550. San Juan: Ediciones Puerto.

_____. 1995a. The Island Caribs: New Approaches to the Question of Ethnicity in the Early Colonial Caribbean. In, pp. 61-89, *Wolves from the Sea: Readings in the Anthropology of the Native Caribbean*, ed. Neil L. Whitehead. Leiden: KITLV Press.

_____. 1995b. The Theme of the Indigenous in the National Projects of the Hispanic Caribbean. In, pp. 25-46, *Making Alternative Histories: The Practice of Archaeology and History in Non-Western Settings*, eds. Peter R. Schmidt and Thomas C. Patterson. Santa Fe, NM: School of American Research Press.

Sued Badillo, Jalil and Ángel López Cantos. 1986. *Puerto Rico Negro*. Río Piedras: Editorial Cultural.

Synnott, Anthony. 1993. *The Body Social: Symbolism, Self, and Society*. New York: Routledge.

Tannenbaum, Frank. 1947. *Slave and Citizen: The Negro in the Americas*. New York: Knopf.

Tapia y Rivera, Alejandro. 1993 [1867]. *La cuarterona*. Prólogo por Edgardo Quiles. Río Piedras: Editorial de la Universidad de Puerto Rico/Instituto de Cultura Puertorriqueña.

Tejera, Emilio. 1977. *Indigenismos*. Santo Domingo: Editora de Santo Domingo.

Telles, Edward. 1999. Ethnic Boundaries and Political Mobilization among African Brazilians: Comparisons with the US Case. In *Racial Politics in Contemporary Brazil*, ed. Michael Hanchard. Durham: Duke University Press.

Thomas, Hugh. 1971. *Cuba, or the Pursuit of Freedom*. London: Eyre & Spottiswoode.

Thomas, Lorrin. 2002. Citizens on the Margins: Puerto Rican Migrants in New York City. Unpublished Ph.D. dissertation, University of Pennsylvania.

_____. 2010. *Puerto Rican Citizen: History and Political Identity in Twentieth-Century New York City*. Chicago: University of Chicago Press.

_____. 2009. Resisting the Racial Binary? Puerto Ricans' Encounter With Race in Depression-Era New York City. *CENTRO: Journal of the Center for Puerto Rican Studies* 21(1): 5-35.

Thompson, Lanny. 2007. Nuestra Isla y su gente: La construcción del "otro" puertorriqueño en Our Island and Their People. Rio Piedras: Centro de Investigaciones Sociales, Universidad de Puerto Rico.

Thompson, Robert Farris. 1983. *Flash of the Spirit: African and Afro-American Art & Philosophy*. New York: Vintage Books.

_____. 1984. The Sign of the Four Moments of the Sun: Kongo Art and Religion in the Americas. In *Flash of the Sprit: African and Afro-American Art and Philosophy*. New York: Vintage Press.

Thurman, Wallace. 1928. *Negro Life in New York's Harlem*. Girard, Kansas: Haldeman-Julius Company.

Tibbets, Celeste. 1989. *Ernestine Rose and the Origins of the Schomburg Center*. Schomburg Center Occasional Papers Series, Number Two. New York: Schomburg Center for Research in Black Culture, The New York Public Library.

Tirado Avilés, Amílcar. 1990. Notas sobre el desarrollo de la industria del tabaco en Puerto Rico y su impacto en la mujer puertorriqueña. *CENTRO: Journal of the Center for Puerto Rican Studies*, 2(20): 19-29.

Torres, Arlene. 1998. La gran familia puertorriqueña 'ej prieta de beldá' (The Great Puerto Rican Family Is Really Really Black). In, pp. 285-306, *Blackness in Latin America and the Caribbean*, Vol. 2, eds. Arlene Torres and Norman E. Whitten, Jr. Bloomington: Indiana University Press.

Torres González, Roamé. 2002. *Idioma, bilingüismo y nacionalidad: la presencia del inglés en Puerto Rico*. Río Piedras: Editorial de la Universidad de Puerto Rico.

_____. 2003. *Preámbulo histórico al establecimiento de la Escuela Normal Industrial de Fajardo: antecedentes metropolitanos e insulares. Revista de Pedagogía* 35: 6-33.

Torres-Saillant, Silvio. 2000. The Tribulations of Blackness: Stages in Dominican Racial Identity. *Callaloo* 23(3): 1086-1111.

Trouillot, Michel-Rolph. 1992. The Caribbean Region: An Open Frontier in Anthropological Theory. *Annual Review of Anthropology* 21: 19-42.

_____. 1995. *Silencing the Past: Power and the Production of History*. Boston: Beacon Press.

Ungerleider, David. 1992. Loíza: más allá y del folclore. In *La tercera raíz. Presencia africana en Puerto Rico*. Lydia Milagros González, ed. San Juan, Centro de Estudios de la Realidad Puertorriqueña [CEREP] and Institute of Puerto Rican Culture.

Urrutia, Gustavo E. 1933. Schomburg. *Diario de La Marina*.

U.S. Bureau of the Census. Thirteenth Census of the United States: 1910, Occupation Statistics. Washington: U.S. Government Printing Office.

_____. 1921. Governor of Porto Rico, 1920-21. Washington: Government Printing Office.

_____. Fourteenth Census of the US: 1920. Washington, DC: Government Printing Office.

_____. Bureau of the Census, Fourteenth Census, Vol. ll -Population 1920. Washington, DC: U.S. Government Printing Office.

_____. 1932. Fifteenth Census of the United States: 1930, Occupation Statistics. Washington: U.S. Government Printing Office.

_____. 1943. Sixteenth Census of the United States: 1940, Comparative Occupation Statistics for the United States, 1870 to 1940. Washington, DC: United States Government Printing Office.

U.S. War Department. Informe Sobre El Censo De Puerto Rico, 1899. Washington, DC: Government Printing Office. [Departamento de la Guerra. 1900. Informe sobre el Censo de Puerto Rico, 1899. Washington: Imprenta del Gobierno.]

Vales, Pedro. 1987. *Justicia juvenil y la prevención de la delincuencia en Puerto Rico.* San Juan: Oficina del Gobernador.

Vales, Pedro A., Astrid A. Ortiz and Noel E. Mattei. 1982. *Patrones de criminalidad en Puerto Rico: apreciación socio-histórica, 1898-1890.* Rio Piedras.

Vargas, Patricia. 2006. Brilla el 'blin blin' de El Cangri en video. *El Nuevo Día* (28 January).

Vargas-Ramos, Carlos. 2005. Black, Trigueño, White...? Shifting Racial Identification Among Puerto Ricans. *Du Bois Review* 2(2): 1-19.

Vasconcelos, José. 1997. *The Cosmic Race: A Bilingual Edition.* Translated and annotated by Didier T. Jaén. Baltimore: Johns Hopkins University Press.

Vega, Ana Lydia et al. 1995. *Historia y literatura.* San Juan: Editorial Postdata.

Vega, Bernardo. 1984. *Memoirs of Bernardo Vega, A Contribution to the History of the Puerto Rican Community in New York.* Ed. César Andreu Iglesias. Trans. Juan Flores. New York: Monthly Review Press.

Vélez, J. 1993. "La Border patrol. *Claridad* 11 November: 40.

Víctima de un discrimen racial. 1996. *El Nuevo Día* January.

Vila Vilar, Enriqueta. 1974. *Historia de Puerto Rico (1600–1650).* Seville: Escuela de Estudios Hispano-Americanos.

Vilar, Miguel G., C. Melendez, A. Sanders, A. Walia, J. Gaiesky, A. Owings, T. Schurr, and the Genographic Consortium. 2014. Genetic diversity in Puerto Rico and its implications for the peopling of the island and the West Indies. *American Journal of Physical Anthropology* 155: 352-368.

Vizcarrondo, Fortunato. 1976. *Dinga y Mandinga (Poemas).* San Juan de Puerto Rico: Instituto de Cultura Puertorriqueña.

Wade, Peter. 1993. *Blackness and Race Mixture: The Dynamics of Racial Identity in Colombia.* Baltimore: Johns Hopkins University Press.

Wagenheim, Kal, and Jiménez de Wagenheim, Olga. 1994. *The Puerto Ricans: A Documentary History.* Princeton and New York: Markus Weiner Publishers.

Wang, Sijia, et al. 2008. Geographic Patterns of Genome Admixture in Latin American Mestizos. *PloS Genetics* 4:3 (March): e1000037. doi:10.1371/journal.pgen.1000037.

Washburne, Christopher. 2008. *Sounding Salsa Performing Latin Music in New York City.* Philadelphia: Temple University Press.

Washington, Booker T. 1994. 1895 Atlanta Compromise Speech. *Vital Issues: The Journal of African American Speeches* 4(3): 34-36.

Watkins-Owens, Irma. 1996. *Blood Relations, Caribbean Immigrants and the Harlem Community, 1900–1930*. Bloomington: Indiana University Press.

Webster, David. 2002. *The Fall of the Ancient Maya: Solving the Mystery of the Maya Collapse*. New York: Thames & Hudson.

Weiss, Kenneth M. and Stephanie M. Fullerton. 2005. Racing Around, Getting Nowhere. *Evolutionary Anthropology* 14 (September-October): 165-169.

West, Cornell. 1993. *Race Matters*. Boston: Beacon Press.

West-Durán, Alan. 2005. Puerto Rico: The Pleasures and Traumas of Race. *CENTRO: Journal of the Center for Puerto Rican Studies* 17(1): 48-69.

Whitten, Norman E. Jr. and Arlene Torres. 1998. General Introduction: To Forge the Future in the Fires of the Past: An Interpretive Essay on Racism, Domination, Resistance, and Liberation. In, pp. 3-33, *Blackness in Latin America and the Caribbean, vol. II*, eds. Norman Whitten Jr. and Arlene Torres. Bloomington: Indiana University Press.

Williams, Claudette M. 2000. *Charcoal and Cinnamon: The Politics of Color in Spanish Caribbean Literature*. Gainesville: University Press of Florida.

Williams, Eric. 1963. *Documents of West Indian History, 1492-1655*. Port of Spain: PNM Publishing Company.

Williamson, Simon. 1938. History of the Life and Work of Arthur Alonzo [sic] Schomburg. *Arthur A. Schomburg Papers*. Unpublished.

Wilson, Samuel M. 1990. *Hispaniola: Caribbean Chiefdoms in the Age of Columbus*. Tuscaloosa: University of Alabama Press.

Wilson, Patricia L. 1984. Puerto Rican Art in New York: The Aesthetic Analysis of Eleven Painters. Ph.D. dissertation. New York University.

Winant, Howard. 1992. Rethinking Race in Brazil. *Journal of Latin American Studies* 24(1): 173-192.

_____. 2001. *The World is a Ghetto: Race and Democracy Since World War II*. New York: Basic Books.

Withey, Ellen. 1977. Discrimination in private employment in Puerto Rico. *Puerto Rican Journal of Human Rights* 1(1): 43-47.

Wolf, Donna M. 1975. The Cuban Gente de Color and the Independence Movement, 1879-1895. *Revista Review Interamericana* 5 (197): 5.

Wolters, Raymond. 1970. *Negroes and the Great Depression: the Problem of Economic Recovery*. Westport, CT: Greenwood Press.

Wright, Gwendolyn. 1983. *Building the Dream: A Social History of Housing in America*. Cambridge: MIT Press.

Yang, Andrew. 2007. Is Oprah Zulu? Sampling and Seeming Certainty in DNA Ancestry Testing. *Chance: A Magazine of the American Statistical Association* 20(1 November): 32-39.

Yelvington, Kevin. 2001. The Anthropology of Afro-Latin America and the Caribbean: Diasporic Dimensions. *Annual Review of Anthropology* 30: 227-260.

Yglesias, Pablo. 2005. *Cocinando! Fifty Years of Latin Album Cover Art, Architectural Series*. New York: Princeton Architectural Press.

Young Lords. 1969. *Palante*. (October).

Zenón Cruz, Isabelo. 1974. *Narciso descubre su trasero: El negro en la cultura puertorriqueña*. Humacao, Puerto Rico: Editorial Furidí.

———. 1975. *Narciso descubre su trasero (El negro en la cultura puertorriqueña)*. 2 vols. 2nd ed. Humacao, Puerto Rico: Editorial Furidi.

———. 1991. Prologue to Juan de Matta García. In *Prietuscos y tarcualitos: Poemas negristas y otros poemas*. Arecibo: Editores GarAndú.

Zimmerman, Warren. 2002. *First Great Triumph: How Five Americans Made Their Country a World Power*. New York: Farrar, Straus and Giroux. Lindsay, Samuel McCune.

NOTES

Introduction

[1] Fuson 1987, p.76.

[2] Lest this statement be interpreted as the Nuyorican generation not considering racial difference among Puerto Ricans (in the United States) as a point of difference, that is, that Nuyoricans were more likely to subscribe to the "racial democracy" creed that pervades much of the discourse of race among Puerto Ricans, reader should also bear in mind the sharp critiques that surfaced among Nuyoricans against the efforts among island-born and –raised Puerto Ricans to diminish those intra-Puerto Rican racial difference and the differential treatment Puerto Ricans of African descent faced within the community both in Puerto Rico and in the United States (e.g., Jiménez-Román 1996; Betances 1972, 1973) precisely because of their exposure to bigotry and discrimination in the United States, which allow them a perch from which to observe with some distance the similarities in the racial regimes Puerto Ricans were exposed to in both Puerto Rico and in the United States.

Chapter 1

[1] In Puerto Rico, "racial prejudice" is popularly conceived of as simply a matter of personal predilection, without any acknowledgment of the racist (usually negative) stereotypes that inform the preference. It is commonly understood and accepted, for example, that "straight hair" (*pelo lacio*) is preferable to very curly or "kinky" hair; indeed the latter is considered "bad hair" (*pelo malo*) that must be "fixed." Similarly, most other phenotypic features that are identified with "Blackness" are deemed inferior; by extension, it is believed that the bearers of these inferior physical traits are "naturally" imbued with inferior intellectual and emotional characteristics.

[2] Díaz was clearly referring to the number of slaves and not to the population classified as Black or *mulato* which, in fact, made up the majority of the island's inhabitants until the 1860 census. Díaz and Alegría's remarks are contained in Bliss (1995).

[3] For a discussion of the exceptionalist logic that informs Latin American racial discourse see Hanchard (1992).

[4] The most significant among these "exceptions" is the two-volume study by Zenón Cruz (1974). Other challenges to the myth of racial harmony in Puerto Rico include Gordon (1949); Betances (1972, 1973); Sagrera (1973); and Nieves Falcón (1993).

[5] An example is the following explanation given by sociologist Rodríguez (1989: 66): "On a social level...Hispanics have a different conception of race, one that is as much cultural or 'social' as it is racial."

[6] One is "Black" in Puerto Rico depending on the degree of conformity to the stereotype of the "pure African," i.e., having physical features which include tightly curled hair, broad nose, full lips, and dark skin color. Even when all the phenotypical criteria seem to fit the stereotype, few Puerto Ricans (past or present) identify, or are identified by Puerto Ricans,

as African. Traditionally, those who were perceived as "too black" were suspected of being "from the islands," i.e. from other (usually English-speaking) Caribbean countries, and thus, not authentically Puerto Rican. More recently, however, and as a consequence of the growing numbers of people from the Dominican Republic who have settled on the island, Black Puerto Ricans are increasingly identified specifically as Dominicans.

7   Regrettably, I have not been able to discover any early writings by women that directly address questions of "race" and racism in Puerto Rico. Indeed, sensitivity to the subject is so great that one of the few contemporary accounts, included in a feminist anthology (Jorge 1979: 134–41) was eliminated from the Spanish translation published in Puerto Rico (see Acosta-Belén 1980).

8   A by-product of minimizing the African/Black presence has been the exaggeration of the Taíno presence. Documentation on the Indian population is clearly unreliable, as the following suggests: the official Spanish census of 1530 reported 1,148 "indios" on the island; the historian Fernando Picó reports that the 1802 census counted 2,300 "indios"—all residing in the southwestern town of San German, the first of the Spanish settlements. If we consider the devastating consequences for the Taínos of close contact with the Spaniards, it is highly unlikely that any Indians would have survived almost 300 years in San Germán, and no where else. Picó reports that after 1802 "indios" were counted as "pardos." (Picó 1988: 57).

9 During the period 1795–1873 there were over twenty planned slave rebellions, most along the northern coast of Puerto Rico. Much more commonplace was *cimarronaje*, the escape into the hinterland or to distant towns where a Black man or woman could "disappear" among the general population (Baralt 1981).

10 The very term *criollo* would reflect this growing national Puerto Rican identity. Originally used to denote the children of Spaniards born on the island, by 1788, when the first comprehensive history of Puerto Rico was published, Europeans were designated simply as blancos or *"hombres de la otra banda"* [men of the other band] and criollo had come to refer to the islander, i.e. the native Puerto Rican (Waggenheim and Jiménez de Waggenheim 1994: 33).

11 The caste system operated throughout the Spanish colonies, although it took different forms. In Puerto Rico, there were fewer caste terms than those used in South America, which probably reflected the absence of Indians on the island. The most commonly used terms, both in official documents and in daily life, were *blanco/a, mulato/a, pardo/a, and negro/a*. One caste term that under-went an intriguing reconfiguration is "jibaro," defined in the early 18th century as someone descended from any of the following combinations: *calpamulo/a and indio/a; africano/a and Indio; calpamul/a and albarazado/a; lobo/a and chino/a; barcino/a and indio/a; tente en el aire and lobo/a*. Each of these terms (with the exception of indio and africano), in turn, referred to other caste combinations; conspicuously absent—or very far in the background—is any reference to European ancestry. Still, since the late 18th century, a Puerto Rican jibaro has been understood to be "White."

12 Term used by Michael Jiménez in his discussion of relations between Colombian peasant women and landowners (quoted in Hanchard 1992: 12).

13 Until the early 19th century, manumission was a common practice of the slaveowners who fathered children with enslaved women and this has been hailed as an indication of the

benevolence of the Spanish slave system. Davis (1996: 281) offers a more persuasive explanation: "Such planters [who freed their mixed children and grandchildren] were unmoved by the plight of slaves or by the degraded position of their mulattos. Always one's own children or grandchildren deserved special consideration, for they were far superior to others of their class; they were of good character and had benefited from Christian training." Economic imperatives, however, were able to override even these egocentric motivations; once slave labor became of fundamental importance for the developing sugar plantations of the 19th century the frequency of manumissions declined significantly,

[14] Denied education and confined to the private world of the family, women had few opportunities for improving their situation beyond marital/sexual alliances.

[15] In the town of Utuado, Pedro Avilés and Andrea Cruz had ten children during the first decades of the 19th century; the marriages of two sons and one daughter were listed in the parish's registry for pardos while two other sons had theirs registered in the ledger for blancos (Picó 1981: 113). Utuado, traditionally perceived as a "White town"— as are all towns in the mountainous interior—was founded in 1739 by a group which "possibly" included a majority of pardos libres, i.e. free mulattos (Picó 1988: 108).

[16] These sentiments, expressed by Major General Nelson A. Miles, commander of the invading forces, just four days after the landing of the U.S. troops, would continue to characterize the North American attitude toward its new colony. For full text of Miles' proclamation, see Waggenheim and Jiménez de Waggenheim (1994: 95–6). For a discussion of the "Othering" of the "natives," see Santiago-Vales (1994).

[17] Barbosa studied at the Roman Catholic Seminario Conciliar de San Juan where, according to his biographer, he was "one of the few students of color who warmed those benches" (Pedreira 1937: 16). In an 1896 response to a particularly virulent racist attack, Barbosa (1896) writes that he "opened the doors" of the Seminary, suggesting that he was the first "hombre de color" to study at that institution.

[18] Reminiscent of an oft-quoted story regarding the onset of Puerto Rican bibliophile and lay historian Arturo Alfonso Schomburg's interest in Black history (in reply to his questions about Black achievements a teacher presumably scoffed that Black people had no history,) Pedreira describes a classroom scene in which a priest asks his students what careers they plan to pursue. When Barbosa volunteers that he wants to be an attorney, the Jesuit laughs and replies, "You must mean a jailhouse lawyer!" Years later the same priest explained to the successful physician that the remark had been meant to "motivate" him in his studies (Pedreira 1937: 19).

[19] The first African American was admitted into the University of Michigan in 1869. In 1875, Barbosa was the first Puerto Rican to attend and, in 1903, the first to receive an honorary Master of Arts degree from the University at Ann Arbor.

[20] The Carroll Commission Report described their meeting with representatives of Puerto Rico's labor movement seven of the nine leaders were "colored men" (Carroll 1989: 51).

[21] For an analysis of the first years of colonial politics under United States domination, see Negrón Portillo (1990).

[22] The Republican Party attracted many Black Puerto Ricans to its ranks, including the attorney and teacher Eugenio LeCompte, who studied with Booker T. Washington

and W.E.B. DuBois; Eulalio García Lascot, who received his medical degree at Howard University; and the labor leader, attorney, and writer Pedro Carlos Timothée, who corresponded with Arturo Alfonso Schomburg.

[23] Barbosa is already expressing, in 1896, his "enthusiasm for democratic principles, the only ones which have been able to help us to partly realize the beautiful dreams and beloved illusions of an awakened spirit." For full text, see Barbosa (1896: 25–8).

[24] *Piti* is most probably a corruption of the French "petite."

Chapter 2

[1] See the excellent introductory essay by Arcadio Díaz Quiñones (1985) for an analysis of his views on race. See also Aparicio (1998: 38–44).

[2] For a critique of Pedreira, see Flores (1993: 13–57). On Blanco, see Díaz-Quiñones (1985: 13–83).

[3] See Frances Aparicio (1998), Vera Kutzinski (1993), and Robin Moore (1997). Clearly, many poems or songs written about mulatas are racist and sexist and don't need too much commentary. But for the likes of Palés Matos, Guillén, Villaverde (and others), there is considerable more complexity (not to mention irony) and a need to sort out that complexity with nuance.

[4] One could claim that Tapia y Rivera's La cuarterona is a tragedy by virtue of wanting to refute Gilberto Freyre' s quote["la negra para trabajar; la mulata para fornicar, la blanca para casar" (black women are [good] for slaving and sweating; mulattas for bedding; white women for wedding)], without Carlos truly seeing the social power that enforces such a perception.

[5] For more on Puerto Rican hip-hop see Flores (2000), Santos Febres (1997), and Rivera (2003).

[6] In the song "Loíza" Calderón addresses issues of racism, identity, police brutality, and equality (or lack of) before the law. Here is an excerpt: "Me quiere hacer pensar/que soy parte de una trilogía racial/donde todo el mundo es igual/sin trato especial/Sé perdonar/eres tú quien no sabe disculpar/no hay cómo justificar tanto mal./Es que tu historia/ es vergonzosa, entre otras cosas/cambiaste las cadenas/por esposas." [Wanna make me think/I'm part of the racial trilogy/ That we are all equal/Nobody treated special/I know how to forgive/you don't know how/no way no how/to justify so much evil/Your history is a shame/that I can name/instead of chains/ you use handcuffs".] (Calderón 2002).

[7] For a critique of González's essay, see Flores (1993: 61–70) and Carrión (1996: 46–66).

Chapter 3

[1] The major defense of "racial democracy" in Puerto Rico remains Tomás Blanco 1942 essay, *El prejucio racial en Puerto Rico*. Río Piedras, Ediciones Huracán, 1985 (with an introductory study by Arcadio Díaz-Quiñones). The more significant analyses of racism in Puerto Rico are Isabelo Zenón, *Narciso descubre su trasero*, 2 vols., Río Piedras, Editorial Furidi, 1974-75; Martín Sagrera *Racismo y política en Puerto Rico*. Rio Piedras: Editorial Edil, 1973. and Eduardo Seda Bonilla, "Dos modelos de relaciones raciales: Estados Unidos y América Latina" *Revista de Ciencias Sociales*, 12(4), 1968, pp. 569-98. For general approach from the perspective of the diaspora, with some affinities with "racial democracy" arguments, see Clara Rodríguez's discussion of Puerto Rican as a "rainbow people" in *Puerto Ricans: Born in the U.S.A.* Boston, Unwyn Hyman, 1989.

2 "Sedoso o áspero".

3 Visiting U.S. researchers, especially in the 1940's-1950's, became enchanted with Puerto Rico's "racial democracy": in time, however, most came to know better. See, e.g. Mintz (1978).

4 In Puerto Rico, even the more common racial terms present large difficulties. Defining who is *negro* or *prieto* ("black"), *blanco* ("white"), *de color* ("of color"), *moreno* ("dark"), *jabao* ("yellow"), *trigueño* ("light-dark"), *cano* ("blond"; partly from "americano"?) or *colorao* (" reddish white"), *jincho* (very light skinned, to the point of a sickly appearance), *mulato*, etc. is daunting, and even more so in translation. The direct, polar terms of *blanco* (white) and *negro* (black) are the least frequently used. The categories and variants themselves clamor for closer attention.

5 "He who is not African on one side, is on the other." The phrase plays with the words *dinga* and *mandinga*, both of which refer to African peoples: the Mandè or Mandingos of the Western Sudan, and the Dinkas further east. But the phrase has a further connotation, using the sense that was given to the term *mandinga* in the Spanish colonial era, as "the devil." Thus, this further translation might read: "He who does not have Africa in him, has the devil.

6 "Hispanismo" has a long and complex history in Puerto Rico that far transcends the field of literature, and which has interesting reworkings in the diaspora. This history should be of interest to specialists in Caribbean, U.S. or Latin American cultural studies, but has rarely drawn their sustained attention. U.S. researchers would find much that is illuminating for understanding the history, in their own country, of anglophilia (the opposite, of course, is also true).

7 Thus "*negroide*" suggests something that is black, but is not even really, deeply black; that would be (too) African. "*Negroide*" also implies something that is perhaps even "abnormally," "pathologically" black. Partly as a result of this, " *lo negroide*" was tacitly expected to spawn no more than minor, "local color" literature. The term "*negrista*," which is used especially with regard to poetry, is preferable but does not necessarily go beyond color.

8 According to Flores (1992: 88): "The real roots of the plena, as is universally acknowledged, are in the bomba; all the early pleneros [...] were originally bomberos, and the most basic features of the plena derive directly or indirectly from bomba."

9 The masked *vejigantes* (costumed, raucous "devils") of Loiza's patron-saint feasts of Santiago the Apostle (St. James) became the best known and perhaps most overworked icon of *cultura negroide*, and *vejigante* masks have been the object of innumerable graphic works. Santiago is akin to the Yoruba deity Ogún, though it is improbable that many Yoruba settled in Loíza. The vejigante coconut-shell masks of Loiza "became a prominent feature of the artistic generation of the 1950's and went on to become a symbol of Puerto Rican culture" (Benítez 1992: 109).

10 Literary critic Julio Ortega has noted: "[I]n Puerto Rico there has been a movement away from privileging the jíbaro peasant to more recently privileging the figure of the black, vindicated and toned variously [matizado] as black [prieto], 'red' [grifo] and *mulatto*" (1991: 29).

11 Not wholly unlike Europeans who acknowledged the "greatness" of Oriental civilizations, Puerto Ricans who primarily identify themselves with a Hispanic heritage are also drawn to negroide music, poetry or graphics arts. However, "the essential relationship [is seen] to be one between a strong and a weak partner" (Said 1978: 40). Cultura negroide is typically disembodied folklore, subject to the same misperceptions as other such phenomenona in folklore in general (frozen quality, ahistoric, asocial, etc.) as of specifically Afro-American

ones (preoccupation with African survivals or innocuous African-European "syncretism," etc.). The rather eerie, enigmatic impression produced by the three-pointed coconut masks of Loíza's vejigantes, when pulled out of their festive context, perhaps captures the perception of lo negroide in AfroPuerto Rican culture.

[12] The immediate impact of *Narciso* was a veritable bomba. Zenón's polemical work played no small part in the crisis of the Ateneo Puertorriqueño, Puerto Rico's oldest and most venerable cultural institution (Silén 1977).

[13] Zenón called his tripartite scheme of Puerto Rican culture "trinitarian.".. with inevitably religious undertones of veracity and authority?

[14] Why are so many of the most defenders of negritud in Puerto Rico supporters of independence, while others (if probably a smaller and less conspicuous group) as strongly in favor of statehood, or commonwealth? How do the discourses of negritud shape and become shaped by political status preferences? This is a Puerto Rican "twist" to the discussion of black culture that needs to be considered seriously, and which only partially resembles the longstanding U.S. debate between black separatism and integration (see Godreau 1995).

[15] Bastide liberally incorporates conclusions of Edith Clarke and M.G. Smith. The Anglophone Caribbean—at least as grasped by Smith and Clarke—had an almost radically different historical experience vis á vis the Hispanic territories in terms of the comprehensiveness, continuity and strength of plantation slavery vis-á-vis heterogeneous form of peasant social relations.

[16] The earlier *Conversación con José Luis González*, published just after *Narciso* and its own storm of debate, anticipated many of the themes of (the even more controversial) next work by González (1980).

[17] One of the most provocative "ethnographic" commentaries in *El entierro de Cortijo* concerned Afro-Puerto Rican surnames from the San Juan-Cangrejos-Loíza region: Verdejo, Cortijos, Paris, Romero, Pizarro, etc.

[18] In general, coastal barrios and coastal municipios in the eastern portion of Puerto Rico have been estimated to have high percentages of blacks: Salinas and Carolina (more than 40 percent) and Guayama and Humacao (more than 30 percent). Both Mintz and Manuel Alvarez Nazario link these high percentages to African slave imports and sugar plantation production. Yet areas where plantation slavery were most important, such as Ponce and Mayagüez, do not figure among the highest percentages; and as we shall see, plantation production was, historically, far less important in Loíza than might be surmised. The large number of free black and maroon squatters in the entire San Juan periphery, the fertility of the sandy loams of the Loíza litoral, the disuasion of insect pests and malaria, and the Loíza litoral's exposure to attacks by Caribs until the seventeenth century, all seem to have been more significant than plantation slavery itself in shaping the durable numerical preponderance of Afro-Puerto Ricans in Loíza.

Chapter 4

[1] In Ferre's novel, Isabel's comments and not her manuscript are presented in italics. In Nolla, Sonia's manuscript is in italics within María Isabel's text.

Chapter 5

[1] I am working from the premise that all history is to a large extent fictional and constructed by the powerful class.

[2] An interesting ethnographic study is Romberg (2003).

[3] A nearly identical version of the Cuban prayer Mayra Santos-Febres uses in pages 71–2 appears in del Río et. al. (1990: 26–7).

[4] For a significant ethnographic study exploring the Institute of Puerto Rican Culture. see Davila (1997).

[5] For an important ethnographic study about San Antón see Godreau (1999).

[6] Suárez-Findlay (2000) makes significant historical contributions to the understanding of prostitution, race, and sexuality in Puerto Rico and in the Ponce of the late nineteenth and early twentieth century.

Chapter 6

[1] Conversations with Carlos Moore, March 1996, Kingston Jamaica.

[2] The questionnaire was filled out in the 1930s for E. Franklin Frazier's 1939 study. Schomburg's completed questionnaire is among Frazier's papers: "A Study of the Negro Family," questionnaire No.2597, E. Franklin Frazier Papers, Moorland Spingarn Research Center, Howard University.

[3] Schomburg to Dabney, August 19, 1937; reel 7, Schomburg Papers.

[4] There is no biography of Colón, but see the helpful biographical sketch in *Centro de Estudios Puertorriqueños*, Hunter College, *The Jesús Colón Papers: Finding Aid* (1991), pp. 6-7. See also Acosta-Bélen and Sánchez Korrol (1993: 22-25), Roger Keeran (1989), and Roberto P. Rodríguez-Morazzani (1995: 24).

Chapter 7

[1] Anthropologist Arjun Appadurai (1991) coined the term ethnoscape, an obvious corollary to landscape, which is useful in the field of ethnic studies as it alludes not only to the ethnic and racial composition of a geographic area, but also to the nature and the character of that area. The documentation of the racism Puerto Ricans encountered can be found in a variety of first person and secondary texts by Colón (2002), History Task Force (1979), Pantoja (2002), Sánchez Korrol (1994), Sánchez González (2001; 2005), and Vega (1984).

[2] I am grateful to Prof. Luis Marentes, who suggested that the library be placed in the context of institutions of resistance. Librarian Isabel Espinal has been a valued sounding board in highlighting the uneven history public libraries have of fighting discrimination and aspiring to be inclusive institutions. I also want to thank the anonymous reviewers of this article for their thoughts on this point and others.

[3] About the Black Puerto Rican community in Puerto Rico, Dr. Mina Perry, an African American who lived and taught in Puerto Rico for 14 years, comments, "I find that many Puerto Ricans do not know that in Puerto Rico there was a small professional class of Blacks who were very clear about their dual links and brought that knowledge to the U.S. There are

distinct family names. They did not speak about it but it does not mean that there was no consciousness" (personal communication 6/20/06).

4 Walter White, an African-American leader, coined the phrase the color line within the color line in an article in the *New Negro*, edited by Alain Locke.

5 Clarence Cameron White (1880–1960) was a well-recognized violinist and composer. He played classical music and in the early 1920s began to work with African-American music and spirituals. His papers are held by the Schomburg Center for Research in Black Culture.

6 Ernestine Rose shares a name with a noted nineteenth-century Jewish feminist, Ernestine Louise Rose (1810–1892). Born in Russian Poland, Ernestine L. Rose has no connection with the Ernestine Rose of Bridgehampton, Long Island, discussed in this article. Due to the shared name, it is logical to wonder whether Ernestine Rose of Bridgehampton was also Jewish. Although her religion is not directly referred to in the biographical information I have consulted, there is mention that a paternal uncle was a minister. After retiring in Bridgehampton, Rose joined the local Presbyterian Church.

7 Of her experience at the Seward Branch library, Rose wrote and published a pamphlet in 1917, "Bridging the Gulf; Work with Russian Jews and Other Newcomers.

8 The author of over 20 published papers and pamphlets, she also authored one book, *The Public Library in American Life*. The only personal papers that survive her refer to her work from 1945–47, after she left the Harlem Branch and worked at Columbia University. Her papers are at Columbia University's library.

9 Children's Registration 1926-1930. New York Public Library 135th Street Branch Records (hereafter NYPLBR), Box 3, Folder 9; Reports 1919-1927, NYPLBR, Box 3, Folder 8; Children's Room Report 1922-1929. Box 2, Folder 17; Children's Registration 1926-1930. NYPLBR, Box 1, Folder 9; 135th Street Branch Adult Education 1932-1950, Advising Readers in Harlem. NYPLBR, Box 1; New and Better Methods for Helping Readers. NYPLBR, Box 1; Readers' Adviser—Annual Report—1932; NYPLBR, Box 1

Chapter 8

1 On racial categories and racial identities in Latin America, see, for example, Candelario (2007), Guerra (1998), Duany (1998), Jiménez Román (1996), Wade (1993) and Skidmore (1993). For an important reminder that Europeans were not "the sole inventors" of the idea of race and racial categorization, see Shoemaker (1997). On the United States, see Nash (1995).

2 On racial categories in the census, see Loveman (2007), Loveman and Muniz (2007), Rodríguez (2000) and Nobles (2000).

3 See testimony by Puerto Rican independence activist Luis Muñoz Rivera before the Committee on Insular Affairs, House of Representatives, 63rd Congress, 2nd Session, on H.R. 138118, p. 61. "Negroes—citizens without rights" is a phrase from historian Barbara Savage, personal correspondence with the author, July 2003.

4 With the passage of the Jones Act in 1917, United States citizenship was conferred on Puerto Ricans in a form that legal scholar and judge José Cabranes refers to (along with many others), as "second-class," since Puerto Ricans on the island cannot vote in Presidential elections, have only a non-voting elected representative in the American Congress, and do not pay federal

taxes. This particular form of American citizenship is explained in the 1922 legal decision Bal-zac v. Porto Rico, 258 U.S. 298 (1922) (Cabranes 1978: 403–4). When Puerto Ricans migrate to the continental United States, their citizenship becomes identical to that of other mainlanders.

[5] On the class composition of the early Puerto Rican community in New York, see generally Vega (1984: 105, 136–44 and passim), Sánchez Korrol (1994: 53–77), Rodríguez- Morazzani (1994: 20–30) and WPA Federal Writers Project, "Life Histories." On the practice of "passing," see Pedro Juan Labarthe, "De Nuestros Lectores," La Prensa, 8 Jan. 1931, 6; and interview with Pedro Cresente, con-ducted by B. Richardson, 13 April 1975, Brooklyn Pioneros Project, LIHS; and L. Thomas (2002: 36).

[6] There is a substantial and diverse literature on the nonwhite "other" racial identities ascribed to various immigrant groups in the US. See, for example, Haney López (1996, 1998), Ngai (1999, 2004), Gutiérrez (1995), Low (1996), Kim (1999), Ancheta (2006). Shaping the racial identities ascribed to nonwhite others in the early twentieth century were new racist discourses of imperialism, lumping the Cuban, Puerto Rican, and Filipino people over whom the United States ruled into crudely differentiated categories of "nigger," "savage," etc. See, for example, Balce (2006), who cites W.E.B. DuBois's 1920 book Darkwater (New York: Washing-ton Square Press, 2007 [1920]), probably the first published book to explore the racist language of empire in America.

[7] "Graves resultados de simple incidente," 21 March 1935, La Prensa, 1; and Complete Report, 10. "1 Dead, 7 Shot, 100 Hurt As Harlem Crowds Riot over Boy, 16, and Hearse," 1, and "Distur-bance in Harlem," 6, New York Herald-Tribune, 20 March 1935, and "Mayor Plans Own Riot Inquiry," Sun, 20 March 1935, 1.

[8] Redbaiting was also an issue in the selection of members of the Mayor's Committee on Conditions in Harlem, established by the LaGuardia in the days following the riot. The Sun pointed to the radical activities of black appointees A. Phillip Randolph, Countee Cullen, and Arthur Garfield Hays ("Indict four more in Harlem riot," Sun, 22 March 1935).

[9] "1 Dead, 7 Shot, 100 Hurt as Harlem Crowds Riot Over Boy, 16, and Hearse," New York Herald Tribune, 20 March 1935, 1,9; "Police Shoot into Rioters; Kill Negro in Harlem Mob," New York Times, 20 March 1935, p. 1; "Mayor Lays Riot to 'Vicious Group,'" New York Times, 21 March 1935, p. 16; "Did Not Know He Caused Riot," Sun, 22 March 1935.

[10] In 1913, a Colombian immigrant founded what would become the colonia's newspaper of re-cord, La Prensa, as a four-page weekly to serve his small community; by 1918, a Spaniard, José Comprubí, started running the paper as a daily to meet the needs of the expanding colonia. Ten years later, La Prensa reported an average daily readership of 15,000. The paper covered headline news from across Latin America as well as local news deemed relevant to its im-migrant readership. In response to the complaints of working class readers, the editors would occasionally make a show of running a front- page interview with a working-class leader, or providing page one coverage of a dock workers strike (many Spaniards and Puerto Ricans were maritime workers). Puerto Ricans in particular also complained, from time to time, about the paper's bias in favor of its Spanish readers. However, by the 1930s, the paper did frequently include news of the skilled working class community—see, for example, the announcement of "Un Ágape," an event at the home of Conchita and Jesús Colón attended by other working class and leftist luminaries in the colonia, including Bernardo Vega; "Un Ágape," La Prensa,

14 Feb. 1934, p. 8. On *La Prensa*'s history, circulation, and readership see Vega (1984: 99); and WPA Federal Writers Project, "Spanish Book," "Spanish Newspapers, Magazines, etc., in New York" at the Municipal Archives, NYC.

[11] See also Rogler (1944) and Fitzpatrick (1959). The contradictory discourses of mestizaje, "racelessness," and "racial democracy" exist in somewhat different forms in many other Latin American societies as well; see, for instance, Wade (1993), Skidmore (1992 [1979]), Wright (1992). On contemporary racial discourse among Puerto Ricans in the United States, see also Rodríguez (1980) and Landale and Oropesa (2002).

[12] This was a reference to the Church of Father Divine. "Tropas para Harlem pedidas ayer; centenares de policías patrullaban anoche el barrio," *La Prensa*, 21 March 1935, 1.

[13] "Los 'motines' de Harlem," editorial, *La Prensa*, 21 March 1935, 4.

[14] *New York American*, 28 Dec. 1930.

[15] Emphasis in original. María Más Pozo, "De Nuestros Lectores," *La Prensa*, 12 Jan. 1931, 6.

[16] Fernando Arjona López, "De Nuestros Lectores," *La Prensa*, 26 Jan. 1931, 6; C. Cedeño Ferrer (writing from Aguadilla, Puerto Rico), "De Nuestros Lectores," *La Prensa*, 30 Jan. 1931, 6.

[17] Gabriel Rivera, "De Nuestros Lectores," *La Prensa*, 27 Jan. 1931, 6–7.

[18] Researchers at the Tuskegee Institute in the 1930s determined that the number of lynchings in the South tripled during the first year of the Depression, from seven in 1929 (down from a high of twenty-three in 1926) to twenty-one in 1930. See Sitkoff (1978: 268–9 and passim); Bunche (1973: 116–7) and Wolters (1970: 337–40). See, generally, Naison (1985). Nationalists frequently responded to *La Prensa*'s stories and editorials on lynching throughout the 1920s and early 1930s.

[19] Marcelino Méndez Pidal, "De Nuestros Lectores," *La Prensa*, 15 Feb. 1934, 7.

[20] Osvaldo Maqueira Calvo, "De Nuestros Lectores," *La Prensa*, 17 May 1934, 4.

[21] See, for example, Naison (1985), Vega (1984), Griffiths (2001). Another interesting development in this moment, to which I can make only suggestive links, was the publication in Puerto Rico of literature scholar Antonio Pedreira's *Insularismo: ensayos de interpretación puertorriqueña*, a seminal meditation on Puerto Rican cultural identity that openly rejected the presence of African "blood" and culture. See Jiménez Román (1996: 2).

[22] See, for instance, transcript of interview with Dona Lucila Padrón, conducted on 12 Jan. 1984 by Ana Juarbe, from the Costureras project of the Center for Puerto Rican Studies, p. 99, in which Padrón describes a cousin trained as a teacher in Puerto Rico who was unable to find work in the city because she was "dark."

[23] Rafael W. Carreras, "De Nuestros Lectores," *La Prensa*, 26 June 1935, 4. Other letters and articles on the "anti-Hispanic campaign" include: J. M. García Casanova, "De Nuestros Lectores," *La Prensa*, 13 June, 1935, 4; "El 'anti-hispanismo' en Washington Heights," editorial, *La Prensa*, 17 June 1935, 4; Richard F. Martin, "De Nuestros Lectores," *La Prensa*, 2 July 1935, 4; and Cosmo Alda Wahl, "De Nuestros Lectores," *La Prensa*, 10 July 1935, 4.

[24] "Las condiciones de vida en Harlem bajo estudio," editorial, *La Prensa*, 13 Dec. 1937, 4.

[25] The *Congressional Record* during the periods of Marcantonio's tenure, 1935–1937 and 1939–1951, is full of such examples.

Chapter 9

[1] Holland Cotter, "A Neighborhood Nurtures Its Vibrant Cultural History," *The New York Times* 16 March 1998, sec. E, 3.

[2] Jorge Soto, "Puerto Rican Art in New York: The Aesthetic Analysis of Eleven Painters," Patricia L. Wilson (Ph.D. diss. New York University, 1984), 128–31.

[3] Point 7 of the Young Lords Organization 13 point program called for "a true education in Puerto Rico's Afro-Indio culture." See *Palante* (October 1969), 19.

[4] Marcos Dimas, "Artist Statement" in *Taller Alma Boricua: Reflecting on Twenty Years of the Puerto Rican Workshop: 1969–1989* (New York: El Museo del Barrio, 1990), 10.

[5] The saying in English can be translated as: "And your grandmother, where is she?" (author's translation).

[6] Soto's baroque imagery can be compared to the work of Carlos Raquel Rivera, whose paintings and prints of the 1960s and 1970s employ allegorical figures and magic realist symbolism to comment on contemporary Puerto Rican life.

[7] Yasmin Ramírez, "Jorge Soto Sánchez," in *Voces y Visones: Highlights from the Permanent Collection of El Museo del Barrio* (New York El Museo del Barrio, 2002), 34.

[8] Flores and Soto became colleagues during a year-long cultural theory reading group that Flores organized at the Center for Puerto Rican studies in 1976. The participants were drawn from various sectors of the Nuyorican arts community such as Neco Otero and Sandra María Esteves from Taller Boricua, and Petra Barreras, an administrator at the Department of Cultural Affairs who later became the fourth director of El Museo del Barrio in 1986. According to Flores the emphasis of the seminar was on applying Marx, Gramsci, and other leftist cultural theorists to examine Puerto Rican culture.

[9] Robert Farris Thompson, "The Sign of the Four Moments of the Sun: Kongo Art and Religion in the Americas" in *Flash of the Sprit: African and Afro-American Art and Philosophy* (New York: Vintage Press, 1984), 101– 60.

[10] Andrés Isidoro Pérez y Mena, *Speaking with the Dead: Development of Afro-Latin Religion Among Puerto Ricans in the United States* (New York: AMS Press, 1991). I was also informed by personal experience gleaned from practicing Bomba, Plena, Vodoo, Afro-Cuban, Brazilian and West African dance traditions and conversations with practitioners of African-Diaspora religions.

Chapter 10

[1] Ballán is a Jewish-American folk singer and music-festival producer. She grew up in the South Bronx, and went to Hunter College of the City University of New York—and Central Park became her backyard. From the mid-1960s to the early 1990s, she was a regular on the Central Park rumba scene. In 1985, she funded the New York City rumba ensemble Los Afortunados with Félix Sanabria and Manuel Martínez Olivera "El Llanero;" they performed nationwide.

2 These jam sessions were also part of two simultaneous ongoing traditions: the Afro-Latin jazz descargas influenced by Cachao y su Combo recording *Cuban Jam Sessions in Miniature* (1957) and the FANIA-style salsa movement. Indeed, the salsa "way of doing" music included a montuno section based on an improvisation also informed by Afro-Latin jazz descargas (Storm Roberts 1999; Fernández 2003).

[3] Musicians specialized in the performance of son music, originally from Cuba but internationalized since the 1920s.

[4] Bongó drum percussionists.

[5] Musicians specialized in the plena, an autochthonous Afro-Puerto Rican working-class musical tradition, based on competitive singing and the use of hand-drums known as *panderos*.

[6] In an interview with Ray Vega, he states that during the 1960s and 1970s, radio was his main connection with Latin music, particularly radio WADO and WRVR. Vega describes how the Sunday's *Latin Roots* show (hosted by Felipe Luciano, co-founder of the Young Lords, member of the Last Poets) covered "the whole spectrum of being a New York City Nation, whether it was politics, music or the arts.... He made everybody aware in the listening audience that everything was connected in one way or another" (Bernotas 1997: 18). Paula Ballán also argues that the 1977 miniseries TV show *Roots*, was an inspirational source of identity, "whether Alex Haley [author] was a fraud or not" (personal communication, 2009).

[7] During the 1960s, Puerto Ricans were the "most destitute" community in New York City; in 1972, they constituted 12.6 percent of unemployment.

[8] Sanders was well known for his artistic crafting of drums and *shekeres*, a percussive instrument made out of a hollowed-out gourd and covered with a net woven with plastic beads or seeds. See Hiss (1976).

[9] Amira became an author and performer of Cuban and Haitian drumming.

[10] Mason is the author of several fundamental books on Regla de Osha.

[11] The Rumberos All Stars became popular for their innovative rumba breaks (called *cierres*), inspired by the *Papín y sus rumberos* (1954) record.

[12] In the U.S. and Latin America, tumbadoras are popularly known as congas. However, conga is the name for the musical orchestra that accompanies the *comparsas* during Cuban carnival.

[13] In general, the Cuban revolutionary regime has promoted Afro-Cuban folklore in order to legitimize the Communist Party's egalitarian commitment towards the inclusion of black people, and the recognition of the nation's African antecedents. Thus rumba has been resignified as an "authentic black" form (Daniel 1991; Knauer 2009; Bodenheimer 2010). Work needs to be done analyzing how this revolutionary discourse differs to the Nuyorican reworkings of traditional Cuban rumba as a vehicle towards their African roots. Certainly Paul Gilroy (1993) would question the embedded discursive logic of "black forms" as symbols of racial authenticity and cultural nationalism. See also Rivera's discussion about "mythologies of liberation" (2010a).

[14] In 1975, Yeyito learned bomba with Heny Álvarez (Joe Cuba's singer); Alvarez had a bomba and plena ensemble operating at El Museo del Barrio. Nevertheless, bomba was mostly performed in special occasions such as the Fiestas Patronales. Bomba was "more elite like, you had to know people who did it privately" (Yeyito, personal communication, 2011).

[15] For a discussion about the role of music in the articulation of Puerto Rican cultural nationalism, see Manuel (1994).

[16] For a discussion of the racial tensions between Puerto Ricans in New York City, see Glasser (1995) and Dávila (1999). For a discussion of the implications of Spanish and U.S. colonial relations in the construction of Puerto Rico's national musical forms, and the 1970s folkloric revival of bomba and plena, see Manuel (1994).

[17] A Puerto Rican doctor and singer living in New York City.

[18] Taíno originally meant "peace" in Arawak but Puerto Ricans are known as Taíno because Christopher Columbus mistakenly called them that after the Arawak used the word to greet him and his men at their first encounter (Santiago 1995: xviii). See Rivera (1996, 2001) and Jiménez-Román (2008) for discussions on race relations between Puerto Ricans and in relationship to African Americans.

[19] Further analysis needs to be done regarding Yeyito's Taíno identification and solidarity with Afro-descendants, particularly in relationship to Dávila's analysis of the role of 1990s Taíno-identity revival movement of Puerto Rican activists in New York City (Dávila 1999) and Quintero Rivera's (1994) argument about the solidarity between Taínos and *cimarrones* during Puerto Rico's Spanish colonialism. For a discussion on Puerto Rican nationalism and the government's cultural and educational policies' mystification of Taíno culture as anti-colonial symbol, object, and as a "mediating symbol between the dominant Spanish and the subordinate African tradition," see Haslip-Viera (1999: 16).

[20] In Cuba, during the mid-1970s, rumba was also undergoing a series of experimentations. The "Chinitos" family invented the rumba *guarapachanguera* style while Francisco Mora "Pancho Quinto" was hybridizing rumba with batá drums into the *"batá-rumba."*

[21] Borrowing from Quintero, improvisation is "a moment of instant inspiration but also a reflection of historical and musical contexts... not individual display but rather the expression of individuality in a collective endeavor..." (2003: 7).

Chapter 11

[1] Elsewhere, I have discussed the broad structures of many of the narrators' life histories, the symbolic effects of their gendered commentaries on Puerto Rican interactions in New York and on the island, the narrators' pain at the distrust they frequently faced on the island, and the San Juan-based organization "Latin New Yorkers" in which thirteen of them were active members (Findlay 2009). I refer to the narrators throughout this article as "New York Puerto Ricans," "New York born-and-bred Puerto Ricans," or "Latin New Yorkers." Fourteen of the fifteen narrators did not generally claim the identity of Nuyorican, probably because of the connotations of poverty, criminality, and "foreign" cultural practices associated with it on the island, particularly in the late 1970s and 1980s. Thirteen of the fifteen preferred to call themselves "Latin New Yorkers," as a way to assert their pride in their New York roots, to distinguish themselves from island Puerto Ricans and to distance themselves from the ongoing poverty of the New York Puerto Rican community. In recognition of the complexity of the actual "Latino" population of New York, I have not consistently used the "Latin New Yorker" term in this article.

[2] Marie Lebrón explained: "It depends on...on...on your surroundings. In certain surroundings, everyone's like you. All the families are mixed, so they accept one another. Now if you go into another area where there might be white...white... white Puerto Ricans, then you might feel that way [discriminated against]. EJF: But in New York, it wasn't that way? ML: Not unless there was a Puerto Rican who was very light-skinned, and their mother didn't want them to hang around dark-skinned Puerto Ricans, but I didn't know of that happening."

[3] For fascinating discussions of the shifting expression and imposition of Puerto Rican racial identities in New York through state-generated documents such as migrant identification and military draft cards, censuses, and birth, marriage, and death certificates, see Haslip-Viera (2009) and Thomas (2009). The racial classification of Puerto Ricans in these documents could change dramatically depending upon the historical moment in which they were produced and who was making the recorded racial ascription.

[4] Lebrón also passionately recalled how her aunt, who was light-skinned, was forcibly separated from her dark-complexioned children when they traveled through the state of Florida.

Chapter 13

[1] First names are used with the approval of informants. In other cases, pseudonyms are used or no name is used at all.

[2] My use of the term "accurate" does not refer to the unbiased application of biological criteria (since no such criteria exists for race) but rather to the application of culturally meaningful categories that make sense to people in the Puerto Rican context

[3] Discourses of blanqueamiento privilege whiteness as a desirable, achievable status that can supposedly be attained through the gradual shedding of African blood and cultural practices via mixture (read assimilation) with white/European biological, or cultural elements (Burdick 1992; de la Fuente 2001; Rodríguez-Vázquez 2004; Stephan 1991; Wade 1993; Whitten and Torres 1998).

[4] The term "Puerto Rican colored" is not a translation as it was originally used in English during the interview.

[5] See other examples of popular sayings and racist jokes in Guerra (1998: 235–8) and Zenón-Cruz (1975: 273).

[6] Robin Sheriff also notes that her informants in Brazil used binary forms of racial identification in jokes and when they talked to her about their encounters with racism (Sheriff 2001: 45). However, she distinguishes these binary conceptions of race from other forms of talk she calls descriptive or pragmatic, which have the deceptive implications of polite speech—or which are plays of language that do not seek to classify people in terms of "race," but merely describe them in terms of color. I, on the other hand, conceptualize all terms of color, no matter whether they are euphemistic or binary, as having possible pragmatic implications in everyday encounters.

[7] In a previous article (Godreau 2000), I established a sharp distinction between slippery semantics and binary forms of racial identification. In that article, slippery semantics was an indicator of people's discomfort with the issue of race and of their efforts to build alternative solidarities based on more socially accepted identities. In this essay, I do not theorize binary forms of classification as being distinct from slippery semantics. On the contrary, I theorize slippery semantics as a much broader, mediating, linguistic mechanism of social interaction that can also include binary forms of racial classification.

[8] For a debate about the imposition of US racial categories and frameworks of analysis on the Brazilian context, see Bairros (1996), Fry (2000), and French (2000).

Chapter 14

[1] Domestic and personal service is the category used by the U.S. Census where much of the data for this paper was obtained. It does not include needle work done in the home. I use the terms domestic work and domestic service indistinctly.

[2] Gainful workers is the term used in the census for workers who worked for wages or their equivalent (U.S. Bureau of the Census 1930).

[3] The only mention of regulations applied to domestic service workers found in the Annual Reports of the Commissioner of Labor between 1900 and 1930 was a reference to Section 1487 of the Civil Code that provided indemnification for domestic servants hired for a fixed time if a master dismissed a servant without sufficient cause. *Annual Report of the Governor of Porto Rico, 1929*, 739. In spite of the observed absence of regulations, various reports by the Commissioner of Labor document cases of domestic workers who requested the intervention of the department of labor in relation to claims that employers refused to pay them. For example see *Report of the Governor of Porto Rico, 1920-21* (Washington: Government Printing Office, 1921) 503.

[4] While attempts were made to prohibit and/or regulate piece work in the needle and embroidery industries during this period, the author found no evidence of this in domestic work. Annual Report of the Governor of Porto Rico, years 1900-1930.

Chapter 16

[1] This figure comes from the 2000 US Census Bureau (www.census.gov). The urban population is calculated based on those that live either in urbanized areas or urban clusters. An "urban area" is defined by the Census as "an area consisting of a central place(s) and adjacent territory with a general population density of at least 1,000 people per square mile of land area that together have a minimum residential population of at least 50,000 people. An "urban cluster," a new category of the 2000 Census, is "a densely settled territory that has at least 2,500 people but fewer than 50,000." The breakdown for Puerto Rico is as follows: 91 percent of the total population live in urbanized areas, 3 percent live in urban clusters, and close to 6 percent live in rural areas.

[2] For a good ethnographic study of the urban underclass of Puerto Rico's slums see Duany (1997) and Safa (1974).

[3] Although other cities have been central to the development of reggaetón (e.g., New York), this paper focuses specifically on the urban experience in Puerto Rico that constructed reggaetón.

[4] Note that here I show the two extremes of inequality, but I am not arguing that there are no other types of spaces, located somewhere inbetween in the socioeconomic hierarchy, that coexist in this urban milieu.

[5] For a discussion of how poverty has been ineffectively approached through the lens of African-American womanhood and mothering, see Kelley (1998).

[6] Parallels to this representation can be made with the military and its training, another space where Puerto Rican males of low socioeconomic means are apt to enter.

[7] For a description of social and spatial fragmentation in the city of San Juan in the 19th

Century, see Martínez-Vergne (1999). In the 20th Century, see Caplow, Stryker, and Wallace (1964).

[8] The intersection of race and class in Puerto Rico is a complex one, and one that falls beyond the scope of the paper. However, there is evidence to support the notion that there has been a racialization of space in Puerto Rico; and that these spaces are attached to class. For example, residents in poor areas tend to identify as Black in higher numbers than residents in more privileged residential areas. See Dinzey-Flores (2005).

[9] In http://www.tegoCalderón.com/.

[10] Hector El Father in the track "Noche de travesuras."

[11] For a discussion on how the use of an "afro" hairstyle by artist Lucecita caused a public politicized debate in Puerto Rico during the 1970s, see Rivero (2005).

[12] Many songs' lyrics reflect this argument, for example, Don Omar and Tego Calderón's "Bandoleros" and Eddie Dee's "Censurarme por ser rapero." Many artists have also made this argument in interviews or newspaper features. Daddy Yankee claimed that his songs are based on his experiences: *"Son vivencias del barrio."* [They're experiences of the barrio.] (Fernández-Soberón 2004). Baby Ranks also expressed in an interview "El reggaetón es algo muy real, tan real como los problemas que existen con las drogas. Hablamos de lo que se ve a diario, de lo vivido." [Reggaetón is very real, as real as the existing drug problems. We talk about what is seen in the everyday, about what is lived.] (Rodríguez 2006: 10C).

[13] Regardless of the songs' subject, most artists make a reference to their sincerity and authenticity. Additionally, many characters in the songs, including the disproportionate number of females referenced in the songs, are evaluated according to their authenticity or their attempts to "trick" or be insincere. I observed this trend as I conducted the content analysis of the 179 reggaetón songs.

[14] Reggaetón shares the trend of depicting everyday life with hip-hop. Butler (2004: 983) has noted that hip-hop, from its beginnings, was considered in the newspaper. Reggaetón, indeed, may be seen in similar ways.

Chapter 17

[1] I am in no way suggesting that prior to the 1990s Puerto Ricans in Chicago had no inter-action with these other groups. There is some evidence that Puerto Ricans had frequent and meaningful social interactions with Mexicans (Padilla 1947) and, to a lesser extent, African Americans (Padilla 1987, 1992) from the very early stages of Puerto Rican migration to Chicago in the 1950s. As Elena Padilla has documented, the Puerto Rican elite that migrated to Chicago in the period between the World Wars tended to have frequent association with whites. Mar-riage between this elite and whites –and other Latin American migrants who shared their social class- was also a strategy to avoid an association with the migration of the Puerto Rican poor and localities marked as "Puerto Rican." Nevertheless, even as recent as the early 1990s, Puerto Ricans' segregation from Mexicans, though falling in the medium-to-high range (an index of .598), still reflected the highest level of Mexican-Puerto Rican segregation of all five cities with significant populations of each group (Massey and Denton 1989:75). A more exhaustive discussion of the production of space and Puerto Rican racialization of African

Americans and Mexicans has been elaborated else-where (Ramos-Zayas 1997, forthcoming: De Genova and Ramos-Zayas 2000).

[2] I am deliberately using "Latino" here, as opposed to "Puerto Rican," because I have included ethnographic data from people whom I interviewed either formally or informally, some of whom were Mexican, Mexican-Puerto Rican, and one person was Dominican. I recognize the potential problems of using pan-Latino rather than nationality-based labels (see Oboler 1995) and try to take these matters into account at critical junctures of my arguments. I will use the nationality-based designator in reference to specific interlocutors, but will continue to use "Latino" when I am outlining broad theoretical concerns.

[3] Virginia Domínguez's essay (1994) eloquently defines racialization as the process by which "differences between human beings are simplified and transformed into Difference.... Racialization is produced and reproduced through ideological, institutional, interactive, and linguistic practices that support a particular construction of Difference" (p. 333). Hence, the term "racialized" describes an instance or situation in which the racial identity of an individual is sharply essentialized or objectified (cf. Hartigan 1999).

[4] People's names in this paper have been changed to protect individual identities. The names of the neighborhoods are the real names. Names of people who may have appeared in newspapers or widely distributed publications have remained the same.

[5] This is based on a 17-month (March 1994-September 1995) ethnographic research project among grassroots activists, white-collar workers in the not-for-profit sector, barrio residents and youth in the Puerto Rican area of Chicago, and a smaller number of suburbanite Latinos. Since most of the Latinos who had contact with whites were the working- or middle-class for the most part, the voices presented in this paper may reflect this tendency. For a more detailed account of the methodological and theoretical propositions of this study, see Ramos-Zayas' *Performing the nation: The Politics of Class, Race, and Space in Puerto Rican Chicago* (forthcoming: University of Chicago Press).

[6] Two edited volumes that are emblematic of the critical white studies field are *Critical White Studies: Looking Beyond the Mirror* (edited by Richard Delgado and Jean Stefancic; Philadelphia: Temple University Press, 1997) and *Displacing Whiteness: Essays in Social and Cultural Criticism* (edited by Ruth Frankenberg; Durham, NC: Duke University Press, 1997). While these edited works have been prominent in the articulation of the field of white critical studies, previous work by Black scholars have provided important foundation for white-ness studies. Two such works are bell hook's (1992) "Representing whiteness in the black imagination" in *Black looks: Race and Representation*, pp. 165-179, and Toni Morrison's *Playing in the Dark: Whiteness and the Literary Imagination* (1992).

[7] While I follow Frankenberg's understanding of whiteness as cultural practice in relation to racial formation and historical process rather than as isolable and static, it is important to examine the ways in which white culture is strategically essentialized among Latinos in Chicago and the purposes of such objectification processes. This is not to obviate how whiteness is complexly and differentially deployed in mediating social relations, but to see how the very essentializing of whiteness constitutes one such mediation.

[8] Yvette Glasgow (1997) uses this phrase to emphasize how much poor whites were willing to

sacrifice to hold on to their property right in whiteness. Racism offers poor whites the illusion of superiority while maintaining the reality for rich whites. As a class stabilizer, racism maintains the status quo of economic exploitation of both black and white victims. Yet the white victims' perverse clinging to racial exclusiveness only serves to divert attention away from economic reform, thereby preventing the potentially powerful coalition they could form with blacks. The concept of a property right in whiteness thus highlights white racial solidarity over class-based interests. There are two sides to this property right in whiteness. For poor whites, it may mean forgoing economic improvement for white exclusivity; for minorities, on the other hand, it may mean gaining economic improvement at the expense of racial solidarity (108).

[9] Pérez's (2000) Mexican interviewee—"Señora González"—used the term *"hilbila"* not only as a translation into Spanish of "hillbillies," but as a *gendered* version of the term. In talking about how Mexican women were not *"rencorosas,"* like Puerto Rican women were, Señora González narrated that she had forgiven her husband for having had an affair with a *"hilbila."* In fact, the Señora González had not only taken her husband back, but had even helped raised the child that had been born from the affair. As she emphasized, the child, now a young woman, called her her "Mexican mother."

[10] Hartigan (1999) demonstrates how anti-"hillbilly" sentiment was broadly expressed across the urban Midwest as white migration from the Appalachian region ebbed through the 1950s and 1960s. Chicago received the largest influx of these white migrants, and it was in Chicago that the racial threat posed by "hillbillies" was more explicitly conveyed. Hartigan analyzes a *Harper's* magazine article entitled "The hillbillies invade Chicago," published in 1958, to highlight that "The city's toughest integration problem has nothing to do with the Negroes.... It involves a small army of white, Protestant, Early American migrants from the South—who are usually proud, poor, primitive, and fast with a knife" (cited in Hartigan 1999:33). Not surprisingly, the image of the ill-bred and barbaric "hillbilly" constituted a "disgrace for the race." The mores and behavior of these hillbillies bore the characteristics of laziness, poverty, and prone to violence—characteristics that working-class and middle-class whites had until then reserved exclusively for blacks. As Hartigan argues, Southern whites were expected to "assimilate" to the dominant cultural decorum maintained by their Northern whites neighborhoods in midwestern urban centers.

Chapter 18

[1] The records of the U.S. Census Bureau, military draft cards, and documents pertaining to the application for U.S. citizenship were obtained from databases on the internet website Ancestry. Com at <http://www.ancestry.com/>. These and other family documents such as birth and death certificates, marriage documents, seaman's papers (etc.) are in the author's possession, and are used throughout this article.

[2] In the 1920 census and despite his dark complexion, Mérida's younger brother, José Peña Centeno, was also listed as "W" or white. In the 1930 census, all of the other persons in the Haslip-Peña household were listed as "NEG" or negro, including two daughters born in the 1920s, my grandmother's Amerindian looking nephew, Tomás Peña, and four boarders, who sublet rooms in the two attached apartments that my grandfather rented at 43 Sackett Street

in South Brooklyn (now Cobble Hill).

[3] "Racially undifferentiated"—meaning that Puerto Ricans or Puerto Rican/ Hispanics were (and are not) usually subdivided into distinct racial groups in official records. However, as we all know, Puerto Ricans and Hispanics (or Latin@s) had become racialized in the public mind as persons of color long before these categories were created as part of the official discourse in U.S. society. See Rodríguez Domínguez (2005) and Thomas (2009). Curiously, the overwhelming majority of Puerto Ricans on the U.S. mainland were defined as white by census enumerators from 1940 to 1970 (87 percent-1940, 92 percent-1950, 96 percent-1960, 93 percent-1970). See Duany (2002: 253–5, 259). This anomaly and the apparent overall failure to apply the one-drop rule begs for further research and explanation.

[4] As far back as I can remember (mid- to late 1940s), my father always identified as a Puerto Rican without making any reference to race, or he resisted the articulation of such references.

[5] On the apparent color-blind internationalist identity of the Colón brothers, see James (1998: Chapter 7) and Colón (2002: 25–9, 294–5 and passim).

[6] In contrast to his siblings, my father's emphasis on a de-racialized Puerto Rican ethnic and cultural identity (he was not a nationalist) was probably based on the fact of his marriage to a Puerto Rican woman who could pass for white and because of his mother's Puerto Rican origins. His adoption of this identity might also have been part of a conscious or unconscious step on a hoped-for path to whiteness. He just as easily could have privileged his Curazaleño, West Indian, or "colored" identity, but he chose not to in contrast to his siblings and other relatives who adopted or accepted different identities.

[7] Two daughters, Felicita and Thelma Haslip-Peña, also made controversial choices. Felicita married an African American but died soon afterwards. Thelma, who had three long-term relationships, initially married Avelino Perry (originally Pereira), a mulato who was judged acceptable to the family because of his "Portuguese" (actually Cape Verdean) background. She then had a relationship with an African American, but subsequently married a dark complexioned Dominican, who was also deemed acceptable because of his Latin@ origins. Needless to say, the racial trajectories followed by the children and grandchildren of these unions has been quite complex.

[8] Meaning in this case that his medium to dark brown complexion and his hair texture were largely ignored.

[9] The daughter also had a child with a Puerto Rican who nevertheless tends to identify or accepts classification as Black.

[10] Justina Santiago, another sister of my maternal grandmother, had also come to New York in the 1920s to work for a wealthy Cuban family. She eventually married an Ecuadorian, Rafael Andrade, the family chauffeur, and had two daughters. In the 1930 census, the Andrades are listed as "IN" or Indians (Native Americans). This classification may have been based on Justina's alleged Amerindian or South Asian appearance and her husband's Ecuadorian origins.

[11] There were occasions when my father would claim an alleged Amerindian ancestry on the matrilineal side of his family.

[12] Results from the National Geographic Society, The Genographic Project, 2007.

[13] Results from DNA Print Genomics, 2007. These tests were originally taken as part of my research on claims that have been made that Puerto Ricans and other Caribbean Latin@s have

significant amounts of Taíno or Native American DNA. See Haslip-Viera (2001, 2006, 2007, and 2008) and Estevez (2008).

[14] I cannot of course be identified as white and would not accept such a classification.

Chapter 19

[1] Dr. Roamé Torres, Professor of Education at the University of Puerto Rico, Río Piedras, provided the author with a copy of this article.

[2] According to Landis (2001) 10,702 students attended Carlisle between 1879 and 1918, including 2,090 who were not classified by tribe or nation.

[3] A total of 60 files of Puerto Rican students have been found. In her research, Landis lists 63 students as members of the "Porto Rico" tribe and Bell (1998: vii) refers to 59 Puerto Ricans as having attended Carlisle.

[4] Navarro's dissertation was published by Routledge in 2002 under the title *Creating Tropical Yankees*.

[5] Letter to S. L. Parrish, from Charles W. Eliot, September 21, 1899. Harvard University Papers, C. W. Eliot, Box 92, Letter Book, C. W. Eliot, January 17, 1898 to March 23, 1903, p. 42 A. Charles W. Eliot (1834–1926) was president of Harvard University from 1869 to 1909.

[6] Booker T. Washington (1856–1915) was born a slave in Virginia. His birth name was Booker Taliaferro. Washington was a leading educational and political figure during the latter part of the nineteenth and early part of the twentieth centuries. He was also a supporter of vocational education and was the first director of the Tuskegee Normal and Industrial School, an educational institution for Blacks founded in 1881 by the State of Alabama.

[7] Letter to John Davis Long from Booker T. Washington. March 15, 1898. The Booker T. Washington Papers (BTW Papers). Vol. 4, 1895–98, p. 389.

[8] Letter to the Editor of the Christian Register. August 18, 1898. BTW Papers. Vol. 4, p. 455.

[9] Duany (2002) argues that during this period there was much ambivalence in the colonial discourse in the United States as it related to the racial identity of Puerto Ricans. According to Duany, this helps explain why the Smithsonian Institution classified Puerto Ricans as Indians (Duany 2002: Chapter 3). It further contributes to our understanding of why Booker T. Washington alleged in his letter that more than half of the population of Puerto Rico was Black, even though the United States Census of 1899 found that two thirds of the population was white. (Duany 2002) For a significant study about race in Cuba see Guridy (2002).

[10] *The Indian Helper*, Vol. XIV, January 27, 1899, Num. 14. See Landis in http://home.epix. net/~landis/portorican.html. Eaton (1829–1906), who was white, served as a Colonel of a regiment of Black soldiers during the Civil War (1863–1865), the 63rd U.S. Colored Infantry Regiment, and was promoted to Brigadier General in March, 1865.

[11] See Navarro Rivera (2000), Negrón de Montilla (1971) and Torres González (2002).

[12] Letter from M.G. Brumbaugh to B.T. Washington. May 7, 1901. BTW Papers, Vol. 6, 1901–2, pp. 106–7.

[13] Even though religious schools were not governmental institutions, their funds came primarily from the State and operated under State control. See Ryan (1962) and Bell (1998).

[14] See document titled Carlisle School, Office of Indian Affairs of the Department of the Interior. RG 75, Records of the Bureau of Indian Affairs, Entry 1349 C, NN 369–71, Records of Nonreservation Schools, Records of Carlisle, Miscellaneous Publications and Records, CA 1908–18, Box 1.

[15] Act of March 3, 1819 (3 Stat. 516). The Act was amended in 1873 (17 Stat. 461). A "Civilization Fund" was established with the same purpose in 1867 (14 Stat. 687). See document titled Carlisle School. Office of Indian Affairs of the Department of the Interior. RG 75, Records of the Bureau of Indian Affairs, Entry 1349 C, NN 369–71, Records of Nonreservation Schools, Records of Carlisle, Miscellaneous Publications and Records, CA 1908–18, Box 1.

[16] See the Indian Citizenship Act of 1924 (8 U.S.C. §1401).

[17] RG 75, E 1323. Records of the Bureau of Indian Affairs, Records of the Carlisle Indian Industrial School. Letters Sent, August 28-Oct. 1900, Jan. 26-May 6, 1901. Box 1 PI-163, p. 345.

[18] See The Carlisle Indian School by F. E. Willard, RG 75, E 1349 C NN 369–71, Box 2.

[19] Bell (1998) estimates that 66 percent of these were captured and returned to the school.

[20] Describing Indians as savages was so prevalent during the Carlisle years that newspapers such as The New York Times used the term "savage" when referring to Indians.

Chapter 20

[1] San Juan Star, April 18, 1999; Caribbean Net News, October 7, 2003 <www.caribbeannetnews. com>; and Associated Press, October 13, 2003 <http//web.lexisnexis. com>. Also, see the reports published in El Nuevo Día, July 11, 1999 and October 9, 2005; El San Juan Star,August 22, 1999; Indian CountryToday, October 6, 2003 <www.indiancountry.com>; Claridad, November 27-December 3, 2003, pp. 29–30; the Orlando Sentinel, December 26, 2003 <www.orlandosentinel. com>; the article by columnist Juan Gonzalez in New York Daily News, November 4, 2003, p. 42; and the supplement "Viva in NewYork" in the New York Daily News, November 20, 2005.

[2] In addition to those who had "Amerindian" mtDNA, Martínez-Cruzado and his team found that 27.2 percent of Puerto Ricans had sub-Saharan African mtDNA, and 11.5 percent had "West Eurasian" mtDNA. See Martínez-Cruzado et al. (2005: 131, 133–6, 150).

[3] See Martínez-Cruzado et al. (2005: 146, 147, 150). For similar quotes, also see Martínez-Cruzado et al. (2001: 491, 500, 503), Orlando Sentinel, December 26, 2003 <www.orlandosentinel. com>; Claridad, November 27-December 3, 2003, pp. 29–39; Indian CountryToday, October 6, 2003 <www.indiancountry.com>; El Nuevo Día, October 9, 2005; and the supplement "Viva in New York" in New York Daily News, November 20, 2005.

[4] Martínez-Cruzado et al. (2001: 492, 493; 2005: 131, 133, 150). In another preliminary study of their sample, Martínez-Cruzado and his team have reported on the 70 percent of Puerto Ricans who have Y-chromosomes that have European traits (passed through the male line), 20 percent that have African traits, and 10 percent that have Indian traits. This is almost the reverse of the ethnic breakdown for the percent ages of female mitochondrial DNA in the same Puerto Rican sample, and demonstrates the overall mixed nature of the island population. See Orlando Sentinel, December 26, 2003 <www. orlandosentinel.com>; Juan Gonzalez in New York Daily News, November 4, 2003, p. 42; Martínez-Cruzado et al. (2005: 147, 149); Martínez Cruzado in El Nuevo Día, October 9, 2005; and the supplement " Viva in New York," New York Daily News, November 20, 2005.

5 New York Daily News, November 4, 2003, p. 42. In their most recent publication, Martínez-Cruzado and his team (2005: 133) claim that their "results conform to most accounts of traditional history, but not at all with the extermination of the Taíno people as early as the 16th century."

6 It needs to be said here that Native American tribal groups in the United States typically

require "one-quarter Indian blood" for membership in the group; however, some tribes "allow as little as one-thirty-second" Indian blood for membership in the group. This demonstrates that identification as an Indian in the United States is based primarily on politics and historical tradition and not on science. See, for example, the discussion in the article "Rejecting 2000 Census Counts, Tribes Are Tabulating Their Own," in New York Times, November 28, 2003, p. 37.

Chapter 22

[1] These figures assume that fifteen generations of thirty years each are being projected back to the 1580s. This conservative figure can be contrasted to those of other demographers who often calculate a generation at twenty or twenty-five years.

[2] Juan González, "Puerto Rican gene pool runs deep," *New York Daily News* (November 4, 2003): 24. Also, see the text and other relevant sources in Haslip-Viera, chapter 20 in this volume (note 4).

[3] Results from the National Geographic Society, The Genographic Project, 20007. Also see the following publications for a critique of this type of research: Duster (nd.), Brown (2002), Elliott and Brodwin (2002), Weiss and Fullerton (2005), Cabrera Salcedo (2006), Brusi-Gil de Lamadrid and Godreau (2007), Bolnick, et al. (2007), Yang (2007), and Nixon (2007), among others.

[4] From <http://www.familytreedna.com/forum/archive/index.php?t-316.html>, February 2, 2004.

[5] From <jimrunningfox@aol.com> to <jimrunningfox@aol.com> March 23-24, 2007 (Messages in author's possession).

[6] In my own case, DNA Print Genomics presented me with the percentages, but without reference to the number of generations. The results despite my alleged Amerindian appearance and my "shovel shaped" incisor teeth (an alleged Indian trait) are as follows: 71 percent European, 29 percent African, 0 percent Asian, and 0 percent Native American.

[7] Mr. Estevez actually quotes Lovén as stating that "Today, there are no pure Taínos," and that "the Taínos were a people that long ago became extinct." It should be noted at this point that persons who claim an exclusive Taíno identity or pedigree are quite vague or tend to ignore the issue of what constitutes a Taíno or Amerindian by definition. When pressed to respond to this issue, they tend to acknowledge the fact of their mixed ancestry, but they soon revert to their claims for an exclusive and privileged Taíno or Amerindian identity. At times, they also claim that the issue of mixture is unimportant or irrelevant. See for example the comments made by Mr. Estevez and Cacike Coqui in response to the concerns articulated by Elder Jim Runningfox in <jimrunningfox@aol.com> to <jimrunningfox@aol.com> March 23-24, 2007 (Messages in author's possession). The issue of what constitutes a Native American has also become controversial and contentious in U.S. society in recent years. See Nagel (1995). Also see Koerner (2005) for the specific connection between race, genetics, and the expulsion of subgroups among the Cherokees and Seminoles, especially the expulsion of those who conform to the physical stereotype of the Black African.

[8] In Puerto Rico, there are quite a number of organized archaeological sites, exhibits in museums, and museums and other institutions devoted to the pre-Columbian Taíno and their legacy, but only one museum devoted to the African experience—El Museo de Nuestra Raíz Africana. This museum was established in 1999 by the Instituto de Cultura Puertorrique-

ña. Prior to this date, there were no official institutions in Puerto Rico devoted to this legacy.

[9] The categories that are used include *Indio lavado*, *Indio claro*, *Indio oscuro*, *Indio quemado*, and *Indio canelo* (washed, light, dark, burnt, and cinnamon colored Indian, etc.).

[10] The crass commercialization and the exaggerated claims made for this kind of research have been debated and roundly criticized in recent years by a number of scientists and social scientists. See for example Duster (nd.), Brown (2002), Elliott and Brodwin (2002), Weiss and Fullerton (2005), Cabrera Salcedo (2006), Brusi-Gil de Lamadrid and Godreau (2007), Bolnick, et al. (2007), Yang (2007), and Nixon (2007), among others. The article recently published by Wang, et al. (2008) is one of the first to insure that research based on admixture testing is subjected to a rigorous peer review process.

[11] As explained in chapter 20 in this volume.

INDEX

abolition 17, 18, 41, 116, 117

acculturation 34, 95, 285, 294

Africa 15, 19, 27, 35, 42, 60, 78, 82, 83, 85, 87, 89, 90, 96, 104, 122, 148, 166, 170, 178, 221, 277, 305, 307, 316, 317

African 7, 12, 13, 16, 17, 19, 22, 23, 24, 25, 26, 27, 28, 29, 30, 31, 35, 36, 41, 42, 43, 45, 49, 50, 54, 55, 56, 57, 58, 59, 62, 67, 68, 70, 71, 73, 77, 78, 82, 83, 84, 85, 86, 88, 89, 90, 91, 92, 94, 95, 96, 99, 106, 114, 117, 118, 120, 122, 124, 125, 126, 132, 133, 137, 138, 139, 141, 142, 143, 145, 146, 148, 149, 150, 151, 152, 153, 154, 155, 156, 162, 163, 165, 166, 168, 169, 170, 172, 173, 174, 175, 176, 177, 178, 179, 180, 181, 183, 185, 186, 187, 188, 189, 190, 192, 217, 233, 235, 240, 252, 255, 267, 273, 274, 275, 276, 277, 278, 279, 280, 281, 287, 293, 297, 306, 307, 308, 309, 310, 312, 313, 316, 317, 320, 321, 323, 324, 326, 327, 328

African American 120, 137, 138, 139, 142, 143, 145, 151, 172, 175, 179, 181, 187, 188, 189, 192, 255, 267, 280

African descent· *See also* African

afroantillanismo 82

Afroboricua 71, 72, 76, 172, 174, 181, 282

Afro-Caribbean 62, 74, 76, 84, 86, 89, 90, 91, 92, 94, 97, 100, 101, 124, 165, 170, 241

Afro-Christian 106

Afro-Cuban 28, 72, 123, 165, 172, 174, 178, 180, 346, 353, 382, 383

Afro-Latino 170, 175, 178, 179, 180, 282, 348

Afro Puerto Rican 23

Afro-Puerto Rican 7, 24, 28, 71, 72, 74, 93, 96, 107, 113, 114, 115, 116, 117, 118, 119, 120, 121, 122, 123, 124, 125, 126, 127, 128, 129, 130, 141, 164, 165, 171, 177, 282

afro-puertorriqueño 80, 81

Afro-Taíno 7, 27, 161, 162, 163, 164, 165, 166, 167, 168, 169, 170, 171

Albizu Campos, Pedro 66, 118

Alegría, Ricardo 41, 241, 316, 317

America 19, 21, 22, 30, 42, 45, 53, 68, 72, 99, 113, 114, 119, 120, 124, 125, 127, 129, 131, 132, 144, 148, 155, 156, 163, 170, 182, 210, 219, 220, 224, 226, 266, 274, 277, 278, 284, 314

American 11, 13, 16, 19, 21, 22, 23, 25, 34, 35, 36, 53, 54, 56, 58, 59, 62, 66, 72, 90, 113, 114, 120, 122, 124, 125, 126, 129, 130, 131, 137, 138, 139, 140, 142, 143, 145, 146, 147, 148, 149, 150, 151, 152, 153, 154, 156, 164, 165, 166, 168, 169, 170, 172, 173, 175, 176, 179, 180, 181, 187, 188, 189, 192, 211, 219, 220, 222, 234, 255, 256, 258, 259, 267, 275, 277, 278, 279, 280, 281, 286, 292, 294, 298, 299, 305, 312, 313, 314, 316, 318, 319, 324, 325

americano 186, 256, 257

americanos 53, 173, 256, 257

Amerindian 8, 35, 36, 281, 285, 305, 306, 307, 308, 309, 310, 311, 312, 313, 314, 315, 316, 317, 318, 319, 320, 321, 322, 323, 324, 325, 326, 327, 328

ancestry 21, 35, 36, 42, 44, 47, 49, 99, 167, 169, 178, 188, 215, 281, 305, 306, 307, 308, 309, 310, 312, 315, 320, 321, 322, 323, 324, 328

anexionista 19

antillanismo 7, 23, 77, 82, 83, 84, 85, 86, 87, 88, 89, 90

anti-miscegenation 50, 58

Arawak 36, 384

Army, U.S. 56, 162, 240, 299, 325

assimilation 4, 33, 34, 180, 292, 299, 310

Atabeya 165, 166

Ateneo 51, 129

autonomismo 17

Autonomista, Partido 50

autosomal DNA 36, 323

Barbosa, José Celso 7, 19, 20, 23, 26, 41, 43, 44, 49, 50, 51, 52, 53, 54, 55, 56, 57, 58, 59, 219

barrio 29, 31, 146, 149, 151, 210, 212, 213, 242, 249, 253, 260, 262, 263, 264, 265, 267

Barrio, El 32, 127, 154, 161, 162, 176, 183, 187

Barrio San Antón 32, 183

Belpré, Pura 7, 25, 26, 124, 133, 134, 135, 136, 137, 138, 139, 140, 141, 142, 143, 144

bias(ed) 31, 67, 92, 273, 312, 318, 325

binary 30, 104, 117, 122, 146, 147, 150, 154, 155, 156, 182, 185, 188, 191, 211, 214, 216, 217, 218, 219, 220, 221, 222, 223, 224, 385

black 11-14, 16, 18-20, 22-26, 29-31, 33, 41, 43-63, 66, 67, 70, 71, 73, 75, 79, 80, 82, 85-89, 91-94, 96-100, 102, 103, 104, 106-109, 113-126, 129, 132, 136, 137, 139, 142, 145-150, 152-155, 166, 168, 175-179, 181, 182, 183, 185, 186, 188-192, 197-200, 202, 203, 207, 208, 210-229, 231-239, 241, 247, 252, 253, 254, 274, 287, 323

black American 26, 149, 153, 155

blackness 14, 20, 23, 32, 41, 43, 67, 69, 78, 92, 107, 108, 117, 119, 154, 155, 178, 183, 184, 186, 188, 189, 192, 212, 214, 215, 217, 218, 221, 223, 226, 232, 252

blanco 19, 47, 48, 51, 99,186, 189, 211, 212, 214, 216, 217, 221, 239, 240, 256, 257, 259, 310

Blanco, Tomás 20, 57, 58, 59, 61, 62, 66, 67, 219

blanqueamiento 199, 215, 220, 223

blanquito 210, 211, 213

blood 46, 47, 48, 49, 52, 53, 54, 55, 57, 61, 66, 96, 97, 116, 128, 153, 166, 200, 202, 205, 219, 226, 297, 321, 324

bomba 28, 72, 164, 165, 175, 177, 178, 241

Borikén 45

bozal 45, 46, 96

British 46, 115, 116, 118, 119, 120, 163, 236, 241, 286

Caribbean 8, 16, 19, 21, 23, 24, 25, 28, 30, 36, 37, 45, 58, 62, 65, 68, 69, 70, 71, 72, 74, 76, 78, 83, 84, 85, 86, 88, 89, 90, 91, 92, 94, 97, 98, 100, 101, 106, 113, 114, 115, 116, 117, 118, 119, 120, 121, 124, 132, 138, 146, 148, 165, 166, 169, 170, 174, 178, 180, 183, 187, 211, 213, 221, 222, 223, 233, 235, 241, 252, 274, 276, 278, 281, 285, 286, 307, 308, 309, 312, 313, 314, 315, 316, 317, 318, 320, 322, 323, 325, 326, 327, 328

Carlisle 8, 14, 34, 284, 285, 286, 287, 288, 289, 290, 291, 292, 293, 294, 295, 296, 297, 298, 299, 300

Carnegie 121, 139

caserío 8, 32, 236, 249, 251, 253

caseríos 32, 234, 235, 236, 241, 248, 249, 250, 252, 253

casta 46, 309

caste 46, 47, 48, 108

Catholic 47, 52, 61, 106, 116, 123, 131, 178, 187, 200

Cayey 127, 128, 218

census 13, 58, 137, 226, 227, 228, 231, 232, 239, 273, 274, 275, 276, 307, 309, 317, 319, 325

Central Park 7, 28, 172-181

Changó 165

Chicago 8, 14, 32, 33, 175, 250, 255, 256, 257, 258, 259, 260, 261, 262, 263, 264, 265, 266, 267, 268

CIIS, Carlisle Indian Industrial School 284, 285, 291, 292, 293, 294, 299, 300

cimarronaje 83

cimarrones 200

civilization 34, 44, 48, 49, 54, 293, 295, 296, 298

civil rights 33, 42, 130, 134, 137, 145, 154, 172, 281

Claridad 163

class 18, 21, 22, 33, 43, 44, 50, 51, 52, 54, 55,

58, 59, 62, 64, 69, 72, 73, 74, 75, 76, 79,
80, 86, 87, 88, 89, 90, 94, 96, 97, 98,
99, 100, 104, 108, 109, 119, 125, 127,
129, 131, 132, 135, 136, 142, 143, 147,
148, 151, 154, 155, 161, 162, 166, 177,
181, 184, 198, 204, 206, 210, 213, 214,
218, 222, 228, 234, 235, 236, 239, 241,
252, 255, 260, 261, 263, 264, 266, 267,
279, 280, 281
cofradías 47
colonial 11, 16, 17, 18, 19, 20, 24, 42, 43, 44, 49,
51, 52, 53, 57, 66, 70, 114, 115, 116, 118,
119, 147, 149, 156, 172, 174, 178, 182,
192, 228, 237, 248, 285, 286, 287, 288,
289, 299, 307, 311, 313, 325
colonialism 18, 19, 44, 63, 66, 70, 116, 153, 177,
178, 223
Colón, Jesús 7, 24, 25, 82, 113, 114, 118, 121,
122, 126-132, 140, 161, 165, 175, 237,
330
color blindness 176
colored 48, 51, 55, 58, 95, 117-119, 149, 150,
151, 152, 156, 211, 213, 215, 226, 278,
280, 285, 290, 291, 297, 308
Commonwealth 18
communist 149
Communist Party 121, 123, 129, 130
Condado 32
conga 169, 170, 177
Cooks, Carlos 120
Cortijo, Rafael 61, 72, 73, 74, 75, 83, 84, 86,
87, 177
Creole 41, 46, 50, 51, 163, 222, 223, 234, 237,
239, 240, 242
criminal 31, 239, 250, 257
criollo 18, 19, 48, 94, 119
Cuba 24, 34, 41, 64, 78, 106, 114-118, 120, 121,
125, 138, 174, 177, 285, 286, 287, 288,
296, 297, 318, 319, 320, 325, 326
Curaçao 274

Danish 46, 118, 122

dark-skinned 32, 66, 70, 71, 73, 99, 104, 106,
153, 155, 156, 188, 189, 190
Darwinism 48, 316
Díaz Soler, Luis 41, 116, 118, 306, 309
dinga 77, 79, 376
discrimination 12, 13, 20, 29, 50, 57, 58, 59, 73,
76, 92, 95, 119, 131, 138, 142, 143, 144,
149, 155, 182, 183, 184, 185, 191, 216,
219, 233, 242, 264, 266, 267
DNA 8, 35, 36, 281, 305, 306, 310, 311, 312,
313, 314, 315, 316, 317, 318, 319, 320,
321, 322, 323, 324, 325
domestic work 30, 31, 225, 226, 227, 230,
231, 232
Dominican Republic 24, 41, 115, 116, 120, 285,
314, 317, 318, 319, 320, 325, 326, 327
drumming 170, 173, 175, 178
DuBois, W.E.B. 51, 56, 59
Dutch 24, 46, 118, 274, 277

Eleggua 88, 96, 168
elite 16, 17, 18, 19, 25, 26, 27, 28, 43, 44, 48,
49, 50, 51, 69, 76, 92, 94, 95, 103, 107,
118, 146, 148, 149, 151, 152, 155, 234,
240, 261
emancipation 18, 89, 108, 119
Episcopalian 123
espiritismo 169, 241
Estado Libre Asociado 17
European 15, 16, 35, 46, 50, 62, 68, 78, 88, 91,
95, 106, 114, 115, 118, 119, 122, 146, 148,
149, 172, 233, 274, 277, 279, 281, 305,
306, 307, 308, 309, 310, 312, 323, 324,
326, 327, 328
exclusion 19, 20, 29, 43, 60, 105, 147, 185, 189,
191, 220

familia, la gran 18, 20, 43, 59, 60, 151, 154,
213, 230, 341, 367
Ferré, Rosario 7, 22, 61, 69, 70, 85, 87, 88, 91,

92, 93, 94, 95, 96, 97, 98, 99, 100, 101,
    332, 340
French 24, 45, 118, 119, 163, 169, 309, 333, 341,
    375, 385
fuerza de choque 30, 204

Garvey, Marcus M. 25, 114, 130
gender 22, 43, 69, 72, 73, 75, 76, 79, 87, 90, 91,
    92, 93, 94, 97, 98, 100, 102, 109, 136,
    185, 214, 222, 225, 248, 251, 262
generación del treinta 12, 20, 26, 44, 66
genomics 15, 34
gente de color 151, 234, 237, 241
gentrification 261, 262
González, José Luis 62, 73, 86, 91, 118
grifo 274, 310
Guayama 23, 67, 83, 96, 274
Guinea 94

hacendados 115, 117, 358
Hampton Institute 34, 286, 287, 288, 289,
    290, 291, 293, 296, 297
haplogroups 313
Harlem 7, 25, 67, 120, 124, 125, 127, 130, 132,
    133, 134, 136, 137, 138, 140-147, 149-
    156, 161, 187, 277, 281
Harlem Renaissance 7, 25, 67, 132, 133, 134,
    138, 140, 143
hermandades 47
hillie-billies 33, 260, 263, 264, 265, 267
hip-hop 32, 72, 241
Hispanic 13, 14, 20, 24, 25, 26, 32, 33, 59, 95,
    113-117, 119, 120, 123-125, 129, 132, 143,
    151, 152, 155, 168, 213, 222, 275, 279,
    280, 309
Hispanicist 62
hispanidad 78
Homar, Lorenzo 164, 167, 168, 169
hostility 50, 134, 143, 185, 190
Humboldt Park 255, 261, 263, 264

identity 4, 11, 12, 13, 15, 16, 17, 18, 19, 20, 24,

27, 28, 30, 33, 37, 48, 61, 62, 67, 71, 76,
    77, 80, 81, 85, 87, 104, 108, 109, 136,
    137, 146, 147, 148, 149, 150, 154, 156,
    164, 165, 166, 168, 171, 172, 174, 175,
    179, 180, 182, 183, 185, 189, 190, 192,
    209, 211, 212, 213, 216, 217, 218, 220,
    222, 223, 252, 256, 258, 259, 262, 265,
    267, 273, 277, 278, 279, 280, 281, 285,
    298, 299, 307, 312, 317, 319, 322, 327,
    328
Indian 8, 14, 34, 35, 36, 41, 45, 57, 66, 78, 106,
    142, 143, 150, 164, 168, 217, 275, 276,
    278, 279, 280, 281, 284, 285, 286, 288,
    292, 293, 294, 295, 296, 297, 298, 299,
    308, 309, 312, 313, 316, 319, 325, 327
indio 211, 215, 318
invisibility 94, 147, 149, 156, 186, 199, 256, 267
Isabel, La Negra see also Luberza
    Oppenheimer, Isabel

jabao 212, 274, 277, 278, 310
Jamaica 114, 117, 120, 316
jibaro 373, 376
jíbaro 18, 87, 91, 95, 179, 266
Jim Crow 42, 54, 58, 59, 61, 124, 144
jincha 211, 376
Jones Act 66

labor force 31, 225, 226, 228, 229, 238
ladino 45
La Prensa 151, 152, 153, 154, 155, 156
Lares 118, 164
Latin America 19, 21, 22, 30, 42, 45, 53, 68,
    72, 120, 129, 131, 148, 170, 182, 210,
    219, 220, 224, 274, 278
Latin Jazz 175
Latino 8, 25, 32, 34, 133, 138, 142, 144, 170,
    173, 174, 175, 176, 178, 179, 180, 241,
    253, 255, 256, 257, 258, 259, 260, 261,
    262, 263, 264, 265, 266, 267, 268, 282,
Latinos 134, 137, 138, 172, 173, 176, 180, 256,
    257, 258, 259, 260, 261, 262, 263, 264,

265, 266, 267, 268, 277, 278, 281
Latin Soul 173, 175
Laviera, Tato 24, 26, 61, 71
Ledru, André Pierre 17, 45
light-skinned 76, 95, 136, 149, 187, 189, 211, 253
Lloréns Torres, Luis 72, 73
Logan Square 255, 258, 263, 264
Loisaida 32, 85
Loíza 23, 31, 32, 80, 81, 83, 84, 85, 86, 107, 164, 183, 237, 247
loro 308
Luberza Oppenheimer, Isabel 22, 103, 105, 106, 107, 108, 109
Luciano, Felipe 118, 174
Lucumí 94
lynching 42, 44, 53, 58, 59, 61, 153

mandinga 77, 79
maroon 84, 87, 222, 237, 316
Martínez Cruzado, Juan C. 285, 305, 306, 312, 313, 314, 322, 323
masonic 124
McKay, Claude 67, 120, 125, 126, 138, 150
mejorar la raza 214, 278
mestizaje 18, 21, 41, 42, 66, 68, 76, 153, 172, 181, 199
mestiza, mestizo 41, 43, 45, 117, 151, 153, 309, 311, 319, 325
migration 12, 13, 16, 24, 25, 80, 134, 140, 142, 144, 166, 167, 182, 186, 263, 266
miscegenation 21, 50, 58, 65, 69, 70, 95, 100
mitochondrial DNA 35, 281, 305, 306, 313
mixed-race 21, 22, 107, 118, 147, 220
mongrel 147
Moore, Carlos 25, 120, 144
morena, moreno 19, 173, 186, 213, 252, 310, 311
mulata, mulato 19, 21, 22, 23, 45, 46, 57, 65, 66, 68, 69, 70, 75, 102, 183, 212, 217, 219, 274, 275, 276, 278, 279, 308, 310, 311

mulatez 67, 68, 69, 83
mulatto 21, 49, 66, 67, 70, 71, 79, 80, 81, 83, 85, 86, 87, 89, 92, 97, 116, 117, 118, 146, 226, 233, 234, 235, 236, 237, 238, 239, 241, 242, 323
multiracial 43, 72, 151, 167, 235

nation 12, 16, 17, 18, 20, 41, 45, 48, 56, 62, 76, 78, 90, 91, 93, 94, 100, 101, 102, 105, 146, 147, 166, 167, 172, 266, 292, 293, 297, 320
nationalist 17, 24, 66, 98, 113, 114, 117, 118, 119, 120, 122, 123, 124, 125, 129, 149, 164, 167, 170, 172, 174, 177, 178, 179, 180, 183, 221
Native Americans 34, 297, 306, 307, 308, 309
natives 48, 53, 170, 236, 318, 324
negra, negro 7, 19, 22, 72, 41-60, 62, 67, 79-81, 85, 86, 91-101, 104, 107, 126, 150, 151, 155, 177, 189, 210-218, 221, 239-241, 252, 274, 276, 309, 310
negrita, negrito 24, 26, 61, 71, 208, 210, 214, 215, 218, 252
negroide, cultura 7, 23, 31, 77, 78, 79, 80, 81, 82, 83, 84, 85, 86, 87, 88, 89, 90, 376, 377
Netherlands 274
New York 4, 7, 9, 25, 26, 27, 28, 29, 32, 33, 71, 72, 80, 81, 82, 84, 113, 114, 120, 121, 125, 128-155, 156, 161-167, 170, 172, 175, 177-182, 184-189, 191, 192, 250, 274, 277, 279, 281
New York Public Library 25, 121, 132, 133, 134, 135, 136, 137, 138, 139, 140, 141, 142, 143, 144
niche 252
Niger-Congo 45
Nolla, Olga 7, 22, 91-101
non-black 26, 104, 217, 221, 223
non-Hispanic 13, 14, 25, 32, 114, 116, 117, 119, 120, 124, 152, 309
non-white 12, 14, 16, 18, 24, 31, 33, 116, 155,

182, 192, 213, 234, 236, 238, 240, 259, 264, 278, 327

Nuyorican 7, 13, 26, 27, 28, 29, 72, 159, 161-181

octoroon 49

Oller, Francisco 166, 167, 168

Orocovis 31, 32, 197, 199, 200, 207

Oshún 106

Palés Matos, Luis 21, 23, 61, 67, 68, 78, 79, 82, 89, 92

Palo 169, 178

Pan-Africanist 113, 122, 132

parda 46, 47, 48, 57, 213, 219, 227, 234, 236, 237, 242, 274, 308, 309, 311, 373, 374

Pedreira, Antonio S. 16, 66, 349, 357, 374, 375, 381

pelo lacio 372

pelo malo 215, 343, 372

peninsulares 19, 118

Perla, La 247, 248

phenotype 16, 44, 81, 151, 182, 187, 192, 253, 257

phenotypes 186, 211

pigmentocracy 119

Piñones 31, 81, 83, 84, 247

plena 28, 61, 72, 80, 82, 83, 86, 87, 164, 175, 177, 178, 241

Plessy v. Ferguson 48, 147

Ponce 32, 80, 82, 96, 103, 107, 108, 166, 183, 210, 212, 214, 228, 229, 241, 251

Porto Rico 48, 286, 288, 289, 290, 297

poverty 14, 32, 72, 136, 182, 232, 234, 240, 248, 249, 250, 251, 252, 253, 254, 262, 266

prejudice 17, 20, 29, 53, 61, 64, 76, 77, 81, 92, 97, 144, 149, 155, 166, 185, 224, 265, 267

prieta 99, 71, 213-218, 310, 367, 376

Prince Hall Lodge 125

public housing 14, 234, 240, 241, 247, 248, 249, 250, 251, 254

Puerto Ricans 1, 3, 4, 7, 8, 11-37, 41- 44, 49, 51-53, 55-56, 58-60, 66-67, 70-72, 77, 82, 85, 90-91, 93-95, 99, 108, 119, 121-124, 129, 131-132, 136-138, 140, 143, 145-156, 162-163, 166-168, 173-175, 177-178, 180, 182-192, 211, 217, 221, 222, 233, 239, 241, 255-257, 259-260, 264, 266, 273, 275, 277, 279, 280, 285-288, 291, 292, 294-300, 305, 306, 308-312, 314, 316, 320-323

Puerto Rico 4, 7, 8, 11-21, 24-36, 41-45, 47, 49-59, 61-86, 88-92, 94-95, 98, 100, 103, 105-109, 114-115, 117-119, 121-125, 127-132, 134, 136, 142, 146, 151, 153, 156, 162-170, 173, 174, 176-179, 181, 183-188, 190, 197-234, 236, 238-241, 247-254, 258, 264, 266, 273-274, 276, 277, 284-289, 291-292, 294, 297-298, 300, 305, 307-322, 325, 326, 328

quadroon 62, 63, 146

race 4, 11, 12, 16-18, 20-30, 33, 34, 37, 41-44, 49, 52-79, 88, 90-94, 97-100, 102, 104-105, 107-109, 113, 114, 116, 118, 119, 120, 129-132, 137, 143, 146, 147, 148, 149, 150, 151, 152, 153, 154, 155, 156, 167, 168, 176, 182, 183, 184, 185, 186, 190, 191, 192, 198, 199, 210, 211, 212, 213, 214, 217, 219-226, 236, 239, 240, 241, 248, 252, 253, 260, 262, 266, 273-278, 280-282, 284, 287, 290, 291, 297, 328

race talk 211, 217, 219, 221, 223, 224

racial democracy 22, 68, 76, 77, 104, 108, 183, 223

racialization 14, 15, 19, 26, 30, 31, 32, 33, 34, 90, 183, 184, 191, 223, 224, 239, 255, 260, 263, 264

racialized 12, 13, 14, 18, 19, 26, 31, 32, 44, 51, 73, 104, 117, 175, 181, 182, 189, 191, 213, 223, 233, 237, 256, 257, 259, 261, 264, 267, 280 racism 29, 30, 41-44, 53, 54-62, 64, 65, 68, 70, 72, 73, 75, 76, 77, 85, 88, 89, 92, 94, 97, 105, 119, 130, 131, 143, 146, 148, 150, 154, 176, 182, 183, 185, 186, 189, 190, 191, 192, 199, 208, 212, 213, 214, 215, 216, 217, 218, 219, 220, 221, 222, 224, 240, 254, 266, 320

racist 20, 23, 42, 43, 44, 54, 57, 58, 59, 62, 67, 74, 75, 79, 85, 86, 92, 120, 121, 133, 147, 148, 156, 183, 186, 212, 216, 218, 219, 220, 221, 240, 242, 253

reggaetón 14, 32, 247, 248, 249, 250, 252, 253, 254

Republican 44, 49, 50, 51, 52, 53, 56

residenciales 32, 234

riot squad 30, 204-206, 208-209

Rivera, Lino 138, 145, 147, 149, 151

Rodríguez Juliá, Edgardo 61, 72, 73, 74, 75, 84, 85, 86, 87, 361

rumba 172-181

Saint Domingue 115

salsa 72, 82, 83, 172, 173, 175, 179, 241, 316

San Antón 32, 107, 183, 210, 212, 216

San Juan 7, 29, 32, 51, 80, 81, 83, 84, 87, 89, 125, 127, 128, 182, 184, 185, 190, 191, 225, 227, 228, 229, 235, 239, 241, 274, 309, 318

santería 165, 166, 170, 173, 241

Santos Febres, Mayra 22, 23, 74, 75, 93

Santurce 86, 136, 232, 276

Schomburg, Arturo Alfonso 7, 24-25, 113-114, 118, 120-126, 129-130, 132, 134, 137, 139-144

scientific 48, 281, 310, 315, 322, 328

segregated 47, 56, 66, 81, 279

segregation 31, 42, 44, 50, 54, 59, 61, 95, 124, 136, 149, 183, 255

Shango 165, 166, 169

slave 17-19, 41, 45-48, 57, 58, 62, 63, 65, 70, 80, 83, 87, 90, 92, 94, 96, 114-117, 168, 169, 180, 199, 200, 210, 213, 215, 217, 222,

223, 227, 228, 308, 309, 313, 318, 326

slavery 17, 18, 41, 57, 58, 62, 63, 64, 65, 69, 85, 86, 89, 116, 183, 200, 213, 221, 223

slippery semantics 211, 213, 214, 216, 219, 220, 221, 222, 223, 224, 385

socialist 113, 121, 129

Socialist Party 53, 121, 129, 132, 149

solidarity 13, 29, 30, 99, 122, 131, 163, 178, 182, 184, 185, 189, 191, 192, 210, 212, 217, 220, 221, 222, 223, 224, 235, 236, 238

Soto, Jorge 7, 27, 28, 161-171

South Bronx 136, 162

Spain 17, 19, 20, 27, 44, 45, 46, 49, 50, 51, 52, 57, 62, 87, 94, 114, 115, 116, 117, 118, 119, 125, 169, 221, 223, 286, 307, 308, 318

Spaniard 15, 17, 19, 41, 46-48, 67, 94, 151, 168, 217, 276, 306, 307, 311, 315, 326

Spanish 8, 17, 18, 19, 20, 24, 25, 26, 36, 41, 44, 45, 46, 47, 49, 51, 52, 57, 58, 59, 62, 63, 66, 70, 71, 72, 73, 76, 85, 91, 94, 95, 96, 103, 114, 115, 116, 118, 119, 120, 124, 129, 130, 131, 134, 135, 137, 140, 142, 148, 151, 152, 155, 156, 162, 164, 167, 168, 169, 170, 173, 174, 176, 177, 178, 180, 181, 187, 199, 202, 204, 209, 222, 226, 227, 248, 258, 274, 275, 276, 278, 285, 291, 298, 309, 315, 316, 317, 318, 319, 320, 321, 322, 325, 326, 327, 328

stereotype 21, 23, 58, 67, 68 74, 75, 98, 137, 175, 232, 325

sub-Saharan African 35, 36, 281, 324

superiority 41, 46, 48, 49, 52, 54, 64, 286

tabaqueros 119, 121, 123, 127, 128, 148

Taíno 7, 8, 14, 27, 35, 36, 44, 45, 78, 85, 91, 94, 161-171, 178, 181, 217, 285, 286, 298-299, 305-328

Taller Boricua 7, 27, 161-171

Tapia y Rivera, Alejandro 61-65

trigueña, triqueño 214, 215, 252

tumbadora 175, 177, 180

turbas republicanas 51

Tuskegee Institute 34, 286-290, 293, 296,⁻
        297, 381, 391

UNIA, United Negro Improvement
        Association 120, 130
United States 4, 7, 11-14, 16,⁻17, 19, 20, 21,
        24-30, 32, 33, 34, 37, 41, 42, 44, 45,
        48,⁻59, 61, 62, 95, 99, 113-132, 134, 142-
        143, 146-148, 154, 161, 168-169, 182,
        185, 202, 207, 221, 226, 231, 233, 239,
        248, 250, 252, 266, 267, 273-275, 284-
        291, 293-300, 307, 325, 328
urbanizaciones 14, 32

Vega, Bernardo 121
vejigante 164-165
Velorio, El 167-168
Virgin Islands 121-124
Vizcarrondo, Fortunato 60, 78-80, 89-90
Voodoo 169-170

Washington, Booker T. 51, 54, 56, 59, 290,
        297
West Indies 274, 277
West Town 32, 255-256, 258, 261-264
white 12-14, 16, 18, 21-24, 26, 29, 31, 33-34,
        41-42, 47-49, 53-55, 57-58, 62-63,
        65-68, 70, 73-74, 76, 79, 83, 86-87,
        92, 93-100, 102-105, 107, 109, 115-119,
        121, 125-126, 131-132, 137, 146, 147-150,
        153, 155-156, 162, 169, 182, 185-192,
        197-199, 201, 203, 208-218, 220-223,
        225-229, 231-232, 234, 236, 238, 240,
        255-268, 274-281, 287, 295, 297, 310,
        323, 327
whiteness 21, 26, 32, 41, 43, 47, 48, 53, 56, 58,
        60, 64, 71, 149, 156, 182, 198, 226, 256-
        267, 276, 280
whitening 69, 70, 93, 95, 180, 181, 199, 214,
        261
Wicker Park 256, 261

¿y tu agüela a'onde ejtá? 60, 79, 80, 166, 328
Yaurel 107
Y-chromosome 35, 36, 323, 328
Yemayá 106
yuppies 32, 33, 260, 261, 262, 263, 264, 266,
        267

Zenón Cruz, Isabelo 16, 20, 59, 62, 73, 125

www.ingramcontent.com/pod-product-compliance
Lightning Source LLC
Chambersburg PA
CBHW070539270326
41926CB00013B/2148